RIKA)
Keep toning
vocal chords
Love Always
Dick

THE PEOPLE'S VOICE

Local Radio and Television in Europe

THE PEOPLE'S VOICE

Local Radio and Television in Europe

Edited by

Nick Jankowski, Ole Prehn & James Stappers

Acamedia Research Monograph 6

John Libbey

LONDON · PARIS · ROME

British Library Cataloguing in Publication Data

The People's Voice: Local Radio and Television in Europe
(Acamedia Research Monograph, No. 6)

I. Jankowski, Nicholas W. II. Series

384.54094

ISBN: 0 86196 322 9

ISSN: 0956-9057

Series editor: Manuel Alvarado

Published by

John Libbey & Company Ltd, 13 Smiths Yard, Summerley Street,
London SW18 4HR, England
Telephone: 081-947 2777 – Fax: 081-947 2664
John Libbey Eurotext Ltd, 6 rue Blanche, 92120 Montrouge, France
John Libbey - C.I.C. s.r.l., via Lazzaro Spallanzani 11, 00161 Rome, Italy

CONTENTS

Part III: Special Themes

ACKNOWLEDGEMENTS

A project of this scope involves many people and organizations. Although we cannot name all of them here, we would like to specifically express our appreciation for the contribution of several individuals and institutions. To begin, Erik Nordahl Svendsen was active in an early phase of the project and played a central role in selecting authors and chapters. He was unfortunately compelled to withdraw as one of the volume editors because of added responsibilities at *Danmarks Radio*.

We were also supported by the critical encouragement of Bob White while he was Director of the Centre for the Study of Communication and Culture in London. Bob wrote extensive commentary on early drafts of several chapters. He also assisted in negotiations with publishers during the course of the project.

Most of the contributors to the book regularly attend conferences of the International Association of Mass Communication Research (IAMCR) and several have held positions within the organization. The IAMCR, particularly the organization's Working Group on Community Media, has provided us with a meeting ground to share ideas and reflect on developments. This book, in fact, is very much a product of the members of that IAMCR Working Group.

The Institute of Mass Communication at the University of Nijmegen has been generous with its support of the project. The Institute granted time to one of the editors to correspond with authors and edit their manuscripts. It also helped finance student assistants and other support activities. Most important, the Institute of Mass Communication is one of the few university centres in Europe where small scale media are a focal point of research. This has contributed to an informed and congenial environment in which this project could be conducted.

We also wish to extend our appreciation to John Libbey and Manuel Alvarado, respectively publisher and series editor. Independence and 'small scale' have virtues not only in the world of media, but also in publishing; we are pleased with the efficiency and professionalism brought to bear in producing this book.

Will Berben and Susan Luijt assisted with translation and typing of texts. Erik van Vulpen and Fred Dijk helped with preparation of the bibliographies and indexes, and with copy editing.

Finally, our greatest thanks are extended to the scholars who have contributed to the volume. They all have demonstrated perseverance and patience in seeing this project to an end. They have put up with many requests for revisions and additional information; they have ungrudgingly shared their knowledge of local media. To all of them we express our warmest appreciation, and hope this project will be but one of many more to come in the area of small scale media.

Contributors

Heinz Bonfadelli (1949) is Researcher and Lecturer at the Institute for Mass Communication, University of Zürich, Switzerland. He received his Ph.D. from the same university in 1980 and has conducted research in the areas of mass media and youth, and reading behaviour. He has also published extensively on the uses and effects of mass communication, videotex and local radio.

Maria Corominas (1961) is Lecturer in the Department of Journalism, Autonomous University of Barcelona, Spain. One of her research interests is the relationship between media and language, which was the topic of her doctoral dissertation: *Language Policy and Media Policy in Europe (Radio and Television)*. Other research interests and publications on which she has contributed focus on radio and television developments in Catalan.

Jan Drijvers (1960) is Research and Teaching Assistant at the Department of Communication Sciences, Catholic University Leuven, Belgium. He lectures on communication policies and broadcasting structures and publishes regularly on local and community media – the topic of his forthcoming Ph.D. He was editor of a community newspaper in Diest and is now a member of the board of a regional television station in Leuven.

Nico van Eijk (1961) is staff member of the Institute for Information Law at the University of Amsterdam, The Netherlands. He is a member of the board of the Dutch Organization of Local Broadcasting (OLON) and of the local broadcasting organization SALTO in Amsterdam. He is also a member of the editoral board of *Mediaforum*, a journal devoted to media and communication law. His primary research interests are related to judicial aspects of electronic media.

Ineke Gooskens (1944) graduated from the University of Amsterdam, the Netherlands, in 1972 with a degree in sociology. She has conducted field research in Mexico and Surinam. Between 1972 and 1986 she worked as a researcher on minority issues for the city of Amsterdam. Since 1988 she is co-director of a research bureau specializing in municipal policy questions.

Peggy Gray (1934) was until recently Research Fellow at Leicester University Centre for Mass Communication Research, England. For the past two decades she has been involved in studies of local and community radio, cable television experiments and the use and social implications of new communications technologies with special reference to their influence within the family. She has served as Administrative Secretary to the International Association of Mass Communication Research (IAMCR) and now holds an honorary life membership of the organization.

Ed Hollander (1948) is Associate Professor at the Institute of Mass Communication, University of Nijmegen, the Netherlands. His research interests include local communication, development communication, local telecommunications and regional media. He has published both theoretical and empirical studies on these media. In the early 1980s he was commissioned by the Dutch government to investigate the emergence of local and community oriented media in Europe.

Lowe Hedman (1942) is Associate Professor at the Unit for Media and Communication, Department of Sociology, University of Uppsala, Sweden. He has for many years conducted research on local communication and has served as an adviser to a governmental committee in this area. He has recently completed a research project on Neighbourhood Radio in Sweden.

Jean-Paul Lafrance (1940) is founder and former director of the Communications Department of the University of Quebec in Montreal (UQAM), Canada. He holds the titles of Professor at UQAM, Associate Professor at the Communications Institute of the University of Avignon, and Associate Research Fellow at *Centre National d'Etudes des Télécommunications* (CNET) in Paris. He has written extensively on cable and broadcasting issues, with emphasis on local media.

Knut Lundby (1948) is Associate Professor and Head of the Department of Media and Communication at the University of Oslo, Norway. During the mid-1980s he served as research officer for a local media project. He is currently involved in investigating the impact of multiple channel cable systems on local media. Another of his ongoing research interests is the sociology of religion and use of mass media by religious organizations.

Birgitte Jallov (1956) holds a degree in Communication Planning from Roskilde University Centre in Denmark. She has made use of media and communication techniques as tools for consciousness raising, development and social change. A former staff member of two of the experimental television stations in Denmark, she also was one of the co-founders of a grass-roots community radio station and a women's radio collective in Copenhagen. She is presently involved development communication projects for the International Labour Organization in Geneva.

Nick Jankowski (1943) is Associate Professor at the Institute of Mass Communication, University of Nijmegen, the Netherlands. Author of *Community Television in Amsterdam*, he has been conducting qualitative and quantitative research of small scale media since the mid-1970s. He is also interested in the introduction of new communication technologies and, in particular, the opportunities for access to these technologies by individuals and social action groups.

Otfried Jarren (1953) is Professor in the Department of Journalism at the University of Hamburg, Germany. He studied political science and ethnography and completed his doctoral thesis on communication structures in the community. He has taught at the University of Berlin and while there managed a long-term qualification project for journalists. His primary research interest is the interconnection between political structures and media.

Peter Lewis (1934) is freelance writer and

broadcaster, and Visiting Fellow at the Communications Policy Centre of City University in London. He was station manager of *Bristol Channel*, one of the experimental cable television stations in the early 1970s. He has been active in the local radio movement and written a number of books on the media. He most recently co-authored (with Jerry Booth) *The Invisible Medium; Public Commericial and Community Radio.*

Birger Nymo (1953) received a degree in sociology from the University of Oslo in 1982 where he also worked as Research Fellow at the Institute for Mass Communication Research. Since 1983 he has been employed at the Norwegian Telecom Research Department (NTR). As NTR Senior Researcher he has recently completed an investigation into user needs for telecommunication and telemedicine.

Frank Olderaan (1959) studied Communication Science at the University of Nijmegen, the Netherlands, and later occupied a research post at the Institute of Mass Communication at the same university. During the period 1984–1988 he conducted a field study of the introduction of interactive cable television services in a small Dutch community. In addition to publications related to this work, he has written on Dutch communications policy and small scale media.

Vibeke G. Petersen (1944) holds a Ph.D. in political science from Copenhagen University. Since 1982 she has been employed in the Department of Broadcasting of the Danish Ministry of Culture, initially as a researcher for the local radio and television experiment and later as staff member of the Ministry of Communication.

Ole Prehn (1952) is Associate Professor at the Department of Communication and Dean of the Faculty of Arts at Aalborg University, Denmark. He has done extensive research in the field of community radio and television and international media policy. He represented the National Research Council of the Humanities in the Committee for Local Radio and Television established by the Ministry of Culture during the trial period in Denmark. He is a member of the governing board of *TV-Nord* (a regional affiliate of one of the national television channels) and is convenor of the Working Group on Local Radio and Television of the International Association of Mass Communication Research (IAMCR).

Michael Schanne (1948) is Director of the *Arbeitsgruppe für Kommunikationsforschung & -beratung AGK* in Zürich, Switzerland. He has been involved in various research projects in the fields of science and environmental journalism, risk communication, news selection and routines, modern newspaper design and audiovisual programming.

Jean Paul Simon (1948) is Researcher at the *Centre National d'Etudes des Télécommunications* (CNET), the research division of *France Telecom*. He has worked as a consultant and publisher of a monthly journal devoted to local government. Along with an ongoing investigation of cultural industries, he has contributed to studies on French public policies, industrial strategies and the regulation of communication systems.

Miquel de Moragas Spà (1943) is Professor in the Department of Journalism and Vice Chancellor of the Autonomous University of Barcelona, Spain. He has also served as Dean of the Information Faculty at the same university. He has published widely on semiotics, communication theory and electronic media developments in Catalan.

Slavko Spichal (1947) is Professor of Communication and Dean of the Faculty of Social Sciences at the University of Ljubljana in Slovenia. He is founder and convenor of the International Colloquium on Culture and Communication, and director of its current project Media Systems in Transition. He was the planner for the conference of International Association of Mass Communication Research (IAMCR) held in Bled, Slovenia, in 1990, and currently serves on the International Council of the organization. Recent English language publications include *Democratization and the Media*

(co-edited with J. Hochheimer and K. Jakubowiez) and *Journalists for the 21st Century* (co-authored with C. Sparks).

James Stappers (1930) is Professor of Mass Communication at the University of Nijmegen, the Netherlands. He studied psychology at the same university and since 1970 has directed the Institute of Mass Communication there. His teaching and research interests involve communication theory, cultural indicators and small scale mass communication. He recently edited a volume of essays on mass communication theory and research with contributions from central figures in the field.

Erik Nordahl Svensen (1945) is Head of Audience Research at *Danmarks Radio* (the Danish Broadcasting Corporation). Prior to joining *Danmarks Radio* he was a researcher at the Danish School of Journalism. During the experiment with local radio and television in Denmark he represented the Social Science Research Council on a committee established by the Ministry of Culture to monitor the experiment. He has also served on the International Council of the International Association of Mass Communication Research (IAMCR).

Peter Widlok (1957) studied communication and literature at the Universities of Berlin and Münster in Germany. He has conducted research projects on German, Western European and North American local radio. He recently completed his dissertation on participation in community radio in the United States. He has worked as a reporter and producer for West German Radio and Television and is currently an adviser at the Northrhine-Westphalian Broadcasting Authority.

Pieter de Wit (1952) studied psychology and mass communication at the University of Nijmegen, the Netherlands. From the early 1980s he has been involved in local broadcasting. In 1982 he began working for the Organization of Local Broadcasters in the Netherlands (OLON) and since 1988 he has served as Executive Director.

INTRODUCTION

In the early 1970s, in both century-old villages and modern housing estates across Europe, people began experimenting with local radio and television. In some instances government authorities had taken the initiative; in others the pioneers were action groups and media collectives enamoured with the communicative potential of video and other alternative media.

Most of these early efforts made use of limited cable television systems installed for distribution of over-the-air radio and television signals. Outmoded television studio equipment and in some cases recently introduced video portapacks constituted the hardware of these early stations. Now, many – but by no means all – community stations have ultra-modern editing and recording facilities for both studio and on-site productions.

Other aspects also distinguished stations of the 1970s from those now in operation. The differences between stations in neighbouring European countries was – and is – considerable regarding objectives, programming procedures, target audiences, relation to national media and local press, and – perhaps most important – the relation to communities served. The differences, indeed, are many and are reflected in the respective legislation and media policies enacted in various European countries.

Similarities exist equally well. Many general trends in media developments seem impervious to national borders: satellite television and the impact of foreign programming on national and local culture, commercialization of radio and television programming at all levels of a media system, and the tension between desire for community involvement in programming and a trend toward more professional production standards. These and other similarities are strikingly evident among local radio and television stations across Europe.

The editors of this volume have been following these developments intensely during the past two decades. As communication researchers we have been intrigued by the impact small scale media usage might have on communication patterns within communities. We were equally taken by the dreams of developing or rebuilding a sense of community within new housing estates and aging neighbourhoods, and applying these new media to that task. Sometimes these new community oriented media were meant to simply inform their audiences of events. Sometimes they went a step further and attempted to mobilize citizens in efforts to bring about change and improvement. Sometimes emancipatory objectives were embedded in station programming.

We have personally studied and conducted empirical research around the emergence of local radio and television in Denmark and the Netherlands. As part of our interest in these developments we established a network of similarily involved researchers elsewhere in Europe which frequently met under the auspices of the International

Association of Mass Communication Research (IAMCR). The initial ideas for this volume, in fact, were sketched at a conference of the IAMCR in Prague in 1984. At subsequent meetings in New Delhi, Barcelona and Bled, papers were discussed and drafts of chapters reviewed.

This volume has, in other words, emerged over a considerable period of time. This has provided ample opportunity for thought and consultation on the development of these small scale media, and we believe the value of this work procedure is reflected in the quality of the contributions.

Our own research and consultations with other investigators around Europe has convinced us that local radio and television are entering a new phase of development. There are strong pressures for decentralizing the national broadcasting monopolies existing in many European countries. The emerging national media policies are taking local electronic media into account. There is also much low power over-the-air broadcasting in addition to cablecasting. And in some places an interface is developing with other, often interactive electronic media: videotex, local teletext services and cable newspapers.

Transition, in other words, is evident in the local radio and television landscape. The intent of this book is to chart and analyse the course of this development in Europe. We have placed emphasis on drawing material from empirically based social science research. We have also included information on media policy, utilization of local radio and television by ethnic minorities and women's groups, and on theoretical perspectives intended to help understand these developments.

The content of this book is arranged in three parts. In Part 1 we treat historical and theoretical issues which underpin the development of community radio and television. In Chapter 1 Ed Hollander traces the historical development of small scale media within the context of the social and cultural upheaval many European countries experienced in the 1960s. In Chapter 2 Hollander and James Stappers examine the theoretical basis of community media. They trace the way mass communications have been conceived and place accent on communication as a form of 'transaction' between people who send and people who receive messages. This discussion is continued in Chapter 3 by Knut Lundby who asks whether electronic media in relatively small geographical localities can serve as tools for strengthening a sense of community. As empirical base for his discussion, Lundby draws on findings from surveys held in two Norwegian villages.

For Part 2 of the volume we asked researchers from around Europe to explore issues particular to developments in their own countries. Eleven countries are represented, and results from experiments in the Nordic countries introduce this part of the book. The Danish experiment with community radio and television was the focus of extensive longitudinal research. In Chapter 4 Vibeke Petersen, Ole Prehn and Erik Nordahl Svendsen distill findings from this work and reflect on recent policy developments in that country.

Chapter 5 examines a special variant of small scale media, 'neighbourhood radio', which has been developing in Sweden since the late 1970s. It was the subject of empirical research conducted by a team of investigators at the University of Uppsala, and Lowe Hedman reviews this material. Finally, to complete contributions from the

Nordic countries, Birger Nymo assesses the community television experiments held in Norway in Chapter 6.

A second cluster of countries treated in this part of the volume are the Netherlands, Belgium, Germany and Switzerland. James Stappers, Frank Olderaan and Pieter de Wit reflect in Chapter 7 on the early Dutch experiments with cable delivered community television and on more recent developments with low power ether radio. In Chapter 8 Jan Drijvers takes on the complex media situation in Belgium, characterized by essentially separate systems for the Flemish and French speaking sections of the country. He traces Belgian policy development for both local radio and television, and the considerable commercial influences on these media. Pieter Widlok and Otfried Jarren were involved in researching the German pilot projects and trace in Chapter 9 what has since happened with local radio in that country. Heinz Bonfadelli and Michael Schanne examine in Chapter 10 the relationship between the local press and local radio in Switzerland.

The third and last group of countries reviewed in this part of the book reflect the range of development among small scale electronic media. In England there is a long history of experimentation with community radio and television, marked by much struggle to gain political recognition. In Chapter 11 Peggy Gray and Peter Lewis analyse this effort to create an electronic form of community communications. Across the Channel in France there has also been much experimentation during the past decade. In Chapter 12 Jean-Paul Lafrance and Jean Paul Simon extract from this history and from experiments with video animation. Community radio developments in Spain are of a rather different nature from those in Northern Europe. The stations, operating without official sanction, often stand in opposition to local political powers. Miguel de Moragas Spà and Maria Corominas focus on these developments in the province of Catalonia in Chapter 13.

Emphasis in this volume, it should be evident from the above overview, is on the development of community oriented radio and television in Western Europe. This is not to say that developments in former Eastern European countries are insignificant or uninteresting. On the contrary, the role these media have played in the tumultuous events across Eastern Europe is extremely significant. That is a topic, however, for another book. Still, we did want to include some material on the very unique media situation in Yugoslavia. Slavco Spichal undertook the task of examining application of the principle of self-management in local radio and of other efforts to democratize local media in that country. Political revolt in 1990 and the ensuing military conflict in 1991 seem to have put an end to Yugoslavia as a unified state. Because of these events, Professor Spichal stresses that his contribution, Chapter 14, must be seen in an historical perspective and not as an analysis of the role of local radio in recent events.

Part 3 of the book consists of five chapters which treat themes overarching the country-specific studies of the previous section. Chapter 15, the first chapter of this section, examines the use of community radio by women in five West European countries. Birgitte Jallov, author of this comparative study, sees striking similarities in utilization of this medium by women's groups. Use of community television by ethnic minorities in the Netherlands is the focus of Chapter 16. In this chapter Ineke Gooskens concentrates on the use of specially produced television programmes for

Surinamers, Moroccans and Turkish residents of Amsterdam. Chapter 17, contributed by Nico van Eijk, surveys judicial developments in several European countries. The final chapter of the book, Chapter 18, compares a number of the developments portrayed in the country studies. Here, Ole Prehn also presents material which could not be included in the individual chapters, such as developments in Italy with 'free radios'. He explicates themes underlying the development of small scale media around Europe: deregulation, commercialization, and the impact of European unification on electronic community media.

In summary, this book, taken as a whole, provides a map or chart of the course community radio and television has taken and is likely to take in the coming years. It is a chart which should not only be useful for mass communication researchers, but also for persons involved in media policy and in station management. Communication students concerned with the the rise of small scale media around Europe will also find the material valuable. There remains, nevertheless, need for much further study; we hope this book will serve as a source of information and inspiration for future researchers of local radio and television.

Nick Jankowski
Ole Prehn
James Stappers

Part I
Historical and theoretical background

1. The emergence of small scale media

Ed Hollander

Institute of Mass Communication, University of Nijmegen, The Netherlands

Community broadcasting in Western Europe, with us for nearly two decades, has shared the historical limelight with developments in media technology, media policy, and specifically the future of European broadcasting systems. The main factors influencing the evolution of community broadcasting were, and still are, national broadcasting systems and policies regarding decentralization and regionalization of broadcasting, social reform movements and the consequences of these movements for media policy and the development of cable television technology.

NATIONAL BROADCASTING SYSTEMS

The historical development of national broadcasting systems in Western Europe can be divided into three periods: the early period of broadcasting systems from 1920 until World War II, the consolidation of national broadcasting systems from 1950 until the late 1960s, and the years since 1970 – the so-called period of crisis and transition. The first two periods are briefly reviewed below; some of the criticisms voiced by various interest groups regarding the broadcasting systems are then presented.

Based on preliminary experiments with radio transmissions held shortly after World War I, a start was made in organizing broadcasting systems within Western European countries. National governments felt that regulation of frequency use was necessary in order to avoid uncontrolled growth of radio stations. At the first European Broadcasting Planning Conference in 1925 an agreement was reached whereby every radio station was assigned one frequency; 16 additional frequencies were allocated for collective use. In this manner each country had at least one permanent frequency and a number of frequencies were reserved for future use (Emery, 1969; Harwood *et al.*, 1966).

By 1930 most countries in Western Europe had organized public broadcasting systems. Broadcasting schedules were subsequently extended and additional radio services were introduced to accommodate cultural and geographic diversity within the respective countries. This diversification in broadcasting stations and programmes was accompanied by better and more sensitive radio receivers, which contributed to the expansion of radio stations and radio audiences.

No major changes occurred in the national broadcasting systems immediately following World War II; in most countries the broadcasting organizations operating prior to the War resumed activity. In this period the number of medium wave band radio stations increased, programme services expanded and the monopolistic position of the public broadcasting systems grew in strength.

In Great Britain, for example, the Charter and License of the *BBC*, due to expire in 1946, was extended until 1951 with little public discussion. In France, the *Radiodiffusion Télévision Française*, founded by Charles de Gaulle, then in exile, was established as a centralized broadcasting company. It replaced the pre-war French broadcasting system which consisted of both public and private broadcasting companies (Thomas, 1976: 2–5).

In Norway, Sweden, Finland and Denmark the existing broadcasting monopolies were extended, and in the Netherlands the Dutch Radio Union was established which co-ordinated several autonomous pre-war broadcasting organizations. In Austria, the Federal Republic of Germany, Switzerland and Belgium, a somewhat different situation developed: public broadcasting companies were organized within nation-wide systems, but in fact each company operated in different parts of the respective country for different language groups or – as in the case of the Federal Republic of Germany – for various member states.

The national broadcasting systems in Western Europe, whether organized as government controlled or as public broadcasting organizations, were all monopolistic in the sense that they held the exclusive right to broadcast nation-wide radio and television programmes.

The 1950s was a period of expansion for broadcasting organizations throughout Western Europe. In the post-war period the economic growth then underway allowed for an increase in broadcasting budgets which permitted construction of relay transmitters and studios and an increase in personnel.

This expansion, together with the introduction of the portable transistor radio and high quality FM programming, in turn contributed to growth in broadcasting audiences. This growth and the overall improvement of broadcasting quality were favourable developments for the eventual political decision to increase broadcasting fees paid by listeners and viewers and, thus, to increase broadcasting budgets.

The introduction of television in the mid-1950s led, in almost every country in Western Europe, to a debate on the introduction of televised advertising. Those countries which eventually chose to permit advertising decided upon a system whereby the advertisements were scheduled between programmes – generally before and after the evening news programme – in order that a certain degree of separation was maintained between advertisements and television programmes. In this way television advertising was introduced, providing an extra source of income, without upsetting the basic structure of the public broadcasting systems. The explosive increase in the number of households having television sets in the 1960s further consolidated the position of the national broadcasting systems in Western Europe.

SOCIAL REFORM MOVEMENTS

The period of growth in national broadcasting came to a standstill in the early 1970s. After the conversion from black and white to colour television and after the introduction of second and third television channels in most European countries, it seemed as if the possibilities for expansion were exhausted. The economic recession during the period prohibited further increase in broadcasting fees. In this context the social reform movements which emerged during the 1960s tended to threaten the stability of the national broadcasting systems.

To help understand this historical situation, Grandi (1978) considers four types of events peculiar to the social and political climate then dominant in Europe. First, many political and social groups began demanding a right to participate in the decision making of broadcasting organizations. Second, a demand for participation was also being heard from within the broadcasting corporations. Staff members argued for decentralized organizational structures, allowing for more autonomy. Third, in those countries where government control over broadcasting was strongest, such as in France and Italy, political parties began arguing that broadcasting should not be a tool for promoting government policy, but for increasing opposition to the government. Finally, economic interests in favour of the introduction of commercial broadcasting also began pushing for decentralization of the entire system, in an effort to dismantle the broadcasting monopolies.

In all four types the drive for decentralization is identical, but not the motive. For cultural and social organizations, decentralization was a method to promote citizen participation in the field of broadcasting. For broadcasting personnel, decentralization was a means for achieving more democratic control of the broadcasting organizations. For political parties decentralization meant gaining an instrument to oppose government policy. And for those in favour of commercial broadcasting, decentralization was a way to gain a foothold in the national broadcasting systems.

In reaction to these events some countries in Europe implemented changes in their broadcasting structures in the early 1970s. In 1975, for example, the French *Office de la Radio Télévision Française* (ORTF) was decentralized. As a broadcasting organization the ORTF was essentially disbanded and seven *Sociétés Nationales* were installed, each with specific tasks in the field of broadcasting. In Italy the monopoly of the *Radiotelevisione Italia* (*RAI*) was reduced in 1974 and again in 1976 by court decisions allowing the operation of commercial local cable stations. In other countries less drastic reforms were carried out or debated (Berrigan, 1977: 145–147; Thurston, 1978). Frequently, offices or special councils were established where citizens or organizations could submit complaints regarding the mass media (Finland in 1968: the Finnish Media Council; Sweden in 1967: the Radio Council; Great Britain in 1971: the Programmes Complaint Commission; Austria in 1974: Council of Radio and TV Customers; Ireland in 1974: Broadcasting Complaint Advisory Committee; Denmark in 1977: Complaints Board).

Broadcasting organizations also began to set up television programmes designated to achieve some form of audience participation: 'Open Door' was created by the BBC in England, 'Auto-Portrait' was produced by *Radio Télévision Belge* and 'Anruf Erwünscht' by the *Westdeutsche Rundfunk*. These programmes were generally broadcast

9

via regional transmitters and could be seen only in the respective regions. It also became standard practice in radio programming to invite listeners to react by telephone.

NEW COMMUNICATION TECHNOLOGIES

In the mid-1970s, concerned persons began reflecting on the future of national broadcasting systems. In France, Great Britain, German Federal Republic, Sweden and the Netherlands, governmental committees were established to study future media developments and their consequences for national broadcasting corporations. The primary motivation for this activity was the expansion of cable television networks and the possibility of local and regional cable services exploited on a commercial basis. A central problem indicated in the studies resulting from this work was incorporation of new developments within the existing broadcasting structures.

Curiously, little attention was paid to the question of how the national broadcasting systems could be modified in light of recent technological developments. The policies which emerged as a result of these studies reflect a conservative attitude toward new media and cable technology. An American report on the broadcasting situation in Western Europe in 1973 states the situation concisely:

> Many governments have been cautious in permitting the development of CATV because the medium represents potential competition to two government controlled monopolies: the national television broadcasting organizations, in terms of programming, and the Ministries of Post, Telegraph and Telephone (PTT's) in terms of communication facilities .... Partially because of restrictive government policies, CATV is presently no more than a supplement to broadcast television. The primary offerings promoting subscriber-interest have been improved reception, use of less expensive tv-receivers and, where allowed, importation of distant signals. The more exceptional capabilities of CATV – such as local programme origination and premium-tv – have not been thoroughly explored. (Stanford Research Institute, 1973: 1)

This policy has only recently undergone change. For years the basic philosophy has been to regard cable as an additional broadcasting facility, supplementing over-the-air broadcasting. In some countries experiments with locally originated cable television programmes were allowed for short periods of time, under strict conditions and with limited funding. These experiments had minor impact on media policy. They were primarily gestures toward citizen groups which wanted to utilize local cable television as a means for promoting community activities and participatory democracy. These experiments did, however, secure additional time for governments to formulate media policies and to contemplate a possible place for community broadcasting in those policies.

The delay in policy development, however, produced more problems than it solved. By the late 1970s satellite television, pay television and pirate radio and television stations had become major issues around Western Europe; the developments could no longer be ignored. Most European countries reacted unilaterally to these developments, with little international consultation. As a result, the original consistency in

Western European broadcasting policy was eliminated as each country attempted to confront the advances of media technology separately.

A complicating factor in the development of an adequate media policy was the supranational nature of much new media technology. Two examples of this are satellite broadcasting and pay television, both of which threatened the non-commercial public broadcasting services. Another complicating factor was that traditional policy fields were – and still are – very much influenced by these new developments and could not be dealt with separately. As formulated by Homet:

> In the stable and relatively simple world of point-to-point communications, broadcasting and the press, this process of policy-making worked rather well....In the past ten years, however, the tranquillity of these European arrangements has been disrupted by a series of technical advances collectively dubbed 'the information explosion'. No longer are communications enterprises fitted into three simple compartments (press, broadcasting and telecommunications); instead many configurations interrelate with and converge on each other. The process of policy decisions has become much more complex, so that it is doubtful any government can harmonize the multiplicity of choices. (Homet, 1979: 98–99)

In this situation, policy making has become too complicated for politicians alone to determine. Other involved bodies – in particular the national telecommunications organizations (PTT's) and national broadcasting organizations – have begun to take initiatives in policy formulation. On the topic of the internationalization of broadcasting, the national public broadcasting organizations have an interest in keeping the frontiers closed for commercially oriented broadcasting satellites. Regarding privatization of telecommunication services, the national PTT organizations have a vested interest in preventing this, which essentially means removing competitors from the market. Under these circumstances, innovative policy formulation is unlikely.

One area of policy activity, however, remains available: decentralization of broadcasting via the cable. It is here that three interest groups – community broadcasting organizations, public broadcasting companies and telecommunication companies – confront each other.

COMMUNITY RADIO AND TELEVISION

During the mid-1970s national experiments were held in England, Belgium and the Netherlands with community television. In Sweden experiments with neighbourhood radio began in 1979 (Swedborg & Svard, 1978). Although announced as early as 1976, the pilot community television projects in West Germany started operation nearly a decade later. And Denmark has recently completed a national experiment with community television (Petersen *et al.*, 1984; Prehn, 1988). Excepting West Germany and Denmark, all the experiments were initiated and completed prior to this decade.

Unlike other community media, community television was confronted at the outset with two obstacles. First, the production and transmission of radio and television programmes was seen as the exclusive domain of the national broadcasting stations.

11

Second, the distribution of those programmes via cable networks was legally in the hands of the national telecommunication organizations – the PTT's.

Community broadcasting stations were dependent upon both sets of organizations, and could only develop within the experimental status allotted by governments. Allowing for such experiments with community radio and television made it possible for the governments to postpone decision making on media policy issues. It also meant that community stations could not claim any rights or privileges until policy decisions, based on these experiments, had been made. This cautious attitude on the part of European governments was rooted in concern for possible commercialization of cable communication facilities. Allowing use of the cable by any non-public broad-casting organization might create a precedent, it was thought, for other, less idealistic uses of the cable.

With the exception of a few countries, such as Sweden, community broadcasting did not emerge from explicit government policy but from continued pressure and activity by the community broadcasting stations once the experimental period had expired. This situation, in which the development of community broadcasting was dependent on government policies in other areas, has continued into the 1980s.

Two areas have been of specific significance to community radio and television: cable television policy and the regionalization of national broadcasting. For a long time, cablecasting of community programmes had been the only 'special' cable service, in addition to distribution of over-the-air broadcasting signals. This exclusive position of community radio and television came to a halt by the late 1980s. Cable television networks have been promoted and new cable services were under development or in an experimental stage. Cable came to be seen as a financially interesting market for new and innovative services such as local teletext, information channels, film chan-nels and interactive videotex services.

Cable policy was no longer aimed at considering the special case of community cablecasting but also had to contend with the increasing pressure from domestic and foreign initiatives (such as satellite television) to commercially exploit the cable consumer market. This change is illustrated in the Netherlands by the involvement of a diversity of governmental ministries (Economic Affairs and Telecom-munications) on media policy, an area traditionally dealt with by the Ministry of Culture. This shift in emphasis further illustrates a change in philosophy regarding the use of cable television networks: less reference to 'communication' and more to 'consumption'.

This change in policy was endorsed by the local governments of the major Dutch municipalities, which, over the last years, had invested substantially in cable televi-sion networks, and wanted to increase the variety of cable services, community television being only one service among the offerings. This development has placed community television in competition with other cable services – satellite tv, informa-tion channels, videotex, public access channels – and has forced community television stations to offer more professional and attractive programming. This, in turn created strain on station budgets.

Community television stations, during recent years, have begun to diversify their budgets by targeting local cable radio programmes to specialized audiences. In this manner community stations have also managed to maintain some continuity between (bi)weekly television productions. Community (cable) radio is relatively cheap and does not require extensive manpower.

Although reception is usually limited to a single radio tuner within the household which is connected to the cable network, community radio is able to maintain more frequent contact with the community than more expensive local television programmes. In view of the advantages of community radio over community television, a tendency can be noted among community broadcasting stations to increase the amount of radio programming and, at the national level, to lobby for utilization of FM frequencies for low power over-the-air transmissions. This strategy resulted in the 1987 RARC conference allocation of frequencies for local low power community radio transmitters. In this way, community broadcasting stations will be able to reach a potentially larger audience with over-the-air radio broadcasts. This move effectively brings community broadcasting outside the areas affected by cable policy, but at the same time places it in another competitive position in relation to the regionalization of national broadcasting.

Regionalization of national broadcasting in Western Europe has been an ongoing affair over the last ten years, although the pace seems to have increased as a result of the activity related to community cable television stations. Instead of developing an integrated policy for regional and community broadcasting, such as done in Sweden, national broadcasting authorities have generally attempted to counter the possibilities for local cable television by establishing regional radio services in large provincial cities.

With the introduction of radio services on the FM band, a decentralized network of FM transmitters was in fact created, and in several countries the possibilities for decentralized programming were already available. Priority, however, was given to national broadcasting and, with the exception of Great Britain, regional radio services were limited to a few hours a day (Wangermee & L'Hoest, 1973). During the past years, however, the number of regional radio stations has increased and air time expanded. The limits of professional radio programming, however, seem to have been set at the provincial level; the cost of equipment and manpower does not enable regional radio services to decentralize further.

The transition by community stations from cable to over-the-air broadcasting effectively creates such a network of local radio stations, which will have to compete or to co-operate with the regional radio services in terms of programme scheduling and production. A new situation may develop should community radio stations decide to work together within a certain region or province. Then, there will effectively be two competing radio services within a province or region.

The prospect of a national network of local radio stations has revived a commercial interest in community radio. In most West European countries governments have tried to block the commercial exploitation of community television since the time of the early experiments with cable television. Now, with the possibility of community radio broadcasted over-the-air and with a shortage of funds for community stations a change in philosophy from 'communication' to 'consumption', and a commercial exploitation of community radio seems more and more probable. The case of community television in Italy has shown the mechanistics of 'networking' community

13

stations into a *de facto* national commercial broadcasting system; the same has been happening in Belgium with community radio stations. In several of the federal states, or 'Länder', in former West Germany major publishing companies already have a share in the commercial exploitation of local radio stations.

Even if community stations manage to resist usurpation by commercial interests and chose for only limited reliance on advertising revenues, this will still bring them into direct conflict with publishers of local and regional daily newspapers, which also depend on those sources of revenue.

As stated earlier, in most West European countries community broadcasting did not develop as a result of explicit government policy. To the extent that community broadcasting has been affected by government policies in other areas – such as policy related to cable television systems and regional radio – the effects have been more detrimental to the cause of community media than beneficial (McCain & Ferrel Lowe, 1990). The reason that, after 15 years, community stations have managed to survive in many European countries is because they have refused to succumb to the considerable problems – in spite of the expectations and hopes of some officials. It is because of that resistance that community broadcasting has secured a small place in national media policies.

But, as has been demonstrated in Italy, Belgium and West Germany, to survive and to live up to the expectations of 'community communication' as formulated in the 1970s, it is insufficient for media policy to simply legitimate community broadcasting. What is needed is legislation that also guarantees a solid financial basis for community stations insuring they are not left to the mercy of regional radio services, local authorities, cable companies and newspaper publishers.

References

Béaud, P. (1978): *Free radio in Italy; report on the visit to Italian experiments*, Strasbourg: Council of Europe.

Berrigan, F. (ed.) (1977): *Access: some Western models of community media*, Liège: Georges Thone.

Bibby, A., C. Denford and J. Cross (1979): *Local television: piped dreams?* London: Redwing Press.

Croll, P. and C. Husband (1975): *Communication and community*, Leicester: Centre for Mass Communication Research.

Emery, W. (1969): *National and international systems of broadcasting*, East Lansing: State University Press.

Grandi, R. (1978): 'Western European broadcasting in transition', *Journal of Communication* 28, 3: 47-50.

Harwood, A., and K. Hunt (1978): *Frequency planning and local broadcasting*, Strasbourg: Council of Europe.

Hollander, E. (1982): *Kleinschalige massacommunicatie: lokale omroepvormen in West Europa*, The Hague: State Pub. Co.

Hollander, E. and N. Jankowski (1984): 'Community television: charting its course in Europe', paper, National Federation of Local Cable Programmers, Boston.

Homet, R. (1979): *Politics, culture and communication*, New York: Praeger.

Jankowski, N. (1982): 'Community television: a tool for community action?' *Communication* 7, 1: 33-58.

Jankowski, N. (1982): *Lokale Omroep Bijlmermeer; eindverslag van een veldonderzoek*, Amsterdam: SISWO.

Jankowski, N.W. (1988): *Community television in Amsterdam. access to, participation in and use of the 'Lokale Omroep Bijlmermeer'*, Amsterdam: University of Amsterdam.

Lewis, P. (1976): *Community control of local radio*, Strasbourg: Council of Europe.

Lewis, P. (1978): *Community television and cable in Britain*, London: British Film Institute.

McCain, T. and G. Ferrel Lowe. (1990): 'Localism in Western European radio broadcasting: Untangling the wireless', *Journal of Communication* **41**, 4: 86-101.

Petersen, V., O. Prehn and E.N. Svendsen. (1988): 'Community radio and television in Denmark', paper, International Association of Mass Communication Research, Barcelona.

Stanford Research Institute (1973): *Cable television in Western Europe*, Menlo Park, California: SRI.

Swedborg, B. and S. Svard (1978): *Neighbourhood radio and community video in Sweden*, Strasbourg: Council of Europe.

Thomas, R. (1976): *Broadcasting and democracy in France*, Philadelphia: Temple University Press.

Thurston, C. (1978): 'Accountability in broadcasting', *Journal of Communication* **28**, 3: 112-119.

Young, I., R. Pye and H. Thomas. (1979): *Evaluation of Channel 40 – Community cable television in Milton Keynes: Volume I – Overview, summary and conclusions*, London: Communications Studies and Planning Ltd.

Wangermee, R. and H. L'Hoest (1973): *L'après-télévision, une anti-mythologie de l'audiovisuel*, Paris: Hachette.

2. Community media and community communication

Ed Hollander and James Stappers

Institute of Mass Communication, University of Nijmegen, The Netherlands

The emergence of community media in the early 1970s brought attention to an area more or less neglected in communication research: the study of communication within the context of the community. Research projects initiated around experiments with community media not only focused on the 'new medium', such as local cable television, but on the geographical setting and, more important, the social setting (Halloran, 1975). The general intention was to include all relevant aspects of the local communication structure in the research, and to evaluate community media performance in relation to that of other forms of local communication and other local media.

Concepts such as 'community media' and 'community communication', apart from their normative connotations (Berrigan, 1979), refer to the study of communication structures and communication processes within a distinct social setting – a geographical community or a community of interest – and therefore focus on both the structural and the process characteristics of mass communications. In addition, communication researchers found that community oriented alternative media were forms of communication and media formats that could not easily be conceptualized in terms of conventional theory and models available for the study of mass communications.

Researchers were confronted with the problem of adequately conceptualizing mass communications within a distinct social setting and with the reformulation of mass communications as such. Two additional problems, accentuated in research on community media, have to do with the need for a more adequate vision of community communication: the interplay between mediated and non-mediated (interpersonal) communication, and the fact that participants in community communication – both senders and receivers – are members of the same social system, the geographical community and/or the community of interest. Conceptualization of participants in community communication in terms of 'audiences' is, from this perspective, inadequate. McQuail (1983: 149) signals this issue in relation to mass media, when he discusses the 'dualistic nature' of the concept of audience. Are participants in community communication an audience that is established in reaction to media content or is the 'audience' an already existing social category, the members of which use media content as well as other sources of information, for their own purposes?

This chapter traces some of the conceptual problems related to the study of community communication back to theoretical issues stemming from the conceptualization of mass communication and explores possibilities for an alternative formulation of community communication.

THE CONCEPT OF MASS COMMUNICATION

When Berelson (1959: 1) made his assessment on the state of communications research as "withering away" he made a wrong diagnosis at the right moment. What he overlooked, or at least forgot to mention, were some really new developments for which he himself had been partially responsible. He ignored Katz and Lazarsfeld's (1954) study *Personal influence* – Riessman and Bauer (1959) commented on that omission – and, more important, he missed the importance of the subtitle of that volume: *The part played by people in the flow of mass communication*.

Nor did he mention the two-step flow hypothesis. This hypothesis – which, as later became clear, would not be confirmed (Cerha, 1967; Lin, 1973: 22–26) – stimulated new areas of research: on the flow of information and influence and the diffusion of news, knowledge and innovations; on the part played by the audience in mass communications. The two-step flow hypothesis, a fine example of serendipity, did focus attention on people and less on media or messages. Thus, the hypothesis was instrumental in a most decisive moment in mass communication research.

Berelson certainly was right in some respects: communications research had come to a deadlock. The old idea of the giant hypodermic needle had become obsolete, as Klapper (1960) showed at about the same time in his comprehensive study. In the early 1960's there was a growing interest in the role of people in mass communications: the part people play in the flow of information and the flow of influence was studied by Katz and Lazarsfeld (1954), Troldahl and Van Dam (1965) and others; homeostatic efforts received the attention of Festinger (1957) and Newcomb (1953); selection principles were summarized by Sears and Freedman (1967) and uses and gratifications were researched by Blumer and Katz (1974), McQuail (1972) and many others.

During this period a new line of thought developed: communication was no longer seen as one-way transmission, but as an interactive process involving both senders and receivers of messages. Communication came to be seen as a combination of the traditional division of labour – the production and consumption of messages – where both activities were considered more equally (Fearing, 1953, 1954, 1962). Communication could thus be seen as a two-dimensional rather than a linear model (Gerbner, 1956). Communication was thought of as a transaction in which two parties, senders and receivers, are each engaged for their respective and different motives (Bauer, 1963, 1964). Once the presumed causal relation between message production and audience effects became less rigid, researchers began investigating not only intended effects, but also consequences – intended or unintended, desirable or undesirable (Gerbner, 1956: 181). In other words, mass communication was no longer seen as an instrument of influence, persuasion or change, but as one factor among many in the social environment.

The trend 'the return to the concept of the powerful mass media' (Noelle-Neumann,

17

1973) signalled the revival in the early 1970's of the notion that mass media ought to have effects, even if they were notoriously ineffective. Under this banner several approaches as different as MacLuhan's media determinism, cultural indicators (Gerbner *et al.*, 1969), agenda-setting (McCoombs & Shaw, 1972), spiral of silence (Noelle-Neumann, 1974) and the knowledge gap studies (Tichenor *et al.*, 1970) could be brought together. Obviously the pendulum had swung once more to the 'powerful mass media' side of the theoretical spectrum. But yet another development was underway.

When Bauer proposed the term 'obstinate audience' in the 1960's, it had dawned on him that people do not behave according to the communicator's wishes, but in accordance with their own motives. Instead of the popular model of an audience being exploited by mass media, he proposed interpreting the action of both partners in communication, senders and receivers, as fullblown problem solvers (Bauer, 1964: 326).

This is similar to the model Shibutani (1966: 9–17) proposed for the study of rumors: communication as a collective attempt to construct a meaningful interpretation in an ambiguous situation. With rumors there is no division of labour between senders and receivers; everybody participating in their dispersion alternately engages in both roles. Shibutani's approach to the study of rumors is also based on the premise that mass communication can best be understood as a collective enterprise in constructing a meaningful interpretation of events relevant for those concerned, and breaks away from a media-centered perspective on human communication. Shibutani and to a certain extent Bauer envisage participation in communications while refering to a general (symbolic interactionist) perspective on social action, and therefore do not limit the part people play in mass communication to the receiver or to audience activities.

More recently, such a theoretical social action perspective on communication activities has been advocated by Altheide (1977) and, in connection with the uses and gratifications approach, by by Davis and Baran (1981). These developments also implicate a more general perspective on mass communication as public communication, and no longer limit the study of mass communication to mass media.

MASS COMMUNICATION AS PUBLIC COMMUNICATION

The most important characteristic of mass communication is that diffusion of information takes place in such a way that information is made public, i.e. is made available to everyone. It may well happen that many people will receive the information. This explains the prefix 'mass' in 'mass communication', but it is not a really important aspect. More than getting information to people, mass communication involves making information available, making information public (Stappers, 1966: 46-62). Also, the means in question regarding the mass media, should not be considered as *conditiones sine qua non* for a definition of mass communication. For the purpose of making certain information or knowledge public, the mass media are one of the most prominent, but not exclusive, communication channels. The spread of rumors demonstrates how information or knowledge can become public in a situation were mass media are not operating, or are engaged in limited activity. There have always been ways of making information available even to entire societies in times when mass media did not yet exist.

Many religions spread across continents before printing had even been thought of. In other words, mass communication – or, to use a better description, public communication – is the diffusion of messages in such a way that in principle no one is excluded from receiving them and no one is excluded from this process by the sender (Stappers, 1966: 47). This conception implies that mass communication is not restricted to communication through the use of mass media, nor to communication aimed at mass audiences.

The emergence of community media in the 1970's demonstrated the inability of the concepts 'mass' media and 'mass' communication to contain this new phenomenon. Here, media were definitely not intended for a mass audience and with no intention of becoming mass media. In studies describing small scale media or community media the expression 'community communication' was introduced (e.g. Halloran, 1975) which stressed the geographical locality and/or a community of interest as an essential context for community media.

When we refer to mass communication as public communication the problem regarding the conceptualization of community communication can be solved: community communication is then a form of public communication, of making public and creating a public within the context of a specific community (geographical and/or community of interest). The fact that community media usually operate on a smaller scale than mass media is an additional distinction between the two types of media, even in view of the efforts of some mass media to cater to specific, limited audiences through audience segmentation strategies.

Community communication should be understood as small scale forms of public communication, i.e. public communication within a neighbourhood, a village, town or suburb. The correspondence with audience segmentation, such as regionalization of national broadcasting and special interest magazines, is that in both cases – community communication and audience segmentation – communication is unrestricted and public, and is calculated to reach a relatively small audience. In fact, the reception will be limited and is intended to be limited because the messages are, qua content and/or form, intended for a limited audience that is interested in specific topics.

The difference between those specialized media and community media lies in the nature of the relationship between senders, audiences and messages. Community communication refers to those 'small scale' forms of public communication such as local cable and over-the-air broadcasting, community press and neighbourhood gossip that are meant for a generally restricted, but open category of receivers who are (usually) not dispersed over a large geographic region. The implicit assumption is that people involved in community communication, both as senders and receivers, have common interests in the double meaning of the word. As members of the same community they have the same concerns *and* they are interested in the same topics because they share the same background. In this sense small scale communication or community communication differs from audience segmentation: communicators in community communication address their audience on the assumption of a shared relevance that community issues have for both senders and receivers because they all participate in the same community. This community, further, serves as a frame of reference for a shared interpretation of the relevance of the topics communicated within the community. It is in the reproduction and representation of common (shared) interests that community media have gained their social and political significance. And it is in this respect that over the last ten years an increasing functional difference between mass media and community media has developed.

COMMUNITY MEDIA AND MASS MEDIA

The difference in scale of operations between community and mass media is relative: it is not possible to distinguish mass communication from community communication just by considering size. Generally speaking, community communication operates on a smaller scale than with mass media, but such a statement hardly suffices as a definition. The kind of communication techniques or the type of medium cannot be regarded as a criterium to distinguish small scale from large scale public communication. Small scale public communication encompasses a whole spectrum of communication forms, styles and techniques.

There is a variety of media involved such as banners, stickers, posters, pamphlets, video, 8 mm film and radio. If this list generates any common characteristics it is that small scale public communication is diverse in type and differs from large scale mass communication and from large, formal and institutionalized mass media. In terms of scale, style and content, small scale public communication is different, especially from institutions like 'the press' and 'broadcasting companies'.

There is a deliberate antagonism towards institutionalized mass media which stems from a historical heritage dating back to the social and political movements of the 1960's, where a critical attitude was expressed regarding most political and social institutions: government, educational institutions, church, industry and mass media.

The image of the mass media as pillars of democracy, as watchdogs of government, came to be questioned because that image presupposed a certain degree of trust in the mass media, like Western democracy presupposes delegated trust in chosen politicians. In the 1960's, a new form of democracy became prominent: participatory democracy. This form implies more co-determination in matters that are relevant to those involved, and more particicpation in the formation and expression of opinions by those directly concerned (Geissler, 1973).

At the national level this development manifests itself in the emergence of various kinds of so-called 'alternative' media such as the underground press and alternative cinema. Gradually, with the rise in significance of political issues at the local level such as environment, housing and welfare, other forms of public communication were used by citizen committees, tenant associations and local political groups. This led to increased use of community media: community press, community radio and community television. These forms of public communication focus at the local level, because the topics have a local significance and are usually dealt with by local government authorities. Community groups would try to draw support from members of the community by pointing out the relevance of the topic for the community as a whole.

These small scale forms of public communication are not necessarily aimed at a confrontation with the establishment, but at trying to create a local forum for articulation and discussion (Dunckelmann, 1975). The established national and regional media, i.e. press and broadcasting, due to their institutionalized character, cannot or will not cater to such specific audiences and local topics. This fact has made community media and small scale forms of public communication an important element in the local community.

CONCEPTUALIZATION OF COMMUNITY COMMUNICATION

The demarcation of small scale public communication from large scale mass media is only a first step towards a theoretical conceptualization of the phenomenon 'community communication'. What we have discussed so far only clarifies that there is more to small scale public communication than just matters of scale or form. All forms of public expression within a specific local social setting come into play, such as public gatherings, communication in neighbourhoods and pubs, meetings, posters and graffiti.

Here, the field of communication has to pay for the fact that communication research usually has been restricted to the mass media and mainly at the national level. When communication research was directed at the local level it usually was intended to study the audience of a single local medium, and not necessarily in relation to other forms of local communication (Brown, 1978). Research on local communication has been limited to specific local media, to specific local media content and to specific local media audiences (Dorsch, 1978; Saxer, 1978).

Research on the process and the structure of public communication within a local setting offers insight into the interplay and the changing patterns over time in and between mediated and non-mediated forms of communication with regard to topics relevant for the individual as a member of the local community. It could also provide insight into the development of structures of relevance, both at the community level and the level of individual community members. Differences in community structure could also be related to variations in communication structure and structures of relevance regarding community issues (Olien *et al.*, 1984).

Such an approach to the study of community communication implies a change in perspective on mass communication – a change from a linear media centered perspective to a more structural *and* dynamic perspective on mass communication as public communication within a specific social context. Such an approach also provides opportunity to explore other theoretical concepts, such as 'community' and the German concepts *Öffentlichkeit* and lokale *Öffentlichkeit* (local public sphere). In an article entitled "Communication and communtity", Chaney remarks that:

> ...the inadequacies of conceptualizing the communication process as one
> of 'exchange' or 'information transmission' has meant a growth of interest
> in the *communal* grounds of communicative interaction (Chaney, 1978: 1).

Chaney opposes the linear 'transmission perspective' on mass communication and stresses the structural dimension which underlies communication processes. In such a perspective public communication, both mediated and non-mediated, is a fundamental human activity, which transforms private individual experience into public collective experience. The context in which this process takes place – the community – is an essential element for understanding the development of collective experience and of the communication process within a specific social setting. Since public communication is such a basic human activity, Chaney opposes the thought that mass media could exclusively contribute to the collectivation of experience, the transformation of individual into social experience.

It is naive to suppose that mass communication has the function of a mirror or telescope through which attention can be brought to important matters. Naive because the image suggests that the importance of events is something that lies in the events, and that all mass communication does is making the importance visible to everyone. Negt and Kluge (1972: 47) came to the same kind of understanding of public communication during a critique on the mass media in their development of the concept *Öffentlichkeit*. To them, *Öffentlichkeit*, or 'public sphere', describes the social organization by means of public communication of authentic experiences and needs that are relevant to a specific group or category of individuals, and transforms the individual experiences into one of the group.

Both concepts – community and *Öffentlichkeit* – do not exclude media use as a possible way of organizing social experience; they merely incorporate media use in public communication, while public communication again is conceptualized at the individual level as an element of a theory of social action. This implies that media use and communicative interaction are not studied as isolated activities but as an integral part of the individual's active orientation towards the physical and social environment.

Although stemming from different theoretical backgrounds, several similarities exist between the concepts community and *Öffentlichkeit* that are of special interest in studying small scale public communication. Both concepts imply a holistic approach to the study of local or community communication, the concepts themselves are not unproblematic. Newby (1980: 13) suggests that essentially three different definitions of community can be discerned: a geographic locality, a local social system, and a sense of identity. When the concept *Öffentlichkeit* is applied to the study of local media and local communication – i.c. *lokale Öffentlichkeit* – the same distinctions can be found. Sometimes *lokale Öffentlichkeit* refers to the relation between communication structure and spatial / geographic structure, sometimes to the relation between communication structure and social structure and, finally, sometimes to the communication structure within a category of individuals for whom specific local topics have a special relevance (Hollander, 1988: 181-186). Both concepts avoid presupposing the existence of one all embracing *Öffentlichkeit* or community as a direct result of mass media exposure. Both concepts stress the existence of several mass media independent or *(Teil)Öffentlichkeiten* and communities. Analytically, they distinguish catgeories of individuals participating in public communication, both as senders and receivers, based on the perceived relevance of topics for those individuals. See also Lindlof's (1987) notion of 'interpretive communities' based on an interest the terms are given in common people constituting a community or an *Öffentlichkeit* through participation in public communication.

The two concepts, although stemming from different schools of thought, are complementary in the sense that the concept community stresses the structural characteristics (social structure, social system), while *Öffentlichkeit* stresses the communication process and the relevance of specific topics as a motive for communication. Essential to both concepts, however, is the element of public communication about matters relevant to those concerned as a process which creates and at the same time presupposes a shared identity.

These concepts can be extended to communication processes at the local or sublocal level. In German literature the concept *lokale Öffentlichkeit* – local public sphere – is used as the conceptualization of an *Öffentlichkeit* that coincides with a geographically based local unit or social system: the municipality, parish, village or suburb. In Anglo-Saxon communication literature the expression 'community communication' refers to the communication structure in a geographical community or in a community of interest. Usually it is taken for granted that such a geographical unit as a parish or suburb is indeed a community of interest in the sense that there exists a local public sphere where relevant issues are communicated. More correct than to suppose that community media will create such a sphere would be to investigate first whether and at what level within the social system – within the city or village – a community of interest exists. It might be the case that at the level of the municipality, no corresponding 'community' or *Öffentlichkeit* in terms of public communication exists, while at another level – neighbourhood or district – a public sphere is present where residents share a concern for specific topics, thus forming the basis for local communication.

In Dutch experiments with local origination cable television programming the degree to which stations developed from initiatives to community stations can partly be explained by the presence of a community or *Öffentlichkeit* at the local level (Stappers, Hollander and Manders, 1977; Stappers and Hollander, 1981; Hollander, 1982).

RESEARCH APPROACHES

Looking at the empirical research concerned with community media over the years, basically three approaches can be identified: the 'localism-cosmopolitism' approach (Merton, 1950; Dobriner, 1958; Lehman, 1986), the 'integration' or 'community ties' approach (Stamm, 1985) and the 'community structure' approach (Tichenor *et al.*, 1970, 1980; Olien *et al.*, 1984).

Localism-cosmopolitism and the community ties approach both take the individual as the point of departure, and attempt to describe and explain the contribution of various factors to the use people make of specific local media. These factors concern the value people place on the community in which they live and on the ties they develop in their community.

In the community structure approach, the structure of the community in which people live (homogeneous *vs.* heterogeneous) is considered a contextual factor influencing both the nature of the community media (content) and the use people make of local media. Instead of the individual, here the point of departure is the community as a social system.

Theoretical concepts such as community communication and *lokale Öffentlichkeit* have drawn attention to the fact that a description and explanation of the use of local media by community residents cannot only be studied at the level of individual characteristics such as length of residence and community identification (see Janowitz, 1952). Nor is it sufficient to study the functions of community media solely from a system approach such as advocated by Tichenor, Donohue and Olien.

What is needed for the study of community media is an effort, as undertaken by

23

Stamm (1985), to integrate several research approaches in order to develop a conceptual model for the study of community media. The main characteristics of such a conceptual model are: integration of community structure and individual factors; a perspective on the use of local media which is not static, but which emphasises the dynamics of local media use as well as the dynamics of the process whereby people are socialized within the community context; and develop a local identity (Dunckelmann, 1975). The study of community media then becomes the study of the contribution community media make to the development of local identity within a specific geographic context.

RESEARCH SIGNIFICANCE OF COMMUNITY COMMUNICATION

Most of the time, mass communication has, by most observers (the general public, but also politicians, social scientists and communication scholars, been considered as an activity engaged in by a small number of professional senders who, through the (mass) media, send messages to the many receivers – the masses – who are then supposed to be influenced by these messages. We have shown that such a view is neither adequate nor tenable. However, this has not inhibited some policy makers and researchers, however, from maintaining this position. It was clear to them that mass communication does something to society, and through misconception of the nature of the communication process, they have clung to antiquated theoretical concepts. Mass communication is, as stated earlier, public communication: a process in which senders and receivers each participate on the basis of their distinct and separate motives.

This process is not merely a matter of isolated media activity, but a comprehensive totality of supplying and obtaining information and knowledge in the social context of a social system. It is easier to demonstrate this coherence by investigation of communication on a smaller scale: in social systems found in villages, suburbs and other geographical communities. The social context and shared interests can be more easily studied in these settings and at this level than at the regional or national level.

Comprehensive research from a holistic perspective on small scale public communication could lead to more and better insight into the process and the structural components of mass communication in general. More insight into public communication on a smaller scale and into commmunity communication could also help move our thinking away from an oversimplified and mechanistic view of commmunication as a linear process, as the transport of information from one point to another. This would be, in itself, a welcome step forward in mass communication theory.

References

Altheide, D.L. (1977): *Creating reality. How TV news distorts events*, Beverley Hills: Sage.

Bauer, R.A.(1959): 'Comments on Berelson's "The state of communication research"', *Public Opinion Quarterly* 23, 1: 14-17.

Bauer, R.A. (1963): 'Communication as a transaction: a comment on "on the concept of influence"', *Public Opinion Quarterly* 27, 1: 83-86.

Bauer, R.A. (1964): 'The obstinate audience', *American Psychologist* 19: 319-328.

Berelson, B. (1959): 'The state of communication research', *Public Opinion Quarterly* 13, 1: 1-6.

Berrigan, F. (1979): *Community communication; the role of community media in development*, Paris: Unesco.

Blumler, J.G. and E. Katz (eds) (1974): *The uses of mass communications*, Beverly Hills: Sage.

Brown, R. (1978): *Characteristics of local media audiences*, Farnborough: Saxon House.

Cerha, J. (1967): *Selective mass communication*, Stockholm: Norstedt & Siner.

Chaney, D. (1978): 'Communication and community', *Communication 7*, 1: 1-32.

Davis, D. and S. Baran (1981): *Mass communication and everyday life*, Belmont, CA: Wadsworth.

Dobriner, W. (1958): 'Local and cosmopolitan as contemporary suburban character types', in W. Dobriner (ed.) *The suburban community*, New York.

Dorsch, P. (1978): 'Lokalkommunikation. Ergebnisse und Defizite der Forschung', *Publizistik 23*, 3: 189-201.

Dunckelmann, H. (1975): *Lokale Öffentlichkeit. Eine Gemeindesoziologische Untersuchung*, Stuttgart: Kolhammer.

Fearing, F. (1953): 'Toward a psychological theory of human communication', *Journal of Personality 22*, 1: 71-88.

Fearing, F. (1954): 'Social impact of the massmedia of communication', in N.B. Henry (ed.), *Mass Media and Education*, Chicago: National Society for the Study of Education.

Fearing, F. (1962): 'Human communication', *Audio-Visual Communication Review 10*, 5: 78-108.

Festinger, L.A. (1957): *A theory of cognitive dissonance*, Evanston: Row, Peterson & Co.

Geissler, R. (1973): *Massenmedien, Basiskommunikation und Demokratie*, Tübingen: Mohr.

Gerbner, G. (1956): 'Toward a general model of communication', *Audio-Visual Communication Review 4*, 3: 171-199.

Gerbner, G. (1969): 'Toward "cultural indicators". The analysis of mass mediated public message systems,' *Audio-Visual Communication Review 17*, 2: 137-148.

Gerbner, G. (ed.) (1969): The analyses of communication content: development in scientific theories and computer techniques, New York: Wiley.

Halloran, J. (1975): *Communication and community*, Strasbourg: Council of Europe.

Janowitz, M. (1952): *The community press in urban setting*, Glencoe, IL: Free Press.

Hollander, E. (1982): *Kleinschalige Massacommunicatie: Lokale omroepvormen in West Europa*, The Hague: State Publishing Co.

Hollander, E. (1988): *Lokale Communicatie en Lokale Openbaarheid. Openbaarheid als Communicatiewetenschappelijk Concept*, Nijmegen: Katholieke Universiteit Nijmegen.

Klapper, J.T. (1960): *The effects of mass communication*, New York: Free Press.

Katz, E. and P.F. Lazarsfeld (1954): *Personal influence; the part played by people in the flow of mass communication*, New York: Free Press.

Lin, N. (1973): *The study of human communication*, Indianapolis, IL: Bobbs-Merrill.

Lehman Jr, E.C. (1986): 'The local/cosmopolitan dichotomy and acceptance of women clergy: a replication and extension of Roof', *Journal for the Scientific Study of Religion 25*: 461-482.

Lindlof, T.R. (1987): 'Media audiences as interpretive communities', in: *Communication Yearbook II*, Beverly Hills: Sage.

McCombs, M.E. and D.L. Shaw (1972): 'The agenda-setting function of mass media', *Public Opinion Quarterly 36*, 2: 176-187.

McLuhan, H.M. (1964): *Understanding media*, New York: McGraw Hill.

McQuail, D. (ed.) (1972): *Sociology of mass communications*, Harmondsworth: Penguin.

McQuail, D., J.G. Blumler and J.R. Brown (1972): 'The television audience: a revised perspective', in: D. McQuail (ed.) *Sociology of mass communications*, Harmandsworth: Penguin.

McQuail, D. (1983): *Mass communication theory. An introduction*, London: Sage.

Merton, R.K. (1950): 'Patterns of influence: a study of interpersonal influence and communication behaviour in a local community', in: P.F. Lazarsfeld and F.N. Stanton (eds) *Communication Research 1948-1949*, New York: Harper & Brothers.

Negt, O. and A. Kluge (1972): *Öffentlichkeit und Erfahrung*, Frankfurt: Suhrkamp Verlag.

Newby, C. (1980): *Community*, Milton Keynes: Open University Press.

Newcomb, T.M. (1953): 'An approach to the study of communicative acts', *Psychological Review* 60, 6: 393-404.

Noelle-Neumann, E. (1973): 'Return to the concept of powerful mass media', *Studies of Broadcasting* 9: 67-112.

Noelle-Neumann, E. (1974): 'The spiral of silence', *Journal of Communication* 24, 2: 43-51.

Olien, C., G.A. Donohue and P. Tichenor (1972): 'Community structure and media use', *Journalism Quarterly* 55, 5: 445-455.

Olien, C., G.A. Donohue and P. Tichenor (1984): 'Media and stages of social conflict', *Journalism Monographs,* nr. 90.

Riesman, D. (1959): 'Comments on Berelson's "The state of communication research"', *Public Opinion Quarterly* 23, 1: 10-13.

Saxer, U. (1978): 'Lokale Kommunikation Anspruch und Realität. Bilanz der Forschung', *Media Perspektiven* 5: 367-379.

Schramm, W. (1959): 'Comments on Berelson's "The state of communication research"', *Public Opinion Quarterly* 23, 1: 6-9.

Sears, D.O. and J.L. Freedman (1967): 'Selective exposure to information: a critical review', *Public Opinion Quarterly* 31, 2: 194-213.

Shibutani, T. (1966): *Improvised news: a sociological study of rumor,* Indianapolis, IL: Bobbs-Merrill.

Stamm, K. (1985): *Newspaper use and community ties. Toward a dynamic theory,* Norwood, NJ: Ablex.

Stappers, J. (1966): *Publicistiek en communicatiemodellen,* Nijmegen: Katholieke Universiteit Nijmegen.

Stappers, J., E. Hollander and H. Manders (1977): *Vier experimenten met lokale kabelomroep,* Nijmegen: Instituut voor Massacommunicatie.

Stappers, J. and E. Hollander (1981): 'Bürgernahes Fernsehen und Kabelpilotprojekte', *Rundfunk und Fernsehen* 29: 13-25.

Tichenor, P., G.A. Donohue and C. Olien (1970): 'Mass media flow and differential growth in knowledge', *Public Opinion Quarterly* 34, 2: 159-170.

Tichenor, P., G.A. Donohue and C. Olien (1980): *Community, conflict and the press,* Beverly Hills: Sage.

Troldahl, V.C. and R. van Dam. (1965): 'Face-to-face communication about major topics in the news', *Public Opinion Quarterly* 29, 4: 626-634.

3. Community television as a tool of local culture

Knut Lundby

Department of Media and Communication, University of Oslo, Norway

Can electronic community media serve as tools for maintaining and strengthening small geographical communities? Are the new media capable of raising and furthering local identity? Politicians and governmental authorities responsible for experiments with community radio and television in European countries have often considered these media to be such tools. Electronic community media, they reasoned, could serve as a defence against encroachment from satellite-delivered cultural influences.

Development of satellite communication is related to an overall tendency in Europe towards centralization and cultural standardization. Local geographical cultures are challenged, among other things, by the specialization required in higher education and the development of interest-oriented communities.

People in smaller geographical communities face problems in maintaining their local identities. This applies in any event to those segments of the local population which are most affected by the processes of cultural standardization and specialization, such as young people and other mobile groups who seek knowledge and cultural impulses outside the geographical community. But also people moving into local communities have more difficulty in acquiring a new local identity than is the case in more stable local cultures.

The electronic community media in Europe have been in operation for too brief a period to be able to give a fair evaluation of their potential as tools for local culture. To change cultural processes takes years. It is simply not possible to measure the impact of new technology or new media before they have become habits in people's lives. To make such evaluations researchers need tools to help understand these media.

In this chapter I describe a set of concepts which can be used in the evaluation of community media as tools of local identity and local culture. I focus on community television, which can be considered the local opposite of satellite-delivered television programming. The findings of a case study are reported, conducted in two local geographical communities in a transitional phase of social and cultural development

27

– a situation in which community television could possibly strengthen the challenged local culture.

TERRITORIALITY AND DISTANCING

How can the social and cultural transition from more closed and stabile to more open and mobile geographical communities be characterized? Within a locality, delimited by its population and administrative borders, a geographical community develops through the interaction and identification among the people living there, and through orientation of the residents towards the community itself. These processes establish and maintain a local culture. In order to strengthen this culture, community television must stimulate the identification, interaction and orientation towards the culture.

'Culture' is here understood as 'milieu of symbols', following the definition of Sorokin. He sees 'culture' as "the totality of the meanings, values, and norms possessed by the interacting persons and the totality of the vehicles which objectify, socialize, and convey these meanings" (Sorokin, 1947: 63).

The media are part of the culture and act as 'vehicles' for communication of shared symbols. New community media represent as such a cultural change as well as channels of communication within a local culture. Communication is woven into the processes of identification, interaction and orientation. Communication is that part of the social interaction where meanings are constructed and messages conveyed. All communication presupposes a common focus of identification in relation to the same culture.

The communication processes in culture make use of symbols – here broadly understood as objects, words and *gestalts* – to which culturally defined meanings are attached. The meaning of a symbol has to be learned by the members of a culture as a matter of convention.

The culture itself develops specific social structures for interaction which function as communication devices or vehicles. Every culture uses a repertoire of such devices. But a specific culture will have a dominant symbolic form, or a dominant combination of forms, within which communication takes place.

Suttles (1972) has characterized two such symbolic forms which give different directions for interaction, identification, and orientation in society and thereby for the shaping of communities: people may interact with each other out of 'territoriality' or 'distancing'. As general symbolic forms they characterize more closed and stable social bonds opposed to more open and mobile relationships between people.

The principle of territoriality is practised within a given area, geographically or symbolically defined. This territory is defined and defended against outsiders. If you are within the territory you are part of the in-group as opposed to the out-group. You either belong or do not belong; there is no position in-between. Communication defines whether you are inside or outside the territory.

Distancing as a principle for social interaction goes together with signals defining how remote or close you want to be to different persons in varying situations. Such communication is quite subtle according to the repertoire of distances one wishes to maintain in relation to others.

Distancing generally fits urban communities better than territoriality because a modernized way of life needs differentiated relations. Territoriality is the symbolic form which suits the traditional, rural community because of the stability in relations and the distinct geographical territory for such communities. But there may be communities based on territoriality even in an urban setting as Suttles (1968) demonstrates in a Chicago-based study.

Territoriality dominates in *Gemeinschaft*, while distancing is the symbolic form mostly found in *Gesellschaft*, to link Suttles concepts to those of Tönnies (1974). Territoriality and distancing usually coexist as symbolic forms in the same society, complementing each other. A person may in some situations act on the basis of territoriality, in other situations on the principle of distancing. But there is a tendency that one or the other symbolic form, or a specific combination of the two, will dominate as an overall principle of interaction within a community.

Territoriality seems to be the basic symbolic form of communication within a limited community, or *lokale Öffentlichkeit*, be it either a geographical community as a cultural whole or a community-of-interest as a subculture within the geographical locality. Even when distancing is the overall symbolic form, smaller communities within the fragmented urban setting will refer to a set of symbols rooted in territoriality for their internal communication. Therefore, to be able to understand use of community media in localities where distancing is the main symbolic form, it is first necessary to study the territorial type.

RESEARCH CONSIDERATIONS

A strategically opportune situation for researching the use of new community media is that where a traditional geographical community is just beginning to progress towards more differentiated social relations at the introduction of the new media, but is still basically rooted in territoriality. The geographical communities chosen for study need to be under the cultural influence of new electronic community media as part of a greater differentiation in the local media system. The ideal cases are geographical communities where there is data collected before and after introduction of new electronic vehicles for community communication.

When there is a change in a local culture from territoriality towards distancing as the dominant symbolic form, it can be assumed that the character of media use in the community will change. When distancing is the dominant symbolic form, 'zapping' and pendeling between media channels will be part of the culture and life style of particular groups. There will be more channels available in each medium and people will maintain different degrees of distance to the different channels, and tend to pendle between them in different situations.

Regarding territoriality, when there is only one or just a few channels available, use of the dominant media channel becomes part of the sense of belonging to the community and of communicating within the community. This provides material for conversation and experience within the territory, and creates and maintains identity in the community. Under territoriality, then, media users should be expected to attend to the dominant medium of different geographical levels, be it the national television programme, the regional radio station or the local newspaper.

29

Under territoriality channel preference, because of this overall stability in media use, may be taken as an indicator of cultural orientation and identification. This is not possible when distancing is predominate. For this reason the ideal situation for research on new television channels in small geographical communities should begin with investigation of a culture at its take-off from a situation where territoriality predominates, towards a culture with more extensive manifestation of distancing.

This take-off from territoriality enables one to understand some of the mechanisms of how modern electronic media function in and for small scale communities. It should thereby be possible to see if and how community television is capable of strengthening local culture through stimulation of the processes of identification, interaction and orientation.

In the empirical research to be reported here, the data are insufficient to provide a definitive answer to whether community television has such a function. It is, however, possible at least to come closer to understanding the process.

CASE STUDIES

Norway provides special opportunity for research on the impact of new television options. Up until now there has been only one national television channel in the country. Although in some regions it is possible to receive Swedish signals, the main television diet – until the advent of cable networks and satellite technology – has been provided on a single channel. There was also only one radio channel in Norway until the early 1980s.

Norway seems to have been and still is (in the 1980s and the early 1990s) in a take-off situation from territoriality to distancing as a dominant symbolic form. According to anthropologist Marianne Gullestad:

> Norwegians have traditionally been a people depending more on territoriality than on distancing as a mode of thought and conduct. The change from mostly territoriality to mostly distancing is in many people's lives taking place at this moment. Having moved to cities or finding themselves in rapidly changing rural centres, they are learning how to cope with these changed circumstances (Gullestad, 1986: 66–67).

The differentiation of radio and television is part of the structural changes behind this general shift from territoriality to distancing. From 1981 to 1986 experiments were conducted with community radio and television in Norway, as well as with satellite television (see Chapter 6 for further information on these matters). Some of the geographical communities involved in these experiments provide excellent cases for research.

I have chosen two localities in different stages of development regarding the influence on culture by a multiplicity of television channels. These two geographical communities, Jevnaker and Elverum, are both located inland in south-eastern Norway. They are both what Gullestad (1986: 67) refers to as "rural centres". The research focuses on the more densely populated cores of these two municipalities: in Jevnaker there are about 4,000 residents and in Elverum about 10,000.

On visiting these two places it becomes clear that distancing as a mode of interpersonal communication is more common in Elverum than in Jevnaker. This is probably due to the size of population and the greater share of mobile academics in Elverum.

With urbanized Europe as a basis for comparison, both Elverum and Jevnaker are rural centres where aspects of territoriality dominate. This is the case also when the sites are compared to the larger cities in Norway. But in relation to the countryside surrounding the two municipalities, both are more influenced by distancing. The point here, however, is not the exact position of these two rural centres on a general scale, but on their relative position to each other. Elverum is, with this perspective in mind, more marked by distancing than Jevnaker. It is neither important nor necessary, however, to determine the exact quantitative difference regarding distancing in this example. What is important here is that the difference between Jevnaker and Elverum demonstrates two stages in the general move from territoriality to distancing as a dominant symbolic form.

New channels in local culture

During the first half of the 1980s cable networks were installed both in Elverum and Jevnaker. In addition to the single national programme, households in the centre of Elverum have had access to Swedish television delivered by cable since 1979. In 1982 the cable company was awarded a franchise to experiment with both community television and distribution of programmes from the OTS satellite, later known as *Sky Channel* (Lundby, 1982).

In Jevnaker The Norwegian Telecommunication Administration established what they called their 'telematic sandbox' for field experiments of new services delivered by cable (Dragland *et al.*, 1985). The first subscribers were able to receive programming from the Swedish television stations, from the community television station and from the French satellite channel *TV5*. Norwegians generally are not proficient in French, and *TV5* was consequently not a major viewing choice of residents in Jevnaker. The Norwegian authorities were unwilling at that time to allow distribution of the more popular English language satellite programming.

This new television programming was introduced earlier and involved more differentiation in Elverum than the later developments in Jevnaker. It is also parallel to the greater emphasis on distancing in social relations in Elverum than in Jevnaker. Residents in the two rural centres had equal possibility to express topics of shared relevance within the community via the newly implemented local television channels. In Elverum access was available through a professional journalist who covered different activities and groups with a small team of volunteers. In Jevnaker groups in the community had direct access and made their own programmes which were co-ordinating by a studio staff member. In terms of form, community television in Elverum was more professional, but both channels were community-oriented regarding programming content. They only transmitted locally produced programming.

For this study localities with cable-delivered television signals were chosen. Cable systems provide an opportunity for comparisons while keeping constant the number of channels available to persons interviewed. The output of television programming is the same for all cable subscribers. (Special services employing decoders, such as pay television, were not in use at the time of the study.)

Two samples

Two samples were drawn from cable subscribers, 15 years and older. The samples are not necessarily representative of the entire populations in Jevnaker and Elverum, but they do demonstrate the contrast in territoriality and distancing between these places.

The Jevnaker sample consists of persons who in 1983 lived in that part of the rural centre where the cable system was planned. In addition, the persons included in the sample had expressed interest in a connection to the cable system (Ulvaer, 1984). Not all of the respondents had actually been connected when the survey was conducted in 1985. Information on social background and television channel preferences are drawn from the first survey, held in 1985 (Lundby, 1986). The respondents in this panel are fairly representative of all adults in the rural centre in Jevnaker, although local orientation is slightly stronger than in the total population of the municipality. The percentage of young people under the age of 20 is in the sample also somewhat smaller than in the total population.

The Elverum sample consists of persons who in 1982 lived in households connected to the cable system (Lundby, 1982). This sample is not representative of the total adult population in the rural centre of Elverum (cf. Werner *et al.*, 1984). There are insufficient elderly respondents and an over representation for the age category 25–44 years. These differences between sample and population probably increases the presence of distancing measured in this locality. Background information for these respondents dates from 1982, a few months before community and satellite television were introduced in Elverum. Preferences for new channels was taken from interviews completed with the same persons a year later (Lundby, 1983).

The two samples, then, exhibit more distinction along the dimension territoriality-distancing than would be found in the total populations of Jevnaker and Elverum. It must be remembered that the results presented below do not characterize these two rural centres as communities. They merely demonstrate social and cultural traits in samples of cable subscribers in the communities at the moment of introduction of new television channels.

Since Jevnaker and Elverum, from a more general perspective, both lean toward territoriality as a dominant symbolic form and only in the first stages of development are aspects of distancing present, it is possible to interpret overall channel preferences here as indicators of cultural orientation.

Cable television provides viewers with an abundance of progamming and assists alternative cultures to interact and perhaps struggle within the same local setting. Every television channel can be seen as an expression of a specific culture. It is produced or edited within the frame of the culture from where it originates. Cable subscribers in Elverum in 1982, for example, met one milieu of symbols in the national television channel, another in the two channels from the neighbouring country, one in the community channel and another in satellite-delivered television programming. These channels use overlapping cultural material, but each of them is edited and presented with reference to one specific culture, be it a geographically-based or interest-based culture.

What merits special concern here are new cultural possibilities introduced in traditional communities through television channels not previously available. In addition to the national television programming, people were able to view a community channel on the one extreme, and transnational channels on the other. Community and satellite television represent opposites in the spectrum of multichannel television. They also suggest two opposite directions of development in new media technology: decentralization and internationalization (Bakke, 1986).

How do people in a geographical community mainly based on territoriality react when cable television brings these new, diametrically opposed cultural opportunities into their homes and local community? The hypothesis is that the kind of relations people have to their community will strongly influence their choice among available television channels. These choices among different cultural impulses, again, will demonstrate whether community television can be considered a tool of local culture or not.

Cultural orientation

A culture is not a static entity, but is constantly undergoing change. This also applies to a local culture. The availability of new television channels in a geographical community is a structural change. The use or non-use of these new possibilities will, over time, contribute to the cultural development of the local community. The direction of cultural change in the collectivity depends on cultural choices taken by the individual members of the community.

The 'cultural orientation' of the individual may be directed out of the community or deeper into the community. A person may react with cultural loyalty or with cultural rejection towards the community. Of course, in everyday life the choices taken are seldom as clear-cut as this, but these opposites suggest the theoretical alternatives.

Orientation towards the community is symbolic because the individual still lives or participates there, even if cultural orientation is outside the locality. Cultural orientation may affect the person's social participation in the community. Cultural rejection of departure may result in less intense social interaction within the community. Stronger cultural loyalty may result in more intense participation and communication within the social structure of the community.

When a community channel and a transnational channel are introduced simultaneously on a cable system in a traditional locality, contradictory cultural impulses are provided to cable subscribers. This situation comes to resemble a kind of quasi-laboratory setting where a cultural experiment may be conducted. What matters here are the expectations people have of the possibilities provided by the new television services. People are generally unable to accurately predict how much use they may make of television channels not yet experienced. Such predictions cannot, therefore, be considered reliable indicators of eventual media use. But when people are asked about their preferences for a new community channel versus transnational channels, the answers can be interpreted as the direction of orientation into or out of the local culture.

Both in Jevnaker and Elverum studies of the expectations of new channels were completed just before community television and satellite television were introduced on the cable systems. In Jevnaker people were confronted with multichannel prospects for the first time; most people had, until then, only watched programming on the single national television channel. In Elverum the cable subscribers had already been introduced to Swedish television, but the programme offerings were new for them. Respondents in Jevnaker were asked in which of the three types of planned channels they had the greatest expectations: the community channel, Swedish television or satellite programmes. At that time respondents did not know that only French language programming would be provided on the satellite channel. More than four out of ten respondents gave priority to Swedish television. Inasmuch as Swedish television was the most familiar and similar to their own national television, it was understandable respondents would have the most concrete expectations about this channel.

In Elverum there were only two alternatives at the time cable subscribers were asked about their expectations. A large number were unable to respond when confronted with two unknown prospects. Of those who did answer, the majority said they preferred the satellite programming (see Table 1).

Table 1. Expectations in new television channels

	Jevnaker per cent	Elverum per cent
Greatest expectations in:		
Community television	22	25
Neighbouring country tv	44	-
Satellite television	21	37
Don't know	13	38
Total	100 per cent	100 per cent
N =	(215)	(266)

Source: Lundby, 1982: **9**; 1986: 107.

In the classic study of 'Rovere', undertaken in the 1940s, Merton (1968) suggests different orientations to community through the terms 'local' and 'cosmopolitan' influentials. The town of Rovere, with 11,000 inhabitants, is comparable to Elverum and Jevnaker. Locals orient themselves into the community, cosmopolitans out of the locality, although they still live there. Merton's distinction between locals and cosmopolitans, then, corresponds to the cultural orientations of 'loyalty' and symbolic 'departure' or rejection.

Merton's study explores "the place of mass communications in patterns of interpersonal influence" (Merton, 1968: 441). Locals and cosmopolitans do not only orient themselves in different ways towards their living environment, but also attend to media in different ways. Locals lean towards interpersonal communication and local media, while cosmopolitans use mass media as a bridge to the wider culture outside the locality.

Stamm (1985: 65–67) has criticized Merton's dichotomy, arguing that it does not adequately cover all persons situated between a clear local or cosmopolitan orientation toward their living environment. This is an important notion, but Merton's concepts may still be fruitful when applied, as Merton himself did, to the dynamics of cultural orientation and not, as Stamm supposes, to static elements of local structure.

There are, as suggested by Rogers (1983: 200), 'cosmopolite' and 'localite' channels. Community television is a localite channel in the sense that sender and receiver are within the same social system. Satellite television offers cosmopolite channels. To study orientations toward local community through expectations to just these alternative new channels, makes the issue very clear.

When the expectations of new television channels are seen as cultural orientations, there are two possible ways of analysing the Jevnaker data. First, expectations of Swedish television could be removed in order to make direct comparisons with Elverum. This is done in Table 2, where allowance is made for persons without a clear local or cosmopolitan orientation, namely the persons who did not know which of the new channels they preferred.

Table 2. Cultural orientation based on expectations of community television versus satellite television

	Jevnaker per cent	Elverum per cent
Local orientation	40	25
Neither ('don't know')	23	38
Cosmopolite orientation	37	37
Total	100 per cent	100 per cent
N =	(120)	(266)

Source: Lundby, 1982: 7; 1987:1988.

But in Jevnaker there was a third alternative introduced at the same time as the local and cosmopolitan prospects, namely Swedish television. Television from this neighbouring country is neither local nor transnational, but an alternative located somewhere between. That this category is most numerous is consistent with findings from Stamm (1985: 66); see Table 3. This, however, does not necessarily make the distinction between those respondents with a local and a cosmopolitan orientation unproductive. Through a larger degree of local orientation (Table 2) or through less pronounced cosmopolite orientation (Table 3), respondents in the Jevnaker data seem more loyal and less in need of a symbolic departure from the local community than the Elverum respondents.

Table 3. Cultural orientation based on expectations of new television channels

	Jevnaker per cent
Expect most from:	
Community television = Local orientation	26
Neighbouring country tv = Neither	51
Satellite television = Cosmopolitan orientation	24
Total	101 per cent
N =	(187)

Swedish television included in above figures; 'don't know' omitted. Source: Based on Lundby, 1986.

Cultural anchoring

While cultural orientation suggests a person's inclination in relation to the local culture, the 'cultural anchoring' indicates position in the social network and milieu of symbols in the community. Cultural anchoring indicates the degree to which an individual is intertwined in the social network and the subculture of the community.

A person who takes part in a community establishes cultural anchoring to that community through its social life. Cultural anchoring is determined by the degree of social interaction (which entails both action or participation, and communication) and identification with or commitment to the community. This applies to essentially every kind of community or human group (Homans, 1950).

People are usually involved in many communities based on specific interests and/or geographical areas of various levels (sub-local, local, regional, national). All these relations imply cultural anchorings. Every person, in other words, is woven into a more or less complicated set of social and cultural bonds. Not all anchorings are activated at the same time, and conflicts between different bonds may develop.

Here we examine the result of cultural anchoring for respondents in the Jevnaker and Elverum communities. The degree of identification with each community was measured by response to a question about the degree one feels connected to the locality. The question presupposes that identification has both a cognitive and affective component. Stamm (1985: 20-21) and Stamm and Fortini-Campbell (1983: 9), in studies of newspaper use and community ties, suggest that the two components can be separated. They reserve the concept 'identification' with a geographical community for the cognitive link and use the concept 'closeness to community' for the affective bonds. Here, these two aspects are treated as a single unit.

The identification with the geographical community was much stronger among respondents in Jevnaker than in Elverum. This was also the case regarding interaction in the community, but to a lesser degree for the concept identification. The level of interaction was measured through a combination of answers to questions about contact with neighbouring households and friends in the locality (Lundby, 1987). These results were confirmed in a recent study encompassing both Elverum and Jevnaker (Futsaeter, 1990).

The outcome of the mix of interaction and identification is a degree of cultural anchoring to the community. Very strong identification to the community, combined with very frequent social interaction, suggests intense and active belonging to the community. A combination of identification and interaction on a strong and frequent level shows a weaker, but still active form of belonging. A person having strong identification to the community, but who is less frequently interacting with others in that community, demonstrates a passive form of belonging.

All people living in a geographical community must have a minimum of social interaction in that locality. Reference based solely on identification is not possible, but a form of attachment may be an option if this minimum level of interaction is combined with a limited degree of identification to the community. If both interaction and identification are minimal, the person has no reasonable ties to the community.

While more than 20 per cent of the Jevnaker respondents seem to have a strong, active sense of belonging to their community, less than 10 per cent of those in Elverum can be similarly described; see Table 4. People seem to have the strongest sense of cultural anchoring in the locality where territoriality is also a pronounced symbolic form.

Table 4. Cultural anchoring and relation to community

	Jevnaker per cent	Elverum per cent
Strong, active belonging	22	9
Weaker, active belonging	31	34
Passive or no belonging	47	57
Total	100 per cent	100 per cent
N =	(215)	(266)

Source: Based on Lundby, 1982: 1.

Relation to community

By combining the variables of cultural orientation and cultural anchoring a measure of relations to community may be constructed. If a person belongs to a community with at least a fairly strong indication of identification and interaction, and has a degree of local orientation, relation to community can be considered 'settled'. The same applies to the situation where a strong and active form of social belonging is combined with a middle-of-the-road orientation.

If, on the other hand, a cosmopolite orientation is complemented by a weak bond of social belonging, the relation to community is 'outward'. This is also the case with an average orientation combined with no form of social belonging to the community.

Between the territorial and the distancing dimensions, there is a more 'contradictory' relation to community. This is the case when a cosmopolite orientation is combined with a strong and active form of social belonging – when a local orientation is combined with no social belonging and when the person is situated between both dimensions. Distribution along the variable 'relation to community' for respondents in Jevnaker and Elverum is presented in Table 5.

Table 5. Relation to community based on cultural anchoring by cultural orientation

	Jevnaker		Elverum
	(*as in table 2*) per cent	(*as in table 3*) per cent	per cent
Settled	39	29	21
Contradictory	21	38	33
Outward	39	33	46
Total	99 per cent	100 per cent	100 per cent
N =	(117)	(186)	(256)

Source: Based on Lundby, 1982: 1

A settled relation to community is most manifest in the Jevnaker data, while the tendency to seek outward from the community is stronger among the Elverum respondents. This seems independent of the manner in which cultural orientation is operationalized (as seen in Table 2 and Table 3).

Settled relations are the most widespread in the community most affected by territoriality. Outward relations predominate in the one population where distancing is more usual. Information about relations to community, based on data collected from individual residents, seems to correspond to the holistic impression of the dominant symbolic forms in the two communities.

Use of new channels

The Elverum cable subscribers interviewed in 1982 were asked a year later about their use of the new channels. Community and satellite television were formulated as opposing services, in a way that respondents were forced to indicate which of the two channels they had preferred during the past year. Such an indicator of media use is admittedly general and vague. The point, however, was to obtain an overall estimation of attractiveness, when viewers were forced to rank these two alternatives, and for this purpose the approach was adequate.

The Elverum data provide a good basis for considering this matter. Inasmuch as distancing was more pronounced in Elverum than in Jevnaker, it would be expected satellite programming would be more appealing there. The cable system in Elverum also provided a more attractive satellite channel, the English language *OTS*, than that which was made available in Jevnaker, the French language *TV5*. Priority in use between the channel alternatives correlates strongly with relations to community, even in this sample where distancing is pronounced; see Table 6.

There are no similar data available for Jevnaker, but there is information about the use of each channel independently. Use of the French speaking satellite programmes on *TV5* is, in a Norwegian setting, not comparable to use of English language television. But the community television channel in Jevnaker was similar to the local channel in Elverum. The findings for both locations were also similar: use of community television increases with the degree of territorial relations to community.

Table 6. Priority given to new television channels

	Settled per cent	Contradictory per cent	Outward per cent	All per cent
Preference:				
Community tv	85	72	41	61
Both/neither	12	17	22	18
Satellite (OTS)	3	11	37	21
Total	100 per cent	100 per cent	100 per cent	100 per cent
N=	(34)	(53)	(68)	(155)

Source: Based on Lundby, 1982.

In 1987, when cable subscribers in Jevnaker were again interviewed, they had been able to receive the more popular satellite channels such as *Sky* and *Super*. The community television channel, however, held its share of the viewers. The 'losers' in the competition for viewers were the national and neighbouring country channels (Vaage, 1988: 11–12). Those respondents with the strongest identification to the local community showed the greatest interest in local television (Skogerbø & Lundby, 1988: 81).

Nearly everyone watches the national channel at least some of the time. But when Elverum cable subscribers were asked to indicate their preference among all channels, the preference for the national channel followed an expected pattern: the respondents which gave the national channel a high rating increased proportionally to the degree of established relations in the community.

Interest in the two neighbouring country channels, in contrast, followed an outward directed pattern. Most people attend to Swedish television occasionally, but the respondents who gave the neighbouring country channels a high rating increased proportionally to their outward orientation regarding the community.

Social correlates of relation to the community

What are the social correlates of 'relations to community'? No significant differences were found between men and women in Elverum and Jevnaker. Age and education, however, show strong correlations with relations to community. Young people tend, as would be expected, to have more outward relations to community than the elderly, who tend to be more settled. There is a similar correlation between education and relations to community. This correlation is maintained when controlled for age. This is illustrated in Table 7 with data from Elverum; data from Jevnaker indicate the same pattern.

A Multiple Classification Analysis (MCA) suggests some differences between the two communities. In Elverum age and education have about the same effect on relations to community; in Jevnaker education has the strongest effect. Age and education are in themselves important variables for explaining media use in a community, but when tested on use of the community channel, another MCA analysis suggests that 'relations to community' in Elverum explains as much of the variance as do age and education, and in Jevnaker even more.

Table 7. Relation to community by education and age

	15-44 years Education		45-79 years Education		All
	Low* per cent	High per cent	Low per cent	High per cent	per cent
Settled	20	14	39	18	21
Contradictory	32	30	36	50	33
Outward	48	56	26	32	46
Total	100 per cent	100 per cent	100 per cent	100 per cent	100 per cent
N =	(84)	(97)	(31)	(28)	(256)

* 9 years of education or less. Source: Based onLundby: 1982

CONCLUSIONS

Is it, from these studies of samples in two Norwegian rural centres possible to draw any more general conclusions about local television as a tool of community? A correlation has been documented between preference for community television and a settled relation to the geographical community in both localities. On the other hand, the priority given to transnational, satellite television corresponds to an outward relation to community.

This result seems independent of the overall local situation in the transition from a more territorial-based mode of interaction to distancing as the predominate principle of social relations. The tendency is the same in both communities studied, though there may be a somewhat stronger connection between channel preference and identification with the community in the rural centre most marked by territoriality (Lundby, 1988).

One conclusion which can be drawn from this is that there can only be real community television in a locality where community relations are already alive and active. Television programming with a restricted distribution area may be termed 'local', but it is only community television if the programming builds upon topics of shared relevance between people with settled relations to the locality. Audience segmented television cannot be community television in this sense, unless the audience constitutes a community with internal relations. An audience constituted upon similarity in taste is not a community.

But is community television capable of preserving and strengthening geographical communities under pressure from satellite television? Community television is usually introduced along with a variety of transnational channels. In this respect the the two rural centres studied in the early 1980s are not typical, with only one satellite channel. Because of the genuine local content of the programming on these two community television stations and because of the strength in community relations, the single satellite channel available received little attention. In one of the rural centres under study, however, data suggest that the community channel is able to keep its share of the viewers even when there is more substantial transnational programming competition.

But this share of viewing will always be small because the quantity of programming on transnational channels is enormous compared to what any community station can provide. The programming quality and local relevance of a well-run community channel may compensate for some of this, but how much?

The final conclusion is rather pessimistic regarding the community option. Local television may be a kind of home intercom for a shrinking base of settled people in a given territory – essentially enclaves in the society at large. The outward-oriented part of the population is growing and seeking new channels in order to feed their more distance-oriented mode of interaction and communication.

It is not possible from this study to reach definitive conclusions about what potential community television may have in smaller European localities. But the evidence presented here, based on the first years of two rural centres in Norway, convinces us that there is a potential of community-building in community television. To be able to build such local relations, however, this new electronic medium must build on relations already present.

References

Bakke, M. (1986): 'Culture at stake', in D. McQuail and K. Siune (eds) *New media politics. Comparative perspectives in Western Europe*, London: Sage.

Dragland, T., K.O. Mathisen and K. Sinkerud (1985): *The telematic sandbox – A field trial with cable television at Jevnaker*, Kjeller: Norwegian Telecommunications Administration Research Establishment.

Futsaeter, K.A. (1990): *Leserundersøkelse indre Østlandet*, Oslo: Department of Media and Communication, University of Oslo.

Gullestad, M. (1986): 'Symbolic "fences" in urban Norwegian neighbourhoods', *Ethnos*, 51, 1-2: 52-70.

Homans, G.C. (1950): *The human group*, New York: Harcourt, Brace & World.

Lundby, K. (1982): *Forventninger til kabel-tv i Elverum*, report, Olso: Department of Sociology, University of Oslo.

Lundby, K. (1983): 'Naer-tv eller satelitt-sendinger? Ett års erfaringer kartlagt', *Forskningsnytt*, 28, 7: 3-7.

Lundby, K. (1986): *Lokalfjernsyn i "den telematiske sandkasse"*, report, Olso: Institute for Mass Communication Research, University of Oslo.

Lundby, K. (1988a): 'Kulturell bakgrunn for mediebruk i lokalsamfunnet', *Pressens årbog*, Copenhagen: Institute for Journalism.

Lundby, K. (1988b): 'Cultural identity as basis for community television', *Nordicom Review of Nordic Mass Communication Research*, 2: 24-30.

Merton, R.K. (1968): *Social theory and social structure*, New York: Free Press.

Rogers, E.M. (1983): *Diffusion of innovations*, New York: Free Press.

Skogerbø, E. and K. Lundby (1988): *Medieutvikling, kultur og regional identitet*, Oslo: Department of Media and Communication, University of Oslo.

Sorokin, P.A. (1947): *Society, culture and personality. Their structure and dynamics*, New York: Harper & Brothers.

Stamm, K.R. (1985): *Newspaper use and community ties: toward a dynamic theory*, Norwood, New Jersey: Ablex.

Stamm, K.R. and L. Fortini-Campbell (1983): 'The relationship of community ties to newspaper use', in *Journalism Monographs*, 84.

Suttles, G.D. (1968): *The social order of the slum*, Chicago: University of Chicago Press.

Suttles, G.D. (1972): *The social construction of communities*, Chicago: University of Chicago Press.

Tönnies, F. (1974): *Community and association*, London: Routeledge & Kegan Paul (first published 1887).

Ulvaer, B.P. (1984): *Kabelfjernsyn på Jevnaker. I/II*, report, Oslo: Press Institute, University of Oslo.

Vaage, O.F. (1988): *Mediebruk i Jevnaker kommune 1987. Tabelloversikt*, report, Oslo: Central Bureau of Statistics of Norway.

Werner, A., S. Höst, and B.P. Ulvaer (1984): *Publikums reaksjoner nå satelit- og lokalfjernsyn*, report, Oslo: Institute for Mass Communications Research, University of Oslo.

Part II
European landscape

4. DENMARK:
Breaking 60 Years of Broadcasting Monopoly

Vibeke G. Petersen,[*] Ole Prehn[**] and Erik N. Svendsen[***]

*General Directorate of P&T
**Institute of Communication, Aalborg University
***Danmarks Radio, Denmark

Until recently, broadcasting in Denmark has been seen as the equivalent of *Danmarks Radio*. A public service institution, *Danmarks Radio* was established in 1925 and until 1981 held the monopoly on radio and television in the country. Denmark is a small country with only 5 million residents, which is one of the reasons for the few electronic media. Another reason is that the broadcasting monopoly has been widely supported within Danish media politics. All the revisions of the broadcasting act, for example, have been passed by a broad majority in Parliament.

Danmarks Radio provides one national television channel, three national and nine regional radio channels. The services are entirely financed by licence fees; advertising and sponsorship have – until recently – been prohibited. In 1990 broadcasting legislation was passed which permits programming sponsorship on *Danmarks Radio*; advertising is still prohibited. As a public service institution *Danmarks Radio* is obliged to offer balanced and varied programming. During the last 15 years, however, a growing dissatisfaction with the monopoly has developed. The institution has been accused of being highbrow, leftist and biased towards the culture of the capital at the expense of provincial life. In addition, the increasing influence of satellite television has reinforced the claim for national alternatives to *Danmarks Radio*.

Audience interest in more television is suggested by the fact that more than half of the Danish households have chosen to subscribe to cable systems which provide over-the-air television programming from neighbouring countries and, more recently, from satellites. The widespread demand for more Danish television was fulfilled by the 1986 act which established a second national television channel, *TV 2*, which started broadcasting in October 1988. *TV 2* offers a national programme with regional slots filled by eight regional stations. *TV 2* is financed mainly by advertising, which covers about two-thirds of the budget, and by licence fees.

An interesting point is that the traditional political consensus in media politics was broken in the case of *TV 2*; the act was passed by Parliament with the smallest possible majority. *TV 2* marks the final breakdown of the broadcasting monopoly of *Danmarks Radio*. But the first move in that direction was taken in 1981 when Parliament passed an act on community broadcasting.

COMMUNITY MEDIA

With the introduction of community radio and television, a development started which has put around 250 small scale radio and 25–30 television stations on the air and on cable systems. Since the experimental period 35 local televison transmitters have been constructed, but many of these are only used to a limited level. In addition there are some 50 local television licences which have been issued only for cable distribution.

The 1981 Act allowing for an experiment with local broadcasting can be seen in part as a result of the general tendency in Western European to dismantle the long established broadcasting order, rather than as a development stemming primarily from pressures in the country itself. Unlike many countries, Denmark has had almost no pirate broadcasters. The commercial lobby, active for decades, wanted access to national rather than local media and thus did not play any significant role in preparing the way for community media.

But like elsewhere in Europe, popular demand for greater social and cultural autonomy for different groups in society had been growing since the late 1960s and early 1970s. Decentralization of *Danmarks Radio*, which led to the establishment of nine regional radio stations during the 1970s, changed little regarding the difficulty for these groups to gain access to the media on their own terms.

The experiment

The legislation and rules governing the experiment contained very little by way of a declaration of intent, and very few restrictions were set as to programme content. Commercial advertising, sponsoring and networking were prohibited. A 'substantial' part of the programming was required to be locally produced; for television this was set at a minimum of 50 per cent. The 10 watt radio and 200 watt television transmitters limited the coverage area of each station to a radius of about 10 km.

During the three-year experimental period a total of 108 community radio and 42 television stations were issued licences. They were run by individuals, newspapers, municipal authorities, trade unions, and a great variety of local associations and interest groups. A modest amount of money was granted by the state and municipal authorities – 6 million DKr by the state and about the same by a number of municipalities combined. By and large, though, stations had to raise their own funding through membership fees, listener contributions and the like.

The fact that the legislation and regulations (with the exception of the requirement for 50 per cent locally produced television programmes) were identical for both radio and television did not prevent the two media from developing along different paths.

The experiment started in a one-channel, non-commercial television setting, and the prospect of being able to provide the first Danish alternative to *Danmarks Radio* television programming – albeit at the local level – attracted licensees who saw themselves as the future contestants in a national commercial television system rather than as local broadcasters. A few of the community radio stations as well soon grew to become genuine competitors to regional stations of *Danmarks Radio*; this and other reasons recommend separate treatment of the development and research findings of community radio and television.

The issues

The main issues addressed in the following discussion are, however, common to both media and can be summed up as follows:

- What happens when non-commercial local forces are given nearly free rein in a well-developed professional media system of public radio and television?

- Is there an interest in producing for, and attending to, these new media?

- To what degree is it possible to find the necessary resources, human and financial, to operate these media?

- What functions emerge regarding these new media? Are the primary functions information and entertainment, making reference to traditional divisions, or are totally new functions developed for community media?

- Is there a tendency towards differentiation or homogenization of station programming?

- Are community media seen as part of the total media system or as something new and independent?

These issues are all related to the media. One could ask similar questions about the experiment in reference to the political system. One such query is whether community media can be seen as an experiment in the sense that the government may evaluate it on completion and then decide whether community media should be permitted and how, or if the social movement set in motion is in fact so strong that the political question narrows down to *how* to regulate community media in the future. Taking this question to task, the experiment can be seen as an arena of tension between political decision making and social forces.

For this chapter, however, issues more immediately related to the community stations are considered: organizational structure, financing, audience and programming produced by participants in the experiment. The results demonstrate that a need for community media has been clearly manifested.

After the experiment

The experimental situation has been replaced by a permanent system of community broadcasting. A law on community radio was passed in December 1985, and in June 1987 it was modified to encompass television as well; new broadcasting initiatives were then invited to participate.

In June 1988 community radio was allowed to carry advertising, and a 'Robin Hood' scheme of subsidy was introduced whereby less financially endowded stations were supported through a levy on the income of other radio stations. In 1989 the ban on advertising on local television was lifted. Since then, stations can carry up to five minutes of advertising daily. In 1990 sponsorship was permitted for both local radio and television. No form of subsidy has been implemented for local television, and in 1991 the subsidy scheme was abolished due to lack of sufficient resources and difficulties in administering the system.

The law decentralizes issuance of licences to local boards, appointed among a wide range of local associations and the municipal councils. The new rules include limitation of licencing to associations and companies which have broadcasting as their only purpose. Business interests, with the exception of newspapers, are not allowed to have predominant influence on a community station. There is no longer any specific requirement for a minimal percentage of local programming. It is stated in the regulations, however, that a station must be rooted in the local area.

RADIO

Of the 179 applicants for community radio stations, 108 obtained licences and 90 actually commenced operation. Only one station closed down during the experimental period. In terms of geographical distribution 25 stations operated in the greater Copenhagen area, 57 in provincial towns and seven in small towns or villages. This concentration in highly urbanised areas reflects both the greater need and capacity for supplementary communication in more complex living environments.

Table 1. Licence holders of community radio stations

	Interest group	Number of stations
1.	Community radio associations	33
2.	Religious communities	27
3.	Newspapers	11
4.	Trade unions	6
5.	Schools and universities	4
6.	Special interest groups	4
7.	Political parties	2
8.	Municipalities	1
9.	Cable network association	1
	Total	89

Source: Ministry of Culture, 1985; 1987a

The radio associations, including those affiliated with grassroot movements, often defined themselves as open stations accessible to everyone interested in making programmes. If organized interests took part they did so through volunteer activists. The experience of these stations was that mainly young people with interest in rock music or in becoming disc jockeys made use of the access opportunity. The radio associations also learned that sustaining a regular service is a full-time operation and that activists come and go. Therefore, the number of paid staff rose from two (out of 25) to six (out of 54) for the average association radio during the experiment. A certain

48

degree of professionalization follows inevitably with experience and with an increase in the number of hours of programming. As for the radio associations, the number of programming hours increased from 19 to 53 hours per week during the three-year experimental period.

Special interest groups involved in the experiment whose main purpose was not broadcasting included religious communities, educational institutions, trade unions, political parties and municipalities. These stations often set out as closed stations in the sense that only members of the organizations were allowed to make programmes. In the course of the experiment most of them relaxed this policy in order to provide more varied programming and to more easily recruit volunteers. The religious stations remained most closed to outside involvement.

Stations operated by newspapers were the most professional from the beginning and had an average of four paid staff members per station. When the number of broadcast hours was extended for these stations, later ranging from 14 to 40 hours per week, more professionals were also required. The average then became 7.5 staff members along with 15 volunteers per station. Daily news, more or less a repetition of news already made available in the newspapers, was characteristic of the programming for this type of station. Music and chat programming, however, were also significant.

Programming

Programming formats and the increase in total hours of programming per week are shown in Table 2 for the main types of stations. The data are based on a week of programming in 1985. Growth is clear: from 2 to 6 hours per day for the average community station after a period of three years. Differences between the formats are not as striking, but still interesting. The more open radio associations are characterized by a mixed programming format, primarily a combination of talk, music and phone-ins. The trade union stations seemed to stick more to the traditional split between 'pure' music or news and talk in other programmes. Finally, the newspaper-run stations are characterized by a high proportion of news, and the religious stations by religious programming. All of the stations seemed to manifest the same degree of growth, but after two years different programming formats were clearly recognizable.

Table 2. Hours of community radio programming

Station type	Music %	News %	Mix %	Religion %	Total hours/week		
					1983	1985	1986
Radio associations	35	26	39	1	19	43	53
Religious	21	28	22	30	10	19	31
Trade Unions	45	30	24	–	6	35	51
Press	22	44	33	–	14	30	40
All stations	35	29	30	6	13	30	40

Source: Ministry of Culture, 1985; 1987a

Community radio audience

At the outset there was serious doubt whether there would be an audience at all for community radio. Looking back, such concern seems ridiculous, but it nevertheless was one of the reasons for conducting survey research in 1984 and 1985. This research, a panel design held in 7 localities in which 30 stations operated, indicated that community radio was quickly able to establish an audience. Average daily listening increased from 20 per cent in 1984 to 26 per cent by the time of the second survey a year later. On a weekly basis, the audience increased from 51 per cent to 60 per cent of the population.

Differences in audience size depended obviously on broadcasting time and type of programming, but less obviously on locality. Listenership was lower in Copenhagen and higher in provincial towns. The sense of community, in other words, appeared weaker in the metropolis than in the town.

Looking at the types of programmes preferred by listeners suggests that the traditional media functions were also fulfilled by community radio. The entertainment function was a primary one: 51 per cent of the audience mentioned music and phone-ins and 18 per cent bingo programmes as favourites. The information function is stressed by the fact that 40 per cent of the audience mentioned news and 24 per cent local debates as programming types especially liked. Religious programmes were only mentioned by 6 per cent of the audience. This last figure was somewhat higher in towns with strong religious stations, but on the whole religion played a smaller role among listeners than among licensees.

The overall opinion among listeners was that they wanted more news and debate, and less music in community radio programming. Nearly three-fourths of the respondents in all localities wanted the stations to continue operation after the experimental period.

Preference for programming types is broken down for age categories in Table 3. The functions of community radio appear to be different for different generations. For young people, music and phone-in programmes are clearly preferred. These programmes are, of course, also appreciated by middle-aged and elderly listeners, but these groups attach more weight to local news programming. The eldest group also favours religious programmes. This generational difference is very similar to the manner national radio is used.

Table 3. Programme preferences on community radio

Age group	Music & phone-in %	Bingo & greetings %	Local debate %	Local news %	Religion %	N %
15–24 years	72	22	22	29	1	283
25–49 years	57	22	25	44	3	889
50+ years	37	18	23	46	11	612
Total	52	21	24	43	5	1789

Note: Figures in columns are percentages of actual number of listeners per age group.
Source: Ministry of Culture, 1985; 1987a

It is perhaps more surprising that programmes in which greetings can be exchanged, games played such as bingo, and local debates attended are equally popular among all age groups. Heterogenious as they may seem, these programmes are all of a true community nature. Music and news can be found on almost any radio channel, but local talk, be it frivolous or serious, is unique to community radio stations.

The general development of listening to community radio can be seen in the annual audience survey conducted by *Danmarks Radio*. The coverage of the population increased from 60 per cent in 1985 to 82 per cent in 1987, at which level it has since remained. Among these potential listeners, community radio programming has been attended to on the average of 7-8 hours per week with no substantial differences noted in the period 1985–1990.

About one hour daily listening to community radio has given a share of listening to the new medium at around one-third, whereas *Danmarks Radio* has maintained about two-thirds of the listening audience, which has increased the weekly time spent on radio from some 14 hours per week before the introduction of community stations to 19 hours (see Prehn, 1990).

It it important to note that community radio listening reached a stable level as early as 1987, a year before advertising was allowed. This indicates that the commercializ-ation of community radio has not really had an effect on the amount of listening, but rather on structural effects and on character and number of stations; see Fig. 1.

Station financing

The financing of non-commercial community radio stations is a mixture of both cash economy and voluntary labour. Cash economy has increased substantially: in 1983

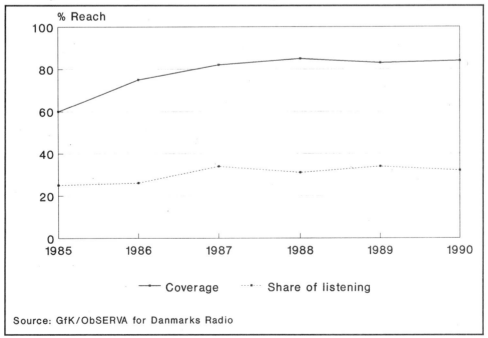

Fig. 1. Community radio 1 week yearly diary (November). Population 15 years+.

about one quarter of the work hours were compensated with payment, and in 1986 this figure had risen to 45 per cent of the total work hours. Four salaried employees worked almost as many hours as 34 volunteers.

The financial accounts of 74 radio stations for 1985 are indicated in Table 4. It is important to bear in mind that the figures only include paid labour; all the voluntary work is excluded from the presentation. The average station had expenditures of 681.000 DKr, 58 per cent of which was for salaries. There is a wide gap between the stations actually paying a staff and the purely voluntary ones: over 1 million DKr as compared to 100.000 DKr. The difference in quantitative output is not nearly as large: 2000 hours compared to 1500 hours of programming per year.

Table 4. The economy of community radio 1988 (average per station)

Type of station	Number of stations	Expenditure (1000 DKr)	of which salary (%)	Expend. per broadcast hour (DKr)	Sources of income (%)				
					State or local government	Listeners	(of which Bingo)	Private subsidies	Sales
With paid staff	33	1.033	58	462	6	44	(20)	42	8
No paid staff	26	112	–	54	3	47	(1)	27	23
Association Radios	26	974	59	334	30	57	(19)	6	7
Religious Stations	26	220	43	150	24	33	(12)	33	9
Trade union Radios	7	965	58	440	21	18	(13)	55	6
Newspaper Radios	10	1.159	65	711	4	20	(15)	72	4
All radios	74	681	58	346	23	38	(15)	31	8

Source: Accounts reported to the Ministry of Culture. 11 Dkr = £1 GB.
Note: 15 radio stations had their staff totally paid by state or local government as grants for job creation or as part of public institutions (schools etc.). The figures for these stations are included in the bottom line (all stations), but are excluded from the top line, which shows the results for stations financing their own staff.

Station income is derived mainly from three sources. Listeners gave 38 per cent, either through receipts collected from bingo programming (15 per cent) or through membership dues to the radio associations. Surveys indicated that one out of five listeners has supported a radio station in some way (Ministry of Culture, 1985; 1987a). The second source of income is the owners or organizations behind the stations (31 per cent). Third, public funding covered 23 per cent of the budgets, mainly as wages for unemployed persons on job schemes and, in some municipalities, free housing for the stations. Finally, stations sold airtime for non-commercial purposes which accounted for the remaining 8 per cent of the budgets.

The radio associations, which included both the very small and very large stations, were characterized by a dependence on listeners' support, accounting for 57 per cent of their budgets. Furthermore, they have attracted many young unemployed people who were funded for 30 per cent of their salaries by the government for a seven-month period.

Although the religious radio stations operated on relatively low budgets, they still relied heavily on their respective religious communities for a third of their incomes. The trade union stations were even more dependent on their owners – for 55 per cent of their budgets – and bingo programming seemed to be the only way these stations could receive support from listeners.

Radio stations owned by newspapers were the most expensive, both generally and per programme hour, and the financial support provided by their listeners was very small. The owners were forced to pay 72 per cent of the budget from their own resources. This investment was hardly based on idealism, but on investment in the future possibility of commercial radio.

Overall, it appeared that community radio was financially manageable for most groups. The average station invested 200.000 DKr in technical equipment during the three-year period, and the annual budget was less than 1 million DKr. In terms of financing, three different types of strategies existed for community radio:

- *Grassroots stations* which subsisted on a shoestring without staff and game programming (e.g. bingo), but which still produced several hours of programming per day with volunteers.

- *Association stations* which operated with both professional staff and volunteers, and were mainly dependent on economic support from listeners. These stations were as a consequence forced to occassionally produce popular programming.

- *Subsidized stations* where the owners (churches, trade unions, newspapers) provided funding for the programming. Because of this affiliation stations strived for large audiences, but usually failed to receive substantional support from listeners.

The future

The question remains: what place can there be for grassroots stations which do not have commercial ambitions or professional resources. 'Place' in the sense of transmission frequency is really the heart of the matter. In most areas of the country there will only be room for one or two frequencies; plans have been made so that all 275 municipalities in the country will have their own frequency, including rural ones with few inhabitants.

With the extreme decentralization of the issuances of licences, political conflicts at the local level can be expected over distribution of broadcasting frequencies. It is doubtful, given this situation, whether grassroots stations will end up with many transmission hours at attractive listening times.

It is difficult to say whether community radio has renewed the cultural communication or political life of local society. But it is certainly the case that the whole process of regulation and allocation has introduced a new permanent issue on the local political agendas. In the future each local community will have the kind of radio it deserves – commercial, grassroots – or, maybe, both (Svendsen, 1987).

TELEVISION

As indicated earlier, the experimental period ran from 1983 to 1986. For television, however, it was extended through 1987. Eight television stations commenced operation in 1983, 25 in 1984, and 1 in 1985.

Prior to the community radio and television experiment the only Danish television alternative was the national channel provided by *Danmarks Radio*. The second national channel, *TV 2*, was then being discussed, but had not yet commenced operation. The satellite channels (e.g. *Sky Channel, Super Channel, TV 5*) were not introduced on Danish cable networks until the last year of the experimental period.

Thus for most of the period community television stations did not have much competition. This may to some extent explain why the stations became quite popular from the outset. But even disregarding this factor it is safe to say that the experiment has demonstrated a real interest on the part of viewers for local programmes. The pessimistic and somewhat arrogant view, quite common intitially, of community television as an amateur pastime was unfounded.

Overview of community television

Of the 150 licences issued by the Ministry of Culture, 42 were for community television stations. Of the 42 licensees 8 failed to commence operation, leaving a total of 34 television stations. They can be categorized according to the organizations running or owning them. As noted earlier, the stations represented a broad variety of organizations and interest groups. The first category, noted in Table 5, community television associations, consists of associations established for the sole purpose of producing community television, while the last category, cable network associations, covers cable network owners[1]. Thus, half of the stations can be characterized as amateur or grassroots projects. The other half consists of different types of organizations with professional or special interest goals.

Table 5. Licence holders of community television stations

	Interest group	N
1.	Community television associations	8
2.	Religious communities	2
3.	Newspapers	4
4.	Trade unions	6
5.	Other organizations	3
6.	Municipalities	2
7.	Cable network associations	9
	Total	34

Source: Ministry of Culture, 1985; 1987a

Two of the stations attracted particular attention during the experimental period. They were both located in the Copenhagen area, available to 1.5 million residents, and they were both highly professional. One, *Weekend TV*, was run by several large

---

1 *In Denmark the cable systems are owned by the subscribers.*

publishing houses and Denmark's largest film production company on a licence issued to a more modest applicant who originally had plans for an open access television station. The attractive location and the relatively large coverage area of the station – serving the most densely populated part of Denmark – made it very interesting for business investors concerned about gaining an advantageous position prior to the start of the second national television channel. *Weekend TV* was closed down in 1986, however, before its licence had expired, primarily because of poor financial prospects for the station.

The other station, *Kanal 2*, was the only pay television experiment in the country and, like *Weekend TV*, its licence was 'taken over' by business interests. In this case it was the Swedish company Esselte (owner of the satellite television company Filmnet) which stepped in as a major financing partner. *Kanal 2* had obtained around 85.000 subscribers towards the end of the experimental period and was concerned, like *Weekend TV*, in becoming involved in plans for the second Danish national channel.

Meanwhile, outside the capital, other stations grew up as genuine community television projects. As shown in Table 6, they were mainly an urban phenomenon. Only four of them were located in rural areas or villages. Fifteen of the stations broadcast over-the-air, while the rest distributed programming through cable systems.

Table 6. Urbanization and number of community TV stations

	Site (population)	No of stations
	Copenhagen (1.5 million)	6
	Provincial cities (more than 100,000)	8
	Provincial towns (less than 100,000)	16
	Rural areas	4
	Total	34

Source: Ministry of Culture, 1985; 1987a

During the experimental period nine stations were shut down. One of them closed as scheduled after one year of operation, but the rest terminated activity due to lack of funding and, perhaps, insufficient interest in the respective areas. The stations were small in size and programming was primarily distributed on cable systems with few subscribers. These developments fit into the overall pattern of events in which the initially large stations became larger and the small stations became smaller, or remained as they were.

Station economy

To illustrate station economy, data from 1985 have been selected because most stations were in operation for the duration of that year. The following tables are based on data collected from 20 stations. The two Copenhagen projects, *Weekend TV* and *Kanal 2*, are excluded because of their larger budgets; the annual funding of *Weekend TV* in 1985, for example, was nearly twice that of all 20 stations.

In Tables 7 and 8 figures are given for stations with and without paid staff. Four of the 20 stations are omitted from this presentation because their staffs were entirely funded through public subsidy. As can be seen in Table 7, about half of the station expenses were staff wages, while expenditures on technical equipment accounted for only 10 per cent of the total budget. Investment in equipment, it should be noted, were made prior to 1985. During that year, the eight stations aired 5,462 hours of programming. The cost per programme hour was 4,279 DKr.

Table 7. Financing of community TV stations with paid staff

Expenses	DKr	%	Income	DKr	%
Wages	2014	(59)	Public subsidy	35	(1)
Other running costs	907	(26)	Membership fees	70	(2)
Equipment	330	(10)	Collections	92	(3)
Housing	146	(4)	Bingo	751	(22)
Depreciation	15	(1)	Airtime sales	405	(12)
Interest	5		Private donations	2075	(60)
			Various	26	(–)
Total	3417	100%	Total	3454	100%

Note: Data is average for eight stations in 1985. Figures in 1000 Dkr (11 Dkr. = £1 sterling).
Source: Ministry of Culture, 1985; 1987a.

Concerning station income, it is important to realize that these eight stations all received substantial support form their parent organizations – 60 per cent of the station budget on the average. Also, revenue from bingo programming and from sale of airtime to third parties contributed to the budgets. Public subsidy, on the other hand, accounted for only 1 per cent of the budget. On the average, then, expenses for a single station with paid staff amounted to 3,417,000 Dkr in 1985.

Table 8. Financing of community TV stations without paid staff

Expenses	DKr	%	Income	DKr	%
Running costs	41	(85)	Public subsidy	5	(11)
Equipment	7	(14)	Membership fees	0	
Various	0		Collections	3	(5)
Depreciation	0		Bingo	1	(3)
Interest	0		Airtime sales	7	(14)
			Private donations	31	(65)
			Various	0	
Total	48	99%	Total	47	98%

Note: Data are for average for eight stations in 1985. Figures in 1000 Dkr. (11 Dkr. = £1 sterling).
Source: Ministry of Culture, 1985; 1987a.

As for stations without staff, the total programming time was 504 hours in 1985, which is equivalent to 653 Dkr per programming hour. These stations relied heavily on support provided by the parent organizations. Most of the community television stations had not reached the break even point during the experimental period.

In Table 9 changes in the amount of personnel is examined for both large (more than five hours programming per week) and small (less than five hours per week) stations.

The tendency for small stations was to become smaller and for large stations to increase the number of staff.

Table 9. Paid and volunteer staff for large and small TV stations

	1984/85			1986			Difference		
	Paid	Volunter	Total	Paid	Volunter	Total	Paid	Volunter	Total
Large	6	6	12	11.4	16	27.4	+5.4	+10	+15.4
Small	0.5	13	13.5	1	9	10	+0.5	−4	−3.5

Note: Large stations broadcast more than 5 hours of programming per week; small stations less than 5.
Source: Ministry of Culture, 1985; 1987a.

Programming

These patterns of expansion and reduction are also evident in the amount of programming during the period; see Table 10. An increase in staff resulted in more hours of programming at the large stations, while the decrease in personnel at the small stations meant less programming output. With an average of only two hours a week, these stations seemed to be below the critical amount of programming required to attract and maintain an audience.

Table 10. Programming hours per week for TV stations

	1985	1986	Difference
Large stations	9	13	+4
Small stations	3	2	−1

Note: Large stations broadcast more than 5 hours of programming per week; small stations less than 5.
Source: Ministry of Culture, 1985; 1987a.

Regarding the actual content of the programmes, Table 11 shows rather distinct differences between different types of stations. The figures are based on a survey held in 1985 among 18 stations. The two professional stations shown in the table indicate a heavy bias towards entertainment programmes. The news programmes also contained much information about the city's entertainment agenda.

Table 11. Programming content of TV stations

Type of station	(N)	News and local affairs %	Studio progr- ammes %	Music/ entertain- ment %	Religion %	Combin- ation %	Total %
1. Professional	(2)	34	4	72	0	0	100
2. Religious	(1)	3	0	51	14	32	100
3. Labour movement	(6)	70	11	16	1	2	100
4. Newspaper	(2)	58	14	25	4	0	100
5. Cable-associations	(7)	71	19	0	11	0	100
All stations	(18)	60	13	19	6	2	100

Note: Figures in columns are average percentages.
Source: Ministry of Culture, 1985; 1987a.

Especially stations funded by the labour movement were able to develop into professional operations with relatively large staffs and distinct programming formats. The programming combined a community angle with the specific labour movement interest in promoting social and health services, as well as issues concerning work conditions and the labour market (Hjort & Prehn, 1987).

Based on programming offered, community television stations either developed into professional stations, and more or less gave up the intention of being open access stations, or into stations barely able to achieve the minimal limits regarding staff, financing and programming. At the same time there was a tendency among stations in larger urban areas to develop a broad spectrum of programming, while stations in smaller cities would continue to provide distinct community oriented programming. This pattern is unique to the development of community television, and is not as clear regarding community radio.

Community television audience

From the very start of the experiment the interest among local audiences for the programming has been relatively high. This is evident in Table 12 which displays 1985 audience ratings for selected stations. The table shows that only 8 per cent of the possible audience never watched the community programmes. On the average 15 per cent watched more than once a week, with the highest rating in the Copenhagen area. This may be due, among other things, to the very popular and entertaining programming offered by the two professionally run stations in Copenhagen.

Table 12. Potential audience of community TV stations

Area	5-7 days a week	Once a week	Never
Esbjerg (cable)[1]	12	68	5
Aarhus (off air)	14	56	8
Svendborg (off air)	7	76	6
Taastrup (both)	21	68	12
Copenhagen (off air)[2]	23	71	8
Average	15	68	8

[1] 3 different stations on the same channel; [2] 3 different stations on the same transmitter.
Source: Ministry of Culture, 1985; 1987a.

Asked about which types of programmes they preferred, half of the viewers mentioned local news and information. In the Copenhagen area about 70 per cent pointed to the entertainment programmes, probably a result of the fact that half of the programming time was devoted to this type of programming.

These rather high ratings must, of course, be considered in relation to the limited television offered in general, and to the fact that the only Danish alternative to this local progamming was that of the national *Danmarks Radio* channel. Nevertheless, more recent audience surveys indicate that the interest among local audiences has risen, even when satellite delivered signals have been made available.

The results of one such survey are displayed in Table 13, data which relate to the seven stations affiliated to the labour movement. Though the findings are based on small samples (100 telephone interviews in each area), the ratings are very high even when compared to ratings from the national channel. For instance, the news programme of *Danmarks Radio* is watched by about half the population 13 years and older.

Table 13. Audience of labour union stations

	Frequency of viewing			Viewing of	
	More than once a week %	Once a week or less %	Never %	News %	Bingo %
Esbjerg	60	12	28	35	15
Fredericia	45	31	24	18	15
Aalborg	55	20	25	34	12
Aarhus	36	18	46	15	26
Odense	20	31	49	11	3
Svendborg	69	14	17	28	21
Bornholm	54	24	22	43	9
Total	48	21	31	26	14

Note: Data collected in 1987 for 7 labour union stations. Respondents 13 years and older.
Source: Instituttet for opinionsanalyse, 1988.

This data seems to suggest growing interest among the audience. One conclusion is that the labour movement stations were able to attract a larger segment of the audience. This 'success' took place relatively long after the introduction of community television, and cannot be explained by the newness of the medium for viewers.

The experimental period demonstrated that there is much interest for locally originated community television programming. This interest may be conditioned by a limited amount of Danish television, but interest in local affairs is nonetheless manifest.

On the other hand, developments during the period have shown several problems for the more 'genuine' community stations operating with minimal financial basis and with only volunteer staff. Eight such stations ceased operation during the course of the experiment. Those remaining had to reduce programming time, and the turnover rate among volunteers was high.

The successful stations were those which were able to expand programming time and staff in order to professionalize the content. This development may partly be explained by the economic problems that especially the smaller stations faced, while the larger stations were kept alive and expanding by heavy economic support from parent organizations. But the development may also be significant in relation to the attractiveness of community stations, both with regard to recruitment of unpaid staff and to the audience. There seems to be a critical limit in programming below which it is nearly impossible to sustain a station, at least in situations where there is no provision for public funding to keep small stations in operation.

Thus, the television experiment has shown the neccessity of professionalizing programme production and creating a distinct station profile which combines community orientation and professional journalism. This development explains why stations have shown a steadily declining interest in 'open access' and workshop productions. Some stations have abandoned this type of programming in order to remain in operation and not to be identified as amateurish.

The experiment has also shown that community stations have to develop a programming mix of genuine community content and more entertaining and middle-of-the-road programmes such as films, series, sports and music videos. To some degree, the more successful stations have danced to the tune of the marketplace in order to survive economically. Even on a community level, television seems to be very different from radio.

CONCLUSIONS

The local radio and television stations started in the early 1980's in a media environment conducive to success: they were the only Danish alternative to *Danmarks Radio* programmes, community concerns were virtually nonexistent on the electronic media, and satellite television had not yet been introduced in the country. The three-year experimental period guaranteed an introductory phase during which the regulatory framework remained stable, and competition was kept at bay.

When the experiment ended in the late 1980s the stations had managed to capture a sizeable audience and to engage a large number of amateur and professional broadcasters. The political question changed from whether or not to allow private stations on a permanent basis, and was redirected to future regulation of the system. This transformation of the political agenda did not pose problematic issues.

As for the broader sociological issues, it is not easy to determine whether the experiment introduced new media, serving different functions, or merely broke the monopoly of *Danmarks Radio* in a traditional way.

There is no doubt that freedom of expression has expanded, if only in quantitative terms, particularly regarding the community radio stations. There are many examples of community communication in terms of locality as well as areas of special interest. It is obvious, however, that this almost unregulated freedom has also brought with it a development in the media of a familiar commercial kind.

The moral of the Danish experiment is that freedom of the media is a coin with two sides: a cultural/political one and a commercial one. It seems impossible to examine one without considering the other. In the end, it will be up to society to use this new freedom or leave it in the hands of commercial interests. The political system, in any event, has left this central issue open.

APPENDIX: Electronic Media in Denmark

The electronic media in Denmark are divided into three distinct groups which operate independently of each other:

- *Danmarks Radio*, established in 1925, is an independent public institution and is financed through licence fees. It provides one national television channel, three national radio channels, and nine regional radio channels (which broadcast a third national programme for a portion of the day).

- *TV2*, on the air since October 1988, is an independent institution and is financed through licence fees and advertising (presently accounting for about

80 per cent of the income, and to increase to 85 per cent before 1994). *TV 2* provides one national and eight regional television channels.

Both institutions are public service broadcasting institutions, and are required to offer balanced and diversified programming. Since mid-1990 both may supplement their financing through programme sponsorship. Their respective shares of the national television audience are roughly equal.

- Local radio and television stations were legally introduced in 1981 and started broadcasting in 1983. As of 1991, about 300 radio and 30 television stations are in operation. They are run by a variety of interest groups, and are financed through advertising, programme sponsorship and donations.

  The local stations receive their licences from local committees. They are not bound by public service requirements, but are required to be situated in the local region in which they broadcast. Networking among stations is prohibited.

Since the mid-1980s foreign television programmes have been an increasingly important part of the Danish media landscape. Viewers who subscribe to cable services (about 55 per cent of the households) have access to about 20 foreign channels, some of which are delivered from neighbouring countries (mainly Sweden and Germany); the rest are satellite delivered. At this point, no Danish broadcasters are distributing programming by satellite.

References

Danmarks Radio (1987): *TV-frekvensundersögelse 2.- 8. november 1987* (Audience Research Report, DR 87), Copenhagen: Danmarks Radio.

Grönholt, L. and F. Hansen (1987): *Reklame i naerradio og lokal-TV* (Advertizing in Community Radio and local TV), Copenhagen: Copenhagen Business School.

Hjort, A. and O. Prehn (1987): *Syv dage med lokal-TV*, Copenhagen: AEM-Invest.

Instituttet for opinionsanalyse (1988): Undersögelse af 7 lokale tv-stationer, Copenhagen: Instituttet for opinionsanalyse.

Ministry of Culture (1987a): *Naerrradio og lokal-TV* (Community Radio and Local TV: Final report), Copenhagen: Direktoratet for Statens Indköb.

Ministry of Culture (1987b): *Status over lokalradioordningen pr. 1. december 1986* (State of Community Radio Administration as of December 1st 1986), Copenhage: Ministry of Culture.

Ministry of Culture (1985): *Naerradio og lokal-TV i fremtiden* (Community Radio and Local TV: Future Prospects), Copenhagen: Direktoratet for Statens Indköb.

Prehn, O. (1990): 'Community radio or just local air waves. The development of community radio in Denmark', paper, International Communication Association, Dublin.

Svendsen, E.N. (1987): 'Community or professionalism: Local radio in Denmark', paper, International Institute of Communication, Local Radio Conference, Rovaniemi, Finland.

5. SWEDEN:
Neighbourhood radio

Lowe Hedman

Department of Sociology, University of Uppsala, Sweden

This chapter examines the community radio service in Sweden known as 'närradio' or 'Neighbourhood Radio.' A service made available to voluntary organizations and associations in the country, the radio programmes can only be received within a three to five kilometre radius from the transmitters. Although Neighbourhood Radio is now an established element of the electronic media system in the country (see appendix for an overview of these media), it has remained independent of the Swedish Broadcasting Corporation.

The decision to introduce this medium in 1979 was taken during a period in which society – and the media – were undergoing substantial change. This period and the accompanying changes are sketched in the first section of the chapter. The remainder of the chapter is devoted to aspects of Neighbourhood Radio: the organization of the medium, the institutional users, programming content, audience attendance to programming, and the relation with other media. A number of general remarks are reserved for the final section.

THE CONTEXT OF CHANGE

As in other Western European countries, radio in Sweden has traditionally been nationally oriented and centrally controlled (Browne, 1984: 36). This approach, although often criticized, has been supported by both the long-ruling Social Democratic Party and the Swedish Broadcasting Corporation. The Broadcasting Corporation has nevertheless been sensitive to these criticisms and has, with the encouragement of Parliament, gradually decentralized many of its programming activities. About half of all radio and television programmes now are produced outside the Corporation's main offices in Stockholm.

Media and societal transformations

The centralized broadcasting system has been part of the larger issue of the monopoly position of the Swedish Broadcasting Corporation. But when the organization of local radio stations was considered in 1973, again preference was given to a centralized body. And a proposal to introduce 36 independent local radio stations was rejected by the left wing parties (SOU 1973: 8).

When a Liberal-Conservative coalition took power in 1976, one of its first tasks was to reorganize the Swedish Broadcasting Corporation. Two years later Parliament approved a proposal made for decentralising the electronic media. Taken as a whole, however, the newly created independent production companies and the parent company are still rather centralized.

During the 1960s and 1970s, discontent with the centralized aspects of society increased. This was especially evident among popular movements and local political parties not represented in Parliament. They believed the broadcasting system had not adequately responded to a multitude of changes in society: the rapid rate of industrialization, the merging of small communities into larger administrative units, the increasing public encroachment into people's private lives, the escalating immigration from abroad to Sweden, and the growing mobility within the country. All of these changes have contributed to concern for a media system which places accent on local information (see Richeri, 1978).

There have also been considerable changes in the Swedish media marketplace, and print media in particular have been the object of these variations. In the 1950s and 1960s newspaper companies experienced considerable decline in circulation and many were forced to shut down. At the same time, the larger newspapers grew larger, and ownership became concentrated in the hands of a smaller group of people and organizations. In more and more regions newspaper monopolies were formed. Inasmuch as Swedish newspapers are generally affiliated with a political party, it was feared this development might have an impact on the democratic functioning of the country. This concern was particularly acute inasmuch as most of the newspapers which went out of business represented just two parties, the Social Democrats and the Centre Party. In 1969 the government appointed a commission to study press concentration and to suggest alternatives for better satisfy the public's informational needs.

Various organizations and associations – particularly among popular and labour movements, adult education associations, temperance and religious groups – had become substantially larger and more powerful since World War II, and felt the Swedish Broadcasting Corporation failed to give them adequate attention. This discontent eventually resulted in the government redistributing shares in the Swedish Broadcasting Corporation. The above mentioned organizations and associations were allotted 60 per cent of all Corporation shares; the press 20 per cent and business groups received the remaining 20 per cent. But these shareholders have no influence on the day-to-day activities of the Corporation, and organizations and associations still lacked a satisfactory medium of expression.

Popular movements were eager either to achieve better possibilities for influencing the Swedish Broadcasting Corporation or to acquire a new electronic medium. As early as 1965 a commission had been appointed by the government to investigate establishment of a 'special radio' for activities which did not easily fit into the existing programmes of the Swedish Broadcasting Corporation. The main intention of this 'special radio' would be to serve educational and teaching needs as well as various demands from popular movements and organizations (SOU, 1965: 20). The government, led by the Social Democrats, considered the proposal too sketchy and postponed consideration until a later date.

Political motives for radio initiatives

So far a number of issues have been sketched as background to why different forms of local radio were eventually introduced in Sweden. In addition, several arguments were offered in the course of political debate on the media. What were, in fact, the political motives behind local radio and Neighbourhood Radio?

In 1973 a government commission proposed establishment of a nation-wide local radio service to satisfy the increasing demand for information of societal concern. Parliament passed a law in 1975 permitting local radio stations to broadcast throughout the entire country. These stations, it was argued, would act as a complement to the local press. The need for such a complementary medium became all the more apparent during the 1960s when large numbers of local newspapers were forced to close down because of financial difficulties. Such closures, it was argued, decreased opportunity for citizens to formulate opinion and engage in public debate. An intense and free flow of information is a necessary condition for a democracy. Objective information and news increase the possibilities for citizens to participate in current affairs, and thus to contribute to the democratic process. The introduction of local radio was motivated mainly by these democratic principles and the belief that communication between a people and its political leaders should be as optimal as possible.

The motives for establishing Neighbourhood Radio were less clear. The 1960 Radio Commission felt that associations and clubs in Sweden needed a more efficient way to communicate with their own members, and that a special radio service would be valuable to them (SOU, 1965: 20). Another government commission concluded that the demand for local information could not be met by public service broadcasting, and suggested further study regarding a special radio service (SOU, 1977: 19).

These developments, however, are not referred to in the proposal eventually made for Neighbourhood Radio and Television. Basically, the responsible ministry simply indicated that there was no longer a need for a law prohibiting low power radio broadcasts since there were sufficient frequencies available for expansion. The reasoning seems to have been that limiting the general public's freedom of expression was unwarranted given the absence of any technical obstacles or problems.

In 1978 Parliament passed legislation permitting 'Neighbourhood Radio' and 'Neighbourhood TV' (the latter only intended for cable systems), to operate on an experimental basis for a three-year period. This period was later extended until June 1985, at which time Neighbourhood Radio became a permanent part of the electronic media system in Sweden. Neighbourhood television has since been replaced by other permanent forms of local cable television.

NEIGHBOURHOOD RADIO – FROM EXPERIMENT TO INSTITUTION

In the autumn of 1978 the government appointed a committee to organize and evaluate Neighbourhood Radio and Television during the experimental period. Altogether, 16 regions in a total of 15 municipalities were given permission to establish Neighbourhood Radio stations (see SOU, 1981: 13; SOU, 1984: 53; and Thomas, 1981). Groups active in these regions could arrange to broadcast on a regular, continuous schedule. The first station went on the air in 1979. During the experimental period new stations were permitted, although the controlling committee followed a fairly restrictive policy.

An important principle of Swedish Neighbourhood Radio is that only certain types of organizations and associations are permitted to make use of the broadcasting facilities. These include: local non-profit associations, including those representing a nation-wide organization; congregations of the Swedish Church; and student unions.

Initially, Neighbourhood Radio, especially in the cities, was largely used by music associations for the sole purpose of broadcasting music, and a number of associations were formed simply to broadcast on Neighbourhood Radio. A law passed in 1982 curtailed this last practice by specifying that the primary activity of applicants may not be broadcasting. Furthermore, associations must have been active in the region for at least a year prior to application.

Neighbourhood Radio provides access, then, to particular organizations and associations active at the local level. Individuals are not allowed to broadcast their own programmes other than through organizations which have obtained permission to make use of Neighbourhood Radio.

Permits are issued by the Neighbourhood Radio Authority which regulates the medium and – until recently – allocates airtime. This broadcasting time is distributed in 15-minute blocks on a weekly basis. Although most organizations make use of more than one such block of time each week, for some smaller associations this amount of broadcasting on a weekly basis has proven to be difficult to fill. In 1990 a proposal for decentralizing distribution of broadcasting time was made. A local authority representing all organizations with a broadcasting permit will probably be authorized to regulate programme scheduling (SOU, 1990: 70).

Neighbourhood Radio is self-supporting; the participating associations pay all costs including operating expenses of the central authority, rental fees for equipment and transmission lines between studios and transmitters, and copyright fees. The costs for each association are determined in proportion to its respective broadcasting time. Broadcasting expenses, in other words, vary according to the number of associations involved in a particular Neighbourhood Radio station, and how long they are on the air.

Most organizations do not have staff in service exclusively for their broadcasting activities. Smaller organizations primarily rely on volunteers, and associations with a large staff generally assign one or two of these persons to oversee the radio broadcasts. In most organizations, working with radio is limited to just a few persons in relation to the whole organization. Except for a small number of primarily religious associations, the organizations do not have people with experience from broadcasting doing the programmes.

Investment in studio and other equipment varies considerably between associations. There are associations broadcasting several hours a week with professional equipment and often with professional staff. There are also small associations broadcasting no more than the minimal 15-minute weekly block of time with very basic equipment (see Hedman, 1981).

Expenses for airtime range between SEK 150 to 175 (i.e. about 16 Pounds Sterling) hourly – not including additional costs for professional staff and programme production. Thus, for not more than SEK 8,000 (720 Pounds Sterling) an association can be on the air one hour a week for a year period (SOU, 1990: 70). Although such broadcasting is inexpensive, many organizations, primarily the larger ones, spend much money on equipment and programming. Other associations, on the other hand, have difficulty raising funding for a minimum radio service.

Advertising in and sponsoring of programmes is prohibited. Associations are also not allowed to promote their own commercial activities. However, they may solicit funds from their own members and from other sources. Some municipal councils, for example, have donated funds and allocated facilities to Neighbourhood Radio stations.

Contrary to the programmes of the Swedish Broadcasting Corporation, there is no requirement that Neighbourhood Radio stations strive to be objective or impartial. The rights and responsibilities Parliament has attached to freedom of expression, however, are applicable and each association broadcasting on Neighbourhood Radio must have a person legally responsible for what is said on the programmes.

The signal range is limited to a radius of three to five kilometres from the transmitter and only in a few municipalities can the signal be heard by all residents in the area. Some stations have requested permission to increase signal strength in order to reach residents living outside the 5 kilometre range. Now, by the 1990s, more than half of the Neighbourhood Radio stations (SOU, 1990: 70) have been granted such permission.

In 1990 it was estimated that between 65 per cent and 85 per cent of Sweden's population is able to listen to a Neighbourhood Radio station in the area in which they live (Hedman, 1990b: 10). Most of the stations, however, are situated in densely populated regions. Some 160 regions now have a Neighbourhood Radio broadcasting service and the number is increasing.

The experimental status remained in effect until mid-1985, at which time Neighbourhood Radio acquired formal approval and entered a new era of permanence. Between 1985 and 1986 the number of stations increased by 26 per cent, and the number of participating associations climbed from almost 1,300 to nearly 1,700, a growth rate of 32 per cent. By 1990 more than 2,200 associations had been issued broadcasting permits.

The amount of broadcasting time did not increase substantially in this period. This is understandable given the preparation required to develop such a comprehensive activity. The average broadcasting time for stations is about 34 hours per week, but the span of time stations broadcast is considerable. Neighbourhood Radio stations in the larger urban areas transmit from early morning until late at night, while stations in small towns may transmit only short periods of the day.

Institutions using neighbourhood radio

Religious associations were the first to realize the informational and propaganda possibilities that Neighbourhood Radio offered. During the experimental period they constituted about a quarter of the total number of organizations on Neighbourhood Radio (see Table 1). The number increased to a third and remained at that level for a number of years. The religious associations were, without doubt, the largest group of associations on Neighbourhood Radio. Their dominance is even more apparent when their broadcasting time is compared to that of other associations. As shown in Table 2, their share increased continually until 1984 at which point it accounted for 59 per cent of the total broadcasting time. With the expansion of Neighbourhood Radio in later years the portion held by religious associations decreased to 29 per cent by 1990.

Political organizations constituted about a fifth of the total number of organizations using Neighbourhood Radio until 1985. During the General Election campaign in 1985 politicians seemed to realize the possibility of Neighbourhood Radio for the first time, and the number of political organizations participating increased nearly 30 per cent. In 1990 they constituted about a quarter of all organizations. Of the 2,240 broadcasting permits issued by October 1990, 581 were allocated to political associations and 544 to religious associations.

Table 1. Distribution of neighbourhood radio permits

	1980 per cent	1982 per cent	1984 per cent	1986 per cent	1988 per cent	1990 per cent
Religious associations	26	32	33	24	22	24
Political associations	19	16	21	27	28	26
Others	54	53	47	49	50	50
	99	101	101	100	100	100
N in hours =	243	298	678	1727	2356	2240

As is shown in Tables 1 and 2, broadcasting time is not proportionally distributed relative to the number of broadcasting permits. Political organizations broadcast fewer or shorter programmes than, for example, religious associations. Despite the fact that the former had more broadcasting permits and that their broadcasting time had almost doubled between 1984 and 1986, they accounted for only a fifth of the total broadcasting time in 1986.

The relatively rapid increase in broadcasting time in 1984 can be explained by the fact that many political parties became interested in Neighbourhood Radio in connection with the upcoming General Election campaign. Active attempts were also made by the committee regulating Neighbourhood Radio to interest organizations other than religious and political ones to participate. Many people expected that a number of political parties would discontinue their Neighbourhood Radio programming once the election was over. This did not, however, turn out to be the case. The broadcasting time of the political associations did drop by 5 per cent between 1984 and 1986, but has since remained constant.

Other organizations than religious and political ones constitute about half of all broadcasting associations participating in Neighbourhood Radio. During the first year of operation these associations broadcasted nearly proportionally to their percentage of broadcasting permits. This situation changed in subsequent years. The tendency seems to be that these other organizations broadcast, relatively speaking, ever fewer and/or shorter programmes. Table 2 shows the distribution of broadcasting time for different types of organizations producing Neighbourhood Radio programming.

Table 2. Distribution of broadcasting time for associations

	1980 per cent	1982 per cent	1984 per cent	1986 per cent	1988 per cent	1990 per cent
Religious	45	55	59	46	37	29
Political	6	5	11	17	19	16
Immigrant	5	7	3	3	3	3
Music	-	8	4	1	1	2
Sport	3	1	2	2	3	2
Adult education	3	1	4	6	9	10
Student	-	6	6	8	7	7
Handicap	-	1	1	*	*	*
Temperance	1	1	1	2	1	1
Trade union	*	-	*	1	3	7
Neighbourhood radio	-	-	3	2	2	5
Others	38	15	8	14	15	29
	101	100	102	102	100	101
N in hours	477.5	726.5	1423	3055.8	3815.3	5466.5

* Less than 1 per cent.

Neighbourhood Radio services vary a great deal between different regions. In 1984 religious organizations used more than 50 per cent of the total broadcasting time on 46 of the 57 stations transmitting at the time. And programming provided by religious organizations accounted for over 90 per cent of the broadcasting time in ten regions. As would be expected, in larger towns there is more varied output and broadcasts from religious associations is not as dominant.

Programming content

That religious associations dominate Neighbourhood Radio does not necessarily mean the content of most programmes is religious. There has not been sufficient analysis of programming content, however, to determine the ratio exactly. For example, a content analysis of all Neighbourhood Radio broadcasts during a single week in 1979, when the service was quite new, indicated that 41 per cent of the programmes were religious in orientation and 9 per cent had a predominantly political theme.

The most common subjects were activities of the association which produced the programme and religion (Wengelin, 1982: 52). The religious associations were responsible for 42 per cent and the political associations for 10 per cent of the total broadcasting time. These figures suggest that dissemination of information about an association's area of activity is one of the main reasons these associations have for participating in Neighbourhood Radio.

Another content analysis conducted a few years later in Uppsala, a university town north of Stockholm, reinforces this conclusion. Questions of religion and faith dominated the broadcasts examined (see Table 3). Entertainment and music contributions are nevertheless large, which perhaps can be explained by the fact that many university student organizations take part in this Neighbourhood Radio station.

Table 3. Distribution of subjects on neighbourhood radio in Uppsala

	per cent
Religion/faith	38
Entertainment/music	27
Upcoming events in the area	9
Association activity	8
Culture/education	5
Social questions	5
Politics/economics/labour market	4
Human interest	3
Energy/environment	1
Sport	0
	100
Total (hours)	26

Source: Atmer, 1984: 26.

Neighbourhood Radio is intended to be a very local medium. Content analyses conducted in 1979 and 1980 suggest that approximately two-fifths of the programmes had a specific local reference. A similarly large portion of programmes made no reference whatsoever to geographical location. Many religious programmes consisted of traditional periods of worship, Bible reading and the like, and contained no local reference. Local writers, musicians and other local talents were seldom heard in the programmes analysed.

Originally, Neighbourhood Radio was not used for mobilizing opinion on local or political questions. Only after some years was this function 'discovered' by certain racist groups which used Neighbourhood Radio for their messages. Another example of this form of use occurred just before the 1985 election when a Neighbourhood Radio station was used by a discontented local political party in one of the country's largest towns, Malmö. The campaign was so successful that the party managed to win several seats in the municipal council. It is generally believed that this electoral success was only possible because of the party's broadcasts on the Malmö Neighbourhood Radio station.

The programming format varies considerably. Many of the programmes are simply presentations of the organizations: their objectives, interests, current and coming activities. Many groups employ call-in programming techniques, either for discussion purposes or for letting audience members express their own views.

In summary, Neighbourhood Radio established itself in a large number of communities around the country. In most locations there was a relatively large population and the service consequently attracted many of the associations active in the regions. There is little reason to anticipate appreciable change in the composition of associations participating in Neighbourhood Radio. The religious associations will most likely continue to dominate Neighbourhood Radio. Political organizations have become more numerous and now broadcast for longer periods than before, but their interest in broadcasting will probably decline between elections.

Audience

The first comprehensive study of the audience of Neighbourhood Radio programming was conducted in 1980, during the first year of broadcasts, in 15 of the 16 experimental regions (see Hedman, 1980). Table 4 indicates that an average of 15 per cent of the residents able to receive Neighbourhood Radio progamming listened at least once a week. On the average weekday 6 per cent of the residents listened to at least one Neighbourhood Radio programme. Slightly more than two-thirds of the population had never listened to Neighbourhood Radio.

This figure should be contrasted with that from a study conducted prior to the start of the Neighbourhood Radio experiment in which only 5 per cent said they did not plan to listen to Neighbourhood Radio programming (Hedman, 1981: 31). One explanation for this discrepancy is that Neighbourhood Radio had not become the kind of service the general public expected. Perhaps a more traditional radio channel with news and other conventional programmes was expected, and less religious programming.

Table 4. Neighbourhood radio listenership

Frequency	1980 per cent	1989 per cent
5-7 days a week	3	6
3-4 days a week	4	3
1-2 days a week	8	8
Less often	14	20
Never	70	37
No reply	2	27
	101	101
N in hours =	4887	4636

Source: Hedman (1980: 39); Hedman & Golborne (1990: 30).

Neighbourhood Radio has thus little by little captured an increasingly larger audience. A study made in 12 areas with Neighbourhood Radio in 1989 concluded that an average of 17 per cent listened to the radio at least once a week (Hedman & Golborne, 1990: 30). Listening to Neighbourhood Radio is much more a primary activity than attending to national radio, given the involvement of local associations and organizations in the programming (Hedman, 1982a: 28).

The general pattern of listening to Neighbourhood Radio does not differ a great deal from the pattern found in studies of national or local radio listening with regard to gender, education and occupation. However, certain differences have been noted in some regions, in all probability because the services there differ in one way or another from those in other areas.

The main variance is found in the listening behaviour of different age groups. Neighbourhood Radio attracts proportionately more people in the younger and older age categories than middle age listeners. The age of listeners also varies a great deal between the different regions. Stations which offer a large amount of music attract many young listeners, whereas stations which offer a large number of religious programmes tend to attract older listeners. This pattern has been reinforced since the introduction of Neighbourhood Radio (Hedman, 1980: 59; Hedman & Golborne, 1990: 55).

The composition and form of the services offered are probably the most important factors explaining differences in listening. Since it is the associations themselves which are responsible for the programming, membership in a transmitting association to a large extent determines whether people listen to Neighbourhood Radio. In 1980 26 per cent of those who were members of a broadcasting association listened each week compared to 12 per cent of those who were not members of an association (Hedman, 1980:63). Since the start of Neighbourhood Radio that difference has become even larger. In 1989 more than half of the members of broadcasting associations listened at least once a week (Hedman & Golborne, 1990: 64), and in some areas with stations broadcasting a large amount of music more than three-quarters of the members listened on a weekly basis (Ekegren, 1990: 42).

The amount that a particular association broadcasts and the size of its share of the total broadcasts offered by a particular Neighbourhood Radio station to a large extent determine how much a member of an association listens. The extent to which the association has other ways of getting in touch with its members is also of significance. Within an association for homosexuals, for example, which regularly broadcasts programmes over Neighbourhood Radio, 60 per cent of the members listened to Neighbourhood Radio each week. More than a third listened to their own association's programme each week. Within another minority group, Arabic-speaking residents of a suburb of Stockholm, 69 per cent listened to their association's Neighbourhood Radio programme each week (Hedman, 1982a: 26).

In one of the experimental regions, where more than 90 per cent of the programmes were of a religious nature, more than half of the residents who were members of some kind of religious association listened each week, whereas only 16 per cent of those who were non-members listened with such regularity. There was also a positive correlation between going to religious meetings and listening to Neighbourhood Radio. Other variables which usually show a correlation with radio listening, such as age and education, were also significant determinants for Neighbourhood Radio listening, but when these correlations were controlled for possible influence from the religious position of listeners, it turned out that age and education had by themselves limited influence (Hedman & Weibull, 1984: 219).

The spread in listening time was larger in 1989 than in 1980. In 1980 the percentage who listened at least once a week varied between 9 per cent and 24 per cent in the different regions (Hedman, 1980: 41), and nine years later the corresponding figures were 5 per cent and 34 per cent (Hedman & Golborne, 1990: 30). The most successful stations are those with associations that have a large membership and which broadcast a large amount of music. It seems, then, as if Neighbourhood Radio stations aim their programming at the general public, and those broadcasting light popular music reach the largest audiences.

Given the nature of Swedish Neighbourhood Radio, it can hardly be regarded as a traditional mass medium. Neighbourhood Radio almost completely lacks local news, which is the most frequently cited reason for interest in local media (Hedman, 1981). Traditional media give people a feeling of security and the media become an integral part of their daily lives (Weibull, 1983). These media are successful due to the fact that general news concerns nearly all persons.

Certainly, a majority of the associations which participate in Neighbourhood Radio want to attract the general public and spread their ideas primarily to people other than their own members (Bertling & Tysell, 1981: 60), but the fact is that most of the programmes attract mainly the members of the transmitting association. It is consequently more reasonable to regard Swedish Neighbourhood Radio as a group medium, and not as a traditional mass medium. A group medium is denoted by having a stable and faithful recipient audience which shares the interests reflected in the medium (Hedman & Weibull, 1984: 225).

Relation to other media

One of the original objections to the introduction of Neighbourhood Radio was that it would compete with the recently started local radio stations. Inasmuch as both local radio and Neighbourhood Radio were locally oriented, overlap was anticipated in the function they would fulfil for listeners. However, as already stated, Neighbourhood Radio differs in several essential respects from local radio and also from the local press. The fear that a competitive situation would develop between local media has been shown to be unfounded.

Yet, the media do compete for the listeners' time, which is, of course, limited. Studies have shown, however, a positive correlation exists between listening to Neighbourhood Radio and listening to local radio. People who often listen to local radio also often listen to Neighbourhood Radio and vice-versa (Hedman, 1980: 69; Hedman & Weibull, 1984: 216; Hedman & Golborne, 1990: 82).

There is also a positive correlation, albeit weak, between listening to Neighbourhood Radio and to national radio. Since no correlation exists between listening behaviour and use of local newspapers, there is reason to suspect that listeners ascribe value to radio use of and for itself.

In comparison to other local media, the local population still spends very little time listening to Neighbourhood Radio. In a study conducted in 1985 in Uppsala, for example, 69 per cent of the public read the largest local paper daily and 30 per cent listened to the local radio station, but only 1 per cent listened to Neighbourhood Radio on a daily basis (Thomas et al., 1987). In a smaller, religious town, Jönköping, similar findings were noted: on a daily basis 75 per cent of the respondents read the newspaper, 35 per cent listened to local radio and 9 per cent to Neighbourhood Radio (Hedman & Weibull, 1984: 216).

CONCLUDING REMARKS

As mentioned at the beginning of this chapter, the idea of Neighbourhood Radio was proposed by the Liberal Party, but could only be realized once there was a non-socialist party coalition in government in 1976. Criticism from the left wing parties was mainly based on four arguments: that Neighbourhood Radio would only become a medium for urban residents, that advertisements and other commercial interests would influence the programming, that only large and economically strong associations would be able to produce programmes, and that Neighbourhood Radio would impede development of local radio.

In 1982, after three years of experimenting with Neighbourhood Radio, the left-of-centre parties regained a majority in Parliament. For some time, there was much anxiety among associations and organizations which made use of Neighbourhood Radio as to what position the Social Democrats would adopt towards the medium. Despite earlier criticisms, the party felt Neighbourhood Radio should be allowed to continue operation providing it became self-supporting.

The objections made towards Neighbourhood Radio are valid, but they do not tell the whole story. Neighbourhood Radio is, and will continue to be, a radio service for urban areas. In 1989 about 86 per cent of residents in the three largest cities in Sweden were able to listen to one or more Neighbourhood Radio stations, compared to only 45 per cent of persons living in the country (Hedman, 1990b: 10). It is in the well-populated regions of the country that there are enough associations able to provide extensive and interesting programming. It is, however, quite possible to produce and transmit Neighbourhood Radio programmes in much smaller areas, and this has been done.

The associations must pay all costs related to Neighbourhood Radio broadcasts. This can, of course, present a problem for small associations which might consider covert commercials or sponsoring, activities prohibited by law. A number of such cases have occurred and the associations involved have been sentenced by the Neighbourhood Radio Authority. In relation to the total amount of broadcasting, however, these cases have been few.

The costs involved may also have the undesired effect that only large well-endowed associations are able to make use of Neighbourhood Radio. It is probable that many small associations have refrained from using the medium for this reason. A study conducted at the start of the experiment suggested this explanation, along with limited personnel, as the most common reasons cited by associations for not using the medium (Bertling & Tysell, 1981: 61). Despite this, there are a number of small associations which successfully broadcast on Neighbourhood Radio, largely because of the interest of a few staff members.

As for possible effects on local radio, there does not seem to have been a decrease in attention to local radio due to Neighbourhood Radio. Nevertheless, there is reason to believe that the introduction of Neighbourhood Radio has in some way affected both local and national radio. From the very beginning Neighbourhood Radio succeeded in attracting young listeners, and many persons within the two larger radio organizations feared they might lose the young generation. Many people within local radio were worried that Neighbourhood Radio would in the future, through advertising or through municipal subsidy, have the economic capability of competing with local radio.

These concerns have certainly played a role in the recent policy of local radio stations to facilitate access to the medium by associations and minority groups, and especially young people (Hedman, 1982b). However, this policy change is also a consequence of a general international trend towards public access radio (see Beaud *et al.*, 1978; Richeri, 1978; Sliepen, 1979).

Once the Social Democrats had come to accept Neighbourhood Radio, and once advertising and sponsorship were seen as unrealistic sources of station financing, Neighbourhood Radio no longer was considered a threat to national or local radio. However, during the last few years the arguments for a 'free' radio (local or regional) have been much more frequent in Sweden, and the non-socialist parties have made several proposals to establish a new form of radio financed mainly by commercials. A limited number of associations within the established Neighbourhood Radio system advocate such 'free' radio and have developed stations very similar to commercial stations in other countries. Common among these stations is the dominance of light music and limited information supplied from organizations and associations (see Hedman, 1990c: 22).

As with many other political concerns, Neighbourhood Radio is a compromize of values and strengths. The Liberal-Conservative coalition might have opened the medium to commercial interests, such as local newspapers, and to allowing financing through advertisements, were it not for a fear of a rejection by the Social Democrats should that party have returned to power in 1979.

Traditionally, the Swedish broadcasting system has been rather regulated and centralized, and this may have had an impact on Neighbourhood Radio. For instance, a proposal for a less centralized system – with the regulating body within the county authorities – was opposed probably because of the experience with and preference for centralized broadcasting.

The main problem with the Swedish approach is the demand for regularity and continuity in broadcasting. Many associations are not interested in using Neighbourhood Radio in such a way and would prefer a more informal method of distributing airtime. The level of association activity often varies, and the present system makes no allowances for this. Neighbourhood Radio procedures favour groups having activities which can be broadcasted live. Such an approach has consequences for how associations schedule their activities, and also explains the limited amount of material from smaller groups.

Neighbourhood Radio has neither been radio 'of the people' nor radio 'for the people'. What it has been is a medium of communication between and within organizations and associations. When newly formed associations have to wait a year before being granted permission to broadcast and when only formal representatives of organizations are allowed to express opinions on the radio, the possibility of Neighbourhood Radio functioning as a lively organ for public debate in the local arena is limited.

The advantages of the Swedish Neighbourhood Radio approach are that even rather small associations have the opportunity to broadcast programmes at nominal costs. Even in locations where many groups are involved, such as in the larger cities and urban areas, small organizations have equal access to preferred transmission times.

Compared to other systems where frequencies must be shared by users, the Swedish

Neighbourhood Radio stations are more likely to have a varied schedule and "a greater degree of 'localness'" (Browne, 1984: 51). How the listener reacts to this variety in programming is not very well known. Traditionally, the listener is not accustomed to sudden interruptions in style and content, which are characteristics of Neighbourhood Radio. Further research may determine whether this has negative or positive effects on listening behaviour.

Swedish Neighbourhood Radio mainly approached the organizations already established and that might explain why Neighbourhood Radio developed rapidly. Inasmuch as general policy and practice have survived scrutiny by both the Liberal-Conservative coalition between 1976 and 1982, and the Social Democrats since 1982, and given the periodic improvement of operating procedures, there is no reason to anticipate dramatic change in the course of Neighbourhood Radio in the future.

APPENDIX: ELECTRONIC MEDIA LANDSCAPE IN SWEDEN

Broadcasting organizations

Public television

The right to broadcast has been granted to a public service company since January 1925. Since 1979 the programme production division of this company, *Sveriges Radio AB*, has been allocated to four independent subsidiaries: *Sveriges Television AB*, *Sveriges Riksradio AB*, *Sveriges Lokalradio AB* and *Sveriges Utbildningsradio AB*.

Two nation-wide television channels within *Sveriges Television AB* (*SVT*):

- *Kanal 1*
- *TV2*

Commercial television
(Swedish speaking)

TV3 owned by Scansat Broadcasting Ltd and based in London. Transmitted through the ASTRA-satellite mainly to households connected to cable networks in the Scandinavian countries.

TV4 produced by Nordisk Television AB and based in Stockholm. Transmitted through the Swedish DBS satellite TELE-X to cable TV households in Sweden and Norway.

Nordic Channel owned by Sanna Holding AB and based in Stockholm. Transmitted through Eutelsat II F1 to cable networks in Sweden and Norway.

Public radio

3 nation-wide radio channels within *Sveriges Riksradio AB*:

- *P1* (serious talk channel)
- *P2* (serious music channel)
- *P3* (light entertainment and music channel)

25 local radio stations organized within *Sveriges Lokalradio AB*.

Radio for associations

239 organizations in 158 areas (November 1990) have permission to transmit what is called Neighbourhood Radio. On the average each organization transmits more than 3 hours per week.

Statistics on media possession and consumption

In Sweden 99 per cent of the households have at least one radio set and 96 per cent of the households are equipped with a television receiver. Some 90 per cent of the sets are colour TVs. More than 45 per cent of the households are connected to a cable network. Some 30 satellite television channels are distributed on these networks. More than half of households have a VCR.

More than 75 per cent of the Swedish population watch television and listen to the radio every day, and they spend about 6 hours a day consuming mass media. Viewing (television and VCR) accounts for a third (32 per cent) and listening (radio, gramophone records and cassette tapes) for almost half (49 per cent) of all mass media consumption. The average viewer watches 2.3 hours a day and the average listener listens nearly 3 hours a day.

References

Atmer, M. (1984): *Närradion i Uppsala*, Uppsala: Department of Sociology, University of Uppsala.

Béaud, P., M. Barret, H. Ingberg and H. L.'Hoest (1978): *Free radio in Italy*, Strasbourg: Council of Europe.

Bertling, E. and I. Tysell (1981): 'Sammanslutningarnas förväntningar pä närradion', in L. Hedman (ed.) (1981): *Utvärdering av närradion*, Stochholm: Liber Förlag.

Browne, D.R. (1984): 'Alternatives for local and regional radio: three Nordic solutions', *Journal of Communication* **34**, 2: 36-55.

Daun, Å. (1981): 'Local communication as counterculture', paper, conference on local communication, Ronneby.

Ekegren, P. (1990): *Närradion – Så tycker vi om det vi hör och gör*, Uppsala: Department of Media and Communication, University of Uppsala.

Hedman, L. (1980): *Närradion och dess lyssnare*, Stockholm: Liber Förlag.

Hedman, L. (ed.) (1981): *Utvärdering av närradion*, Stochholm: Liber Förlag.

Hedman, L. (ed.) (1982a): *Närradion – Innehållet, Medlemmarna och Invandrarna*, Stockholm: Liber Förlag.

Hedman, L. (1982b): *Lokal närradio eller nära lokalradio*, Uppsala: Department of Sociology, University of Uppsala.

Hedman, L. (1990a): 'Radioutvecklingen i Sverige', *Medienotiser* nr. 1/90, NORDICOM-Sverige, pp. 1-6.

Hedman, L. (1990b): *Närradiolyssnandet i riket*, Uppsala: Department of Media and Communication, University of Uppsala.

Hedman, L. (1990c): *Nära radio för föreningar*, Uppsala: Department of Media and Communication, University of Uppsala.

Hedman, L. and L. Weibull (1984): 'Lyssnandet på närradio', SOU **53**: 201-226.

Hedman, L. and G. Golborne (1990): *Närradions publik*, Uppsala: Department of Media and Communication, University of Uppsala.

Proposition 1977/78: 91, *Radio & TV 1978-86*.

Richeri, G. (1978): 'Italy: A democratisation of the media', paper, IIC Annual Conference, Dubrovnik.

Sliepen, A. (1979): *Experiments with local cable television and local/regional radio in the Netherlands*, Strasbourg: Council of Europe.

SOU (1965: 20): *Radions och televisionens framtid i Sverige*, Stockholm: Allmänna Förlaget.

SOU (1973: 8): *Radio i utveckling*, Stockholm: Allmänna Förlaget.

SOU (1977: 19): *Radio och TV 1978-1985*, Stockholm: Allmänna Förlaget.

SOU (1981: 13): *Närradio*, Stockholm: Allmänna Förlaget.

SOU (1984: 53): *Föreningarnas radio*, Stockholm: Allmänna Förlaget.

SOU (1990: 70): *Lokalt ledd närradio*, Stockholm: Allmänna Förlaget.

Thomas, M. (1981): *Neighbourhood radio – a new medium in Sweden*, Uppsala: Department of Sociology, University of Uppsala.

Thomas, M., L. Hedman, and P.G. Holmlöv (1987): *Upsala Bornas Massmedievanor*, Uppsala: Department of Sociology, University of Uppsala.

Weibull, L. (1983): *Tidningsläsning i Sverige, Tidningsinnehav, tidningsval, läsvanor*, Stockholm: Publica/Liber Förlag.

Wengelin, K. (1982): 'Innehållet i närradioprogrammen 1979 och 1980', in L. Hedman (ed.) *Närradion – Innehållet, Medlemmarna och Invandrarna*, Stockholm: Liber Förlag.

6. NORWAY:
Deregulation of broadcasting and community television

Birger J. Nymo

Norwegian Telecommunications Administration, Norway

HISTORICAL REVIEW

Since 1933 broadcasting in Norway has been controlled by a public monopoly, the Norwegian Broadcasting Corporation (*NRK*). *NRK* is based on a public service broadcasting model in which the state determines organizational structure and controls finances, and the *NRK* maintains a large degree of freedom concerning formulation of programming policy. *NRK* programming is transmitted on two radio channels and one television channel to Norway's four million inhabitants.

The broadcasting monopoly was established in the Broadcasting Act, and since World War II this Act has seldom been the topic of political debate. Until 1981 the monopoly was all encompassing, except for the exchange of programming from neighbouring countries and for a few permits allowing occassional transmission of student broadcasts and training programmes.

In the 1980s this relatively stable situation changed drastically. Influenced by technological advances related to distribution and production, the concept of broadcasting has taken on a new meaning in Norway. The broadcasting monopoly has partly been replaced by a more liberal model with increased freedom for community and international broadcasting, independent of the *NRK*.

The first signs of political dissatification with the broadcasting monopoly came when the Conservative Party published a report in 1980 on the future of broadcasting. The report recommended deregulation of the state broadcasting monopoly. The political situation in the country, however, precluded a sharp break with the 40-year-old political consensus on broadcasting policy. Changes would have to be introduced step by step, and in the initial phase permission was given for limited experiments with community broadcasting outside of the *NRK*, and for distribution of satellite television. The reason for holding community broadcasting experiments was to gain experience in order to establish principles for the future organization of broadcasting in Norway.

Within the framework of the Broadcasting Act, 50 licences were allocated in 1981 for community radio, seven for community television and seven for distribution of satellite programming. All the television licences required programme distribution through cable networks. In 1984 the Broadcasting Act was modified to allow extension of the experimental activities. The number of licences increased to 381 for community radio, 129 for community television and 50 for satellite programming.

At the same time as these experimental activities were taking place questions on other policy aspects of broadcasting – advertising on radio and television, cable television networks and a new nation-wide television channel (*TV 2*) – were on the agenda of several governmental committees. All of the political parties were forced to formulate or reformulate their views on these topics. This resulted in a new political consensus in which the *NRK* monopoly was broken. In 1988 a new Broadcasting Act took force which formally separates community broadcasting from the *NRK*.

BASIS FOR COMMUNITY TELEVISION EXPERIMENTS

Historically speaking, Norway is a country with a stable media system and broadcasting policy. Questions about the media which have prompted debate since World War II include the financing of broadcasting through advertising and the support provided by the state to maintain a geographically and ideologically differentiated press structure. State grants to the press have come to constitute considerable financial outlays, and these investments have contributed to the situation in which the local newspaper is considered the most important local news medium in Norway. There are a total of about 155 newspapers edited by around 120 publishers in the country.

Reluctance to finance broadcasting by means of advertising is closely connected to the tradition of public service found in radio and television. Many people have regarded the state monopoly without advertising as the most important guarantee for a serious, non-commercial form of broadcasting which would benefit the country as a whole. What, then, challenged this position and the stability in the broadcasting system with initiation of a seven-year experimental period with community television?

The general development within broadcasting technology in the 1970s is one important external factor in helping explain these events. In general, distribution of television via satellite has resulted in a new broadcasting situation throughout Europe. Television has become an international medium. At the same time, video technology improved and distribution via cable networks opened up the possibility for television to become a local medium. In Norway this resulted in pressure against the established monopolistic form in which broadcasting was organized, especially regarding competion from commercial foreign television stations.

These developments coincided with an increase in the political strength of the Conservative Party and with growing interest in cultural policy among the liberal members of this party (Vaagland & Østbye, 1982). Politicians envisaged increased opportunities for business in the wake of the new broadcasting technologies.

Cable companies also encouraged transformation of broadcasting policy. Since the 1960s development of cable networks has taken place in the densely populated areas in southeastern Norway. Distribution of Swedish television to Norwegian viewers was the motivating factor of these activities. Towards the end of the 1970s these companies saw the possibility of providing customers with a wider range of cable delivered services which they felt would further stimulate expansion of the networks.

In Norway broadcasting, and in particular television, has been nationally oriented. At the same time, decentralization of broadcasting has been an important factor in Norwegian policy considerations. In the last decades regional radio programming has developed which covers the entire country. In the middle of the 1980s *NRK* also carried out experiments with regional television.

Decentralization and democratization of television have been vital issues in the debate on community television in a number of countries. In Norway, pressure from 'grass roots' organizations and from others striving for democratization and decentralization was minimal prior to the experimental period. In this context democratization has come to mean access to the medium for groups with special information needs in the local environment. However, democratization and promotion of public involvement became important arguments in favour of the experiments. Television was seen as a means for creating local identity, counter-balancing trends toward centralization and for increasing freedom of expression.

Another reason given for holding the experiments was to help safeguard the national culture. The coming of satellite delivered television implied further internationalization of television programming available in Norway. Until recently, about 40 per cent of *NRK* programming has been of foreign origin. Community television was meant to stem further impact from abroad.

All in all, the authorities were not faced by strong demands to experiment with community television. The source of the experiments, rather, is found in a political desire to deregulate broadcasting in Norway and to adapt new developments within broadcasting technology. Democratization, decentralization, increased freedom of choice, variety and counter-balancing the influence of foreign television constituted the basic arguments for the experiments.

CONDITIONS OF EXPERIMENTATION

The Ministry of Cultural and Scientific Affairs, the licencing authority of the Broadcasting Act, set the limitations and outlined the requirements for the experiments. These conditions were generally effective for the entire experimental period, although some were altered during the course of events.

First, community television was closely linked to distribution via cable networks because of limited frequencies available for wireless transmission. This requirement excluded the possibility of providing community television in large parts of the country where such networks have not been constructed. The requirement also led to the unintended consequence that the right of ownership to limited channels in a cable network could result in a monopoly on community television if the network owner and transmission company were unable to reach an agreement on use of the channels. Access channels with limited resources could especially become victims of such situations. In 1984, in response to this criticism, a few licences were granted for over-the-air transmission of television programming.

Programming was not to be financed through commercial advertising, and public grants were not awarded to support programming activities. This meant community television was not a real possibility for the less financially resourceful licensees. It was, however, permitted to distribute programming sponsored by private companies, but reference to such sponsorship could not be made during the programming. Sale of transmission time was also allowed providing the amount of time sold did not exceed 25 per cent of the total broadcast time.

Second, restrictions were made as to which organizations could qualify for a licence. Nation-wide organizations, businesses and and private individuals were prohibited from holding licences. During the initial phase of the experiment, beginning in 1981, newspapers were formally excluded from participating. This was done to curb creation of local information monopolies. In the second phase of the experiment, from 1984, newspapers were allowed to apply for licences.

Third, programmes were to meet certain editorial requirements. The content had to conform to Norwegian law. The programming editor, intended to be a resident within the licence area, was legally liable for the programming transmitted. The arrangement was an effort to prevent non-local interests from gaining control of the stations. The responsible editor was also to abide by the code of ethics established for the Norwegian press. In this manner, the licencing authorities incorporated ethical requirements which exceeded provisions in the law – a situation not previously encounter in Norway. The programming was to be local in nature, i.e. either produced locally or dealing with local issues. In practice, this meant that at least 50 per cent of the transmission time was to consist of local programmes.

Fourth, if any of the licencing rules were violated, the licence could be suspended or withdrawn by the authorities. If ethical infractions were suspected, a complaint could be submitted to a national committee. This committee was established pursuant to the Broadcasting Act and was originally intended for handling complaints about programmes of the Norwegian Broadcasting Corporation. During the experimental period the committee was also to handle complaints concerning community broadcasting.

Finally, in order to monitor the experiments the Ministry required that the licensees submit information on their activities at regular intervals, such as financial accounts and programming schedules. In order to assess the experiments, a community broadcasting committee was established, and in 1986 this committee submitted its report.

Participation in the experiments

Once community television had been made politically feasible, a large number of organizations expressed interest in participating in the experiment. During the entire experimental period more than 200 applications for licences were submitted. The applications came from all parts of the country, but inasmuch as the licences required signal distribution via cable networks, more than half of the applications came from the southeastern and the most densely cabled parts of the country. Oslo, the capital city, accounted for more than 20 per cent of the applications. Some 550 organizations, groups and institutions – alone or with other candidates – submitted applications. On the average, 2.7 organizations were represented by each application, but the majority of applications came from single organizations. See Table 1 for a list of the main licence applicants.

Table 1. Major applicants for station licences

Group of applicants	Representation of the total number of applications (N=203)
1. Newspapers	26%
2. Religious organizations	16%
3. Housing cooperatives	15%
4. Cable companies	15%
5. Private persons	11%
6. Political parties etc.	10%
7. Public bodies	9%
8. Business and trade	8%
9. Film/video companies	7%
10. Humanistic/idealistic organizations	7%

When the applications were considered in 1984, 40 experimental regions around the country had been selected, based on an equal geographical distribution, pattern of settlement, economic, social and cultural variations. Within these areas all applicants were granted a licence. In areas where a newspaper or a political party was granted licence, all newspapers and political parties in this area were offered a licence in order to avoid possible criticism regarding unfair competition. A total of 129 licences were granted.

The general picture which emerged was that the higher the number of co-operating parties applying, the easier the application was accepted. With the exception of companies and video manufacturers, the largest group of applicants was newspaper publishers. Newspapers, indeed, played a dominant role: individually or together with other applicants, newspapers were represented in every third licence.

What purpose did the licensees have in mind for community television? The applications reveal a large range of utilization of community television. Four types of purposes stand out (Syvertsen, 1987):

1. Focus on the community. This implies objectives such as strengthening the local community, supporting local cultural activities and creating a buffer against commercial foreign cultural influences.

2. Focus on organizations. This implies working for the objectives of certain organizations, distributing information on groups in the community such as religious denominations and language groups, and generally relating to the viewers of the television programming in much the same was as a newspaper relates to its subscribers.

3. Focus on news and information. The most important aspect of stations with

this purpose is to provide a professional journalistic news service for the communities. Stations with this purpose also strive to serve as a training ground for journalists.

4. Focus on alternative or critical information. This purpose involves establishing an alternative to other media and striving to foster a critical attitude to news media.

Both training and professional journalistic coverage of the community (type 3 above) are important objectives of the largest group of licensees – the newspapers. These are also the most commonly found objectives among all licensees. The second most commonly stated objective is orientation towards the community (type 1). Few stations cite focus on alternative or critical information (type 4) or on local organization (type 2) as the purpose of their activity – a situation resulting from the fact that the experiments did not originate from initiatives by local action groups but from governmental authorities.

The applications were also influenced by the fact that few people had a well-conceived notion of the different aspects of community television before the experiments. Once the experiments began, however, many were eager to participate. This transformation is reflected in plans made for the amount of broadcasting, and the forms of organization and financing considered. Three-fourths of the applicants planned to broadcast less than three hours per week. Only a couple of the religious group licensees had plans to transmit substantially more programming: between 70 and 168 hours per week.

The majority of the applicants made use of people already employed in the parent organizations so that community television would become part of their daily work. A third of the licensees intended to allow all persons interested to participate in production activities, and about a fifth planned to engage specialized employees.

A majority of the licensees planned to finance the stations with a multitude of sources, but quite a few of the licensees also intended to finance the stations from the resources of the parent organization. Other financing possibilities often mentioned include voluntary licence fees, donations, pay television, lease of equipment and sale of studio services.

FROM PLANS TO PRACTICE

In the first part of the trial period, between 1981 and 1984, all seven licensees started broadcasting programmes. Although the newspapers were excluded from being licensees, they became the principal agents in these trials, together with the cable companies. The cable companies which were granted licences faced a situation where distribution networks and permission to distribute local programmes were regulated, but they did not have the equipment and experience required to produce programmes. The cable companies, thus, joined forces with the newspapers. The result was that the newspapers partly bought shares in the cable companies and arranged agreements on programme production.

The experiments in this period were strongly characterized by the influence of professional information workers responsible for programme content (Nymo, 1984a;

1984b). None of the newspaper dominated experiments had any clearly formulated programming philosophy; the programmes mainly consisted of news magazines and documentaries. In addition, some programmes of a non-local character were distributed, especially sports and entertainment programming. The national television channel was the primary source of inspiration for these experiments.

Whereas all of the licensees offered programmes during the first experimental period, this is far from the case in the second period. Then 49 of the 129 candidates for licences eventually came to produce community television programmes. The programmes were distributed via cable networks which vary in size from 200 to 160,000 connections. Some of these licensees broadcast very few or sporadic programming. By the beginning of 1986 only 10 of these licensees were providing weekly or monthly programming. There was, in other words, a large discrepancy between the optimism expressed by many of the applicants and the programming actualized during the Norwegian experiments with community television.

Those who did not utilize their licence fully cite one main reason: insufficient financial basis. This explanation refers to both funding required for production equipment as well as to day-to-day operations. Many people had underestimated the funding necessary to be able to launch a community television station. Inasmuch as no public grants were awarded and advertising was not allowed, the basis for operating community television quickly disappeared. Also, it should be noted that a number of those who did not use the licences fully only intended to indicate interest and did not seriously plan to launch a station at that point in time.

Distribution of programming was another problem which prevented a number of people from starting community television. By linking licence to distribution via cable networks, a number of licensees became dependant on agreements with cable television companies. Conflicts of interest occurred, particularly in areas where a number of people intended to distribute community television on the same network. In Oslo, with the largest cable television network in Scandinavia, time-consuming negotiations on prices, channel leases and distribution of transmission time resulted in a number of parties abandoning plans for community television.

NATURE OF THE EXPERIMENTS

In the experimental period no funding was made available for systematic scientific evaluation. It is thus difficult to give a balanced picture of the period. Case studies of several stations, however, were undertaken by individual scientists and research institutions. One general impression which emerges from these studies is the diversity of experimentation which took place. There were stations operating with very limited technology and a handful of volunteers; there were also stations with considerable resources at their disposal and where programming was produced by professional television companies.

At one extreme are the stations found in housing cooperatives. Here, emphasis was placed in engaging residents of the housing estates in station activities (Bomann, 1983). A central objective of these stations was to activate other residents to become involved in community activities. Also, stress was placed on using volunteers and relatively simple production equipment. Although production costs of the programming of these stations was minimal, continuity in programming remained problematic.

A position more in the middle is found in stations organized and run by local volunteers, but where teams of professionals coordinate activities and provide technical support for productions. One station exemplifying this position is Jevnaker Community Television (JTV) and has been the object of scientific evaluation (see discussion in Chapter 3).

Jevnaker Community Television was part of an experiment with new telecommunications services carried out by the Norwegian Telecommunications Administration in the municipality of Jevnaker about 80 km north of Oslo. This station offered weekly programmes lasting about an hour to approximately 800 households. The equipment could be used free of charge by residents of the community.

Residents were able to organize and determine programming content without interference from the Norwegian Telecommunications Administration. All persons in Jevnaker wishing to share information were able to produce programmes for the station. The cultural secretary of the town was responsible for editorial content and three employees co-ordinated activities. During the period of study around 70 persons attended local courses on production of community television, and about a fifth of this group formed the nucleus of the volunteer production staff.

Some 90 per cent of the content in this access channel was produced locally and reflected cultural life in the community. The station did not provide a news service, but city council debates and other local events were broadcast live.

A contrasting example of a community television station can be found in Oslo. Several newspapers, a church and a production company associated with Scandinavia's largest cable television company were among those most active in community television. Oslo and other major cities in the country constituted the 'local area' for these organizations (Naerkringkastingsnemnda, 1986). Newspapers participated in the experiment in order to gain experience with the medium. They generally considered community television as a potential outlet for their news and information resources. Inasmuch as advertising was not allowed during the experimental period, the newspaper companies financed station activity. Programming here was produced in close co-operation with the newspaper company, particularly with the news department. Not surprisingly, programming was characterized by a professional approach to selecting and presenting news.

These news programmes focused regularly on local events. Although the approach seemed influenced by national television, the topics were often subject to more thorough commentary than is generally the case in national television progamming. The point of departure was that community television should play the same role for the local community as the role played by the Broadcasting Corporation for Norwegian society as a whole.

Community television stations organized by religious organizations were different from other stations in that they received support from Christian media companies with much experience with television. These companies produced professional television programmes which were sold to the community stations. 'Community' for these stations did not refer primarily to a geographical region, but a 'community of interest', i.e. the religious community. Much of the programming for these stations came from the United States and was subtitled in Norwegian.

In Oslo, the company Janco Vision A/S has produced programming for community stations since 1981. This company was established when Scandinavia's largest cable television company was granted a community station licence. Janco Vision was allowed to programme eight hours of 'prime time' on the Oslo cable network. Today, this network reaches about 130,000 households. The programmes are also relayed via satellite for use by other community television stations elsewhere in the country. In all, programmes produced by this company may reach more than a million viewers.

Contributions from the owners (a large industrial company and a major newspaper) constitute the financial backbone of the station, but the intention in the future aim is to support station activities through advertising, public grants and production support from the industry. An objective of Janco Vision is to provide programming suitable for regional television, and in that sense is extending the meaning of what was characterized as a conventional geographic region for community television in the country.

In summary, about 60 per cent of the programmes on the community stations in Oslo are produced by the stations themselves; the remaining 40 per cent are purchased, mainly from foreign distributors. A general programming profile consists of three main elements: sports, music and feature programmes. The first two categories consist mainly of purchased programmes; feature programmes are usually produced by the station itself.

PUBLIC RESPONSE

Only a small portion of the Norwegian population has had opportunity to view community television. In 1985 a total of 9 per cent of the population was able to watch community television (Lund, 1986). Following expansion of cable networks and co-operation on programme distribution between stations, this has increased to 15 per cent in 1986 and 20 per cent in 1987 (Haraldsen & Lund, 1987).

Attendance to community station programming is unevenly distributed throughout the country. The majority of those who can view this programming are located in the densely populated areas around the capital. Elsewhere in the country stations tend to be found only in town areas because that is where cable systems have been built.

Considering the country as a whole, only 1 per cent of those who are able to watch community television do so on a daily basis. This figure suggests the degree of competition community television faces from other television channels. The percentage is misleading, however, regarding the number of viewers attending to individual programmes. Most local stations do not broadcast daily, but once or twice a week in addition to replays. The number of people who can view community television daily, therefore, is much less than those able to view in the course of the week.

Whether importance should be attached to the number of viewers watching the programmes depends on the purpose of the activity. To the typical access station a better measure of impact is the degree of production related activity generated. Nevertheless, no one is interested in distributing information which does not have an audience, and audience surveys have been carried out by many of the stations.

These surveys suggest that community television is watched by more viewers in small rural communities than in urban communities. Findings from audience surveys noted in Table 2 illustrate this relation (Werner *et al.*, 1984; Lundby, 1986).

Table 2. Viewers of community television

		Percentage of viewers who viewed last programme:
*Oslo, March 1984**		
	Newspaper television	11–14% (N > 171; N > 143)
	Janco Vision	10–22% (N > 30)
	SLGTV	13–16% (N > 53; N > 234)
Rural communities		
Elverum community television (March 1984)		37% (N = 335)
Jevnaker community television (October 1985)		47% (N = 234)

*The noted percentage vary because, during the period in which the surveys were conducted, a number of programmes were broadcast. Both the lowest and highest percentage obtained during a week period are noted.

In general, community television has a lower viewer rating in the capital, Oslo, than in Jevnaker and Elverum. These two places are smaller towns functioning as administrative service centers for the local municipalities. At the time of the surveys all three locations offered viewers nearly the same number of television channels along with a community television channel. This suggests that the character of a community is a more significant factor influencing public interest than the nature of the programming. The three stations referred to in Oslo have a somewhat different programming profile, but there is still little difference between the number of viewers for each station; see additional discussion in Chapter 3.

THE FUTURE OF COMMUNITY TELEVISION

The original objectives of the experiment with community television were only to a limited extent realized. The possibility of organizations and individuals becoming involved in the operation of community television prompted much initial interest. This was not, however, sufficient basis to achieve the original objectives. Even when the unrealistic hopes regarding citizen participation are disregarded, insufficient funding to generate variety in programming and to promote democratization of the medium remained major obstacles. Established media enterprises, especially newspapers and cable television companies, dominated the stations during the experimental period. As a consequence, little was achieved in the effort to strengthen Norwegian television culture against competition from foreign producers.

The experiment did result in reformulation of Norwegian broadcasting policy, and the state broadcasting monopoly in that process was broken. A new Broadcasting Act was ratified in May 1988, and since then community broadcasting can be permanently operated outside the *NRK*. This Broadcasting Act enables authorities to grant licences for community broadcasting to schools, local groups, non-profit organizations, and other groups with activities directly related to community television. Licences are not issued directly to media companies, national organizations, private individuals, businesses and municipal institutions. And when these entities are participants in a station, they may control no more than 49 per cent of the shares.

Licences are granted for a period of seven years and a state authority has been established for processing applications. In order to stimulate focus on local issues licences are normally granted to single municipalities and licence holders are required to reside within the respective station transmission area. Over-the-air broadcasting has also been expanded since the experimental period. This has made community television possible in areas of the country without cable systems.

The community television experiment demonstrated that financing is a key issue for the future of community television. Neither democratization of the media nor increased variety in programming is possible without sufficient funding to run a station. Regarding community radio, the Broadcasting Act of 1988 opened the way for advertising. Three years later, in April 1991, advertising was also legalized for community television. The introduction of advertising at the local level, together with the planned introduction of advertising on the national television channel in 1992, has resulted in a major transformation in Norwegian broadcasting policy. During this period restrictions on reception of foreign satellite channels have also been abolished and, as a consequence, the competition prevelant on the international television market has made its debut in Norway.

Community television is now, since the Broadcasting Act of 1988, permanently established in Norway. The experience of the trial period suggests, however, that the medium will not expand substantially as long as opportunities for profit making are limited. On the other hand, there is a steady increase in applications for new stations. In 1988 and 1989 some 103 licences were issued, and by 1990 about 200 applications had been submitted for licences; not all, as of this writing in late 1991, have reached the stage of broadcasting, however.

With the introduction of advertising on community television in 1991 the medium may become more interesting for newspapers, publishers and other media enterprises. In the future Norway may also experience, once advertising becomes well established, a division betweeen professionally-run commercial local channels and those which are volunteer-run and non-profit. As has been experienced in other European countries, non-profit channels may be difficult to finance in the long run inasmuch as there is no guaranteed form of public support.

A fund has been established for community television similar to the one for community radio, but the limited resources allocated to this fund are primarily targeted for special projects, and minority and educational programming. The daily operating expenses of stations must come, in other words, from other sources such as the local authorities, locally based companies and organizations, sale of airtime to third parties, legalized forms of gambling like bingo, and advertising.

In summary, the Broadcasting Act, along with the growing commercial influence, has brought about many changes in the environment of community broadcasting in Norway. Community broadcasting here is clearly entering a new and different phase of activity than during the experimental period.

APPENDIX: ELECTRONIC MEDIA IN NORWAY

Television

The *Norsk Rikskring Kasting (NRK)* is a public service broadcasting institution financed by licence fees. It runs the only national television channel which also includes regional outlets. In 1992 a second, privately owned and advertising financed national channel is to be launched. A limited number of licences have been issued to companies using satellite transmission, of which the largest is *TV-Norge*. Approximately 200 licences for community television have been issued.

Radio

NRK runs two national radio channels and regional services. *NRK* plans to launch a third channel in the near future, and a fourth channel is being considered as a private company. At the local level 458 licences have been issued for community radio stations.

Cable

Approximately 25 per cent of the Norwegian households are connected to cable networks. In addition to other programming, Swedish channels are generally made available.

References

Bomann, A. (1983): *Intern-tv: Selvstyrt medieutvikling i boligmiljøer*, Oslo: Institutt for samfunnsforskning.

Haraldsen, G. and S. Lund (1987): 'Fjernsynsseing vinteren 1987', report 4/87, Oslo: *NRK*.

Lund, S. (1986): 'Lyd- og billedmedier februar 1986', report 8/86, Oslo: *NRK*.

Lundby, K. (1986): 'Lokalfjernsyn i "den telematiske sandkasse"', report 82, Oslo: Institutt for pressforskning.

Nymo, B.J. (1984a): *Forsøk med lokalfjernsyn i Norge*, Copenhagen: Pressens årbog.

Nymo, B.J. (1984b): 'Publikum og fjernsyn over kabel: Nabolandsprogram, satellittsendinger og lokalfjernsyn', report 17/84, Oslo: Televerkets forskningsinstitutt.

Naerkingkastingsnemnda (1986): 'Forsøk med lokal radio og fjernsyn i Norge', report 1, Bergen: Universitetet i Bergen, Institutt for masskommunikasjon.

Syvertsen, T. (1987): 'Ny teknikk, ny politikk og "nye" medier', report nr. 4, Bergen: Universitetet i Bergen, Institutt for masskommunikasjon.

Werner, A., S. Host, and B.P. Ulvaer (1984): 'Publikums reaksjoner på satellitt- og lokalfjernsyn', report nr. 75, Oslo: Universitetet i Oslo, Institutt for presseforskning.

Vaagland, O. and H. Østbye (1982): 'From non-policy to policy – Notes on the development of Norwegian media policies', Bergen: Senter for mediaforskning.

7. THE NETHERLANDS:
Emergence of a new medium

James Stappers,[*] Frank Olderaan[*] and Pieter de Wit[**]

University of Nijmegen
**Organization of Local Broadcasters in the Netherlands (OLON), The Netherlands*

Broadcasting in the Netherlands has always been a political issue. Governments have fallen and political parties have regrouped along lines distinct from traditional political divisions. It is not surprising, then, that new techniques enabling diversification and decentralization of broadcasting have been hindered by issues alien to broadcasting itself. In this chapter we explore the rise of local radio and television in the context of the Dutch system of broadcasting. Initially, local broadcasting was intertwined with cable networks and early experimentation with local origination programming in the 1970s was dependent on this infrastructure. Since then, many developments have come about, including low power ether radio. Predicting what is yet to come is, of course, difficult, but as we note in the final section of the chapter the original blue sky expectations of local broadcasting have given way to a more modest notion of what local broadcasting can contribute to local communication.

DEVELOPMENT OF BROADCASTING

During the period radio broadcasting became established in the Netherlands the country was characterized by a social phenomenon known as 'pillarization'. Society was divided into so-called pillars: Catholics, Protestants and Social Democrats – each representing about one third of the population. These pillars had their own organizations, labour unions, schools, sport clubs. More important, each pillar had its own political parties. Members of the pillars cultivated social contacts within their respective pillars. Each pillar also had its own media – newspapers and magazines initially, and later radio and television companies.

This pillar system had several advantages. It provided emancipatory groups opportunity to develop and it contributed – via the media – to pluriformity of expression. There were also difficulties; not everyone belonged to one of the three original pillars. This led to formation of a fourth division: a neutral or universal pillar. This fourth pillar, however, lacked the ideological unity present in the other three. A diversity of political and religious groups were brought together in this new pillar, thus making it difficult to identify a common theme or basis.

The 1960s was a decade of much social upheval in the Netherlands which resulted in many institutional transformations. Secularization was taking hold like elsewhere in Western Europe and contributed to a weakening of the traditional link between religious denomination and political preference. Moreover, during this decade people began to feel less need for church affiliation and for religious education of their children. Most of the identifying characteristics of the pillar system either eroded naturally or were intentionally dismantled. The broadcasting system, however, remained impervious to this transformation.

During this period Dutch broadcasting was basically a form of public broadcasting consisting of several public corporations which shared radio equipment, transmission frequencies and programming time.[2] Later, the same form of cooperation developed for television. But in the 1960s political opposition arose to this 'club scheme'. Commercial television became seen as the lance with which the system could be opened up. Publishers, who had been prohibited from sharing the fruits of broadcasting in previous years, hoped to become involved through the introduction of commercial television. However, the political majority in the country was still in favour of the basic tenents of the public broadcasting system and were able to forestall introduction of a commercial form.

Still, with the Broadcasting Act passed in 1966, some changes were introduced. Cooperation between the different broadcasting organizations was expanded. A sizeable portion of broadcasting time was allotted to an organization for producing programing of general interest such as news bulletins, sports events, song festivals and educational and minority related issues. A new clause was also appended to the broadcasting law which enabled new groups unaffiliated with the traditional societal pillars to enter broadcasting.

The revised broadcasting law also permitted for the first time advertising as a source of income for public broadcasting. A new institution, STER, was established to coordinate advertising intended for radio and television. The purpose behind this construction was to limit the influence of advertising on programming, while at the same time generating additional revenue. To further restrict possible influence, commercials were only allowed to be aired in time blocks before and after the evening news broadcasts.[3]

Shortly after these changes cable television networks began to be built. Since these networks originally provided no more than a relay service of over-the-air signals, they can be considered as extensions of the broadcasting system. In the 1970s these networks began to be constructed on a large scale around the country (Brants &

---

2 *English language publications which provide an overview of the Dutch broadcasting system include Brants (1986), Brants & Jankowski (1985), Van der Haak (1977), Olderaan & Jankowski (1988) and NOS (1990).*

3 *The amount and placement of commercials on television have been continual topics of debate and (contd. from previous page) considerable increase in the number and flexibility in placement has come about since the period discussed here. See NOS (1990) for recent information.*

Jankowski, 1985). The flatness of the terrain and the relatively small geographical size of the country enabled community antenna systems to provide quality reception of a variety of channels. In addition to the two Dutch channels, most systems could receive three Belgian, three or four German, and one or two English channels.[4] Availability of these foreign stations provided a substantial extension of television programing for the Dutch viewer, and this programming variety is attributed as one of the reasons for the popularity of cable television (Olderaan & Jankowski, 1988).

There was much interest in developing special programming to be transmitted on these cable systems. Both traditional publishers and hardware manufacturers were interested – publishers because they saw an opportunity to break into broadcasting, and hardware manufacturers because of their concern for market expansion. Both groups expected that local origination cable television programming could serve as a product testing ground and as a warming up exercise in preparation for the anticipated introduction of commercial television.

Community workers, on the other hand, believed that local radio and television were ideal instruments for promoting social change. Some enthousiasts seized the opportunity and experimented with the medium, producing and transmitting programming to cable subscribers. This led, in 1971, to a government mandate prohibiting use of the cable for broadcasting local programmes.

At the same time, the government promised to initiate and subsidize an experiment with the new medium. A change in government postponed initiation of this experiment until 1974. There was also a shift in policy and uncertainity arose as to the purpose of the experiment. Some persons came to feel the government had announced and later authorized the experiment in order to postpone making a decision on the use of cable systems for distribution of locally produced programming. It was believed to be no more than a tactic for buying time before determining the future of broadcasting.

EXPERIMENTING WITH LOCAL ORIGINATION CABLE PROGRAMMING

The promised experiment with local origination and cable distribution of radio and television programming took place in six Dutch municipalities between 1974 and 1978. The number of residents in these municipalities able to receive the cable delivered local programming varied between 6000 and 60,000. Conditions in the six localities also differed substantially. In the smaller communities – the towns of Dronten, Deventer, Goirle, and Melick-Herkenbosch – there was general agreement and cooperation between local authorities and the persons involved in setting up the stations.

In the two larger localities – Bijlmermeer and Zoetermeer – the difficulties and differences were more fundamental. Bijlmermeer, a modern high-rise housing estate situated on the perifery of Amsterdam, was at that time not yet officially part of the city, but was nevertheless within the city's jurisdiction. Amsterdam authorities were much more interested in establishing a radio station able to serve the entire city with

---

4   *The number of cable-delivered channels has since expanded considerably. In 1991, for example, 19 television and 37 radio signals were distributed on the cable system in Amsterdam.*

over-the-air programming than concentrating on a cable station only able to serve a portion of a single housing estate. Ultimately, the Ministry of Culture ruled that the Bijlmermeer housing estate, because of its unique characteristics, should participate in the experiment (Jankowski, 1988: 45–55).

Zoetermeer, another 'new town' located near The Hague, was originally a small village with no more than 6,000 residents. By the start of the experiment, however, the population had mushroomed to 60,000 and was still increasing. The Zoetermeer authorities, like those in Amsterdam, were also less than enthousiastic about a local television station. They believed the money could be better spent on facilities which a larger portion of the population could enjoy, such as a community swimming pool. As in the case of Bijlmermeer, the Ministry of Culture pressed for participation of the station in the experiment and the local government in Zoetermeer eventually consented.

Several conditions defined and limited the activities of the stations selected to participate in the experiment. First, only non-profit organizations considered culturally representative for their respective communities were eligible as candidate stations. Licensing of stations was done by the Ministry of Culture, with advice from the respective local governments of the municipalities in which the stations were to operate.

Second, station programming activity was restricted to the community for which the license was issued. The content of the programmes were also to be related to that community. Third, each station was provided a fixed amount of funds for facilities and programming expenses. Advertising or sponsored programming was not permitted. Once a station officially commenced with programming activity, it was allowed to continue for two consecutive years. The amount of programming per week during that period was not to exceed three and a half hours for each medium, radio and television. This programming was not allowed to interrupt or replace programming from the Dutch national channels distributed on the cable television systems. And, finally, the experiment was to be monitored by social science research.[5]

The six stations participating in the experiment officially started transmission of programming in the period 1974-75. The experiment was officially terminated in 1978. Although not specified in the conditions of the experiment, the limited funding made available precluded hiring extensive professional staff. Most of the stations did employ a station director, usually with broadcasting experience, who coordinated activities of volunteer programmers.

Many of the problems which organizations dependent on volunteers face – personnel with limited experience, inconsistent level of reliability, and high turn-over rate – were present in the stations. Still, the stations managed to produce continuous programming of acceptable technical quality with a staff of about a hundred volunteers per station.[6]

---

5   *The major reports emerging from the three research projects include: Stappers et al. (1976, 1978), Koole et al. (1976) and Jankowski (1982b). Two other Dutch language volumes also consider the experiment: De Bruin et al. (1983) and Bierhoff & Van Hooidonk (1984). Portions of this work have been presented in a number of internationally-orientated publications: Stappers (1978a, 1978b, 1979a, 1979b), Stappers & Hollander (1981), Jankowski (1982a, 1988) and Sliepen et al. (1978).*

One of the central tasks of the research projects which monitored the experiment was to assess audience awareness, use and appreciation of the programming. The research designs of the three projects differed considerably: from a panel survey research design to an anthropological participation observation study. Given these differences elaborate comparison of findings is not possible. Nevertheless, a number of comments can be made based on the survey research conducted in most locations.

Generally, residents in all six sites became aware of station activities during the course of the experiment. Regular viewership varied from place to place, but ranged between 20 per cent and 30 per cent for all of the stations. The higher percentages were recorded in the smaller locations – the towns of Goirle, Dronten and Melick-Herkenbosch – and the lower figures in the larger 'new towns' of Zoetermeer and Bijlmermeer. In the smaller sites the local stations were much more important as sources of information on local affairs than in the larger ones where daily newspapers tended to serve that function.

It seemed, based on surveys held before the experiment, that most people would have little interest in programming related to politics. Once the experiment started, however, programming on local politics proved to be very popular. One reason for this popularity was that it was possible to broadcast discussions in full without regard to the customary time restrictions imposed by national broadcasting. Also, local politicians were sceptical whether amateur staffed stations would be able to adequately summarize council meetings and preferred integral rather than edited transmissions. These local council meetings, broadcast live, became one of the more popular programs. More than 50 per cent of station audiences attended to at least a portion of these cablecasted meetings. Technical conditions prevented this type of programming at some stations, but even there programming of political issues drew large viewership.

All six stations concentrated on producing television rather than radio programming. Some stations later experimented with cable delivered audio programming which could be received on television sets. This programming never commanded much audience attendance and appreciation, but it was inexpensive to produce and provided training opportunities for volunteers.

Programming policy varied from station to station. The smaller stations tended to blend different types of information with local culture. The informational programming concentrated on local politics and on club and recreational activities. In the larger sites, especially in Deventer and Bijlmermeer, there was more tendency to focus on community related issues and problems in an effort to inform and mobilize viewers. There was also effort to involve residents in programming activities as done on American public access channels.

Audience attendance and appreciation was highest in those communities with the following characteristics: (1) a cable infrastructure available to most households, (2) transmission of programming on at least on a weekly basis, (3) a homogeneous

6   That an experiment which relied on volunteers and allowed highly decentralized decision-making in programming affairs was even possible evoked astonishment amongst delegations of visitors from neighbouring countries. One explanation for this success is that the Dutch have a long tradition of living and working with people of different opinions – one of the characteristics of the pillar conception of Dutch society.

population in the area served, (4) prior awareness among residents of community concerns and problems and (5) an already thriving media culture within the community.

Once the experiments were under way, the Minister of Culture published in 1975 a memorandum on media policy intended as a step towards formulation of legislation which would encompass all media. Although local broadcasting was not specifically mentioned, distribution of radio and television signals via the cable were noted. Following the description of regional broadcasting as a welfare service of and for the region, local broadcasting was considered in the memorandum as a form of community work. This implied that funding had to be secured locally and stations would have to compete with other locally funded welfare activities such as youth clubs and libraries. Such an arrangement was detrimental to stations wanting to establish a secure financial base.

LOCAL BROADCASTING AFTER THE EXPERIMENT

In 1978 the experiment formally ended and government financing ceased. The national government was willing to allow local broadcasting activities to continue provided financing for stations was locally secured and, as during the experimental period, advertising was prohibited. Five of the six stations acquired funding elsewhere which allowed them to continue programming, albeit more modestly. One station, for example, was forced to discontinue television programming and concentrated on radio productions.

By the early 1980s, nearly two-thirds of the Dutch households had been connected to cable delivery systems, and initiatives to start local radio and television activities were increasing. In 1981, at the opening of the first color televison studio at a local station, an organization for such stations was formed – the OLON (Organization of Local Broadcasters in the Netherlands). OLON membership grew rapidly: from 14 in 1981, to 156 in 1985, to over 300 stations and initiatives by 1991. The OLON was eventually recognized by the government as the official representative of local broadcasting and was allotted an annual subsidy to finance its activities.

The OLON believed that local station programming should not be restricted to distribution by cable, but over-the-air transmissions should also be permitted. The OLON was opposed to the regulation then under consideration that would have given local authorities responsiblity for licensing local stations. Such a procedure, it was argued, would create a dependent relationship between a station and local government, and would hinder station efforts to provide objective news and information about local events. Such journalistic activity was considered the primary objective of local stations by the OLON.

In 1982 the Minister of Culture published another memorandum which adopted many of the OLON's standpoints. By then, however, a conflict in the government forced the Cabinet to resign which postponed enactment of the recommendations. In the same period the number of illegal pirate stations increased substantially. These stations mainly provided popular music programming without – in the pirate tradition – payment of royalties. In some cities the number of pirate stations created havoc on the airwaves by transmitting on frequencies reserved for legal stations. Perhaps the most flagrant violation of these stations, from the perspective of the government, was that they broadcast advertising.

Once a new government was in power effort was made to curb the pirate stations and to permit other services on cable systems. The pirate stations were eventually shut down, and in 1984 new regulations were brought into effect, allowing issuance of licenses to new local cable stations.

Further development of local broadcasting was basically determined by three conditions formulated in these regulations. Although the regulations were new, the conditions dated back to the experimental period a decade earlier. First, stations were to be representative for the cultural and social life within their respective communities. Second, only one station license per municipality was to be issued. Finally, advertising was still prohibited.

These regulations have remained in effect, although modified slightly in the Media Act of 1988. In that Act, local broadcasting was explicity mentioned for the first time; local radio was no longer considered a subunit of regional broadcasting and local television was no longer classified under the management of cable television systems. Since September 1990, advertising is permitted on local radio and television programming provided an agreement is reached with the local press regarding involvement in advertising exploitation compensation for revenue loss.

Station types and activities

These regulations, including the problematic requirement regarding cultural representativeness, provided an adequate framework for development of a large number of stations engaged in a diversity of activities. The stations came to differ in many respects, but generally speaking three types can be distinguished. First, there are stations where local broadcasting functions predominantly as a *hobby* for those involved. Volunteers are active in these stations for a variety of reasons: for the pleasure of making popular music programmes, for playing record requests or hit parade tunes, for operating the studio equipment. To a large extent, this station type is a continuation of earlier pirating activity and is often dependent on a few central persons.

Second, there are stations which serve as a communication *tool for special interest groups*. These stations are based on the philosophy dominant in the 1960s and generally find support among diverse groups in the community. Specific local events and problems are discussed in the programming and the interests of specific groups are often defended. There are usually strong ties with minority groups such as the elderly, the unemployed and ethnic groups. This type of local broadcasting places much value on encouraging programming contributions from diverse groups in the community.

Third, there are stations which attempt mainly to serve as a *local news and information service*. Providing news and information is the main activity of these stations. The underlying principle is that much local news, not deemed relevant to the other traditional local media, still deserves attention. In addition, there are many local events which receive little or no interest from other local media. Providing a journalistic product to the station audience is the intention of these stations. Although the product may differ in terms of the content found in other local media, it is similar in that journalistic procedures have been employed to produce it. This station type emerged as a reaction to earlier government policy which attempted to cast local stations in the role of community work facilities.

Most stations are, in fact, a mixture of the above three types. Smaller stations tend to be of the first type, stressing the hobby aspect of broadcasts. The second type of station – a tool for special interest groups – has become less prominent than in previous years. Now, this type is found only in stations with ethnic oriented programming; such stations are located in the four largest cities of the country. The third station type, emphasizing local news and information, is found nearly everywhere, but this type has also been the force behind development of professionally staffed stations in the major cities. Rotterdam launched such a professional television station in 1989 and Amsterdam plans to introduce *City TV*, a similar form of professional television, in 1992.

By September 1991 some 255 local broadcasting stations were in operation. Of those stations 168 produced only radio programming, 6 only television and 81 stations both radio and television programming. Local stations are found relatively more often in the larger municipalities; see Figs. 1 and 2.

Stations are not confined to specific geographic areas. They are in operation in the densely populated urban areas as well as in rural parts of the country; and see Fig. 3.

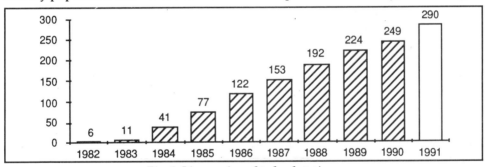

Fig. 1. *Licences issued to local stations.*

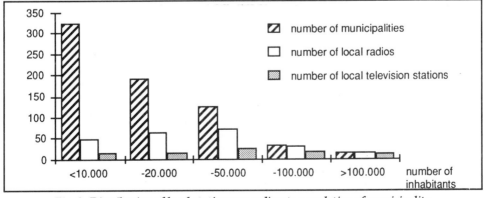

Fig. 2. *Distribution of local stations according to population of municipality.*

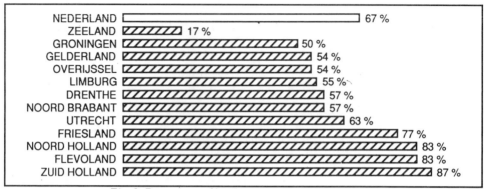

Fig. 3. Percentage of local stations per province, 1990.

Only in the province of Zeeland (a group of islands situated in the southwestern part of the country) the number of stations is lagging behind development in the rest of the country.

Present-day local stations differ in several respects. Table 1 gives an overview of basic features of six local stations and provides an illustration of some major differences regarding broadcasting time, staff size, budget, and programming activities. Some stations concentrate their energy on producing a single television programme each month, while other stations produce several hours of both radio and television programming on a weekly basis. The degree of programming activity depends, of course, on the amount of funding available. The financial latitude of stations is in almost all cases determined by local authorities. A few stations receive an annual subsidy from the local administration. Most stations, however, are dependent on an initial grant or periodic financial aid.

A final difference worth noting is that some stations not only produce radio and television programs, but also are involved in providing forms of videotex – local teletext, electronic newspapers[7] and interactive videotex services.

Table 1. Characteristics of six local stations

City	Groningen	Tilburg	Gouda	Meppel	Weert	Helmond
Population	167,000	153,000	61,000	23,000	40,000	63,000
% on cable	80	98	94	98	80	88
Volunteers (app)	100	80	100	40	50	50
Activities:						
Radio	7 hr/d	5 hr/d	14 hr/wkend	14 hr/wkend	10 hr/wkend	none
TV	1 hr/2 wk	none	little	little	none	1 hr/mn
Videotex	none	none	none	none	yes	yes
Budget, Dfl/yr	100,000	20,000	15,000	15,000	12,000	10,000

Source: Mol, 1988.

7 *These 'newspapers' consist of alphanumeric text supplemented with graphic or photographic illustrations in which each screen constitutes a story or advertisement. These screens revolve in carousel fashion; an entire 'edition' of the newspaper lasts around 15 minutes and is updated once or twice a day. Current government restrictions prohibit transmission of moving images or audio signals intended to accompany the images (Becker & Jankowski, 1986; Mol, 1988).*

Table 2. Viewership of local television in Zaltbommel

	1985	1986	1987
less than once a month	35	42	43
1–3 times a month	40	37	42
4 times a month or more	25	21	15
Total (N = 193)	100%	100%	100%

Source: Stappers et al., 1989.

Table 3. Financial budget for 22 local stations

City	Population	Hours radio	Hours tv	Budget radio	Budget tv	Budget total
Dinteloord	5587	400	18	2500	500	4000
Fijnaart	6165	660	3	5000	2500	7500
Mill	8000	368	16	6000	15,000	30,000
Landsmeer	8629	8760	80	17,800	1000	18,800
Haaksbergen	22,690	280	30	2500	13,000	38,000
Geldermalsen	21,239	2652	25	6000	60,000	66,000
Skarsterlën	23,015	754	38	21,900	49,700	95,000
Rucphen	20,475	1300	5	16,000	4000	20,000
Steenwijk	20,947	1846	15	62,125	67,875	130,000
Wageningen	32,358	1698	200	19,127	1268	36,203
Wijchen	35,000	704	8	7500	5000	28,575
Roermond	38,000	350	10	20,000		20,000
Enschede	144,052	72	10	3600	10,650	20,000
Sneek	29,500	890	3	15,750	3800	32,600
Geleen	34,254	352	20	5000	10,000	51,000
Bergen op Zoom	46,091	590	7	10,000	7000	25,000
Rijswijk	48,886	540	9	25,000	6000	68,300
Amersfoort	89,596	8760	40	70,000	100,000	170,000
Apeldoorn	147,375	574	1	53,500	21,000	74,500
Nijmegen	147,131	536	20	20,000	20,000	106,000
Eindhoven	190,900	351	98	2446	12,850	15,000
Den Haag*	443,851	13,800	900	50,500	61,000	210,000

*Station in Den Haag uses more than one channel.
Source: Wit, 1990.

Until recently local broadcasting was confined to distribution of programming on cable systems. In April 1987, however, a technical experiment was initiated to determine the number of low power radio transmitters which could operate without signal interference. Results of that experiment allow for as many as 500 low power transmitters to be licensed around the country. In March 1988 three stations began transmitting programming over-the-air. By 1991 the number had increased to 200, and 300 more of these low power radio stations are projected for the near future.

Audience reactions

A topic of obvious importance is how the public responds to the local radio and television programmes. Since the experimental period limited audience research has been conducted. An exception was the experiment with interactive cable television in the town of Zaltbommel.[8] One of the new services introduced on that town's cable system was local radio and television programming. Each week two and a half hours of television programming was cablecasted. The programming was repeated once during the same week. Table 2 indicates the frequency of attendance to this programming over the period 1985–87. As can be seen, the percentages are relatively constant across time. More than half of the residents indicated they watched local television programmes at least once a month.

It is difficult to compare these figures with information from other local stations, often gathered from *ad hoc* telephone surveys and personal reactions to programs. The impression, however, is that the results in Zaltbommel are typical of those found elsewhere.

In Table 3 an overview is provided of radio listenership for a number of stations. In nearly all cases large majorities of the community residents are aware of the radio programming and sizeable numbers of residents – 20 per cent to 40 per cent – say they listen to the programmes regularly. In general it seems that local broadcasting is attended to on a regular basis but not very frequently. As confirmed in recent research, most people are aware of the programming, particularly in the smaller communities.

CONCLUSIONS

As far as the future of local broadcasting is concerned, local radio stations will, in all likelihood, eventually capture a larger share of the listening audience. This change is largely due to recent government regulation permitting stations to employ low power ether transmitters. Growth in both the number of stations and attending audience will undoubtedly play a major role in continuing discussions about advertising. As stated earlier, the local and regional press were originally opposed to lifting the ban on advertising, but the number of advocates grew, particularly within the political parties. This created a climate for new regulations passed in 1990 which allow advertising, providing an agreement is reached with the local press regarding division of the income.

Another factor of influence on the future of local broadcasting is the general increase of media operating at the local level. People no longer need to depend on community newspapers and broadcasting stations for local information. In a growing number of communities electronic newspaper services are being provided, and plans are also being made for local teletext systems and for interactive videotex services. This increase in local media may stimulate community stations to provide better programming, but maintaining a portion of the audience will also become more difficult.

The decade and a half of experience with local broadcasting in the Netherlands has yielded a number of insights. But it is difficult, if not dangerous, to attempt to apply these insights to situations in other countries. The Netherlands is a small and densely populated country, aspects which influence the relation between regional and local

---

8   *The final report of this research (Stappers et al., 1989) details the four-year experiment in detail. Shorter English language presentations of the work include: Jankowski & Olderaan (1986) and Jankowski & Mol (1988).*

media in the country. The particular Dutch political situation has been of major influence on the development of local and regional press and broadcasting which has obstructed a more 'natural' development.

A question posed frequently is whether the country is too small to support three different levels of media: national, regional and local. There is much debate on this matter, but on one point there is agreement: community residents have much interest in local news and information. Local political issues, even more than local cultural affairs, command large audiences on local television. Programming devoted to local political topics seldom receives much interest from national or regional media; regional radio, for example, is simply unable to spend a comparable amount of time on local issues.

A preference evident both during the national experiment with local cable programming and during later experience is that the audience tends to look at more local television than it listens to local radio. The fact that listening to local radio, until recently, was hampered by government restricting only allowing cable delivery of programming and the fact that only a limited number of receivers are connected to the cable may account for this preference. There remain indications, however, that audiences prefer to look rather than to listen.

The major insight of the Dutch experience with local broadcasting, however, is that the optimistic and idealistic expectations of many early experimenters with local broadcasting have not materialized. They conceived of local television as becoming a major force in community development. There was ample opportunity to create awareness and involvement among residents in the new towns via these new media – many of the experiments took place in such communities, and were guided by staff of welfare and community agencies – but this did not happen to any sizeable degree.

While it has been demonstrated that it is possible to produce radio and television programming with and by volunteers, that alone was unable to build a sense of community. Where a lively community and local press already prospered, local broadcasting also thrived. Where an active public sphere[9] already existed, there was also space for another medium of communication – local broadcasting. Where such public sphere was absent, neither the population nor the local authorities became enthusiastic about the medium. If one thing has became clear during the past years of experience, it is that solidarity and community are not created by community broadcasting, but community broadcasting does flourish in a climate of community and solidarity.

APPENDIX: ELECTRONIC MEDIA IN THE NETHERLANDS

At the national level eight independent broadcasting organizations produce programming for five radio and three television channels. These eight organizations collectively form the NOS, the Dutch Broadcasting Foundation, which is also responsible for a portion of the national programming. In addition to these nine organizations there are some 30 smaller independent organizations – from religious groups to political parties – which provide programming.

---

9 *The German terms* Öffentlichkeit *and* Kommunikationsraum *come closest to describing this concept (see discussion in Chapter 2).*

At the regional level there are 13 radio stations, one for each of the provinces in the country (with the exception of the highly populated province of South Holland which has two regional radio stations). Most regional stations transmit programming for about five hours per day; in the remaining hours programming from one of the national radio channels is broadcasted. The amount of transmission time for the regional stations is increasing, in part because advertising has been permitted since 1991.

At the local level some 300 of the 670 municipalities in the country have local radio or television stations. Inasmuch as local stations primarily operate in larger communities, nearly two-thirds of the residents in the country can receive local radio or television programming. Only one local station is permitted for each municipality, however, and it is the station which is responsible for the programming broadcasted. In addition to low power radio, both radio and television programming is distributed by cable systems; some 80 per cent of the households in the country are connected to such a system. The stations are required by law to reflect the cultural, religious and social life of the respective localities in which they operate. This regulation stems from an effort to create a form of equal representation within the stations.

All three levels originate from a public service broadcasting philosophy. The introduction of commercial electronic media has, however, been an issue of debate for decades. In 1989 a Dutch language commercial television channel was established in Luxemburg in order to circumvent restrictions in the Netherlands. This development accelerated discussion in the country for institution of a form of commercial broadcasting in addition to that based on a public service philosophy.

National broadcasting is funded for approximately 60 per cent from listener and viewer fees and 40 per cent from advertising. Regional broadcasting is funded from regionally collected fees. Many municipalities provide subsidies for their local stations and, in addition, some stations collect funds from their viewers and listeners, from local businesses through programme sponsoring, and from selling broadcasting time to third parties. Since September 1991 advertising is permitted as a source of funding for both regional and local stations.

References

Becker, L. and N. Jankowski (1986): 'Use and assessment of cabletext services', *Massacommunicatie* 14, 245-258.

Bierhoff, J. and G. van Hooijdonk (1984): (eds) *Lokale omroep; problemen en perspektieven*, Utrecht: Stichting Welzijns Publikaties.

Brants, K. (1986): 'Broadcasting and politics in the Netherlands: from pillar to post', in R. Kuhn (ed.) *Broadcasting and politics in Western Europe*, London: Frank Cass.

Brants, K. and N. Jankowski (1985): 'Cable television in the Low Countries', in R.M. Negrine (ed.) *Cable Television and the Future of Broadcasting*, London: Croom Helm.

Bruin, M. de, T. van Doormaal and N. Jankowski (eds) (1983): *Kleine media: lokale omroep en video*, Boskoop: Macula.

Haak, C. van der (1977): *Broadcasting in the Netherlands*, London: Institute of Communications.

Jankowski, N.W. (1977): *Lokale Omroep Bijlmermeer in het proces van samenlevingsopbouw*, SISWO: Amsterdam.

Jankowski, N.W. (1982a): 'Community television: a tool for community action?', *Communication* 7: 33-58.

Jankowski, N.W. (1982b): *Lokale Omroep Bijlmermeer, eindverslag van een veldonderzoek*, SISWO: Amsterdam.

Jankowski, N.W. (1988): *Community television in Amsterdam: access to participation in and use of the 'Locale Omroep Bijlmermeer'*, Amsterdam: University of Amsterdam.

Jankowski, N. and A. Mol. (1988): 'Confused objectives and organizational difficulties: an experiment in home language instruction', in F. van Rijn and R. Williams, (eds) *Concerning home telematics*. Amsterdam: North Holland.

Jankowski, N. and F. Olderaan. (1986): 'Two-way cable in Zaltbommel. An exercise in implementation', in C. Ancelin, J. Hartley, F. Pichault, Pl Pop, and L. Qvortrup (eds) *Social experiments with information technology*, Brussels: Fast.

Koole, T., J. Oorburg and W. Wartena (1976): *Lokale televisie in Deventer*, Groningen: University of Groningen.

Mol, A.l. (1988): *Verslag van het onderzoek naar het introductieproces van nieuwe diensten in lokale gemeenschappen*, The Hague: NOTA.

NOS (1990): 'National broadcasting in the Netherlands', brochure, Hilversum: NOS.

Olderaan, F. and N. Jankowski (1988): 'The Netherlands: The cable replaces the antenna', in L. Becker and K. Schoenbach (eds) *Audience responses to media diversification. Coping with plenty*, Hillsdale: Lawrence Erlbaum.

Sliepen, A., J.G. Stappers and F. Duursma (1978): *Experiments with local cable television and local/regional radio in the Netherlands*, Strasbourg: Council of Europe.

Stappers, J.G. (1978a): 'Kabelfernsehen in den Niederlanden', in: U. Paetzold (ed.) *Kabelkommunikation*, Munich: Ølschläger.

Stappers, J.G. (1978b): 'Lokales kabelfernsehen in den Niederlanden', *Mediaperspektiven* 12: 877-886.

Stappers, J.G. (1979a): 'Das Beispiel Niederlande', in W.R. Langenbucher (ed.) *Lokal Kommunikation; Analyse, Beispiele, Alternativen*, Munich: Olschläger.

Stappers, J.G. (1979b): 'Lokales kabelfernsehen in den Niederlanden', *Mediaperspektiven* 1: 51-52.

Stappers, J.G. and E.H. Hollander (1981): 'Bürgernahes Fernsehen und Kabelpilotprojekte', *Rundfunk und Fernsehen* 29/1: 13-25.

Stappers, J.G., E.H. Hollander and H.J. Manders (1976): *Onderzoeksprojekt lokale kabelomroep, interimrapportage*, Nijmegen: University of Nijmegen.

Stappers, J.G., E.H. Hollander and H.J. Manders (1978): *Vier experimenten met lokale omroep*, Nijmegen: University of Nijmegen.

Stappers, J.G., F.G. Olderaan and N.W. Jankowski (1989): *Interactief op inactief. Een onderzoek naar de ontwikkeling van experimenten met het kabelnet in het kader van het kabelkommunikatieproject in Zaltbommel*, Nijmegen: Institute of Mass Communication.

Wit, P. de (1990): *OLON Vademecum lokale omroep 1990-1991*, Nijmegen: OLON.

8. BELGIUM:
So many ways to run a railroad

Jan Drijvers[10]

Catholic University, Leuven

BELGIAN MEDIA POLICY: MANY VOICES, DIFFERENT WORLDS

Belgium is not only the most densely cabled country in Europe, it is also blessed with the densest networks of railroads and motorways. These 'communication networks' have turned Belgium into a labyrinth of tracks, signposts and stations – and of bridges without any function and roads leading to nowhere. In spite of these closely inter-woven infrastructures and the many possibilities to interconnect and communicate, people in Belgium breathe and live in 'worlds apart'.

On the cultural map of Europe, Belgium is situated at the intersection of the Latin and Germanic worlds. Instead of turning Belgium into a melting pot of intermingling cultures, this collision of cultural traditions has divided the country into two separate Communities. The border between them runs in a straight line, from west to east. The Flemish Community in the North and the French speaking, or Wallonian Community in the South have, indeed, very little in common.

Already very distinctive in terms of geographical, political, religious, economic and social characteristics, both Communities also speak different languages – Dutch in the Flemish section and French in Wallonia. A fact of which very few Belgians are aware is that all of these differences are reflected in the media of both Communities, for people from one Community hardly read magazines and newspapers or watch television and films from the other community (Fauconnier, 1984: 325–327).

In addition to these two main Communities, the outcome of World War I endowed Belgium with yet another but smaller German Community located in the Eastern region of the country. And Brussels, originally a battleground for the French speaking and Flemish inhabitants, has become a modern version of Babel with the influx of rich European bureaucrats and poor North African immigrants.

---

10 *The title of this chapter has been inspired by Landry et al. (1985):* What a way to run a railraod. An an analysis of radical failure.

The distinctive media landscapes in these Communities are not only a logical conse-quence of cultural differences, but are also a product of politically divergent media policies. Regarding politics, the Belgian railroad system metaphor no longer holds. While almost all of the railroad tracks in Belgium lead to or run through Brussels, the capital is gradually losing its aura as the central seat of government, parliament and administration. Today the nearly 10 million inhabitants of the Belgian Kingdom are ruled by six different governments and 60 ministers or secretaries of state.

This Kafka-like situation is the result of a continuing process of 'federalization' in which, since the 1970s, institutional powers have been shifted from the nation to the Communities. Throughout the phases of this continuing process the Communities have been invested with a large degree of political autonomy over their respective regions. Because radio and television are regarded as important instruments in the construction of this cultural and political autonomy, broadcasting policy has been one of the most illustrative arenas of this process of federalization. In 1960 a law divided the National Broadcasting Institute (NIR) into two separate public corporations: *BRT* (now *BRTN*) and *RTB* (now *RTBF*). Since 1971 the respective Communities have gained legislative powers over the cultural aspects of broadcasting, and in 1980 the entire field of broadcasting was entrusted to the legislative and executive powers of the regions. That is, with the exception of broadcast advertising and some technical aspects related to distribution of frequencies, both of which were transferred only recently (1988-1990) to the Communities by the national government.

In this way broadcasting has been caught in an institutional joust and has succumbed to the tensions that have traditionally characterized the Belgian political landscape. First of all, broadcasting policy reflects the powerplay between the nation state and the Communities, and between the Communities themselves. When politicians from the north and the south both claim hegemony over a particular region – be it the metropolitan capital Brussels or the tiny border village of Voeren – the media are employed in the power struggle. In such a manner, Flemish governors obstructed the start of a French speaking community television experiment in Brussels from 1976 until 1985 (Van Apeldoorn, 1985: 68).

In the second place, media policy in Belgium cannot be understood without reference to 'pillarization,' (Drijvers, 1990c: 6) or 'ideological segregation', a notion marking the cultural and social landscape which divides the Belgian population according to their religious or ideological beliefs. In an era labeled by some as 'the end of ideology' (Bell, 1962), ideology still plays a key role in media policy debates. This is the case even though in present-day Belgium insurance companies, newspapers, youth movements and gymnastic clubs no longer recruit their members or clients within the same 'ideological family' as was common a few decades ago. From this perspective of ideology, it is possible to explain why the 'socialist' south runs a more state oriented media policy than the Catholic dominated north. At least partially, because there are important exceptions to that majority rule.

In order to establish a form of social and political pacification between the different groups in each Community, almost every media decree contains a clause which prohibits discrimination of 'ideological' minorities. This clause guarantees minority opinions a form of representative access to programmes and the management of a public broadcasting organization.

Thirdly, it is important to consider the central role played by political parties in both language groups. In each Community the fight between political parties for power over the region has led to a high degree of politicalization of the media, and – *a fortiori* – of television (Burgelman, 1990). On the national as well as local level, directly or through the so-called 'pillar organizations', political parties appoint the governors of the broadcasting institutions and members of advisory bodies. They also set up local radio stations and attempt to control them through umbrella organizations.

As in every other country, all such political aims must be enacted through the proper mechanisms and evolutions of the media system. Because of its central geographic position between larger European neighbours, Belgium is unable to escape the pan-European evolution towards a media landscape where the divisions between media types and between nations are disappearing at an astonishing pace. In such a situation, every political objective related to the media must be examined yet again, this time with respect to supra-national rules and regulations.

The effects of these processes can be reinforced or neutralized by the way they interact. This helps explain why Belgian media policy – and broadcasting policy in particular – appears as unnerving and complex as one of Escher's labyrinths.

Several elements, mentioned above, are vital to understanding the way in which local or regional broadcasting in Belgium has been moulded.

First of all, local broadcasting policy in Belgium has a very segmentary character (Drijvers, 1988: 137). The legal framework for local broadcasting is not only different for the Flemish and the French speaking Community, but in each Community radio and television have been dealt with separately. For this reason Belgian literature on the topic seldom overlooks both media and the term 'local broadcasting' is quite uncommon (Drijvers, 1985, 1990c; Selleslach, 1990).

Secondly, the bulk of laws and regulations on local radio and television are the result of short-term planning. Especially in Flanders, where no opportunity existed for local radio and television stations to experiment with programming formats, legislation seems to trail behind technical, cultural and economic developments. National laws and decrees within the Communities mainly aim to legalize existing situations (Drijvers, 1988: 136).

In political debates on broadcasting, local radio and television have hardly ever been considered and judged on their own merits. Plans to introduce broadcasting locally have been linked with and made subordinate to other themes and issues on a larger, i.e. national, scale. Local television today, for example, does not have a proper legal framework, but in both Communities it has been noted in decrees that serve wider objectives, such as breaking the monopoly of the public broadcasting system (Drijvers, 1990c: 12).

Since media concentration has become so commonplace there no longer is a clear distinction between the local, regional, national or even international scales of operation. The local broadcasting scene has been invaded by actors heretofore strange to local communities. And the nationally oriented actors – political parties, trade unions, press groups, advertising companies – often play a decisive role in the way local broadcasting is organized and regulated.

In the following sections I intend to illustrate how this complex process of policy making has given birth to the present local broadcasting landscape in Belgium. For the reasons mentioned above, it is necessary to tell four different stories: one about local radio, another about local television, and then for each medium another story about its place in the two main Communities of the country. In the final section I will attempt to fit the pieces of this puzzle together and draw a few general conclusions.

LOCAL RADIO: A COMMON PAST, A DIFFERENT FUTURE?

Local radio in the Flemish and French speaking communities share a common past and similar present, but may face a different future.

A common past

Although before World War II some smaller private stations were allowed to broadcast over the frequencies not used by the *NIR*, the post-war period was characterized by a strengthened monopoly of the public broadcasting organizations (Burgelman, 1990). This situation lasted until the end of the 1970s when a number of ideologically oriented groups and geographical communities discovered that relatively inexpensive radio technology provided a means to express themselves autonomously. From 1978 to 1981 the Belgian airwaves were flooded with illegal radio stations, each with a unique – but often comparable history (De Meyer, 1984; Driesen, 1981; Govaert, 1988; Herroelen, 1986; Selleslach, 1985; Van Pelt, 1986).

The radio pioneers came from a variety of movements and groups – heirs of the social revolutions of the late 1960s – who had exchanged their mimeograph and copying machines for electronic media. For them, radio became an instrument to mobilize their members or their local communities around particular issues or actions (Drijvers, 1988: 133). The tone for this activity was set by ecologist groups in the French speaking Community (*Radio Eau Noire, Radio Activité*), but the format of this 'action', 'combat' or 'militant' radio as it came to be known was soon imitated by other groups in both Communities. Before long, students challenging rising enrollment fees (*Radio Scorpio*) and workers trying to prevent the closure of a factory (*Radio Sylvania*) were users of this type of radio.

A second group of radio activists were concerned with the use of the medium as an instrument for integration and communication within an existing or planned community. This format of 'community', 'animation' or 'local' radio – most of these communities were seen as geographically defined units – differed substantially from the first group in that the radio programming was aimed at a larger public. As a consequence of this approach, concepts such as 'programming' and 'schedules' entered the vocabulary of local radio (Herroelen, 1986: 6). The Belgian prototype of this model was *Radio Louvain La Neuve*, a station which tried to breathe life into a new but isolated university campus.

A third group of radio stations is often neglected in academic writing, but is nevertheless quite important in terms of number during the early period of development and in terms of the role they later played in the 1980s. This group could be labelled 'amateur' or 'hobbyist' radio. These stations were often run by individuals, fan clubs and even families, and seemed to take Stephenson's (1988: 45-65) dictum "communication is pleasure" quite literally. This group considered radio, much like users of citizen band equipment, a fascinating toy. The names given to these stations suggest the exotic and exciting: *Radio Tropical, Radio Palermo, Radio Fun, Radio Relax.*

Radio was taken more seriously by a fourth and last group which found inspiration in the adventures of the North Sea pirate stations during the late 1960s and 1970s (De Meyer, 1984: 168). These stations contrasted sharply with the three other types in that their ambitions were clear and unbounded: to be national, professional and commercial. The aim of these stations – examples are *Radio Maeva* and *Radio Contact* – was to reach the largest possible audience for their advertisers through a mixture of all that 'public' radio refused to broadcast: popular music, songs in the national languages, dj chatter, late night programming and – perhaps most importantly – commercials (De Meyer, 1984: 166; Selleslach, 1985: 23).

Between 1978 and 1981 each of these groups of radio stations developed its own programming format, defended its definition of the medium and attempted to impose that definiton on others (Selleslach, 1985: 7–10). Above all, the groups fought each other for the best spot on the FM band – a fight without rules inasmuch as all of the stations were illegal.

The chaos caused by overloaded frequencies and illegal advertising forced the government to act. The first move was one of repression; stations were shut down by the police and equipment was confiscated. In these raids a remarkable preference was shown for the 'action' or 'militant' radio stations (Herroelen, 1986: 7; Selleslach, 1985: 24).

By reducing the complex issue of local radio to the question of breaking the monopoly of the public broadcasting system – a priority of the center right parties – the bigger commercial radios and their lobbies succeeded in moving the item of 'local radio' from the agenda of the judicial authorities to that of the political world (Chateau, 1980; Driesen, 1981; Herroelen, 1986: 578). Furthermore, the growing popularity of the stations gradually forced the government to allow some kind of 'private radio' (Herroelen, 1982: 204). In order to regain control of the airwaves (Voorhoof, 1986: 7), the national government created a legal framework for radio communication in mid-1979 which legalized local radio and required stations to acquire two types of licences (Voorhoof, 1986: 1–6). The first type – a technical licence – could be obtained from the national Minister of the PTT when a station adhered to the technical conditions laid down by a Royal Decree. This decree, issued in 1981, limited signal range to a maximum of 8 kilometers, transmission power to 100 watts and frequency of transmission to channels in the upper section of the FM band (100–104 MHz and later 100–108 MHz). Advertising was banned.

The recognition of radio stations with the above licence, however, was contigent on a second organizational licence. Issuance of this licence was vested in the Community governments. Since 1980 the federalized Constitution had empowered the Communities to create their own rules regarding station statutes, organizational structures and programming policies. It was up to the Communities, then, to decide how many and which types of local radio they wanted to allow or forbid, to foster or to obstruct.

The decrees adopted in the respective Communities expressed a clear preference for small scale local radio stations with a community perspective (Voorhoof, 1986: 7). The Wallonian decree on local radio in 1981 as well as the Flemish decree on non-public radio a year later imposed similar conditions. Radio stations should be operated by non-profit organizations, independent from political or commercial organizations and from other radio stations. The programmes were to focus on a neighbourhood or geographically situated community (Bolis, 1984: 9). One of the central objectives was to stimulate participation of citizens in their communities.

The Wallonian decree, however, expressed a more leftist accent by allowing local governments to participate indirectly in the stations, and by reserving frequencies for stations with a non-permanent character (Govaert, 1988). This type of 'action' or 'militant' radio was completely disregarded in the Flemish decree (Selleslach, 1985: 50).

In spite of these decrees, the gap between reality and legality only increased in subsequent years (Selleslach, 1990: 4). The lawmakers contributed to this situation through inactment of inadequate rules and regulations. In the Flemish Community, most of the station applications were approved perfunctorily, and no fewer than 428 licences were awarded without consideration of the committment or involvement of licensees in their respective communities (Govaert & Lentzen, 1986, 15; Voorhoof, 1986: 7–8).

In some larger cities as many as ten stations were recognized, while in other towns none were approved. The advisory bodies installed in both Communities were incapable of performing the task for which they had been created. They had, as in the Flemish Community, been appointed and manipulated by political parties (Selleslach, 1985; Wylin, 1986: 859) and so-called 'representative organizations' which judged station applications on the basis of membership or political alliance (Van Pelt, 1986: 3). In the French speaking Community, the Executive of this Community granted some 100 provisional licences without consulting advisory commision, because the advisory body could not decide in time (Govaert, 1988: 15).

Frequently, the process of licencing took more time than the two-year duration of a licence. There was no budget or personnel to control whether stations obeyed the vaguely defined conditions concerning programming, access and independence. The national government and the Community Executives were neither able nor willing to coordinate assignment of frequencies with licences, particularly in the region of Brussels.

The main defect of both decrees, however, was the lack of any provision for financing the stations (Selleslach, 1985: 47). In spite of the public function of the stations, no government funding was provided, and private resources were severely limited by the ban on advertising.

Such defects were exploited by the large commercial stations. Without substantial interference from the authorities, these stations exceeded the maximum transmission range and power, disregarded the ban on advertising, broadcasted syndicated programming and initiated networks of local stations. By absorbing large numbers of the 'amateur' radio stations with financial difficulties, the commercial stations soon outnumbered and overpowered the 'association' or 'community' radio stations (Govaert, 1988: 47–48; Selleslach, 1985: 32; Wylin, 1986: 859).

A similar present

Since 1985 commercialization, concentration and expansion have become dominant themes in both Communities (Govaert, 1988: 17–20). Emphasis on media concentration affected the local radio landscape in two consecutive periods. The first period began when the centre-right national government issued a Royal Decree in 1985, which allowed local radio stations to broadcast advertising without a licence. From that moment on, local radio became an attractive prey for press groups and advertising agencies which, until then, had shown only marginal interest in the medium. These 'external' actors, operating on a national level, created forms of association which undermined the local character of the stations (Lentzen, 1988: 7; Selleslach, 1985: 25).

Although a wide range of companies, social organizations and churches offered syndicated – and often sponsored – programming to stations, the most important role was played by news and advertising agencies. News agencies, most of which had been constructed by newspaper publishers in the two Communities, delivered primarily national and international information to their subscribers, who paid for the service with air time (Van Overbeke, 1986). Advertising agencies signed exclusive contracts with the most popular or demographically most interesting stations in order to offer advertisers airtime on a provincial or nationwide chain (Govaert, 1988; Schamp, 1986).

In Flanders, the most important advertising agencies were run by the same press groups, while their pendants in the French speaking Community were controlled by the financial world or by commercial services of national media (Govaert, 1988). The influence of these professionally run news and advertising agencies gradually grew stronger until they no longer were clients of the radio stations, but controlling units – sometimes to the point of ownership (Govaert, 1988: 49; Lentzen, 1988: 11).

Although a new Royal Decree in 1987 made advertising on local radio contigent on issuance of a licence, the years since then are marked by a second period of concentration even more fierce than before. Increasing competition for national advertising budgets between the largest networks has drawn new actors into the field and prompted others to leave.

Most Flemish press groups, for example, have recently dismantled their news agencies, such as Cobra and Radio Service, and some have even discontinued their advertising interests in order to concentrate on involvement in nationwide commercial television. The largest advertising agencies (as Transistor-IP) have gained power over the majority of the radio stations, while a new form of networking has been developed: franchising (Lentzen, 1988: 35-38).

Under this system, station management is handed over to a franchising company. This company gives the stations a common name, forms a single promotional campaign, sells airtime to advertisers and recruits station staff. Such franchising companies, however, also impose a computer controlled standard format for music and informational programming, and for announcer presentations. These companies (as Contact) have one remarkable characteristic: they operate on both sides of the language barrier (Lentzen, 1988).

Local radio in Belgium is now entering an era of internationalization. Because of the largely deregulated and privatized radio landscape in France and Luxemburg, this move towards internationalization is more evident in the French speaking Community than in Flanders. With an eye for the European audiovisual market, French media groups have been showing interest in Belgian radio. Havas, for example, has taken over the biggest advertising agency Transistor-IP; French radio networks like *Nostalgie, NRJ, FUN* and *Métropolis* have been closing franchising contracts with Belgian radio stations and networks; and peripheral stations such as *RTL* and *Europe 1* are attempting to capitalize on their popularity with Wallonian listeners in order to gain a larger portion of the Belgian advertising market.

The main threat to local networks in the Flemish Community, however, emerged from within the Community itself. Concerned by the initial popularity of the local radio stations, the public broadcasting company *BRTN* launched a counter offensive (Wylin, 1986: 861). Programmes were rescheduled and given a more popular format, regional and local information increased, a part-time service for commuter listeners in the capital was revamped into a full-time pop station, and late night programming was initiated. Most significantly, since September 1990 the *BRTN* has begun broadcasting advertising on a legal basis – to the detriment of the private stations which are facing a decline in both listeners and advertisers. A similar policy by the public radio in the French speaking Community RTBF, did not achieve the same success, in spite of the creation of some *radios de base* in Charleroi, Spa and Arlon and the start in 1991 of *Radio Capitale* in Brussels.

A different future?

This increase in media concentration has prompted the Community governments to think about new ways to bring reality and legality closer together. Although the two Communities are facing similar situations in that they are – since January 1989 – additionally responsible for broadcast advertising, they seem to be opting for opposite remedies.

The policy of the French speaking Community is one of 'adjusting law to reality.' In 1987, the center-right Executive placed local radio within a broader decree intended for the audiovisual sector. This decree demonstrated a clear liberal and deregulatory character. The term 'local radio' was changed into 'private radio' (*radios privées*), commercial companies were allowed, and the duration of the licence was extended to four years. Furthermore, a single company was allowed to control as many as five stations, government participation was prohibited, and private radio stations could apply for a licence to broadcast commercial and non-commercial advertising as well as sponsoring.

In February 1990, 183 of the 247 licensed stations had access to these commercial resources. The Executive, run by a socialist majority, has as yet shown no inclination to change this policy radically. The revised decree for the audiovisual sector, passed in July 1991, has tightened the property rules slightly and also expresses support for maintenance of the *radios associatives d'expression*. At the same time, though, the decree legalizes the so-called 'radio service organizations' through separate licences and allows for different categories of stations, varying in transmission power and range from a single neighbourhood up to several city districts. The new decree also facilitates the start of *BEL-RTL*, a community-wide commercial radio station run by a joint venture between *RTL-Radio, TRL-TV* and the two largest radio networks *Contact* and *Rossel FM* (*Le Soir*). This is a clearcut indication of how the European marketplace has bridged the gap between radio, television and the press as well as the long-standing divisions between local national and international media.

Caught between the demand by networks of national origin for protection against French intrusion and the interests of independent community stations, the Community Executive seems to have chosen for a pragmatic solution. The community stations are pacified with funding for production of informational programming, documentaries and cultural magazines designed to extoll the cultural virtues of the French speaking Community.

The Flemish Community, however, has chosen for an alternative scenario and is attempting to 'adjust reality to law'. In late 1990, a few months after the renewal of 394 licences, the Flemish Council adopted a new decree on local radio to replace the eight-year-old decree on 'non-public radio.' The main measures include: limiting the transmission range to eight kilometers; requiring that 80 per cent of the programmes be produced locally and that half of the news items have a local origin; prohibiting control of more than one station per company; requiring registration of all contracts with news, advertising, and programming agencies; curtailing franchising policies through registration of station name and jingle; and limiting advertising to what is termed "region-bound publicity and sponsoring".[11]

These measures signify the Community's determination to eliminate forms of concentration and commercialization in local stations. There have also been improvements in licencing procedures and an extension of licence duration to nine years.

In spite of these measures it remains uncertain whether government determination can stand up to the powerful chains of radio stations operating in the Community.

If the nine 'free local radio stations' in the German Community are included, there are presently some 650 local stations in the country. Belgium, then, is not only blessed with the most cable, railroad and motorway networks in Europe, but also with the most finely woven structure of local radio stations. The presence of 650 stations, however, by no means implies 650 different voices.

LOCAL TELEVISION: A DIFFERENT PAST, A COMMON FUTURE?

Local television is only a few years older than local radio in Belgium. From a European perspective, however, the Wallonian Community may be considered among the pioneers who introduced the Quebec community television model on the Continent. The extensive cable infrastructure, the interest of social and cultural organizations for the possibilities of lightweight video equipment, and the supportive stance by the Community government all facilitated introduction of community television in the French speaking Community in 1976 (Béaud, 1980; Collard, 1990: 1; Hollander, 1982: 60-61; Van Apeldoorn, 1985: 3–8).

Although identical technical conditions existed as well as similar interest by Flemish cultural workers, the Community government in this part of the country prevented

---

11 *Decreet van 7 november 1990 houdende organisatie en erkenning van lokale radios (B.S. 29/1/1991), artikel 5.*

experimentation with local television until a decade after the French speaking Community. Small scale television in Flanders, introduced in 1987, was thus confronted with a totally different political and media context, factors which determined the course it has followed.

A different past

Local television began in 1976 when a Royal Decree legalized within the boundaries of the French speaking Community experiments with audiovisual programmes of local importance, restricted to social and cultural activities. In the experimental period, lasting from 1976 until 1985, 12 sites were approved, ranging from well populated agglomerations such as Liege, Namur, and Charleroi to rural areas such as Rochefort, Gembloux, and Ottignies (Béaud, 1980: 47; Govaert & Lentzen, 1987: 6; Van Apeldoorn, 1985: 9–14).

Although situated in different regions and operated by a variety of organizations (video groups, trade unions, universities), all of these experiments met the requirements of a 'community' model. In order to create "a true instrument for communication at the disposal of the local community," (Béaud, 1980: 46) all experiments had to provide local information, animation and permanent education in a way which encouraged active participation by the population. The stations were run by non-profit organizations with a board of directors which was both pluralistic and representative for the respective localities. The majority of the staff were volunteers. The Community government subsidized the costs of equipment and exploitation, and advertising was prohibited (Barrett, 1978: 2; Bolis, 1984: 12; Hollander, 1982: 63-64).

Within this common framework, each station developed its own unique accent – sometimes stressing local information, sometimes promoting public access or permanent education (Béaud, 1980; Mikolajczak, 1987: 27; Van Apeldoorn, 1985). The most specific experiment in this respect was 'Canal Emploi' in Liège. A joint initiative of the local university and trade unions, this station directed its programming at unemployed residents. Canal Emploi considered primarily social and economic topics in its programmes, but the station also developed material for vocational training and adult literacy projects (Canal Emploi, 1980; Hollander, 1982: 72-73; Mikolajczak, 1987: 28; Van Apeldoorn, 1985: 57-59; Van Oss, 1986).

Through combination of a private structure with a public mission (Collard, 1990: 2), these stations created a new model within broadcasting theretofore unknown: *la télévision locale et communautaire* (TVC). This 'community model' was institutionalized by a governmental decree in 1985. This decree marked the end of the experimentation period and secured a place for local community television in the audiovisual landscape of the French speaking Community.

The rules laid down in the decree consolidated the non-profit and pluralistic character of the organization and required local production of programming. Provisions were also made for creation of programming committees and public funds were allotted to cover a substantial part of personnel expenses and equipment. In order to prevent domination of these stations by local goverment, no more than half of the members of the station's governing body could come from government agencies (Collard, 1990: 5).

Since 1976 the government in the Flemish Community had shown little interest in any form of local television. The minister responsible for broadcasting refused to extend the Wallonian experiments to the Flemish Community, or to Brussels. The justification given was that "experimentation and regulation required further research" (Fauconnier, 1984: 327; Van Aerschot, 1979: 160). However, no research project was funded and local television was reduced to a theoretical topic at academic conferences.

By 1980 a sphere of political passivity was transformed into one of repressive hostility when, after a pirate cable transmission in Heist-op-den-Berg, the responsible local videogroup was arrested and sentenced for misuse of radio equipment. Already distressed by the chaos surrounding local radio stations, the government wanted to maintain the public monopoly of the BRT rather than allow locally oriented and controlled television on the cable.

The early 1980s, however, were marked by a radical shift in broadcasting policy, when a majority of Christian Democrats and Liberals, unhappy with what was considered politically biased reporting by *BRT* journalists, decided to break the monopoly of the public broadcasting company. For the period between 1981 and 1987, both political parties and their supporters produced a plethora of proposals and alternatives (Drijvers, 1990a: 11). In this manner local and regional television were placed, once again, on the political agenda. One perspective, however, remained dominant: that of privately owned and commercially run nationwide television, financed through advertising and operated by press conglomerates. The link between local television and private commercial television had been made and, from then on, was never to disappear.

A converging present

In 1987, the two-year old decree of the French speaking Community was amended to include a section on local and community television within the general framework of the audiovisual sector. The revised decree preserved the spirit of the original document (Collard, 1990: 7) by maintaining the non-profit character of the stations, limiting their range of operation to a single district ('arrondissement') and requiring that 65 per cent of the productions originate locally. Licences were issued for five years and government representation on the governing boards and programming committees was limited to no more than a third of the seats. The new decree, however, revealed its deregulating character more fully in another section which delineated yet another model: private regional television.

In contrast to the community model TVC stations, these private stations were to be commercial enterprises without any public partnership or funding. These stations were to be allowed to transmit to neighbouring provinces and a small *cahier de charges* was to be imposed in exchange for a nine year licence. Only 20 per cent of the programmes had to be locally produced.

In spite of these attractive conditions, no proposals were submitted. The local TVC's supported with public funding and a decade of experience, along with the new Community-wide private station *RTL-TVI*, had reduced the commercial opportunities.

In the meantime, in 1987, the centre-right majority in the Flemish government adopted a long awaited cable decree. Rules were set for distribution of foreign satellite channels, and "non-public television organizations"[12] were also legalized. Public debate over this decree focused on a proposal for creation of a press-owned station for the entire Flemish Community (VTM) and paid little attention to another section in the decree which provided for creation of "non-public television organizations aiming at a local or regional community"[13] and at specific social and cultural target groups spanning geographic localities. The text of the decree, however, was unclear regarding the possible functions and conditions of these local and regional television stations (Drijvers, 1990a: 11).

More explicit rules were laid down in subsequent regulations, but the overall text came to resemble a legal patchwork and left many questions unanswered. The 'non-public' entity of the organization, the large and imprecise demarcation of the transmission zones, the unclear separation between local and regional initiatives, the absence of any regulation regarding representation, the implicit possibilities for networking, the vague selection criteria to assess applications and, finally, the unrestrained competition between stations in the same transmission area. All of these factors and uncertainities provided opportunity for the commercialization of broadcasting on a large scale.

On the other hand, there were also signs of concern for small scale local initiatives: the admittance of non-profit organizations; the obligatory 'local' character of all programming, in particular news; the minimum percentage of local productions, to increase from 50 per cent to 75 per cent over a five-year period; the restriction of airtime to two hours a day; and the restricted scheduling (Drijvers, 1990a: 12).

Above all, this legal framework remained vague about how stations should be financed. The Flemish government showed no intention whatsoever to subsidize these local/regional stations, but at the same time it was held hostage by the Community-wide commercial channel VTM, which had been promised a monopoly on advertising resources.

In mid-1988 the Flemish Executive, under pressure by the positive advice from the Media Council, issued the first licences for regional television (covering transmission zones from a city district to an entire province) to four initiatives in Antwerp (*ATV*), Leuven (*RTVL*), Eeklo (*AVS*) and Waregem (*RTVO*). Issuance of these licences prompted a flood of new applications. Some 20 organizations, located throughout the Community and representing a wide range of actors applied for licences. Out of fear for an impending chaotic situation and aware of the regulatory impotence of the cable decree, the Executive decided to halt all further initiatives. No new licences were granted and the four stations that were already recognized were denied permits to

---

12 *Decreet van 28 januari 1987 betreffende het overbrengen van klank-en televisieprogramma's in de radiodistributie- en teledistributienetten en betreffende de erkenning van niet-openbare televisieverenigingen (B.S. 19/3/1987), hoofdstuk III.*

13 *Decreet van 28 januari 1987 betreffende het overbrengen van klank-en televisieprogramma's in de radiodistributie- en teledistributienetten en betreffende de erkenning van niet-openbare televisieverenigingen (B.S. 19/3/1987), artikel 7,2.*

broadcast advertising. Without public or private resources, the holders of these licences were unable to initiate regional television.

A common future?

Today, 11 local and community stations are broadcasting television programming in the French speaking Community, covering about 160 communes, mainly in the more densely populated northern part of the Wallonian provinces. Reaching some 3 million people, the stations are very popular (Collin, 1986: 24). Research findings suggest that 90 per cent of the local population knows about the existence of the TVC's and 30 per cent describe themselves as "regular viewers" (Collard, 1990: 7).

Almost all of these stations, however, are facing financial problems. Although they receive about two-thirds of their resources from local and Community government funding (Collard, 1990: 7), this does not cover the rising costs of equipment and of daily programming. In 1988, lack of financial resources and internal problems caused the demise of *Canal Emploi*. With an annual budget ranging from 8 to 50 million Belgian Francs (Micolajczak, 1987: 29), almost every station has to secure supplementary funding. For that reason, some of the stations have created audiovisual companies, producing and selling commercial productions.

Since 1985, the majority of the stations also rely on advertising resources, a practice that is neither forbidden nor formally allowed. The specific target group and the popular acclaim of the community oriented TVC stations make them an attractive medium for advertisers (Collard, 1990: 7), but also draw the attention of the big advertising agencies and national television stations (through its regional production center the *RTBF* already exchanges images and equipment with the TVC stations in Liege, Charleroi and Namur) (Collin, 1986: 2; Govaert & Lentzen, 1987: 7).

With the inevitable professionalization of technicians and journalists, there is less reliance on a voluntary work force. This transformation has brought with it a decline in commitment and involvement of the population (Collin, 1986: 22; Govaert & Lentzen, 1987: 7; Van Apeldoorn, 1985: 73). Local community television in the French Community nowadays is still local but hardly 'community' television, for no more than 10 per cent of the programmes is made by local groups or non-staff individuals (Micolajczak, 1987: 31). The 'local angle' might well be the next to go. While abolishing the private regional television model, the new Reform Decree permits TVCs to expand into neighbouring areas with common cultural features, to extend their licences up to 9 years and to reduce the minimum local production from 65 per cent to one third.

The question is whether the unique character of the TVC stations will be able to withstand this growing industrialization, commercialization and professionalization of the audiovisual industry. This question is even more pertinent in the Flemish Community where local and regional television initiatives must develop in an unprotected environment (Vidéotrame, 1989: 10-12).

Without the experience of an experimental period, without strong and supportive legislation, and without financial resources, regional television in Flanders has been at a standstill for a long time. From the four licensed stations, only one (*AVS*) is broadcasting regular programmes, but for a time it was forced to sell most of its airtime to a Dutch commercial production company because of financial problems.

A second station (*RTVO*), facing bankruptcy, was sold to a commercial production company and has recently been taken over by a joint venture, controlled by one of the strongest national press groups (Drijvers, 1990c: 11).

On the policy level, a majority of the Flemish Council finally agreed upon a new decree in October 1991. This decree allows, among other things, for recognition of eleven regional television stations in Flanders and one Flemish station in Brussels. Each station will have a monopoly within its own transmission area. The stations can be financed through regional advertising and may also be supported by public bodies. Media concentration is prohibited, but stations are allowed to work together within the same province.

Although the decree suggests a certain inclination towards the 'community' or 'participatory' model, both politicization and commercialization remain imminent threats. Press groups, national broadcasting organizations, advertising agencies, production companies, radio networks, cable distributors and community governments continue to circle around regional television like vultures eager to pluck the best pieces (Drijvers, 1990a: 13).

COMMUNITY BROADCASTING: AN UNPROTECTED SPECIES

Community broadcasting, intended as a third model of broadcasting (Lewis & Booth, 1989), alongside and between the state controlled public system and the commercial private models, has never really existed in Flanders and is currently under threat in the French speaking Community. The distinguishing features of the community model are either missing in the contemporary local broadcasting landscape or are gradually fading away (Drijvers, 1990b).

With the exception of local television stations in the French speaking Community, local broadcasting is organized as a private enterprise with no guarantees for democratic control. The residents of a locality are not represented, nor can they claim any right to participation. Even in the case of most TVC stations, representation is mainly seen as a way to balance the interests of political parties.

The legal regulations, demanding stations to provide the local population with access (not only to management and control, but also to the programming and production) have been skipped (for radio in Wallonia), toned down (for radio in Flanders) or are not precise enough to be enforced (for television in Wallonia). Local television and radio in Belgium has, in effect, been slowly regressing toward the classical conception of one-way communication common for most mass media.

The main cause for the decline of an open access philosophy is the concern for professionalism. The introduction of regular or continuous programming, the public demand for technical quality, the professional and expensive equipment and the need for a stable organizational structure, have left little space for a philosophy of voluntarism. Volunteers are leaving local broadcasting and being replaced by production companies, franchising organizations, advertising agencies, and press groups.

The additional costs required by a policy of professionalism have weakened the non-commercial character of the initial local radio and television stations. Introduction of advertising as a legal (in the case of radio throughout the country) or tolerated (in the case of local television in Wallonia) financial resource represents a point of no return in this process. When there is no public funding (as with local radio around the country and with Flemish local television) or when subsidies dwindle (as with local television in Wallonia), advertising resources are essential for survival. The evolution of local radio in both Communities has undermined the illusion that these commercial resources have no influence on programming or control and ownership of stations.

Both politicians and industry share responsibility for the absence or disappearance of the community broadcasting model. Several governments have shown either little or belated attention for the local dimension of broadcasting. And when they did, the resulting policy was often unclear, no choice was being made between one of the three models.[14] Contradictory options, incomplete regulations, and short-term planning have crippled the legal framework. Laws which cannot be enforced play into the hands of commercial groups who are in favour of deregulation and privatization.

Above all, the political world has never wanted the community model to work. Particularly in Flanders, Brecht's (1930/1983) dream of people taking the communication processes of their community into their own hands seems to have nightmarish qualities for the main political parties who play a central role in the coordination and control of the ideological 'pillars' constituting Belgian society and culture. In the French speaking Community, where the community model has been tolerated by the government regarding radio and even promoted regarding television, protective measures to allow the community model sufficient breathing space in its struggle with the public service or commercial model are insufficient.

Although in the early period of development governments showed a permissive attitude toward illegal commercial practices, they now have become active accomplices by gradually dismantling the protective rules designed to reduce this market dependency: larger transmission zones, more private resources, legalization of networks, allowance of multi-ownership, decline of compulsory local production, and removal of open access obligations. In this evolution towards deregulation, the actual re-regulation policy of the Flemish Executive on local radio, constitutes a remarkable anachronism.

In an era where broadcasting is perceived primarily as an industrial activity, local broadcasting is unable to escape the laws and mechanisms of the market. Local radio and television unfold their activities on a marketplace where other suppliers are already active. They become active competitors in a media landscape where concentration has grown so narrow that borders between local, regional and national communities have disappeared.

The consequences of this embracement by large scale commercial groups on local community broadcasting is two-fold. In a first phase, the 'community' philosophy with its cultural values is replaced by the criteria of profitability and cost effectiveness. In a second phase, the remaining local broadcasting loses its local perspective. Media concentration has come in successive and growing waves: first regional, then national and, finally, international.

The rate of this concentration differs according to place and medium. Until now, local

---

14 *One exception to this statement is the clear choice made for TVC stations by the Wallonian government.*

television stations on both sides of the language border are developing different kinds of commercial and non-commercial regional networking within their respective Communities. The majority of Flemish local radio stations are controlled by national groups, while private radio stations in the French speaking Community have already entered a phase of internationalization.

There is little doubt that this evolution towards internationalization will increase, for recent European legislation on transfrontier broadcasting[15] leaves very little room for protective measures by national governments, while the continuing process of federalization obstructs a coordinated Belgian media policy to answer this new challenge (Drijvers *et al.*, 1988).

Due to changing policies of national and Community governments and the autonomous evolution of the marketplace, the variety of experiments with local radio and television which marked the early stage of development, have now been reduced to and concentrated around the two models on which traditional broadcasting in most Western European countries tends to focus: the public service model and the commercial model (Drijvers, 1990c: 13). In between, the space remaining for a community oriented approach, is becoming narrower by the day. Survival, it seems, will largely depend on the ability of local stations to function in a claustrophobic environment.

APPENDIX: ELECTRONIC MEDIA IN BELGIUM

BROADCASTING ORGANIZATIONS

Flemish community

Television

Public: *BRTN*:   2 Community-wide channels: *TV1* and TV2

Private: *VTM*:   1 Community-wide channel

FilmNet: 1 pay-TV channel (film)

4 regional TV stations:

- *AVS* (Eeklo)
- *ATV* (Antwerp) (on paper)
- *RTVL* (Leuven) (on paper)
- *RTVL* (Kortrijk) (on paper)

Radio

Public: *BRT*:   5 national channels:

- Radio 1 (information)
- Radio 2 (popular & regional)
- Radio 3 (classical & culture)

---

15 *See, for example*: E.G. Richtlijn van 3 oktober 1989 betreffende de coördinatie van bepaalde wettelijke en bestuursrechtelijke bepalingen in de Lid-Staten inzake de uitoefening van televisie-omroepactiviteiten + Europese Conventie (Raad van Europa) van 15 maart 1989 inzake grensoverschrijdende omroep.

	- Studio Brussel (youth & pop)
	- World Service
Private:	- 394 'local' radios

French speaking community

Television

Public:	RTBF: 2 Community-wide channels: RTBF 1 and Télé 21.
Private:	*RTL-TVI*: 1 Community-wide channel
Canal + TVCF:	1 pay-TV channel
Community:	11 local and community TV stations (TVC):

- *Antenne Centre* (La Louvière)
- *Canal C* (Namur)
- *Canal Zoom* (Gembloux)
- *No Télé* (Tournai)
- *RTC Tele Liège* (Liège)
- *Télé Bruxelles* (Bruxelles)
- *Télé M/B* (Mons)
- *Télésambre* (Charleroi)
- *Télé Vesdre* (Verviers)
- *TV Com'* (Ottignies)
- *Vidéoscope* (Rochefort)

Radio

Public:	RTBF: 4 national channels: *RTBF 1*, *RTBF 2*, *RTBF 3*, *Radio 21* (youth)

1 international channel: *Radio 5*
1 agglomeration radio: *Radio Capitale* (Brussels)

3 *radios de base* (local):
- *Fréquence 4* (Arlon)
- *Canal 13* (Charleroi)
- *Radiolène* (Verviers-Spa)

Private:	247 'radios privées' (local)

German community

Television —
Radio

Public:	BRF: 1 channel
Private:	9 *freie lokale Radios*

MEDIA POSSESSION AND CONSUMPTION

In Belgium, 98 per cent of the population has at least one radio receiver (4.5 million sets are in the country); 96 per cent has a television set, of which 25 per cent more than one (3 million sets). More than 90 per cent of the television sets is connected to one of the 37 cable networks, providing between 15 and 25 channels for viewing. Some 25 per cent of the households are equipped with a video recorder.

Between 70 per cent and 80 per cent of the Belgian population listens at least 15 minutes per week to the radio. The average listener attends between 3 and 3.5 hours per day to radio programming. Between 80 per cent and 90 per cent of the population watches television for at least 15 minutes per week; the average viewer watches about two hours per day.

References

Aerschot, E. van (1979): *Lokale televisie in Nederland en België*, dissertation, Brussels: RITCS.

Apeldoorn, R. van (1985): 'Les télévisions locales et communautaires', *Crisp-Courier Hebdomadaire* 1075-1076.

Barrett, M. (1978): *Etudes de cas sur la télévision locale en Belgique*, Strasbourg: Council of Europe.

Béaud, P. (1980): *Médias communautaires. Radios et télévisions locales et expériences d'animation audiovisuelle en Europe*, Strasbourg: Council of Europe.

Bell, D. (1962): *The end of ideology*, New York: Free Press.

Bolis, L. (1984): *Local radio and television stations in Europe*, Strasbourg: Council of Europe.

Brecht, B. (1930/1983): 'Radio as a means of communication: a talk of the function of radio', in A. Mattelart and S. Siegelaub (eds) *Communication and class struggle: 2. liberation, socialism*, New York: International General.

Burgelman, J.C. (1990): 'Post war broadcasting developments in Belgium: formal discourse versus political reality,' *Medien Journal* **14**, 3: 122-132.

Canal Emploi (1980): *Canal Emploi: formation à distance*, Liège: Canal Emploi.

Chateau, B. (1980): 'Monopole de la RTBF et radios libres en Belgique', *Etudes de la radio-télévision* 27: 205.

Collard, S. (1990): 'Les télévisions communautaires et locales en communauté française de Belgique', *Guide des Médias* 4.

Collin, Y. (1986): 'Lokale omroepen in Wallonië', *Koepel Vijf* 2: 21-27.

Crookes, P. and P. Vittet-Philippe (eds) (1986): *Local radio and regional development in Europe*, Manchester: European Institute for the Media.

Meyer, G. de (1984): 'Opkomst en ondergang van de vrije radio. Belgische lokale zenders tussen commercie en politiek', in J. Bierhoff and G. van Hooijdonk (eds) *Lokale omroep: problemen en perspectieven*, Den Bosch: NIMO.

Driesen, P. (1981): *De vrije en lokale omroep in opmars tegen het nationale omroepmonopolie*, Brussel: RITCS.

Drijvers, J. (1988): 'Kleinschalige media tussen pleinvrees en claustrofobie', in L. Heinsman and J. Servaes (eds) *Hoe nieuw zijn de nieuwe media? Een mediabeleid met een perspectief*, Leuven: Acco.

Drijvers, J., P. Dhondt and J. Servaes (1988): 'Televisie zonder grenzen: commercie of cultuur'. in L. Heinsman and J. Servaes (eds) *Hoe nieuw zijn de nieuwe media? Een mediabeleid met een perspectief*, Leuven: Acco.

Drijvers, J. (1990): 'De private televisie in Vlaanderen', *Mediagids* 14.

Drijvers, J. (1990): 'Local television and adult education: two worlds apart?' paper, International Erasmus programme on adult education, Leuven.

Drijvers, J. (1990): 'Local and regional community broadcasting: a solution for the media policy of small European countries?' paper, Bled, International Association of Mass Communication Research.

Fauconnier, G. (1984): 'Serving two cultures: Local media in Belgium', in G. Gerbner and M. Siefert (eds) *World Communications Handbook*, New York: Longman.

Geerts, C. (1982): 'Der lokale Hörfunk in Belgien', *Mediaperspektiven* 3: 178-183.

Govaert, S. (1988): 'Les radios privées en communauté française', *Crisp-Courrier Hebdomadaire* 1201-1202.

Govaert, S. and E. Lentzen (1986): 'Les médias en Flandre II', *Crisp-Courrier-Hebdomadaire* 1108: 3-17.

Govaert, S. and E. Lentzen (1987): 'De private televisie in de Franse Gemeenschap', *Mediagids* 4.

Herroelen, P. (1982): *1,2,... veel? Kroniek van 20 jaar Belgische radio en televisie*, Leuven: Acco.

Herroelen, P. (1986): 'Lokale radio: van actievoerder tot stationmanager', *Politica* 1: 3-12.

Hollander, E. (1982): *Kleinschalige massacommunicatie. Lokale omroepvormen in West-Europa*, The Hague: State Publisher.

Landry, C., D. Morley, R. Southwood and P. Wright (1985): *What a way to run a railroad. An analysis of radical failure*. London: Comedia.

Lentzen, E. (1988): 'Les médias dans la Communauté française', *Dossiers du Crisp* 29.

Lewis, P.M. and J. Booth (1989): *The invisible medium: Public, commercial and community radio*, London: MacMillan.

L.'Hoest, H. (1975): *La vidéo d'animation en Belgique francophone*, Strasbourg: Council of Europe.

Mikolajczak, C. (1987): 'Onze télévisions sur un plateau', *Media Magazine* 29: 26-31.

Oss, F. van (1986): 'Canal Emploi: televisie voor werklozen', *Opvoeding* 4: 5-7.

Overbeke, J. van (1986): 'De nieuwsregieën – een nieuw fenomeen bij de niet-openbare (lokale) radio's in België', *Massacommunicatie* 2: 165-169.

Pelt, H. van (1986): *De niet-openbare radio in Vlaanderen: veel geblaat, weinig wol?*, Antwerpen: U.I.A.

Schamp, W. (1986): 'Na het kluwen der radio's, het kluwen der radio-netwerken', *Politica* 1: 45-51.

Selleslach, A. (1990): 'Regionale TV-omroepen: een standpunt over problemen en perspectieven', *Mediagids* 13.

Selleslach, G. (1985): *De niet-openbare radio benaderd vanuit het dekreet van 6 mei 1982. Werking en evaluatie van de Raad van Niet-Openbare Radio's*, Brussels: Free University Brussels.

Stephenson, W. (1988): *The play theory of mass communication*, New Brunswick: Transaction.

Vidéotrame (1989): 'Les télévisions locales et régionales dans la CEE', colloque internationale, Namur.

Voorhoof, D. (1986): 'De niet-openbare radio-omroep: de wettelijke omschrijving nader bekeken', *Mediagids* 2.

Wylin, W. (1986): 'Hoe lokaal zijn de lokale radio's nog in Vlaanderen?', *Gids op Maatschappelijk Gebied* 858-863.

9. GERMANY:
From idealistic pilot projects to commercial local radio

Peter Widlok[*] and Otfried Jarren[**]

[*] *LfR, Landesanstalt für Rundfunk Nordrhein-Westfalen*
[**] *University of Hamburg, Germany*

Germany is without doubt a developing country, at least regarding media politics. While local radio is an established part of the media scene in almost all of Germany's European neighbours to the west, the development of local broadcasting is still in its infancy in what before reunification was called respectively the Federal Republic of Germany (FRG) and the German Democratic Republic. In this chapter the development of local radio is described basically from the perspective of the former Federal Republic. In the former socialist part of present-day Germany the media – electronic as well as print – operated under the strict influence of the Communist Party. Since reunification in October 1990 this situation has changed considerably, and expectations concerning new independent local radio stations in this part of the country will be briefly discussed at the end of the chapter.

The first local radio station in the former FRG, *Stadtradio Freiburg*, started operation in October 1984. But after two years of transmission this pilot project, administered under the umbrella of a public law radio network, was terminated. From the perspective of media politics there was no further interest in continuing this otherwise successful radio station.

Since then, a boom in local radio has developed, albeit under different circumstances. The new radio stations, presently numbering around 180, are almost all commercial stations. These stations were launched once private radio was authorized in the FRG.

There were several reasons why the introduction of local radio was delayed in Germany as compared with other European countries. These reasons relate to the discussion of the introduction of new (electronic) media, and this discussion centres on the issue of political power.

'MEDIA SEPARATION OF POWERS'

For a long time, the phrase 'media separation of powers' (*Publizistische Gewaltentei-lung*) has characterized the parallel existence of private publishing houses and pub-licly controlled and financed radio, a combination introduced by the Allies after World War II. This phrase refers on the one hand to the existence of print media as the domain of private publishers operating commercially, and on the other hand to radio networks with a mandate to serve broad cultural interests and diverse groups in society. The interplay of these two systems is meant to ensure programming variety and freedom of expression.

Radio organized under public control, called 'public law radio' or *öffentlich-rechtlicher Rundfunk*, took on the role of an integrative medium meant to offer something to everybody. On the basis of the regulations enacted in many states economic criteria constitute only a part of the broadcasting mandate. Second German Television (ZDF), founded in 1961, is the only nation-wide broadcasting station; see appendix to this chapter for further information.

Advertising is an important source of funding for public broadcasting. As a counter-vailing force to the economic pressure which might result from sole reliance on advertising revenue viewer and listener fees are also collected.

During the past years major changes have occurred in this area. Today some broad-casting systems, ZDF for example, finance almost half of their activities with revenues collected through advertising. Since the government establishes the amount of viewer and listener fees (at present this amounts to DM 19 per month [about $10] for both radio and television), this form of dependence has been frequently used to exert political pressure on public law stations. State parliaments must approve proposed fees, which means that considerable influence can be exerted by the states in the form of national regulation of public radio broadcasting.

Foregoing local radio

Political balance between the press and radio was maintained for several years. In 1972, the structure for separation of powers among the media received additional support when, in a moratorium, the directors of the nine state-wide broadcasting networks informed publishers of daily newspapers that the networks would forego airing local programmes and operation of local radio stations. They also said they would not include advertising in their regional programmes. In return, the broadcast-ing directors expected publishers to give up plans to establish private radio stations, an interest of some publisher since the late 1950s. This moratorium was acknowledged by publishing interests in the country, but without an explicit agreement to relinquish all interest in local radio stations.

Initially after this moratorium no substantial change took place regarding the repor-ting of local events. But even without electronic media competition, the press market began to change in many communities. In the late 1960s and early 1970s, press concentration increased. Smaller publishers were taken over by larger companies or merged with others. This resulted in a reduction of the number of independent local papers. In addition, more media monopolies were formed and citizens became increasingly dependent on a single newspaper for information about local events.

More than a third of all Germans now receive information about local happenings from a single newspaper. The number of independent publishing entities – newspapers with their own editorial staffs – decreased from 225 in 1954 to 119 in 1989, and the number of publishers who also function as newspaper editors diminished from 624 to 358 during the same period (Schütz, 1989: 754).

In spite of mounting concentration, daily papers maintained a monopoly position over news reporting in their respective communities. Other print media, such as advertising circulars, present no serious competition for daily papers.

The dualism in the media – the 'media separation of powers' – has remained uncertain. While the commercial press has occasionally been criticized, public law radio stations have been under almost constant political pressure. Some critics have disparagingly asserted that the principle of media separation is no more than an unwanted 'child of the Allies'.

State influence

State influence of radio stations and policy began in the 1950s, shortly after the Allies relinquished control of the airwaves. The federal government, then controlled by the conservative party CDU, developed a proposal in 1952 to regulate radio and to introduce private FM radio stations.

These new radio stations were to be financed mainly by advertising, and would thus have to compete with local newspapers for revenue. But this proposal failed to carry, in part because of the lobbying efforts of newspaper publishers. For a long time afterwards, no further mention was made of structural innovations regarding radio. However, early discussions about local radio programming demonstrated that "controversies did not arise over social benefits, opportunities for local programming content, or even the interests of listeners, but only over the political question of who should have how much influence on radio" (Starke, 1985: 45).

Additional efforts to develop radio in the FRG were later attempted again by the Christian Democratic Party (CDU) government under Konrad Adenauer, first Chancellor of the FRG. Effort was made to establish, in addition to the ARD (Standing Conference of German Broadcasting Networks), a second nation-wide television channel.

This 'German Television Company' was meant to operate under private ownership, but was to be instituted by the state. A decision by the Federal Supreme Court in 1961 aborted this attempt to establish state television in the country. The basic message of this historic ruling, sometimes termed the 'Magna Charta' of Broadcasting in the FRG, was that the proposed German Television Company would be entirely under state control, and the constitutionally mandated separation between broadcasting and the state could not be guaranteed. The Court further held that broadcasting should not be in the control of the state or a single social group.

With this unequivocal Court decision all plans for privatization and commercialization of electronic media were – at least temporarily – thwarted. The establishment of the German Television Company became not only an interest of the federal government but also of a large number of private economic interests, including publishers.

Radio deregulation: the dual system

This Supreme Court decision in 1961 was not the only ruling which affected the status of radio. In 1971, in 1981, in 1986, and most recently in February 1991, the Federal Supreme Court has considered diverse issues pertaining to the medium. In the 1981 decision, for example, the Court in a sense reversed a previous ruling by permitting, in connection with the introduction of new media, other organizational forms in addition to that provided for in public law radio networks.

Although the Court also emphasized in this decision that any kind of radio organization must be independent from the state or particular social groups, the court also ruled that the FRG Constitution did not explicitly prescribe a particular system of broadcasting, either public law or private. The current structure of existing broadcasting networks, where internal pluralism was safeguarded through a board representing 'socially relevant' organizations, was not the only possible way to organize radio.

The primary concern was that radio, by including socially relevant groupings in the organizational structure, would help citizens formulate opinions on public issues, unhindered by either the state or private interests. Legislators at the state level would have to ensure that radio would not be misused by particular economic or journalistic concerns.

The Court also noted that the situation in which radio operated was different from the press because of the limited number of frequencies available and the larger financial investment required for radio productions. As long as these differences existed, the Court argued, all stations should be expected to satisfy the criteria for producing quality programmes.

Although these conditions have changed in the course of time, they have not become altogether invalid. Some technical developments have modified the situation. For example, an international conference for regulating frequencies held in 1979 established new frequencies on the FM band. Satellite technology has also had an impact on radio, and large numbers of households have been hooked up to cable systems. Production and distribution costs, however, continue to be high.

The Federal Supreme Court decision regarding radio in 1986 was as significant as previous rulings. For the first time the Court referred to a 'dual structure of radio and television', to the parallel existence of private and public law radio stations. In the opinion of the Court, public law networks have the task of providing basic and comprehensive programming. But such programming and a guarantee of pluralistic balance, need not be demanded from private radio stations. Still, the individual states may require private radio stations to provide a pluralistic perspective in programming.

Thus, particular social groups may be given neither preferred treatment nor discriminated against, according to the Court. Referring to the 1961 decision, the Court ruled that all views and opinions – also those of minorities – must have a place in private radio programming, and that dominance by any particular viewpoint should be counteracted through legislation and supervisory commissions.

Cable pilot projects

The introduction of locally oriented programming on public law broadcasting networks was slow in coming, in spite of the increasing concentration of the local press and the development of local electronic media elsewhere in Western Europe. Both scholars and proponents of increased citizen participation in political affairs began to take note that the media failed to satisfy basic human communicative needs. "It is unfortunately the case," argued Teichert (1981: 117), "that newspapers and radio stations only imperfectly satisfy these expectations." Support increased for the position that local and non-commercial radio – community radio – could perhaps help reduce existing communication deficiencies, strengthen the sense of identity within communities, and further participation by citizens in local affairs.

In the 1970s, political power and party politics prevented experimentation with local radio in a manner similar to that emerging in neighbouring countries. Only within the framework of four 'pilot projects' – held in Berlin, Munich, Dortmund, and Ludwigshafen – were new forms of communication considered. On the basis of recommendations proposed in 1978 to the state governments these projects were developed, making use of cable systems.

Private stations were allowed to participate in the pilot projects in Munich, Ludwigshafen, and Berlin. *Kabelfunk Dortmund* was organized under the public law auspices of West German Radio (WDR). In Dortmund procedures were also introduced to provide communities with local radio programming. In the other three participating cities local radio programming was also provided for a brief period by the private commercial stations, but this activity has since been suspended.

Opportunity for innovation and experimentation within these pilot projects was not taken to any great extent. The projects, although tokenly supported by all of the state governments, was weakened by political compromises which undermined the initial intentions. Before completion of the projects and the research which accompanied them, the states with CDU governments passed media laws permitting commercial radio and television. These state governments wanted to secure the new information and communication technologies primarily for private interests. Social Democrats, in contrast, favoured creation of public law institutions for these new media.

Experiments with local radio programmes were initiated in the Munich pilot project, and once legislation was passed after completion of the project local radio stations were also started in other communities. The majority these local radio stations, however, were purely music stations.

Regionalization of radio

The expectations of radio listeners became increasingly embarrassing for public law radio network programmers by the end of the 1970s. According to one study three-fourths of those questioned were interested in programmes dealing with local events, and only 19 per cent were primarily concerned with coverage outside the locality (e.g. Eckhardt, 1979: 706). This and other studies emphasized the substantial interest of citizens for more locally oriented programmes.

The radio networks, however, were not prepared for this task. Plans to launch local radio stations under public law sponsorship had been put to rest with the moratorium of the network directors in 1972. For political reasons the radio networks had shown restraint in the discussion about local radio out of fear that such plans might be realized by newspaper publishers or other commercial interests. The policy of the public law radio networks concentrated on a development they perceived as headed in the direction of local radio – regionalization.

The argument for regionalization rather than for emphasis on local communication was convincing, but it was also identical to the argument for local radio: the need on the part of listeners for what has been termed *mediale Nahweltberücksichtigung*, or media coverage of local events. It is interesting to mention in this regard the 'tactics of demarcation' employed by policy makers of the state radio networks during the period of the moratorium. They then introduced plans for regional radio with the argument that there was no question that this might 'strictly speaking' be local programmes or local radio. These explanations took into account the interests of the publishers of local newspapers, even if defining the difference became increasingly difficult (Leudts, 1985: 53).

Regionalization actually means that one broadcasting area is subdivided into several smaller regions for which special regional programmes are produced. This happened and still happens as a rule in the form of so-called *Fensterprogramme*, or 'window frame' programmes. At certain times of the day, the statewide broadcasts are split up into independent regional stations. During these periods the regional stations broadcast their own window frame programmes. Critics say that with this procedure the networks have essentially relinquished the original goal of social integration with this emphasis on programming for target audiences – emphasis also found in the region-wide programmes.

PRIVATE RADIO IN THE FRG: MODELS AND CONCEPTS

Local radio in the FRG lacks uniformity. The state media laws which are different from one state to the other have led to highly differentiated models of organization for private radio stations. In some states there is and will be no local radio at all. In northern Germany new private radio stations were introduced which operated statewide and thus covered large areas. In the states Schleswig-Holstein and Lower Saxony the private sponsors were combined into associations of programming suppliers who were given a statewide frequency. The same model recently has also been introduced in the state of Hessia. These licensed associations are made up of the publishers of daily newspapers in the state or region. These newspaper publishers not only dominate opinion in the print media, but also on radio.

The radio stations in Lower Saxony (*Radio ffn*) and in Schleswig-Holstein (*Radio Schleswig-Holstein*) may be received not only in the particular state where they are licensed, but also in the cities of Hamburg and Bremen. And, in the case of *Radio ffn*, reception extends to parts of the most densely populated state in the FRG, Northrhine-Westphalia. Because of the large areas these stations serve, it is difficult to consider them local radio stations in any sense of the term.

In Hamburg the situation of 'local' radio is particularly complex. Listeners can choose between the four radio programmes broadcast by the public law network North German Radio (NDR) as well as programmes transmitted by *Radio Schleswig-Holstein*, *Radio ffn*, and the private stations *Radio Hamburg* and *Radio 107*.

Since the end of 1987 two additional local radio stations transmitted on the FM band for a brief period, namely the public law but yet profit oriented stations *OK Radio* and *Radio Korah*. Shortly after beginning activity financial difficulties ensued and forced *Radio Korah* from the air.

A unique aspect of these last two Hamburg stations was the clear division between the non-commercial organizational structure, comprised of clubs and associations active in the city, and the companies which supplied the technical equipment. These companies are profit oriented and are entitled to solicit advertising.

Because of the organizational structure these two stations come closest to what can be termed community oriented broadcasting. The primary aim of *Radio Korah* was to provide extensive local news from various sections of Hamburg. Programming included much background information and timely reaction to current events. This programming format clearly distinguished the station from other commercial radio stations with top-40 music programming targeted at large groups of listeners, and is also preferred by many advertisers. *OK Radio*, under new management, has changed into a format radio mostly for young people.

In Bavaria and Baden-Württemberg there still is more emphasis on numerical variety. In Bavaria, the largest federal state of the FRG, the licensing authorities pressed for realization of a plan to establish some 90 local FM stations in 78 different locations, as well as a new state-wide broadcasting corporation (*Antenne Bayern*). In the major Bavarian cities, Munich and Nuremberg, and in smaller towns fierce competition has been taking place between several licensed private local stations, all of which are exclusively financed through advertising. A recent study has suggested that these stations are in financial difficulty. The privately owned local radio stations in Bavaria as a group have lost a total of DM 30 million (about $ 15 million) (Röper, 1990: 756).

One of the problem these stations face, particularly in the larger cities, is the sharing of a single frequency by several suppliers of programmes. This means that it is difficult for each of the suppliers to achieve a distinctive profile or identity for their programming. Another problem is programming quality; some observers criticize the absence of journalistic standards and emphasis on programming directed toward audience segments with limited purchasing power (Schmitz-Borchert, 1988: 76). Popular music and advertising spots, along with the chatter of disc jockeys, seems more important to these stations than serious coverage of local news. "With the help of 'swinging music' (from the current hit parade) and an abundance of participatory games, these programmers search for an audience, while their journalistic contributions are particularly limited" (Jarren, 1987: 15).

The fact that large number of radio stations provide the same kind of programming has served as an incentive for other stations to initiate programming oriented toward small target groups. *Klassik Radio* in Hamburg, *Jazz Welle Plus* in Munich and *Kultur-Radio* in the Bavarian town of Aschau have applied this strategy with success.

In the state of Baden-Württemberg, there were initially plans to license more than 50 local and 20 regional radio stations. Another 22 frequencies were to be added later and shared by two or more stations per frequency. This plan would have at least provided the potential of diversity through quantity. However, realization of this plan has been delayed. In the spring of 1991 there were 23 local radio and 22 regional programmes in operation (cf. DLM Jahrbuch 1989/1990: 200-220; see also appendix to this chapter).

But many of these stations were suffering from severe financial problems due to the competitive situation caused by several stations having to share a single frequency. The advertising market is not large enough for so many stations, and media experts are already discussing plans to combine individual broadcast areas in order to reach more listeners. Instead of many smaller and autonomous radio stations programmes will be tailored to large geographic areas, making use of local and regional 'window frame' programmes. The majority of the radio stations in Baden-Wurttemberg is already linked to regional networks; they are not independent stations, but affiliate members with only small time slots for their own locally produced programming.

The difficulty of achieving the original plan for Baden-Württemberg lies in the fact that outside of metropolitan areas commercially oriented local radio stations are not economically viable. Advertising revenues in rural areas are too small for adequate operation of one or several competing programme suppliers. Operating costs for a local radio station are between DM 1.5 to 5 million (about $1-3 million). These figures, although approximate, make clear that only larger corporations are able to build up and maintain local radio stations. In Baden-Württemberg – but also in other federal states – newspaper publishers are heavily involved in the radio business and have come to be termed regional "media multis" (Jens, 1989: 23-37).

In Baden-Württemberg there is one community radio station operating without involvement of publishers or other businesses. In Freiburg *Radio Dreyeckland* (RDL), which had been on the air illegally for several years, was finally awarded a licence in 1988. *RDL*, one of the few genuine community radios stations in Germany, is interested in developing a concept of 'free radio', following the principles of community and participatory radio found elsewhere in the world. This approach involves working without commercial interest and providing broad access for citizens and groups to participate in programming aimed at political, social, and cultural issues in the region. The station intends to offer music programmes which cannot be heard elsewhere and report news underplayed or withheld by other media. Active audience participation in the operation of the station and financial support from listeners is seen as essential (RDL, 1990).

RDL is currently the only licensed station in the Federal Republic that is attempting to achieve such a far-reaching community and listener participation. Two other stations, *Radio 100* in Berlin and *Radio Z* in Nuremberg, have somewhat similar objectives. These stations are also providing access to groups and individuals interested in producing programmes. The stations are not commercially motivated organizations, although both are selling and airing advertisements, unlike *RDL* in Freiburg. *Radio Z* broadcasts only a few hours a day because of the limited time available on the shared frequency.

There are various other models in practice around the country. One model involves several programme groups sharing a single frequency. This situation is present in Bavaria, Baden-Wurttemberg, and Rheinland-Pfalz (the Palatinate).

Another model or construction involves an 'alternative' radio station and a commercial radio station sharing a single frequency. This situation has been implemented only in Berlin, and then only for a short period of time. A consortium of private, commercially oriented groups on the one hand, and on the other "independent media groups wishing to improve Berlin's rigid newspaper and radio scene" (description provided by *Radio 100*) were using the same frequency to air their programmes. Since 1989 an additional frequency has been made available and was awarded to the 'alternative' leftist station *Radio 100*. It ceased operation in 1991, but later continued under the name *Radio Energy*. As a music and commercially orientated station, it is now directed towards younger listeners.

Local radio – competition for local newspapers

A special government commission argued against involvement of daily newspaper publishers in private radio stations. The advice of this commission was not followed by the state governments which are responsible for media legislation. In many areas – such as in Schleswig-Holstein and Lower Saxony – newspaper publishers were given privileged access to local and regional radio. The argument for this policy was that publishers could in this manner be compensated for possible losses to their advertising revenues.

This development, however, is detrimental for promotion of journalistic variety inasmuch as many newspaper publishers already have a print media monopoly in their regions. Allowing publishers to own radio station creates the added danger of double media monopolies.

Is the threat of competition, either in the journalistic or economic sense, which newspapers fear from new electronic local media real? Media experts (e.g. Teichert, 1981) agree on the need for journalistic competition. They feel local radio provides this, and further competition is anticipated once local television is introduced in major cities around the country. This form of competition, however, is seen as beneficial in the promotion of journalistic diversity, local communication and democratic government.

Opinions differ regarding economic competition, however. One development seems probable: in locations where several newspapers are operating additional competition for the limited advertising funds could hurt the smaller papers.

It can generally be said that because of media-specific differences between newspapers and local radio stations the two media complement and supplement one another. While local radio may initially pose no direct journalistic competitive threat with economic consequences, indirectly and in the long run, a situation could develop with substantial journalistic and economic competition between the two media. This will develop especially if current negative trends for newspaper publishing increase. There is a danger that local newspapers may lose more young readers – who subscribe, buy and read newspapers less today than previously – to electronic media.

Northrhine-Westphalia: innovative concept in local radio

Genuine community radio, we have argued, does not exist in the Federal Republic. The electronic media scene in the local area is largely made up of commercial radio stations. As shown above, only some radio models are different in that respect: in

Hamburg these were only the stations *OK Radio* and *Radio Korah*; in Baden-Württemberg it is *Radio Dreyeckland*; in Nuremberg it is *Radio Z* and in Berlin *Radio 100*.

In addition to these examples, a different form of radio has been introduced in Northrhine-Westphalia where the first local radio station (*Radio DU* in the city of Duisburg) started operation in April 1990. By mid-1991 about 25 to 30 stations are expected to be on the air in this region. In this most densely populated state of Germany (17 million people), currently governed by the Social Democratic Party (SPD), there is a chance – more than in the other states – for development of a diversity of local radio stations oriented toward local conditions.

In keeping with the Northrhine-Westphalia broadcasting law, programming responsibility in the local stations must be strictly separated from the (profit oriented) technical operation. An association of sponsors, in which social and cultural groups are represented and have voting rights, becomes the programming agency and licensee. The company operating the station, in which local publishers and local governments are free to join, is responsible for financing the station – which may be solicited through advertising – and for technical support and equipment maintenance. The company is not permitted to determine programming policy or content.

This arrangement of strict separation of programming and financial responsibility was strongly criticized by most local publishers; they were obligated to pay the piper, but not to call the tune. Although this legal regulation was introduced to avoid development of local or regional media monopolies some observers (e.g. Prodoehl, 1989), anticipate the danger of increasing influence by publishers who make financial investments in local stations.

The conservative Christian Democratic Party (CDU), opposed to this arrangement, took the case to court. The Supreme Court, in a ruling handed down in February 1991, supported the Social Democratic radio concept which is, as the Court explained, intended to ensure high quality programming on local radio stations.

The economic situation in Northrhine-Westphalia differs with that in Hamburg, Bavaria and Baden-Württemberg in the sense that only one local station is to be licensed per broadcasting area. There is no plan to share a frequency between two or more radio programming groups.

There are also to be no stations with uninterrupted music and an abundance of commercials, and little or no reporting on local events. In contrast to the north and south of the FRG, citizen groups and local initiatives in Northrhine-Westphalia will have the opportunity to make programmes themselves. This innovative concept in the Northrhine-Westphalia broadcasting law provides that 15 per cent of the broadcasting time must be reserved for contributions from groups with non-commercial interests. This offers the possibility to publicize concerns of people who are not covered by the local newspaper or public law radio. This also provides a chance to produce – for the first time in the history of German radio – participatory programmes attentive to citizens interests, albeit limited in duration and within the framework of a commercially financed station. This will be, then, local radio of a type without precedent in or outside the FRG.

AFTER REUNIFICATION: AN EAST GERMAN PERSPECTIVE

Regarding the print media, the process of integration between East and West is proceeding rapidly. It began just after the opening of the borders and formal reunification. Western publishers are extensively investing in old and new newspapers and creating, once again, monopolies (see Röper, 1990).

The situation of print and electronic media in the five new states between the cities of Rostock in the North and Dresden in the South can appropriately be characterized as the 'Wild East'. For the existing state-wide broadcasting network this means transformation into public law radio and television. Since early 1992 three public corporations operate in the five federal states: *Ostdentscher Rundfunk* (*ORB*) in Brandenburg; *Mitteldeutschur Rundfunk* (*MDR*) in Saxony, Saxony-Anhalt and Thuringia, and *Norddeutscher Rundfunk* (*NDR*) in Mecklenburg-Vorpommern.

The future of the other organizational forms of radio and television is unclear. The official Reunification Act between West and East Germany simply states that the parliaments in all of the five new states must pass new federal broadcasting laws by the end of 1991. In four state parliaments the conservative CDU has a majority; only in Brandenburg are the Social Democrats in power. The possibility for independent groups to form community radio stations therefore is small.

Although the European Federation of Community Radios (FERL) is involved in formulation of charters for the 'free radio' stations in the city of Erfurt in Thuringia and elsewhere (see FERL, 1990), it seems unlikely that *Radio Free Erfurt* will obtain a licence in 1992 under the new media law. The same must be said for the community radio movement in Leipzig. In this city, in the state of Saxony, local pressure groups are attempting to establish a station modelled on a community-oriented structure. The intent of these groups is to create a system allowing direct citizen participation in radio policy and programming similar to the system in operation in Northrhine-Westphalia (Bora, 1990). It is more likely, however, that the conservative state government will introduce commercial radio on a local or regional level.

CONCLUSIONS

There are several reasons why local radio stations in the FRG emerged late in comparison to elsewhere in Europe. From the beginning, the public law broadcasting networks attempted to prevent competition from private radio and, therefore, did not produce local programming or, for some time, work toward regionalization. This strategy was meant to restrain newspaper publishers from becoming involved in private radio stations. This explains why there was no journalistic competition between radio and the press in the regions and local communities. It was not until the late 1970s that public law networks started with regionalization. But these programmes can only be heard for a few hours every day.

The newspaper publishers did not follow this strategy of the public law networks, however. After the demise of the social-liberal coalition government in 1982, the introduction of private radio in the FRG was placed on the political agenda. Newspaper publishers were very much interested in this development and managed to gain a foothold in these new radio stations.

The pilot projects, which dated from the social-liberal era, lost their function of trying out new programme offerings in the local communities. The projects served to introduce commercial radio, and the public funds appropriated for these projects were used in fact to further private radio. Once people realized that it would take considerable time to make a profit from advertising linked to programmes disseminated by cable, more and more terrestrial frequencies were allotted to private radio stations.

In the context of these developments locally or regionally oriented radio stations were initiated in many places around the FRG. The great majority of these stations is exclusively geared to making a profit. Local radio has become very much a business enterprise. Only a few groups with alternative stations have managed to hold their own in this privately organized local radio scene. Often oriented toward the model of community broadcasting, these stations will have to demonstrate in the coming years whether they can survive in a competitive situation. Although the chances are slim, the local radio stations in Northrhine-Westphalia may prove to be the exception.

The situation in the eastern sector of Germany since reunification in October 1990 is generally characterized by a strong and profitable development towards privatization and concentration of the media. While this is undoubtedly the case in the print sector, the expected new state broadcasting acts, currently being prepared and discussed but not yet passed by the state parliaments, will probably allow only commercial radio stations. Perhaps in the state of Brandenburg, given the Social Democratic party presence in the government there, another form of local radio may be possible – like the Northrhine-Westphalian model: a commercial radio framework that provides opportunity for people to produce and air their own programmes.

APPENDIX: MEDIA LANDSCAPE GERMANY

National level

Television

1.   ARD; (*Arbeitsgemeinschaft der Rundfunkanstalten Deutschlands*; (First German Television), Federation of the statewide public law corporations:

Bayerischer Rundfunk (BR), *Hessischer Rundfunk* (HR), *Norddeutscher Rundfunk* (NDR), *Radio Bremen* (RB), *Saarländischer Rundfunk* (SR), *Radio Freies Berlin* (SFB), *Süddeutscher Rundfunk* (SDR), *Südwestfunk* (SWF), *Westdeutscher Rundfunk* (WDR), *Ostdeutscher Rundfunk* (ORB) and *Mitteldeutscher Rundfunk* (MDR).

All of these corporations also air radio programming on a statewide level.

2.   *Zweites Deutsches Fernsehen* (Second German Television), public law corporation (only television, no radio programming).

3.   Four major private, commercial corporations: *RTL plus, SAT 1, Tele 5* and *Pro 7* (distributed via cable and terrestrial hookups). Additional national and international television corporations available on cable and satellite.

Radio

Private commercial radio corporations nation-wide only available on cable.

State level

Television

Public law corporations, same as above under National Level.

Radio

1. Public law corporations, same as above under National Level.

2. Private commercial radio companies in Bavaria, Hessia, Schleswig-Holstein, the Palatinate (one per state). In Lower Saxony there are two companies. All signals are distributed over-the-air.

3. Regional/local level

Television

1. Regional 'window frame' programmes by public law corporations (see National Level above).

2. In some regions there are private companies.

3. Local (private) radio models in the federal states: state-wide private, commercial corporations as in Schleswig-Holstein and Lower Saxony; private stations as in Hessia and the Palatinate; and one state-wide and many smaller stations as in Bavaria.

In Baden-Württemberg: instead of many local stations as originally planned, there is now a tendency to develop regional networks because of intense competition at the local level. In Northrhine-Westphalia an innovative radio model has been introduced: only one commercial station per local reception area with a strict separation between programming responsibilities, assigned to a non-commercial local board, and the financial and technical matters (a responsibility mainly taken on by local publishers). It is legally required to allocate 15 per cent of the local programming time for citizen participation. *Radio DU* in Duisburg started as the first of this type of station in April 1990; some 30 of these stations are anticipated by the end of 1991.

In the former German Democratic Republic change is from a state controlled network to the creation of commercial radio and television in the new Eastern federal states with the exception of Brandenburg.

Radio

1. Regional 'window frame' programmes provided by public law corporations.

2. In some regions, such as Schleswig-Holstein, private companies have 'window frame' programming.

3. Local private radio stations are found in various states:

    in Bavaria: 45 stations;

    in Baden-Württemberg: 23 local programmes and 22 regional programmes provided by private companies;

    in Berlin: 4 commercial local stations (*RTL Radio, Radio 100,6, Info Radio* and *Radio Energy;*

in Northrhine-Westphalia: 25 local stations on the air in mid-1991 and about 40-46 stations expected by 1992.

in Hamburg: 3 private stations in addition to the 4 programmes provided by the public law corporation NDR.

4. Community radio

Only 2 community oriented stations exist:

Radio Dreyeckland, with its own frequency, in Freiburg (State of Baden-Württemberg);

Radio Z in Nuremberg, Bavaria, sharing a frequency with other broadcasting groups;

Radio 100 in Berlin, with its own frequency.

As for the former DDR, or East Germany, the previously state-controlled radio and television system has been changed into three public law corporations. There are also plans to introduce private radio and television stations.

References

BORA (1990): (Bundesverband Offenes Radio; 'Federation of Open Access Radio'), press release, Aug. 8th.

DLM Jahrbuch 89/90 (1990): *Privater Rundfunk in Deutschland*, edited by the State Broadcasting Authorities (Landesmedienanstalten), Munich.

Eckhardt, J. (1979): 'Bürgernähe garantiert Hörererfolg. Eine Studie zur regionalen Berichterstattung im Hörfunk des WDR', *Media Perspektiven* 10: 703-708

FERL (1990): ('European Federation of Community Radio'), newsletter, Forcalquier, Sept. 25th.

Jarren, O. (1987): 'Senden in der Region. Lokalradios in der Bundesrepublik', *Das Parlament* 70, 50 (Dec. 12th): 15.

Jens, C. (1989): 'Privater Hörfunk – eine Verlegerdomäne. Ergebnisse einer Dokumentation über Verlagsbeteiligungen an Privatradios in der Bundesrepublik Deutschland', *Media Perspektiven* 1: 23-37.

Leudts, P. (1985): 'Die Regionalisierung des Rundfunks. Ein Modell für den Lokalfunk?', in O. Jarren and P. Widlok, (eds), *Lokalradio für die Bundesrepublik Deutschland*, Berlin: Vistas.

Prodoehl, H. (1989): 'Mit dem "Zwei Säulen-Modell" gegen multimediale Meinungsmacht', *Der Landkreis* 59, 1: 12-14.

RDL (Radio Dreyeckland) (1990): *Ein Stück Luft*, Freiburg: RDL.

Röper, H. (1990): 'Formationen deutscher Medienmultis 1990', *Media Perspektiven* 12: 755-774.

Schmitz-Borchert, H. (1988): 'Pluralität aus Wettbewerb oder "format radio"? Anmerkungen zu den Entwicklungsbedingungen eines "neuen Radio"', in H. Schmitz-Borchert (ed.), *Lokal funk. Anmerkungen und Statements zur Hörfunkentwicklung*, Köln: Hayit.

Schütz, W.J. (1989): 'Deutsche Tagespresse 1989', *Media Perspektiven* 12: 748-775.

Starke, J. (1985): 'Der Kampf um den Lokalfunk – ein "altes" rundfunkpolitisches Thema. Anmerkungen zum Diskussionsverlauf in der Bundesrepublik', in O. Jarren and P. Widlok (eds), *Lokalradio für die Bundesrepublik Deutschland*, Berlin: Vistas.

Teichert, W. (1981): 'Regionalisierung im Rundfunk. Erwartungen und Defizite', in M.W. Thomas (ed.) *Die lokale Betäubung oder der Bürger und seine Medien*, Berlin: Dietz.

10. SWITZERLAND:
Attractive and successful, but not very local

Heinz Bonfadelli and Michael Schanne

University of Zürich, Switzerland

Switzerland is a small, alpine country located in the heart of Europe. Its multilingual population has been served by a public broadcasting monopoly, the Swiss Broadcasting Corporation, since the early 1930s. The service of this monopoly has been the source of considerable protest, some of which was expressed in the establishment of alternative radio stations. This activity led the Swiss government to authorize experimentation with local radio programming. This experiment, and the accompanying research, is the focus of this chapter. Although the primary data collection transpired in the mid-1980s and the experiment was officially completed in 1988, the findings remain relevant for the contemporary state of local radio in Switzerland.

After a brief sketch of the country and its media system, the organization of the experiment is outlined: the initial regulations, station organization and financing. Analysis of station programming is examined in the next section, indicating the degree of localness in programmes and opportunities for audience participation. Audience use of the programming is considered in terms of station functions within communities. Next, various forms of the impact local radio stations have had on society are noted: on newspapers, on social and cultural services, and on community participation. Finally, in the concluding section, reflections are made on both the experimental period and developments with local radio since then.

BACKGROUND

The 6.5 million residents of Switzerland are divided among four major language groups: German (74 per cent), French (20 per cent), Italian (5 per cent) and Romansch (1 per cent). The mountainous terrain of the country contributes to an uneven distribution of the population. Nearly one-quarter live in 16 cities, each with more than 30,000 residents (Bundesamt für Statistik, 1986). The country is composed of a con-

137

federation of 26 regional states or Cantons. A stable democracy, Switzerland has highly developed mechanisms for consensual politics which provide opportunities for political participation by its citizens (Saxer, 1986).

As a result of liberal ideology and cartel forming, the press is reliant upon the market economy and, politically, on freedom of commerce and trade as well as freedom of the press. Radio and television, in contrast, have been organized as state monopolies. The number of Swiss newspapers is very large relative to the size of the population – a result of the cultural and political segmentation in the country. Geographical divisions and the small size of the three main language markets reduce newspaper circulation to minimal figures. The number of newspapers has declined from 406 to 310 between 1939 and 1971, and to 275 in 1989. Three-quarters of the newspapers have circulations less than 10,000; only 7 have more than 100,000 readers. The over-whelming majority (188) are published in German; the remainder are published in French (68), Italian (14) and Romansch (5).

Broadcasting is organized as a public service monopoly, as is the case in most European countries. Radio and television, for decades without proper judicial foun-dation, are now written into the Swiss constitution after receiving citizen approval in a plebiscite held in 1984. This constitutional act states that the legislation of broadcast media is an obligation of the confederation. It further states that provision of infor-mation, education and entertainment are the main objectives of radio and television. The act guarantees independence for these electronic media and at the same time requires forms of consideration for other media, especially the press. It also provides for an independent board to consider complaints.

Radio and television in Switzerland have been run by the Swiss Broadcasting Cor-poration since 1931, a non-profit company characterised by a dual structure: the politically autonomous professional organization which produces the programmes, on the one hand, and the non-professional organization representing the different regions and organized interests of the country, on the other. The cultural and linguis-tic diversity of Switzerland is mirrored in the federal structure of the Swiss Broadcast-ing Corporation which produces three television programmes – one each in German, French and Italian – and three radio programmes in each of these languages. All of the television programmes are distributed throughout the country. The Swiss Broad-casting Corporation and its programme production is mainly financed by licence fees and television advertising; advertising on radio is prohibited.

Since the 1970s technological innovations, market forces and changes in media policy have altered the media landscape in Switzerland. The installation of cable systems and satellite delivery have increased the number of television programmes available from foreign countries. As a result, commercialization and internationalization are on the rise. The diffusion of video recorders has further stimulated time delayed viewing and programme alternatives. New information and entertainment services have been created for a public with increasingly specialized and fragmented interests. The older electronic media, television and radio, have penetrated new areas thanks to ex-perimentation with local radio and television. Decentralization, concern for local programming and more public participation are results of this transformation (Bon-fadelli & Hättenschwiler, 1989b).

EXPERIMENT WITH LOCAL BROADCASTING

Several factors contributed to experimentation with private local radio stations: the Swiss Broadcasting Corporation, the national media policy, publishing interests, technical developments and radio pirates abroad.

For a long time, the Swiss Broadcasting Corporation was the only producer and distributor of radio and television programmes in the country. Since 1961 the corporation began transmitting regional programmes on a limited basis; daily regional radio programming was not institutionalized until 1978. Public broadcasting not only neglected the growing interest in local affairs, but by providing only two programmes per language region – one with popular and folkloristic music and another with classical music and cultural programming – it spurred increasing numbers of young listeners to abandon the Swiss radio channels in favour of the new youth oriented radio programmes in neighbouring countries.

In 1979 a former journalist from the public broadcasting corporation launched a radio station across the border in Italy (Schawinski, 1982). The FM signal could be received 130 kilometres to the north in Zurich, and became very popular with young people. The station was eventually shut down by Italian authorities, but not before thousands of young people in Zurich and Bern had expressed their support for the station. In 1983 the station was sold and the journalist applied for and received a license to operate a station in Switzerland. These efforts resulted in the popular *Radio 24* now operating in the region of Zurich.

In the 1970s the liberal political parties (FDP and SVP) began to criticise the Swiss Broadcasting Corporation, claiming their programming was biased. The SVP, the conservative party of the trade associations, founded an organization to monitor progamming of the Public Broadcasting Corporation, and also launched a major anti-public broadcasting campaign. The long run objective of these activities was to create a political climate to deregulate broadcasting. In this manner the 'public monopoly' of the Swiss Broadcasting Corporation was broken and private broadcasting introduced.

Since 1972 the federal government has occasionally permitted short-run experiments with local television. In 1977 an official ordinance was passed allowing experiments with local television, but without advertising. Experiments took place in Renens (1977-78), Fribourg (1973, 1975, and 1978), Lucerne (1978), Geneva (1979 – 1982), Solothurn (1981) and in Wil and Zug (1980 – 1981). Although these experiments were received positively by the audiences, and in most cases research findings indicated public interest in the programming, the experiments were stopped because of insufficient funding (Hunziker & Schors, 1983; Slivinski & Dembinski-Goumard, 1984; Hättenschwiler & Jedele, 1987).

The above mentioned factors, particularly pressure from the conservative parties and a change in the minister responsible for the media, resulted in a governmental decree in 1982 which authorised extended experimentation with private local radio and television until 1988 (RVO, 1982).

Local radio ordinance

The formulation of the Local Radio Ordinance (RVO) was preceded by a controversial political debate which eventually focused on five issues: the number of local radio stations to be allowed, the signal range of the new radio stations, the degree of local orientation in the programmes, the role of the local press in the stations, and whether advertising should be allowed.

The Social Democrats and labour unions in particular argued strongly for experiments with community radio that would be local and non-commercial in nature. In contrast, the liberal political parties and financial interest groups favoured private radio stations with as few restrictions as possible, to be funded through advertising. The position of the print media, especially the press, was ambivalent: they supported deregulation of the electronic media, but they also feared possible losses in local newspaper advertising. This was the main reason for the fact that many newspaper publishers later applied for radio licenses. Experiences with different forms of non-profit community radio in other countries, such as Sweden, were not publically discussed or considered serious alternatives.

As a result of the power balance in the federal government it was hardly surprising that the Local Radio Ordinance of 1982 was based mainly on a commercially oriented model of private local radio with only minimal restrictions. The programme oriented requirements were formulated in a vague manner to make control nearly impossible.

The goals of the experimental period were fourfold: to assess interest in producing and using local radio programming, to measure possible impact on other media, to consider possibilities for audience participation in programming, and to consider appropriate policy measures for these media.

There was a large variety of regulations instituted for the experimental period. In the first place, the stations operating on the FM band were to restrict the broadcasting area to that of a 10 kilometre radius. This signal area could be extended in rural areas. Some 15 minutes per day could be reserved for advertising. In 1984 this limit was increased to 20 minutes daily and compensation was permitted for seasonal variations. Certain types of advertising on which print media relied were also prohibited. These included advertisements for alcoholic beverages, tobacco products, financial institutions, employment, housing rental and sales, and used automobiles.

The private radio stations were also obliged to comply with fairness and programme variety rules, and to cover local issues. A certain amount of programming was to be produced by the stations themselves, but co-operation in production activities and exchange of programmes was allowed. Stations were intended to operate as non-profit organizations, but surplus capital could be reinvested in other media ventures.

As a form of control, each station was to establish a board to handle complaints. The stations were to carry out their own research activity. To coordinate these efforts and to provide additional data, a research programme was established nationally and received funding from the Media Department of the federal government.

Local radio landscape

Some 269 individuals and organizations applied for licenses in 1982, 197 of them for local radio stations. Of these applicants, 36 were granted a license, and seven radio stations commenced transmission in November 1983. In 1987 there were 33 radio stations and some small scale local television experiments without advertising (e.g.

in Zug and Niederhasli) which provided programming in all three languages; see Table 1.

The criteria employed for selecting licensees included technical and geographical considerations, and assessment of the feasibility of the proposed projects. The criteria themselves were not questioned, but there were objections to the stations selected (Haldimann, 1984). It turned out that only a few community oriented stations were chosen as opposed to a large number of service and youth oriented music stations. Newspaper affiliated stations were also granted licenses. Most stations were situated in urban regions where advertising resources are plentiful, and few projects were established in rural and mountainous regions of the country.

Table 1. Local radio landscape in German region of Switzerland (1985)

Name of station	Region	Listener potential[1]	List-eners[2]	Annual budget[3]	Station characteristics
Radio Z	Zürich	511	174	4330	Large; supported by banks, unions, industries; financial problems
Basilisk	Basel	282	178	2680	Only station in Basel; large public; financial success
Radio 24	Zürich	511	215	2450	Leading youth oriented station; former pirate
Eulach	Winterthur	156	59	1380	Traditional programming; supported by liberal (financial) groups
Extra Be	Berne	244	105	1340	Leading station in Berne; financial problems; newspapers involved in station
Pilatus	Luzern	141	79	1350	Only station in central Switzerland; financial problems
Zürichsee	Stäfa	154	46	1230	Station owned by leading local newspaper; competed with R24
Sunshine	Zug	68	38	1000	Cooperated with R24; financial problems
Aktuell	Gallen	154	62	995	Only station in Eastern Switzerland; owned by local newspapers
Raurach	Sissach	64	17	715	In rural Baselland; large financial deficit; few listeners
Munot	Schaffhausen	55	32	687	Only station; cooperates with local newspaper
Thurgau	Frauenfeld	127	16	–	Run by local newspapers
Gonzen	Buchs	53	30	–	Run by local newspaper
Canal 3	Biel	106	42	566	Founded by local journalists; bilingual programmes
Förderband	Berne	244	41	444	Cultural programming; financial problems
Matterhorn	Zermatt	5	5	247	Tourist oriented; listener success
LORA	Zürich	470	19	216	Only left-wing station; no advertising
Sarine	Freiburg	17	7	172	Bilingual; financial problems
Total		2337	1165	19,802	

(1) Listener Potential: People living in the licensed area in thousands;
(2) Listeners: occasional and frequent listeners in thousands;
(3) Budget: in thousands of Swiss francs per year.

Financing

All private local radio stations are financed by advertising with the exception of *LORA*, an alternative station in Zurich supported by donations and subscribers. Still, there are major differences between the radio stations noted in Table 10.1. Of the 16 stations in the German speaking region of the country, three have annual budgets of more than two million Swiss Francs (Sfr). Five stations have a budget of 1-2 million Sfr. and seven stations manage with less than a million Sfr. annually. The 15 stations in this region together spent nearly 20 million Sfr. in 1985, but nearly half of this money was shared by three stations: *Radio Z, Radio Basilisk* and *Radio 24*.

The total sum spent on advertising in local radio was 18 million Sfr. in 1984, and had increased to 30 million Sfr. by 1985. Especially the medium-size and small stations experienced difficulty in securing sufficient advertising at the beginning of the experimental period. As a consequence, most stations lost money during the first two years. Acceptance by national advertisers of this new medium was slow in coming and, in the French speaking region of the country, stations are still losing money where competition from the French-based *radio libre* stations is strong.

Introduction of local radio caused a partial increase in advertising funds, but also some redistribution of advertising budgets (IBFG, 1986). Some 70 per cent of the firms surveyed redistributed advertising money and 30 per cent increased budgets. Firms operating on a national basis tended to redistribute their funds, while regional firms favoured an increase in their advertising budgets. The IBFG study estimated that three-quarters of the 20 million Sfr. spent for local radio advertising were redistributed. About 5 million Sfr. was considered funding stimulated by the introduction of this new medium.

It was also estimated that the Swiss press lost about 7 million Sfr. – about a half per cent of the annual revenue from advertising. Newspapers directly affected by local radio stations reported a loss of about 2 per cent. It seems that the press is but one of the media affected by the introduction of local radio, and apparently not as severely as other media.

Organization and personnel

Most radio stations are organized as joint stock companies. The financial problems, especially for the medium-size and smaller stations during the early years, resulted in reorganization and loss of independence of some stations. Newspaper publishers and some local companies as well as nationally operated food chains took advantage of this situation to purchase stock. Consequences of this situation was an increased trend to intermingle programming with advertising, including the now widespread practice of placing advertising in programmes related to particular products.

In 1985 there were some 320 persons employed in 250 full-time positions in the stations. About two-thirds of these staff worked in stations in the German speaking region of the country. Much programming is still produced by volunteers in most of the stations. In general, four to seven journalists work for the larger stations. *Radio Z*, for example, has 13 full-time paid positions for programme production and presentation, *Radio 24* has 12 staff members, and *Radio Basilisk* 14. *Radio Pilatus*, one of the smaller stations, operates with 6 paid staff members. Most journalists involved in news reporting tend to have a press or broadcasting background; programme announcers have generally been trained on-the-job.

PROGRAMMING

Analysis of the content of radio programming has been conducted on a regular basis by the research team commissioned to monitor the experiment. General features of the programming are first presented below, followed by an indication of their local character and the degree of participation evident.

General features

An overwhelming percentage of the programmes consist of middle-of-the-road music, design to capture the largest possible audience. Approximately 90 per cent of all programmes, and more than 50 per cent of the news magazines dedicated to local information, are of the 'easy-going easy-listening' variety and include advertising, jingles, jokes and games. This programming variety is not what was originally intended when legislation for the experiment was passed. The Local Radio Ordinance was intended to encourage programmes in a traditional sense of community media: local programming in which participation is encouraged and where communication in the local community is facilitated. At the end of the three-year experimental period, there was little evidence that local radio stations had attained these objectives.

There were, in any event, no innovations with programming formats or journalistic procedures. Such expectations may have been unwarranted given the unfavourable economic situation many stations experienced, but this does not explain the lack of success in meeting the minimal objectives established by the governing authority of the experiment.

'Localness' in station programming

An analysis procedure was developed to differentiate degrees of local emphasis in programming. Variables were clustered into geographic, societal and journalistic dimensions.

Table 2. Geographic level of items in local radio news programming

Geographic level	Percentage of time		
	1984	1985	1986
Local News	59	62	64
National News	21	16	18
International News	15	15	13
Unspecified	5	7	5

On the geographic dimension, local radio stations reported events mainly from the studio and from within the transmission area. National and international news, in contrast, were presented as flash announcements. This emphasis is less a result of an intent by stations to fulfill a 'local mission', but of their inability to compete with the

Swiss Broadcasting Corporation in the area of national and international news coverage.

Table 3. Time of items per geographic level in local news programming

Geographic level	Time of item in minutes (mean time period)		
	1984	1985	1986
Local News	2' 12"	2' 03"	2' 03"
National News	1' 04"	1' 02"	1' 05"
International News	50"	44"	0' 44"
Unspecified	1' 16"	1' 13"	1' 10"

As would be expected from the above remarks, the societal and journalistic dimensions of local reporting are relatively weak. A 'hard' and 'mild' version of local reporting were constructed by combining dimensions. The 'mild' version consisted of the original geographical dimension combined with either the societal or journalistic dimensions; the 'hard' version consisted of all three original dimensions – geographical, societal and journalistic.

The two versions suggest both an increase in the percentage of time and in the number of cases, as well as a substantial decrease in the time each news item is on the air. It appears from this material – see Table 4 – that local radio stations report local events in the same routine manner as the local press. There is no apparent gain in new and critical local reporting with the presence of local stations.

Table 4. Substantive local reporting – 'hard' and 'mild' versions

	1984	1985	1986
'Hard'			
Percentage based on cases	4%	9%	16%
Percentage based on time	10%	19%	27%
Mean length of unit in min	3' 53"	2' 55"	2' 29"
'Mild'			
Percentage based on cases	25%	29%	39%
Percentage based on time	38%	46%	51%
Mean length of unit in min	2' 10"	2' 08"	1' 53"

Encouragement of participation

Journalism research suggests that reporting tends to focus on the upper strata of social hierarchies and especially on the most powerful political leaders. Journalists tend to offer such leaders opportunity to express their opinions immediately and directly on the air. To what extent, it can be asked, do local radio stations deviate from this procedure?

Local radio stations are a popular site for public appearances by politicians, directors of public and private organizations, public relations and communication specialists, and figures in the leisure industry. These persons are generally given the opportunity to express their opinions and views on the radio for a relatively long period of time (an average of five minutes per appearance). The setting is generally congenial and the interviewing journalists tend to offer supportive rather than critical comments.

Table 5. Expression of opinion by 'leaders' and 'ordinary people'

'Leaders' & 'Ordinarypeople' in local radio news magazines		% cases	% time	Time in minutes
1984	'Leaders'	12	43	4' 57"
	'People'	2	8	6' 45"
1985	'Leaders'	12	47	5' 16"
	'People'	1	5	5' 49"
1986	'Leaders'	11	42	5' 16"
	'People'	2	7	4' 50"

It should be made clear that 'ordinary people' and 'women and men in the street' are generally only considered suitable for an appearance on radio or television when they have an opinion or view which deviates from the ordinary. It is in this respect surprising that in 1984 local stations provided an average of seven minutes per unit of analysis in programming situations devoid of dramatics or special programming effects. Such programming opportunities, however, remain rather limited. Other opportunities for expression of opinion are offered through phone-in programmes, a programming format which nearly every local station employs. In a single week during the research period there were 254 such programmes, for a total of 279 hours of transmission.

Table 6. Phone-in programmes on local radio

Type of phone-in programmes	No. of programmes per week		Hours of programmes per week	
Games	74	29%	106	38%
Music requests	61	24%	70	25%
Classified Ads	46	18%	26	9%
Congratulations	24	9%	23	8%
Discussions	17	7%	22	8%
Advice	15	6%	10	4%
Community Radio	7	3%	8	3%
Contact & 'Radio sex'	2	1%	4	1%
Other	8	3%	10	4%
Total phone-in programmes	254	100%	279	100%

Approximately 20 per cent of the phone-in programmes, based on their number and duration, can be attributed to participatory programming of a community media type

145

in which mutual exchange of opinions is facilitated. The remainder, some 80 per cent of all phone-in programmes, can be associated with marketing stategies of the stations – efforts to link listeners to 'their' radio station.

AUDIENCE: USES AND FUNCTIONS

On the national level two data sources allow comparison of the audiences of the local radio stations in Switzerland. The research department of the Swiss Broadcasting Corporation has been monitoring local radio activity since the start of the experiment with an annual radio listener survey conducted in the three main language areas of the country (e.g. SRG-Forschungsdienst, 1981–1990; SSR, 1981–1990). In addition, a panal survey has been conducted by the research group responsible for evaluating the project (Bonfadelli, *et al.*, 1984; Bonfadelli & Hättenschwiler, 1985; Hättenschwiler & Bonfadelli, 1987; 1988).

Needs and expectations prior to experiment

About a third of the radio audience expressed interest in additional stations and programming prior to the start of the experiment with local radio. As a consequence of dissatisfaction with the existing two public radio programmes, an opinion expressed mainly by young people, attitudes and expectations concerning the new private local radio stations were very positive in 1983. In addition to other issues, the panel survey mentioned above examined community oriented information needs and deficiencies experienced by citizens. People in the regions investigated were mainly interested in the following topics: environmental questions; consumer, tenant and work related problems; and leisure and cultural events. Surprisingly, the majority of people expressed only moderate or low interest in the traditional local institutions such as the church, community clubs and unions or parties. The three information deficiencies perceived as most intensive were: consumer, tenant and work related problems; issues related to community planning and development; and transportation problems.

People expressed a wide range of expectations concerning the programmes and functions of the private local radio stations. There was strong interest in more local and regional news and service information. In addition, young people and listeners living in urban areas expressed preferences for more pop music. Radio programmes spoken in the dialect of the region and 'listening to familiar voices' were also noted and suggest expression of functions related to social integration. These expressions ranked especially high in the German speaking region of the country.

After introduction of private local stations

After its introduction in 1983 the Swiss private local radio stations were quickly accepted, in particular by younger audiences in the German speaking region. The private radio stations in France, *radio libre*, remain a leading competitor for them in the French speaking part of Switzerland.

Introduction of local radio in 1983 stimulated an overall increase in time spent on audio media per weekday from 151 minutes in 1983 to 176 minutes in 1984. The time spent on foreign radio stations, e.g. *SWF1/3* in Germany, decreased from 37 to 16 minutes per day. Due to the start of the new third public radio programme *DRS3*, designed for a younger audience, the overall position of the Swiss Broadcasting Corporation stabilized, although radio listeners continued to spend some 31 minutes per day attending to the private Swiss local radio stations.

The introduction of private local radio stations as well as the *DRS3* by the Swiss Broadcasting Corporation have caused severe audience fragmentation, particularly between age groups. Listeners in the 15 to 29 age bracket strongly prefer the new radio programmes. The time spent per day attending to local radio programming was 47 minutes, compared to 57 minutes for *DRS3*. The traditionally oriented main radio programme, *DRS1*, experienced a decrease in listener attendance from 67 minutes per day in 1983 to 42 minutes in 1984.

Table 7. Shifts in radio use between 1980 and 1989 in German region of Switzerland

Daily use of radio (min)		1980	1982	1983	1984	1985	1987	1989
Swiss programmes	DRS1	96	90	84	83	74	88	91
	DRS2	8	7	12	8	4	3	3
	DRS3	–	–	9	24	25	23	21
	Other	8	6	0	11	8	12	6
Swiss public programmes		112	103	104	126	110	121	120
Swiss local radio		–	–	–	31	39	42	45
German radio	SWF1–3	25	23	25	12	10	25	11
	R24	5	3	7	–	–	–	–
Other foreign stations		4	5	6	4	3	6	12
Foreign radio in min/day		34	31	37	16	12	18	22
Records/cassettes		12	13	10	8	12	8	12
Total use of audio media		152	146	151	176	171	189	199

Notes: Swiss local radio stations operational since 1983;
DRS3, youth oriented public channel since 1983;
R24, Swiss pirate station Dec. 1979–1983.
Source: SRG-Forschungsdienst, 1981–1990.

Degree of success of private local stations

The new private local radio stations have been able to attract a considerable audience in quite a short time and are accepted in the different regions, although their success varies considerably. Over half of the population in the German speaking part of Switzerland switch from time to time to a private local radio station, and about 30 per cent are regular listeners. Some 40 per cent of the population, however, does not listen to the local stations at all.

Table 8. Size of daily audience of local radio stations

Radio station	Daily audience Local radio audience			Audience structure				
	Occas- ional	Local radio	All radio stations	Males	Females	15–29	30–49	50–74
Basilisk	63	34	72	53	47	37	37	26
Radio 24	42	20	72	44	56	59	36	5
Radio Z	34	10	72	43	57	18	64	18
EXTRA BE	43	10	77	41	59	66	30	4
Zürichsee	30	11	74	43	57	40	51	9
Raurach	27	13	80	40	60	31	42	27
Aktuell	40	21	72	73	27	45	46	9
Eulach	38	15	63	58	42	28	63	9
Munot	59	30	83	56	44	40	43	17
Pilatus	56	18	82	56	44	52	48	0
Sunshine	56	22	75	41	59	31	54	15
Canal 3	40	8	75	27	73	36	57	7
Sarine	42	4	90	62	38	20	63	17
Matterhorn	94	69	85	52	48	42	39	19
Förderband	17	0	77	–	–	–	–	–
LORA	4	0	72	61	39	59	41	0
Total	43%	18%	76%	49%	51%	39%	48%	13%
(weighted)	57%	25%	74%	47%	53%	41%	47%	12%

Note: Weighted by populations for different regions of stations.
Source: SRG-Forschungsdienst, 1986.

Radio as a medium reaches 75 per cent of the adult population each day in the German and 70 per cent in the French and Italian speaking regions of Switzerland. In comparison, the local stations in the German region reach only about 20 per cent of the adult population daily, and in the French region 8 per cent. If one looks at the time spent listening to radio, some three hours per day, 25 per cent of that time is spent listening to local stations in the German region and 10 per cent in the French region of the country. The success of the different private local radio stations, in other words, varies considerably and is generally higher in the German than in the French region. In the latter region the third radio programme of the public broadcasting system in Switzerland, *Couleur 3*, and the *radio libre* private foreign stations are still very successful.

Among the most popular Swiss stations are two large, urban based operations: *Radio 24* in Zurich and *Radio Basilisk* in Basel. A very small amateur-run station in the mountain region of the Canton Valais, *Radio Matterhorn*, is also popular. Particulary important for the intended target groups are the two alternative stations: *Radio Förderband* in Berne and LORA in Zurich.

In 1985, 43 per cent of the listening time was spent attending to *Radio Basilisk* in the region around Basel, 40 per cent to the three public radio programs, and 17 per cent to radio stations broadcasting from Germany. The situation is much different in Bern, where only 13 per cent of the listening time was spent attending to the two local stations, *Radio Extra Be* and *Radio Förderband*; the three public programmes from DRS1-3 dominated the market with 83 per cent of the listeners. The situation in Zurich is between these two extremes: the three local stations – *Radio 24, Radio Z* and *LORA* – command 41 per cent of the listening time; *DRS1-3* 51 per cent; and foreign based stations 8 per cent.

Smaller stations like *Radio Zürichsee* and *Radio Raurach* in the urban or suburban areas of Zurich and Basel are in strong competition, both for listeners and advertising, with the large stations in these areas. The influence of foreign radio stations is still considerable along the country border – not only in the French, but also in the German region. In Basel and Schaffhausen, for example, 17 per cent of daily radio use is devoted to foreign stations, and in the Canton Neuchatel and the area of Lausanne this share is 49 per cent and 39 per cent, respectively.

The success of the private local radio stations is especially high among the young, but the age and sex distribution of the audiences vary considerably. *Radio 24* and *Radio Extra Be* are good examples of stations oriented towards a young audience. They reach as much as two-thirds of the 15 to 29 age group each day, but only 5 per cent of the listeners 50 years and older. There are other stations, however, in the more rural areas which need to appeal to a wider segment of the audience. Some of them – *Radio Matterhorn* and *Radio Munot* in Schaffhausen, for example – reach almost 20 per cent of the residents older than 50 everyday, and attendance by listeners in the age groups 15–29 years and 30–49 is about equally divided.

Functions of private local stations

Local stations perform functions which differ widely from region to region and from group to group. Young people, living in urban areas, listen to the stations principally for two reasons: the youth oriented music and the free and spontaneous atmosphere generated in the programmes. Programmes with local information and those with integrative functions – as found in programming broadcast in the dialect of the region – become more important when people are already to an extent integrated and involved in community life. Furthermore, there are considerable differences between the German and French language regions regarding the functions local radio performs for listeners (see Table 9).

Table 10 indicates that local radio performs different functions for various listener groups. Listeners with moderate and low local levels of community identification[16] attend to local programming mainly because of the youth oriented music, familiar voices and the popular disc jockeys (the previously mentioned free and spontaneous programming atmosphere). On the other hand, community identification and integration correlate significantly with the use of local radio as a means for strengthening

16 *Community integration' is an index based on survey responses to questions directed at amount of interest in community life, participation in community events, community-orientated knowledge and emotional ties to the community.*

ties to the community: for obtaining information about what is happening in the community, and for keeping track of local life and events. These functions are often rated highly by listeners because the programmes are presented in the regional dialects.

Table 9. Reasons for listening to local radio

"I listen to local radio because..."	Language regions	
	German %	French %
Local radio informs you well about what's happening in the community and region	66	63
I try to keep track of the local life and events	60	57
I especially like the music	58	76
Their programmes are unforced, free and spontaneous	57	73
You get information about important events you have to be informed	57	45
There is much music and little talk	51	62
Programmes are spoken in the dialect	50	26
I like the special way they present the news	44	53
Local radio is often a topic of conversation	41	31
I like to listen to familiar voices	32	47
Local radio gives you a lot of buying/leisure tips	31	49
I especially like the programme announcers	26	49
One can participate in the everyday life of people	26	39
I have the feeling local radio is made for me	26	27
Local radio has a watchdog function, e.g. it controls influential people and reports on abuses	25	18
Ordinary people like me are allowed to speak	23	45
There are chances to participate in programme production or to call into programmes by phone	22	28

Source: Hättenschwiler & Bonfadelli, 1987.

Another question of concern is whether the relationship between community oriented use of local radio and community integration of the listeners is also evident at the macro level in the communities investigated. Data from the panel survey show that use and acceptance of local radio (rank order correlations of +0.56 and +0.74 respectively) and motivations for listening such as 'local information' (+0.72), 'dialect' (+0.53) and 'everyday life' (+0.67) are generally higher in communities where the overall social integration already is high. Music (−0.28) as a general motivation for listening, however, is higher in communities with a low level of integration.

SOCIETAL IMPACT

Impact on local newspapers

Even after the introduction of private local radio in Switzerland local and regional newspapers have remained the most important source of news. Some 60 per cent of the adult population reads a local newspaper or the local section of a regional newspaper to become informed about local and regional events. In comparison, only

21 per cent listens to local radio programming. The figures for obtaining local information via public radio and television channels are a little higher. The importance of the local radio stations in comparison to that of the regional magazines broadcast on the public radio station *SRG* (Regionaljournale) as a source for locally oriented information varies significantly from region to region. 'Regionaljournale' commands more than 25 per cent of the listenership in the regions of Zug, Berne, Schaffhausen and Fribourg, but only 9 per cent in Zermatt and 13 per cent in Basel where the private local radios, *Radio Matterhorn* and *Radio Basilisk,* are exceptionally successful.

Table 10. Listening motivation related to community integration

	Listening Motivation (%) "I listen to local radio because..."	Community integration		
		Low	High	Diff.
Emotional functions	I especially like their music	78	64	−14
	There is much music and little talk	69	58	−11
	Of spontaneous atmosphere	71	69	−2
	I like to listen to familiar voices	42	38	−4
	I especially like the programme announcers	41	36	−5
Local information	About what's happening in the community	55	71	+16
	To keep track of the local life/events	65	76	+11
	Short information about important events	53	62	+9
	Of buying and leisure tips	39	39	+0
Control	Local radio has watchdog functions	23	26	+3
Local integration	Programmes in the dialect of the region	40	53	+13
	Participation in everyday life of people	31	35	+4
	Local radio often a topic of conversation	37	43	+6
	Feeling that local radio is made for me	28	31	+3
Participation	Ordinary people like me allowed to speak	31	35	+4
	Can participate in programme production	27	28	+1

Source: *19 regions with private local radio stations*, 1985, N = 2500.

Table 11. Regularly used sources for local information

	"I regularly use" (%)	Language regions	
		German %	French %
	The local newspaper	60	58
	The local section of the regional newspaper	54	53
	The private local radio	27	25
	The regional programs of the public radio	26	25
	The regional programs of the public television	26	32

Source: Hättenschwiler & Bonfadelli, 1987.

Listeners of local radio were asked to assess the influence of the introduction and use of local radio on their local knowledge and newspaper reading behavior. About two-thirds who listened at least occasionally believed they were better informed

151

about local and regional issues (Bonfadelli & Hättenschwiler, 1985). In contrast, a third did not notice any such change in local awareness. Some 58 per cent were not aware of any effect on their newspaper reading behaviour due to listening to local stations. About 8 per cent felt the news obtained from local radio made them less inclined to read newspapers, and 29 per cent believed that local radio news actually stimulated their newspaper reading more. In summary, local radio news does not seem to affect newspaper reading severely, and to the extent a relation does exist it appears that reading is more stimulated than suppressed.

Impact on social services and cultural animation

The private local radio stations serve as a source of social and cultural information for a majority of the listeners. A third of the occasional and regular listeners went to an exhibition, 30 per cent to a movie and 20 per cent to a concert or participated in a local event because of an announcement heard on local radio. The effects of this type of function of the local stations vary from region to region. Radio announcements for community events are typical in the rural areas, whereas suggestions for movies and other cultural events have more impact in urban areas.

Besides these cultural and social service functions there are also consumer magazines broadcast on the local radio stations as well as advertising. About a third of the listeners follow product or market information and 20 per cent have purchased products heard about on local radio. Some 20 per cent said that they listened frequently and 38 per cent occassionally to local radio advertising. In contrast, 27 per cent, do not listen to the advertisements and 9 per cent switch to another station when they are broadcast.

Impact on local participation

How do listeners of local radio stations respond to possibilities to participate in the programmes? Generally, only a minority of about 10 per cent of the radio listeners have participated in the programmes or have attended an event organized by the local stations.

Almost 20 per cent personally know people working at the stations and about 20 per cent said that they had made telephone calls to the stations. About 10 per cent of the listeners have attended an event organized or sponsored by the stations and about as many have participated in a contest or game show or have sent greetings to friends via the radio. Less than 5 per cent, however, had personally participated actively in programme production.

CONCLUSIONS

Local radio stations – at least the economic successfully ones – are located in Switzerland's urban areas where the largest advertising markets can be found and where extensive media enterprises already exists. Only two or three local stations have contributed to eliminating deficiencies in local information. In the mountainous regions of Switzerland, where the markets are not favourable to substantial profits resulting from advertising, minimal interest has been demonstrated for this medium.

Legislation, furthermore, has not encouraged a less commercial development of local radio.

The stations are listened to by an audience which is generally young, urban and male. Local radio seems to serve as a form of companionship to listeners; music programmes are attended to in a more or less incidental manner. The stations satisfy demands for easy-going, easy-listening programming directed at a young audience whose needs were long neglected by the Swiss Broadcasting Corporation. Structurally identical audiences and market conditions contribute to the similar programming produced by the stations.

Local radio stations in Switzerland have not succeeded in contributing in any sigificant way to local reporting. Until now they have not met the expectations of a politically interested local public which has expressed interest in programming devoted to environmental, consumer, housing and labour issues. Furthermore, they have only partially met expectations of the legislator looking for new voices in local information and asking for more substantial local news. Considering these aspects, it is not surprising that local newspapers have been able to sustain a leading role in the media market.

Swiss local radio programmes are produced by professionals. The programmes are market oriented and styled to capture the largest possible audience. Programming directed towards minorities or programming offering significant forms of participation are rare. Local stations do call people's attention to cultural and social events in their respective communities.

The government decree which established experiments with local radio terminated at the end of 1988. The licenses for the local stations, however, were not suspended inasmuch as a new federal law for radio and television was – and still is – being debated by the Swiss Parliament. This law will presumably be ratified in 1992. The minister in charge of radio and television maintains that, on the whole, the experiences with local radio stations have been positive. It is expected that the new federal radio and television law will permit licensing of privately owned and operated local radio stations in the country.

One of the main trends of the Swiss experience with local radio is the increasing importance of economic considerations at the expense of journalistic and societal goals and values. At the start of the experiment, most private local radio stations were loosely organized amateurish undertakings. At the end of the experimental period the stations could be characterized as joint stock companies and as divisions of multimedia corporations financed and controlled by newspaper publishers. In spite of an orientation increasingly determined by the profit motive and comparatively favourable advertising conditions, only a few of the stations have begun to make money and been able to repay initial investment loans.

In 1989 the final research report on the experiment was published (Saxer, 1989), along with a series of supplementary studies (Haas & Corboud, 1989; Schanne *et al.*, 1989; Bonfadelli & Hättenschwiler, 1989a; and Blum, 1989). From this wealth of material the government drew four conclusions regarding formulation of the new federal law for radio and television. First, the need for (private) local radio has been demonstrated. Second, local radio stations should not be limited by a technically determined transmission zone, such as the 15 kilometre radius prescribed during the experiment. Other factors such as topography, economics and social structure must also be taken into consideration. Third, the separation between advertising and programming has to be more precisely regulated. And finally, incentives are necessary to encourage development of local stations in remote and mountainous regions.

Contrary to findings from the research project, the federal ministry of media has proposed measures which stress economic aspects of the stations. Given this bias, it is not surprising that local broadcasting came to be dominated by the principles of free enterprise near the end of the experimental period. A more socially oriented goal of media policy – the stimulation of participation by residents in their communities and promotion of communication diversity within localities – was dismissed by the government. Social and political objectives were no longer considered relevant as guidelines for media legislation. This transformation marks an end to the originally socially-based conception of local radio in Switzerland, and introduces, with legislative approval, a commercially grounded philosophy of community media.

References

Blum, J. (1989): *Die Lokalradios und ihr Umfeld. Ergebnisse aus Expertengesprächen und Panelbefragungen zu den lokalen Rundfunkversuchen in der Schweiz 1983-1988*, Zürich: Arbeitsgruppe RVO-Begleitforschung am Seminar für Publizistikwissenschaft der Universität Zürich.

Bonfadelli, H., M. Gollmer, and W. Hättenschwiler (1984): *Lokalradio-Nullstudie. Teil 1: Lokalräume im Vergleich*, Zürich: Arbeitsgruppe RVO-Begleitforschung am Seminar für Publizistikwissenschaft der Universität Zürich.

Bonfadelli, H. and W. Hättenschwiler (1985): *Lokalradio-Nullstudie. Teil 2: Soziale Strukturen*, Zürich: Arbeitsgruppe RVO-Begleitforschung am Seminar für Publizistikwissenschaft der Universität Zürich.

Bonfadelli, H. and W. Hättenschwiler (1989a): *Das Lokalradio-Publikum. Ergebnisse der Publikumsbefragungen zu den lokalen Rundfunkversuchen in der Schweiz 1983-1988*, Zürich: Arbeitsgruppe RVO-Begleitforschung am Seminar für Publizistikwissenschaft der Universität Zürich.

Bonfadelli, H. and W. Hättenschwiler (1989b): 'Switzerland: A multilingual culture tries to keep its identity', in L.B. Becker and K. Schoenbach (eds) *Audience responses to media diversification*, Hillsdale, NJ: Erlbaum.

Bundesamt für Statistik (1986): *Statistisches Jahrbuch der Schweiz*, Basel: Birkhäuser.

Haas, J. and A. Corboud (1989): *Die Lokalradio-Organisationen. Struktur und Entwicklung der an den lokalen Rundfunkversuchen in der Schweiz beteiligten Lokalradio-Organisationen*, Zürich: Arbeitsgruppe RVO-Begleitforschung am Seminar für Publizistikwissenschaft der Universität Zürich.

Haldimann, U. (1984): 'Kommerzialisierung mit Bremsversuchen. Lokalradio in der Schweiz', *Medium* 14: 7-8, 18-23.

Hättenschwiler, W. and H. Bonfadelli, H. (1987): *Lokalradio-Verlaufsstudie '85*, Zürich: Arbeitsgruppe RVO-Begleitforschung am Seminar für Publizistikwissenschaft der Universität Zürich.

Hättenschwiler, W. and H. Bonfadelli, H. (1988): *Lokalradio-Verlaufsstudie '87*, Zürich: Arbeitsgruppe RVO-Begleitforschung am Seminar für Publizistikwissenschaft der Universität Zürich.

Hättenschwiler, W. and M. Jedele (1987): 'Akzeptanz von Lokalfernsehen und Bildschirmtexten in der Schweiz', in F. Fleck, U. Saxer and M. Steinmann (eds) *SGKM-Jubiläumsband*, Zurich: Schulthess Polygraphischer Verlag.

Hunziker, P. and W. Schors (1983): *Lokales Bürgerfernsehen. Die Wilstudie*, Aarau: Sauerländer.

IBFG (1986): (Interdisziplinäre Berater- und Forschungsgruppe Basel) *Lokalradio-Werbestudie. Bedingungen, Auswirkungen und Funktionen der Lokalradio-Werbung*, Basel: IBFG.

RVO (1982): *Verordnung über lokale Rundfunk-Versuche*, Bern: EDMZ.

Saxer, U. (1986): 'Switzerland', in H.J. Kleinsteuber, D. McQuail and K. Siune (eds) *Electronic media and politics in Western Europe*. Frankfurt: Campus.

Saxer, U. (1989): *Lokalradios in der Schweiz. Schlussbericht über die Ergebnisse der nationalen Begleitforschung zu den lokalen Rundfunkversuchen 1983-1988*, Zürich: Arbeitsgruppe RVO-Begleitforschung am Seminar für Publizistikwissenschaft der Universität Zürich.

Saxer, U., H. Bonfadelli, M. Gollmer, and W. Hättenschwiler (1983): *Lokale Rundfunk-Versuche. Vorstudie zum Design der Versuchsphase und zu den vorgesehen Begleituntersuchungen gemäss der Verordnung über lokale Rundfunkversuche*, Aarau: Sauerländer.

Schanne, M., A. Diggelmann, and K. Luchsinger (1989): *Die Lokalradioprogramme. Befunde aus den Programm- und Sendungsanalysen zu den lokalen Rundfunkversuchen in der Schweiz*, Zürich: Arbeitsgruppe RVO-Begleitforschung am Seminar für Publizistikwissenschaft der Universität Zürich.

Schawinki, R. (1982): *Radio 24. Die Geschichte des ersten freien Radios in der Schweiz*, Zurich: *Radio 24*.

Schweizerische Journalisten-Union (1983): *Über Werbefinanzierte Lokalradios- Absage und Warnung*, Basel: SJU.

Slivinsky M. and D. Dembinski-Goumard (1984): *Etude evaluative d'un media locale. Le cas de la télévision par câble à Avanchet-Parc*. Genève: Université de Genève.

SRG-Forschungsdienst (1981-1990): *Die Medienstudien 1980-1989. Die Beachtung der SRG- und Lokalradioprogramme in der Deutschschweiz*, Bern: SRG.

SSR-service de la recherche (1981-1990): *Etudes medias SSR 1980-1989: Impact des programmes de la SSR et des radios locales en Suisse romande*, Bern: SSR.

11. GREAT BRITAIN: Community broadcasting revisited

Peggy Gray[*] and Peter Lewis[**]

[*]*Leicester University Centre for Mass Communication Research*
[**]*Communications Policy Centre, City University, London, UK*

Broadcasting in Britain until the late 1960s was limited to essentially a national service with only minor regional variations. In 1967 the first *BBC* Local Radio stations were opened. These were followed in 1973 by independent local radio stations (ILRs), and in 1976 by the first community radio programming on cable. Experiments in community television began in 1972. However, development in community radio and television has been a long time in coming. As of 1991 a new Broadcasting Act has come into force. This legislation is likely to bring about radical changes affecting all domestic communications, and it is difficult to see what the future has in store for the embryonic community broadcasting sector.

In this chapter we begin by outlining the structure which has existed for the past forty years and which, for convenience, we refer to as the period of the *BBC/IBA* 'duopoly'. After a survey of the mainly short-lived community initiatives that did occur during the duopoly period and the campaigns and contexts that brought them about, we discuss the newly created structure and possibilities for the future.

THE BBC/IBA DUOPOLY

Between 1954 and 1990 all public broadcasting in Britain was provided by the *BBC* (British Broadcasting Corporation) and the *IBA* (Independent Broadcasting Authority). The *BBC* is governed by a Royal Charter and the *IBA* by an Act of Parliament. The *BBC* is financed by the television licence fee, the level of which is fixed by Parliament. The *IBA* was financed by a levy on advertising profits from each of the 15 independent television companies contracted by the *IBA* to serve 14 different regions of the country, and from the commercial radio companies each of which, like the television companies, paid a rental fee to the *IBA* for use of the transmitters.

The *BBC* provides two television channels, five national radio networks, three national regional networks (Scotland, Wales and Northern Ireland) and 30 local radio services which reach approximately 85 per cent of the population. The first local radio stations began in 1967 and it was intended that they should be locally financed and serve 'identifiable communities'. However, the 30 *BBC* stations now in existence serve a much wider area and are financed from the licence fee.

Since 1973 there have been commercial local radio stations (known as *ILR* stations), generally covering slightly smaller areas than their *BBC* counterparts. There are now 50 *ILR* local radio stations, which together also reach about 85 per cent of the population. However, a number of these stations are owned by the same company and link up on air for large parts of the day, opting out for local news and information and some other programmes. In 1985 hopes were raised for the establishment of 21 community radio stations, but they were dashed when the government cancelled the experiment before any licences had been granted. Pressure from the pirate stations and from organizations like the Community Radio Association mounted, so that the *IBA* reconsidered the situation and decided that they would issue two dozen so-called 'incremental' licences. These are described later in this chapter.

In addition, there are a number of other small scale radio stations licenced by the Home Office. These are hospital or university stations, operating on the induction loop principle. Throughout the period there have been two community radio stations operating on cable. Development of cable has been slow in Britain, but is now taking off so that other such community radio and television channels are beginning to come into operation or are planned in those areas where cable is being developed.

PRE-HISTORY

The steps by which the present system was arrived at were taken in response to pressure, almost inadvertently, and in a period where the main focus of attention was television.[17] The first of the post-war committees on the future of broadcasting, the Beveridge Committee (1949), recommended development of local radio, possibly separate from the *BBC*. However, the minority report recommendation for commercial competition in television eventually led to the breaking of the *BBC*'s monopoly by ITV in 1954. The Pilkington Report (1962) was severely critical of ITV and dismissed the case of the commercial radio lobby in favour of the *BBC*'s proposal for 250 local radio stations. Once again, television claimed the limelight, the *BBC* being allowed to develop *BBC-2* but not local radio.

It took the arrival of the North Sea pirates in 1964 to force a change in the situation. A Labour government's response was to legislate against piracy, order the *BBC* to introduce a specialized pop music channel (*Radio 1*), and launch a cautious pilot project with eight local radio stations. The Conservatives, then in opposition, were impressed by the commercial and popular success of the pirates and promised to introduce commercial radio. In government from 1970, this they did, but in local form and the first Independent Local Radio (ILR) stations opened in 1973 under the supervision of the *IBA*.

By the end of the 1970s, each half of the *BBC/IBA* duopoly controlled an equal number

17 *For a fuller description of this period see Chapter 6 in Lewis & Booth (1989).*

of stations, reaching some three-quarters of the population. Four features distinguished this dual service. First, it fell far short of the original intention, both in the *BBC* and the commercial radio lobby, to provide hundreds of small stations. Political and economic constraints limited the total number of stations, whose coverage areas were consequently enlarged.

Second, all British radio, national and local, provided the same service on two or more frequencies, 'simulcasting' on VHF as well as on medium wave. Third, neither half of the local service was a network, though *BBC* stations used *Radio 2* as a sustaining service, and *ILR* stations made use of Independent Radio News (IRN). The consequence on the commercial side was poor uptake of national advertising. Even when *ILR* was expanded after the return of the Conservatives to government in 1979 to the point where commercial local radio, with over 50 stations, outnumbered *BBC* by two to one, the proportion of national advertising devoted to radio remained low, at around 2 per cent.

Fourth, the *BBC* decided, and the *IBA* was obliged by legislation, to provide a scaled down version of public service programming at the local level: 'serving neighbourhood' was equivalent to 'serving nation' in an approach that can be traced back to the discussion of local radio in the Pilkington report. Specialized radio was confined to the BBC's national networks and local audiences became accustomed to 'strip programming' formats, disc jockey talk, phone-ins and a top-40 playlist filling out the schedules around local news (Local Radio Workshop, 1982).

Both *BBC* and *ILR* claimed to serve the whole community. As a consequence, their ability to satisfy specialized tastes within their coverage areas, for example in music or minority language interests, was severely limited. The *BBC*'s attitude to community access fell far short of the hopes contained in its 1966 local radio blueprint (BBC, 1966), while the *IBA* failed to support with any conviction the one community-based franchise it granted in Cardiff (Lewis & Booth, 1989).

The Annan Report (1977: 205) described local radio as a "mess" and proposed a local broadcasting authority. However, once again, a television proposal absorbed public attention and reforming energies, and the now highly successful *Channel 4* was the outcome.

The campaign for community radio which gathered support in the latter half of the 1970s, taking its cue from the Annan Report, levelled the criticisms summarized above at local radio, but also drew on the experience of the cable experiments held during the first half of that decade.

CABLE IN THE SEVENTIES

In 1972 licences were granted for an initial three-year experimental period to five cable companies to provide local television in Greenwich, Swindon, Wellingborough, Bristol and Sheffield (see Lewis, 1976; 1978).

All five stations were owned and operated by commercial companies who were required to bear the full financial cost of the experiment. Four of the licensees were cable companies who were exploring ways of expanding business because improved over-the-air reception was leading to a drop in subscription levels. The other licence holder, EMI, was interested in exploring the potential market for television software in the event cable operators were granted a concession for pay television. The differences in wealth and attitude towards cable television by the licencees inevitably affected the operation of the stations, and significant differences were to be found between the stations.

The size of their professional staffs varied from six to 16, the type of premises they occupied ranged from a converted terraced house to a smart suite of offices, the quantity and quality of equipment varied from secondhand and barely adequate to new and plentiful, and the amount of regular output varied from four and a half hours of original programming a week to daily sports, news and local feature programmes in addition to special weekly features.

One station saw its task as providing a local television service of high technical quality based on national standards. It included information about community life as well as programmes made by local residents, and provided opportunities for members of the local community to appear and to express their views. Another station sought to identify the gaps in major network output and to fill those gaps, thus providing a local alternative to national television. Other stations intended to provide community television in which members of the local community could be initiators, participants and programme makers.

The degree of control retained by the professionals, the structure of the organization intended to encourage community involvement, the design and type of the involvement, the amount of access to equipment and programming time were matters which varied considerably between stations. Had a proper research programme been built into the experiment, the various operations could have been compared, and a model might have been developed indicating the type of organization most likely to foster community involvement. However, there was no such research programme. The only independent research undertaken was a study of Swindon *Viewpoint* (Croll & Husband, 1975).

The five experimental stations each experienced difficulties in attracting and sustaining community participation over a period of time. Where there was a significant level of community participation in production, a great deal of staff time had to be devoted to train, assist and advise community participants.

From the beginning Swindon *Viewpoint* operated a 'neutral resource' policy by which the staff were facilitators enabling people to exploit the medium. Local people were encouraged to take part at all stages of programme making. Portable video equipment was readily available without cost or paperwork, and a community editing facility was provided. During the experimental period there was sufficient local material to sustain programming. *Viewpoint* attracted an audience, established itself as a topic of conversation, and involved a large number of individuals and groups in various stages of production. Research findings suggest that participation gave personal satisfaction to many, enhanced the sense of group identity, and increased the visibility in the community of some groups. There was an increase in the level of knowledge, interest and involvement in local affairs and a subjective sense of being better informed among viewers in a way not shared by nonviewers (Croll & Husband, 1975).

The terms of the licences did not allow for experimentation with different forms of financing for local television, and so no information was made available about the

159

possibility of local financing and accountability. By the end of the experimental period four of the five stations had terminated operation. In the same year a sixth licence was granted for Milton Keynes (Young, 1978; see also Bibby *et al.*, 1979). Swindon *Viewpoint* was taken over by a locally elected board of directors and became the first television station to be owned and operated by the community it served (Dunn, 1977).

During the next three years most of the serious problems encountered by *Viewpoint* were financial in nature, and many of those involved believed that a radio service might be a more realistic community medium. Radio might achieve the declared aims (both wider access and participation, and community building) with less staff and funding requirements.

THE COMMUNITY RADIO MOVEMENT

If the cable companies discovered that a local programming service did not in itself provide sufficient force to reverse declining subscriber support, the experience of the community media lobby taught it to press more strongly for locally-based, non-commercial ownership, and to explore radio rather than television. In radio, as well as being more affordable, nonprofessionals could more easily achieve production standards acceptable to audiences, and politically there seemed more possibility of success in campaigning for a separate sector of community radio (see Booth, 1980; Partridge, 1982).

During the 1960s and 1970s many people had become aware of the possible influence of the mass media in bringing social issues to the notice of a wide and diverse public. They had begun to demand opportunities through the media to raise their own special concerns and present their own particular arguments in their own language and in their own way.

Some concessions were made by the duopoly regarding these aspects: phone-in programmes became quite common on radio; access programmes, whereby a group of people were given the opportunity to present a special project on television, were introduced; and local radio gave various individuals and groups a chance to become involved in broadcasting. However, editorial control was always retained by the broadcasters and their professional values often got in the way of the work of the 'amateurs'. Persons participating felt frustrated and some complained. There were complaints about misrepresentation due to the editorial process and time constraints; other complaints concerned the unattractive time slots made available, and in many cases the total unavailablity of airtime.

In its plan for local radio in 1966 the *BBC* stated that:

> the active cooperation of each community would have to be enlisted to an extent not previously experienced in Britain. The opportunity to speak on the air would come to great numbers of people who had never broadcast before because the stations' staff would be continually seeking out new citizens with something to contribute. (BBC, 1966: 13)

At first many people who were new to the medium did participate either as interviewees or, in some cases, as initiators or even producers, but rather quickly local radio became more professional. The trade unions objected to the use of nonunion labour and professional broadcasters criticised the work of the volunteers and worried about the retention of *BBC* standards. The role of volunteers became marginal and the local population became once again passive: submitting information to be broadcast by the professionals, taking part in phone-in programmes, and making record requests. A few people became 'broadcasters' and others contented themselves with serving on advisory bodies or making themselves available to be interviewed on matters on which they had specialist knowledge or could be regarded as local spokespersons.

Cable radio

Another opportunity for people to participate in broadcasting arose out of an experiment in cable radio. A number of new towns and other municipalities had expanded rapidly in order to provide housing and work for their fast growing post-war populations. Local authorities or housing corporations were anxious to find ways of exploring "...community development with regard to the overall social aspects of developing a new town" (Aycliffe Licence Application, 1978: 11). They wanted to use every tool available to them, and radio was one such tool. Telford Development corporation looked at the community cable television experiments and decided that they would like to use the cable for a sound-only service. In response to that initiative the Home Office agreed in 1976 to grant seven cable radio experimental licences.

The stations were subsequently established at Basildon, Newton Aycliffe, Telford, Thamesmead, Greenwich, Milton Keynes and Swindon – the last three were towns which had also been involved in the previous community television experiment. Again, as in the case of the television experiment, the stations operated very differently in terms of, among other things, use and role of professional staff and volunteers, type of programming, and amount of time on the air. No provision was made for comparative, independent research, and it is, therefore, impossible to judge the value of the experiment.

Of the seven stations only one, in Newton Aycliffe, was the subject of social science research. The resulting report suggests that, although a wide audience was reached and generally enjoyed the station's programming, there was a very low level of active involvement in the station by people from the community. This was probably mainly due to the manager's personality and his view of the role of a community station. He set great store on high technical standards and professional presentation so that it developed as a station "for the community but not to any substantial extent *of* or *by* the community" (McCron & Dungey, 1980: 67).

At Telford, however, at least in the early days, there was active participation of local residents encouraged by a station manager who had worked as a producer in Australian public (community) radio (Peterson, 1981). Had other stations been studied the results may have been quite different, but towards the end of the experiment all of them had come to depend heavily on commercially recorded music. In any case, one serious limitation of every station was distribution of programming via the cable, which meant residents whose radios were not connected to the cable system were unable to receive the service.

More recent campaigns for community radio have concentrated on the use of low power transmitters and the pirates, referred to later on, have demonstrated how effectively these facilities can be used. Community radio stations which distribute programming via the cable still exist in Milton Keynes and Thamesmead. The latter was the subject of a small scale research project (Gray, 1988) which highlighted some of the problems – structural, financial, policy, and personnel – encountered by a community radio enterprise attempting to involve the community and volunteer labour in the operation of the station.

Third force radio

As a result of the experiences described above demand grew for a 'third force' in radio. The third force was to be separate from the *BBC* and the *IBA*, and was not to be concerned with making profits or maximizing audience size. In this climate the Community Communications Group (COMCOM) was formed in 1977 with support from the Calouste Gulbenkian Foundation to coordinate a response to the Annan Report from an alliance of community media and community arts activists. COM-COM's Local Radio Working Party was the most active of the organization's sections and its evidence to a Parliamentary Select Committee in 1978, along with that of Local Radio Workshop, was instrumental in securing the first official proposal in favour of community radio. This proposal stated that future frequency plans should take account of the possibility of "voluntary radio services within small communities" (SCNI, 1978: 125).

In 1979, COMCOM published a Community Broadcasting Charter, adapted from the station membership rules of the American sister organization, the National Federation of Community Broadcasters, and two years later it provided start-up funds for the magazine *Relay*, devoted to coverage of community radio experiences abroad and campaigns in Britain. The Community Radio Association took over the activities of COMCOM and coordinated a coalition of initiatives including hospital and student broadcasters, the cable radio licencees which had survived from the mid-1970s, radio workshops, and some of the new generation of radio pirates operating from land-based stations.

A report by the Home Office Local Radio Working Party (1980) contained several pages of discussion of the case for community radio. For the next few years, however, developments in cable television and satellite broadcasting were to occupy the attention of the Home Office and Cabinet ministers, and not community radio.

Social action broadcasting

During the 1970s there were a number of initiatives by the duopoly to explore ways in which people could use broadcasting to stimulate community action. Some such programmes showed what was involved in voluntary work, others showed how self-help schemes could operate and others exhorted people to contract the broadcasting company to offer their services or contribute to a charitable cause. There were many problems associated with these programmes, not the least of which was coping with the response.

Some of these programmes were deemed a success in terms of audience ratings and high levels of response, but how effective were they really? The University of Leicester Centre for Mass Communication Research was commissioned to undertake an independent study of a social action television in a series called *Reports Action*, produced by Granada TV and shown throughout the country. The study examined the aims of the various agencies involved, the operation of the programme, the forms of presentation employed, the follow-up systems and relationship between the broadcaster and others involved, and the long-term involvement of volunteers. Possibly the most valuable contribution of the study was to stimulate "full discussion of the major issues" (McCron, 1978: 150).

The nature of social action broadcasting may be said to have changed over the years (for an early conception, see Coleman, 1975), but it is still very much alive. Much of the programming is related to consumer problems, and is broadcast on both television and radio. Small local initiatives with the aid of community media may prove very effective and the research in Thamesmead, referred to above, indicated that the local community expected this type of service.

CABLE IN THE 1980s

Mention has already been made of cable and satellite television, and in this section we look at the community programming on cable that has resulted from the Thatcher government's plans for cable development. These plans were based on four assumptions: (1) that the economy would be increasingly dependent on the information sector, (2) that new technology held the key to expansion in that sector and that there are obvious benefits for any country whose electronics industry can gain a lead over competitors in the field, (3) that private capital had to finance the expansion, and (4) that the profits resulting from the increase in entertainment channels which cable could provide would be the prime motor for starting the process – or, in the words of an often cited phrase, the process would be 'entertainment-led.' The overall context was set by the government's belief in competition within a free market, assisted by the privatization and deregulation of telecommunications and broadcasting.

Within such a strategy, community programming was obviously not a priority for companies facing heavy capital outlay to install broadband networks. Nor did the Cable and Broadcasting Act of 1984 require the Cable Authority to do more than merely take into account the plans of an applicant for community programming before awarding a franchise.

Cable expansions did not at first proceed at the pace originally predicted by the report of the Cabinet's Information Technology Advisory Panel (1982) for a variety of reasons: caution among financial backers in the City, the strength of broadcasting interests within consortia whose efforts were targeted on control of satellite channels, and the slower than expected development and installation of optical fibre cable and new switching systems. Perhaps also the relatively high penetration of home video recorders, along with broadcasting services of reasonably good quality, resulted in less pressure by consumers for cable than has been the case in the United States.

By the end of the decade, however, cable prospects had improved and some community programming could be found. The reason for the upturn in cable's fortunes was the presence of North American investment and expertise. With their home markets approaching saturation level, companies like the American U.S. West and the Canadian MacLean Hunter calculated that the low penetration of cable in Britain offered good possibilities for expansion. Their experience had taught them that local and community channels are a good marketing tool, and the profit motive rather than regulatory requirements was the reason for their interest in this type of programming. The 1984 Cable and Broadcasting Act merely require the Cable Authority to "take into account" when granting a licence, the extent to which the applicant proposes:

> to ... include ... programmes calculated to appeal specially to the tastes and outlook of persons living in the area and programmes in which such persons are given an opportunity to participate. (Cable and Broadcasting Act, Chapter 46, section 7)

The last Annual Report of the Cable Authority (1990), before it became part of the Independent Television Commission (ITC) in January 1991, indicated that 311,647 homes were connected to cable systems – 2 per cent of all households – and 9 per cent were passed by cable systems. The total of number of households located within franchise areas was 14.5 million (Cable Authority, 1990). Of the 136 cable licencees, only 17 were operating, and of these half a dozen were producing regular local programming, with several more transmitting textual or text-with-picture services as a first step towards local origination programming. Many cable operators consider 20,000 subscribers the minimum necessary before a local service can be considered financially viable.

The local services vary in the extent to which they invite access and participation of local people, give suitable training to volunteers, and create structures for policy input from the local community such as advisory boards. Some local producers see their role as suppliers of high quality, professionally produced local news. The services they provide are virtually indistinguishable from the local programmes of the commercial ITV companies. Others give priority to local expression and interests in whatever form it might take. Different funding strategies include the parallel production of corporate videos to finance community production, the leasing of facilities for the same purpose, or the formation of partnerships with charitable trusts or business enterprises. The channel in Aberdeen, launched in 1985, is the best developed, and Clyde Cablevision in Glasgow until recently operated both professional and community access services. Coventry has a strong interest in educational programming, while Croydon employs a local company to produce a seven-day-a-week local news programme. *Laser TV* in Basidon runs an hour and a half breakfast show on weekdays which contains a large portion of advertising, there being no regulatory limit beyond EC rules on the amount allowed.

The Institute of Local Television in Edinburgh takes a critical view of these developments. Its local surveys show a high level of demand for local services, but also indicate the uneven quality and poor availability of community programming [which] together with the low levels of cable take up and slow rate of build, have to date provided an inadequate base for advertising (Rushton, 1990: 6).

Subscription, the Institute suggests, may be a better source of revenue for local channels. The Institute has published an overview of all the franchise committments on local programming, has helped form the Association of Local Television Operators (ALTO) and hopes to strengthen the resolve of local authorities to demand control of or guaranteed access to local channels on behalf of local communities. This last activity is especially relevant in that there are a large number of operators yet to start services who must still negotiate wayleaves and other permissions with local authorities in their areas.

COMMUNITY RADIO:
AN 'EXPERIMENT' AND 'INCREMENTAL' FRANCHISES

In this section we pick up the story of the campaign for community radio. Supporters of this campaign saw a significant precedent in the creation of a lightly regulating Cable Authority. For the first time an authority outside the *BBC/IBA* duopoly had been entrusted with the responsibility for programming.

This may have been a factor which led to the Home Secretary's acceptance in 1985 of the case for community radio. The Community Radio Association's arguments also had undoubtedly been gaining ground with the Broadcasting Department of the Home Office, and the documentation of their case was assisted by the support given to community radio workshops and the funding of research studies by the Community Radio Development Unit of the Greater London Council (GLC) before the GLC's abolition in 1987 (Broadcasting Research Unit, 1985).

Radio piracy was also persuasive. By the end of 1984 there were indications that in the London area the pirates were encroaching on the commercial radio audience. Despite increased fines for illegal broadcasting and confiscation of equipment, around 50 stations could be heard in the London area on weekends, and several in each of the major cities. Most offered music unrepresented or insufficiently heard on *BBC* and *ILR* stations. Many carried advertising. The financial plight of some of the smaller *ILR* companies also created pressure. This was less due to the pirates than to the difficulties of meeting the *IBA*'s rental requirement during an economic recession. But *ILR* made much of the injustice of pirates escaping scot-free while legal stations strained to meet their regulatory obligations. The announcement of the conditions for a community radio experiment in mid-1985 had the intended consequence that piracy was for a time considerably reduced.

Twenty-one locations were specified from the Shetland Islands to Penzance, Cornwall, and 266 applications were received for the two-year experimental licences. In early 1986 an advisory panel had sifted through them and made its recommendations. By then a new Home Secretary had replaced the original author of the experiment and summarily cancelled the plan. The pretext given was that "the exact form of the experiment was still causing difficulty...." (Hansard, 1986) and that the government had decided to postpone community radio until its Green Paper on radio, due later in the year, allowed this type of broadcasting to be considered in the context of other issues. But one researcher has written of the "cynicism and caprice of the government," commenting that the cancellation reflected "the absolute lack of any coherent policy in this area" (Bredin, 1986: 99)

The Green Paper (1987) did indeed clarify the government's position which clearly owed much to the philosophy of the Peacock Committee, if not to the actual structural recommendations of its Report. Set up in 1985 to advise the government on whether the *BBC* should be financed by advertising, the Peacock Committee's very existence constituted a pressure on the *BBC* and the notion of public service broadcasting. Most of the report, published in July 1986, was devoted to television. The proposals to sell off *BBC Radio 1* and *Radio 2* met with little favour, not even from the government.

The Green Paper's recommendations remained intact as part of the government's general plans for broadcasting as a whole, and for the most part are to be found in the provisions of the 1990 Broadcasting Act (Home Office, 1990) which came into effect in early 1991. Before summarising those provisions that concern radio, we should mention an *IBA* initiative which anticipated the new, less regulated future.

It will be noted that three years had elapsed between publication of the Green Paper and the starting date of the new legislation, with yet another year before new stations and channels were likely to be operational. Mindful of the frustration this delay was causing the community radio movement (which had already suffered a cancelled experiment in 1986), and concerned about the renewed activity of pirates, the *IBA* Radio Division secured Home Office approval for the award of some two dozen 'incremental franciscs.' These were intended to "provide programming directed towards communities of interest including ethnic groups and specialist music interests, or smaller geographical communities" (*IBA* press release, March 6, 1989). The stations were located in already existing *ILR* areas – hence 'incremental' – and did not have to provide the broad range of services expected of *ILR* stations.

Once again the number of applications was, as for the cancelled experiment, far in excess of the licences available – 163 applications for 21 licences. A further two extra London-wide franchises attracted 40 applications and were won by an easy listening music station, *Melody*, and a former pirate programming soul/dance music station, *Kiss FM*. Ten of the licences went to groups who, as members of the Community Radio Association (CRA), could be said to be committed to community programming. Most of these, however, quickly encountered financial problems. The size of the licence fee, the high technical specifications and the limited time allowed to raise the money required led groups to adopt commercial structures or join forces with existing commercial broadcasters. As *Airflash* (Community Radio Association, 1989: 1), the CRA's journal, commented "The hybrid status of many applications sits uneasily with the *IBA*'s stated intention of licensing 'new entrants'."

From late 1989, the 23 new licencees began to come on the air, but a year later only four – *Wear FM* in Sunderland, *East End Radio* in Glasgow, *RTM Thamesmead* and *Belfast Community Radio* were still community controlled, and the status of the last was in some doubt. In the rest of the so-called 'community' bids, ownership takeovers had reduced community control and input to virtually zero. Nevertheless, the incremental franchise operation had renewed the interest kindled by the cancelled experiment of 1985-86. Encouraged by the CRA, there were community radio groups in most areas of the country willing to put in bids for the new licences.

THE STATE OF DEREGULATION

In discussing the opportunities for community broadcasting under the new legislation, we think it best to concentrate on radio. We have already covered cable television earlier in this chapter, and broadcast television seems less likely than radio to offer the space or size of units capable of responding to community-based demands. Two exceptions to this generalization must be made: *Channel 4*, required as it is to cater for minority interests, has been successfully able to serve nationwide communities of interest, whether of ethnic or cultural taste (for example, films, rock music, the gay and lesbian communities). Even under the new Broadcasting Act, *Channel 4* may continue to succeed in serving these communities. Secondly, the remit of the proposed

Channel 5, may yet be interpreted locally and could thus offer as much potential for community-oriented programming as local cable channels (Rushton, 1990).

Overseeing radio, then, a new Radio Authority took over from the *IBA*'s Radio Division in January 1991. In fact, most of the *IBA* staff transferred with their Director of Radio. The Authority chairperson, known for his right wing views, has admitted that "community radio needs some kind of non-commercial funding if it is to succeed" (Community Radio Association, 1990: 1). Attempts at committee level and later during debate of the Broadcasting Bill in the House of Lords to strengthen the position of community radio, for instance by creation of a Radio Fund, failed. The Broadcasting Act makes no distinction between commercial and community radio.

The Radio Authority will be inviting bids for three national commercial licences – the first, for a 'non-pop' FM music station, was advertised soon after the Authority took over – and for 'hundrends' of local licences. As of mid-1991 the first 28 locations for the latter have been named and there are likely to be community bids in each of them. The national licences will be auctioned to the highest bidder (subject to the Authority's broad definition of the format for each), while local licensees will be chosen on the basis of their proven research into local needs and what the Authority judges as applicants' ability to carry out the proposed programming objectives. The Act's intention is that the Radio Authority should use a 'light touch,' a style modelled on the former Cable Authority, functioning more as a licensing rather than a regulatory body. As noted in the Green Paper of 1987 "Whether stations flourish or not will depend in the main on their own efforts: their own programme choices and judgements and the support of the audiences they aim to serve (Green Paper, 1987: 28).

The phrase might also stand as a prescription – or epitaph – for the *BBC* whose local radio stations have often claimed to serve the community, and whose health generally must affect a community radio sector which sees itself as redefining public service broadcasting at the local level. The *BBC*'s licence and Charter is due for renewal in 1996. Before then the present government expects the television licence fee to be phased out and a subscription fee to be introduced as the main means of funding. (A Labour government would preserve the licence fee.) In the move to subscription, no mention is made of how radio would be funded (hitherto the *BBC*'s radio services have received an internally calculated portion of the television licence revenue), and the medium is bound to suffer in the cuts which the *BBC*, under this scenario, will have to make as the licence fee drops below the official Retail Price Index. The Green Paper expected that some local radio stations in each area should continue to be part of public service broadcasting. The *BBC* was to be the organization which would provide this service, but that, in an ominous phrase, "the *BBC* will have to judge the size of its committment to local radio alongside the other claims on its resources" (Green Paper, 1987: 40). Already the *BBC*'s three large metropolitan stations, in London, Manchester and Birmingham, have been put 'on probation' to see whether they can increase their audience share. As competition at national and local level bites into the *BBC*'s listenership and as financial stringency takes effect, we expect that the non-commercial sector of radio will shrink. *Radio 1* (pop music programming format) might be forced to take advertising or be sold off; local stations, already sharing a proportion of programming in regional groups, might become even more regional or be shut down altogether.

Where is the future for community radio in all this? It is possible that in some localities these stations may profit from a weakened *BBC* presence, and some Radio Authority licences could go to community radio applicants in under-served rural areas or to applicants offering to reach minority ethnic communities scattered across large conurbations. Perhaps, too, community radio in Britain may want or need to take advantage of the newly emerging patterns of European broadcasting. One of us has suggested elsewhere that:

> as transnational pressure forces the old national broadcasting systems and monopolies to jettison some of their public service broadcasting obligations under the necessity of competion, the mantle could well be picked up by cross-border alliances of those who have formerly called themselves free or community broadcasters (Lewis & Booth, 1989: 204).

References

Annan Report (1977): *Report of the committee on the future of broadcasting*, London: HMSO.

BBC (1966): *Local radio in the public interest*, London: BBC.

Beveridge Committee (1949): *Report of the broadcasting committee*, London: HMSO.

Bibby, A., C. Denford and G. Cross (1979): *Local television, piped dreams?* Milton Keynes: Redwing Press.

Booth, J. (1980): *A different animal: local radio and the community*, London: Independent Broadcasting Authority.

Bredin, M. (1986): *Organising alternative communication: the context of community radio in Britain*, Leicester: Centre for Mass Communication Research.

Broadcasting Research Unit (1985): *The audience for community radio in London*, London: Broadcasting Research Unit.

Cable Authority (1990): *Annual Report & Accounts 1989-90*, London: Cable Authority.

Community Radio Assosiation (1989): *Airflash* 33.

Community Radio Assosiation (1990): *Airflash* 37.

Croll, P. and C. Husband (1975): *Community and communication; a study of Swindon community television experiment*, Leicester: Centre for Mass Communication Research.

Dunn, R. *Swindon viewpoint: a community television service*, Strasbourg: Council of Europe.

Gray, P. (1988): *Radio Thamesmead: survey of a community radio station*, Berkhamsted, Herts: Volunteer Centre.

Green Paper (1987): *Radio choices and opportunities. a consultative document*, London: HMSO.

Hansard (1980): *Record of parliamentary proceedings* (Parliamentary Written Answer to Written Question), London: HMSO.

Home Office Local Radio Working Party (1980): *Third Report*, London: HMSO.

Home Office (1990): *Broadcasting Act*, London: HMSO.

Information Technology Advisory Panel (1982): *Report on cable systems*, London: HMSO.

Lewis P.M. (1976): *Bristol channel and community television*, London: IBA.

Lewis, P.M. (1978): *Community TV and cable in Britain*, London: British Film Institute.

Lewis, P. and J. Booth (1989): *The invisible medium. Public commercial and community radio*, London: Macmillan.

Local Radio Workshop (1982): *Nothing local about it: London's local radio*, London: Comedia.

McCron, R. (1978): *Reports action: a case study in the promotion of social action*, Leicester: Centre for Mass Communication Research.

McCron, R. and J. Dungey (1980): *Aycliffe Community radio: a research evaluation*, Leicester: Centre for Mass Communication Research.

Partridge, S. (1982): *Not the BBC/IBA. The case for community radio*, London: Comedia.

Peterson, A. (1981): 'Doing it for Themselves,' *Relay* 1 (Autumn): 10-11.

Pilkington Committee (1962): *Report of the committee on broadcasting*, London: HMSO.

Rushton, D. (1990): 'Take 5: Where will the programmes come from?' *Television*, Journal of the Royal Television Society, 6.

SNCI Report (1978): *Tenth report from the select committee on nationalised industries*, London: HMSO.

Young, I. (1978): *Local access television in Milton Keynes: Channel 40*, London: Communication Studies & Planning.

White Paper (1988): *Broadcasting in the 90s: competition, choice & quality*, London: HMSO.

12. FRANCE:
Broadcasting in turmoil

Jean-Paul Lafrance[*] and Jean Paul Simon[**]

[*]University of Québec at Montréal
[**]National Centre of Telecommunications (CNET), Paris

Is there a French model of community media? How can local media exist in a country with one of the most centralized broadcasting systems in Europe? Are experiments with alternative media even possible inasmuch as the communications sector in France has been subjected to the monopolistic regime of public service for so long?

Although it is always risky to remove ideas from their original context, a number of French intellectuals nevertheless traveled during the 1960s to Québec in order to study experiments then underway with community radio and television (Barbier-Bouvet et al., 1979). They returned to France with ideas about media and direct democracy, television as a tool for promoting town hall debate, local communication, 'self media', 'people's video' and 'guerilla video'. This visit stimulated excursions to other experiments, and in the course of time almost all city councilmen in France responsible for communications policy in their respective districts have visited experiments like those in Canada (see Lafrance, 1990).

Some people (e.g. de Gournay, 1986) claim that the 'myth of the community' has obscured rather than clarified debate about communications, and that the phrase is often given a narrow North American interpretation. Similarly, the term 'deregulation' has often obscured public debate on government liberalization policies (Simon, 1991b). These matters make it sometimes difficult to explain the meaning of public access channels to a French public because so much of the discussion about media policy is politically sensitive and discussion about free speech often results in polarized dispute.[18] For years, public debate around the creation of local television has

---

18 An example of this difficulty was experienced in Cergy-Pontoise, a suburb of Paris, where efforts to apply the notion of public access to one of the cable channels resulted in the establishment of a committee which instituted such strict access regulations that local video craftsmen eventually stopped using the channel.

been entangled in arguments about the right of local authorities to control such stations (see Simon, 1984, 1987).

These issues make it difficult to define the nature of community media without studying them in a specific context and from the perspective of contemporary social relationships. It is also important to distinguish the various functions these media can fulfill (see Charon *et al.*, 1990; Simon, 1990, 1991a). Before concentrating on some of these themes, however, the legal and political background of broadcasting in France must be sketched.

THE POLITICS OF BROADCASTING

Direct operation of broadcasting by the state was the rule in France as in most other European countries for almost 40 years. Nevertheless, French public service broadcasting displays specific features which are not a direct consequence of legislation.

There is a monopoly over programming maintained by a monopoly over the distribution of television signals. There is also direct and strict political control of broadcasting exercised from the executive branch of government. In addition, trade unions in the country constitute a third powerful component controlling the French broadcasting system.

The 1950s and '60s was a period of relative consensus among the representatives of these components despite apparent conflicts. This led to a political division between governmental control of information (especially instituted and maintained by the Gaullist administration) on the one hand and the defense of artistic expression and employment by the trade unions and the Communist Party on the other. The Communist Party was then very influential among artists and intellectuals.

Representatives from these divisions generally shared the same basic values and beliefs regarding broadcasting as an instrument for further education, parallel and complementary to the public education system. Broadcasting was meant to bring 'high-brow' culture to the masses.

Newspapers did not object to a system of broadcasting that prevented confrontation with such a potentially powerful competitor. On the contrary, reform forces active in the mid-1970s and early 1980s shared a similar distrust of the public service system although it was more or less hidden since the consensus over the value and role of public service was still strong, at least in terms of ideology. The Socialist Party was particularly attached to these values, and a large number of its members and political personnel were employed in government offices (Dagnaud & Mehl, 1988: 356).

The political as well as economic translation of this belief in the positive role broadcasting could fulfill in society was encapsuled in the notion of *économie mixte*,[19] where a balance is maintained between state control of operations and the influence exerted purely by market forces. This form of state economy came into dominance after World War II and was promoted again by the Mitterrand administration as a kind of French compromise between socialism and capitalism. The notion is deeply rooted in French legal culture for reasons which go beyond the scope of this chapter. Suffice it to say that it derives from an overlap of the national interest as represented in the continuity

---

19 *A mixed economy is a very common pattern in utilities, low income housing and public transportation*

of the state with the general political will as manifested in the electoral process (Rosanvallon, 1990).

What is striking in the case of broadcasting is the contradiction between official or ideological commitment to principles which bears little or no relationship to the practice of these principles. A task force was instituted in 1981 to investigate some of the contradictions between ideology and practice as related to broadcasting, but its recommendations were not followed (Moinot, 1981). Eventually, though, the work performed by the task force contributed to a compromise which reduced pressure from the trade unions to reorganize the state-run broadcasting company ORTF. Most channels authorized since then, however, (in 1984 the fourth channel, and in 1985 the fifth and sixth channels) were far removed from the earlier model of television as an instrument to educate the masses.

The introduction of the fourth channel (*Canal Plus*, a scrambled subscription channel) is highly illuminating in this regard. Early studies advocated an educational or cultural channel following the public service model. This proposal, however, was labeled unrealistic by President Mitterrand's former head of cabinet, A. Rousselet, then chairman of Havas, a private but state-owned communications firm. Rousselet proposed an entertainment channel devoted to sports and movies that was shortly afterwards adopted by the President without governmental hearings or public debate.[20]

The second striking point is that the contradiction between liberalization and political control remained in effect. The example of the 1974 divestiture and 1982 reforms showed that they, too, were instruments for eliminating political opponents and weakening other parties. This highlights another belief held by French politicians: the media, and especially television, are considered central determinants in the fate of political figures.[21] Politicians are consequently reluctant to release their power over the media. In a country without a First Amendment the almost natural tendency is to attempt to control the media, but this is not the same as state control of the direct operations of the media. The British Broadcasting Corporation is an example of a state operation without direct political control. France, however, then had both a state operated and politically controlled broadcasting system.

The contradiction between liberalization and political control remained at the very core of a succession of legislative acts although it became less and less visible; see Table 1 for a overview of legislation related to media policy. A good indication of this progressive loss of visibility can be found in the consequent appearance of a regulatory body. From 1974, when the idea for such an entity had not even been conceived, to 1989 when the *Conseil Supérieur de l'Audiovisuel* (CSA) was given maximum authority on broadcasting, an avalanche of legal changes accompanied these regulatory bodies. In 1982 the first body to be created, the *Haute Autorité*, which was inspired by

20 *André Rousselet is a key figure in French communications policy. After having left the President's cabinet, he maintained direct access to the President and power to influence policy on broadcasting issues. He remained Chairman of the Board of Canal Plus, a subsidiary of Havas even after the privatization of the channel. Canal Plus is now considered a driving force in broadcasting, if not all forms of broadcasting.*

21 *For a critique of this conventional political wisdom see Blumler et al. (1978).*

the British model, tried desparately to assert its moral and legal authority. In 1986, the *Commission Nationale de la Communication et des Libertés* (CNCL) attempted to regulate broadcasting and telecommunications with a mandate going beyond mere local regulation. The CSA maintained its own mandate, but lost power over telecommunications.

Table 1. Chronology of communications acts

– May 8, 1837: Creation of state monopoly for telegraphy

– December 28, 1926: Creation of a radio department within the PTT; state to buy out private broadcasters after 1933

– August 10, 1933: Board of directors of public radio to be divided into three units: public service, non-profit organizations ans public authorities

– February 13, 1935: Mandel's decree to regulate public broadcasting and form advisory agency *Conseil Supérieur de la Radiodiffusion* (CSR)

– July 29, 1939: Executive order requiring creation of a national broadcast administration

– April 1, 1940: Creation of the Ministry of Information to supervise the media

– March 23, 1945: Ordinance requires repeal of all private broadcast licenses

– July 30, 1949: License fee instituted for broadcasting

– December 31, 1953: State monopoly instituted for programme production

– February 4, 1959: Creation of *Radio-Télévision francaise* (RTF) under authority of the Ministry of Information

– June 2, 1964: Creation of *Office de Radiodiffusion-télévision francaise* (ORTF)

– July 3, 1972: Revision of *ORTF*, chairman to be nominated by government; creation of advisory body *Haut Conseil de l'Audiovisuel*

– August 7, 1974: *ORTF* divested into seven public firms – TF1, *Antenne 2*, FR3, *Radio-France, Société Francaise de Production, Télédiffusion de France*, and *Institut National de l'Audiovisuel*

– July 28, 1978: State monopoly over broadcasting reasserted

– November 9, 1981: Local non-profit organizations granted waiver for local radio

– July 29, 1982: New status for audiovisual communication; creation of regulatory body *Haute Autorité de la Création Audiovisuelle*; empowered to nominate chairperson of public broadcasting

– December 6,1983: Havas (then a public firm) granted franchise to operate over-the-air scrambled channel *Canal Plus*

– August 1, 1984: Regulation of cable networks

– January 18 and February 21, 1986: Franchises awarded to private operators for the fifth and sixth channels

– September 30, 1986: Creation of regulatory body *Commission Nationale de la Communication et des Libertés* (CNCL) with mandate also covering telecommunications and privatization of TF1

– January 19, 1989: Third regulatory body, *Conseil Supérieur de l'Audiovisuel*, restricted to broadcasting

In all instances, these regulatory bodies have not been creations of Congress, but of the executive branch of government. The main reason for this is that in the tradition of French public service law, an independent entity is a contradiction per se, and close to being unconstitutional. Since the legislative and judicial branches of French government are much weaker than the executive, it is far more difficult to remain independent and still be given a real part to play in government. One observer, commenting on these regulatory bodies, summarized the relationship succinctly: "The CNCL stood for regulation without independence and the CSA and the Haute Autorité stood for independence without regulation" (Cohen-Tanugi, 1990: 31).

However, the means of control changed as they were adapted to altered conditions. Instead of being direct, the mode of control became more and more indirect and followed arcane financial channels. Seen in this light, the revival of the notion of a 'mixed economy' was an elegant way of dressing old ideas in new clothes. At the beginning of the 1980s, even with a new 'freedom of broadcasting' law (Article 1 of the 1982 law), government control did not lessen.

After 1982, the focus of control shifted from the government itself to financial holdings or state controlled firms. The two pillars of indirect intervention became the *Société Financiere de Radiodiffusion* (SOFIRAD) under the total control of the state and Havas in which the state owns 51 per cent of the shares. The first organization controls operations abroad, mainly radio stations and networks located on the periphery of France (*Europe No. 1*, *Radio Monte-Carlo*, *Sud-Radio*). The second is the invisible hand of the government in a variety of communications firms, among which is the *CLT* (*Compagnie Luxembourgeoise de Télévision*), the 'grand old lady' of European commercial broadcasting (Dyson, 1990) and parent company of France's most popular radio station, *RTL*. As will be seen, radio also exemplified the same contradiction between an emerging will to liberalize broadcasting and, at the same time, to perpetuate control of the media.

THREE CENTRAL ISSUES

Three major issues related to the development of local, community and alternative media are democratization of broadcasting, concern for maintaining cultural identity, and decentralization of territory. The first, *democratization of broadcasting*, has only recently been an issue in France although it had been promoted for a long time. There is, it must be emphasized, a tendency for political parties to demand pluralism when they find themselves in the opposition and then to justify monopoly when in the government majority. Broadcasting has always been an instrument of propaganda even when not in the hands of the party in power. After each election, the political victors have not hesitated to change the board of directors of the broadcasting companies and to fire the leading news anchormen appointed by the previous political victors. Without exaggerating the influence of politics on the media, it must be admitted that there has been, and still is, a lack of reasonable distance between government and broadcasting. People often tend to confuse public service with monopoly, and political power with civilian society.

To attack the monopoly of *Radio France* at the end of the 1970s, many opponents formed a coalition even though there was difference of opinion, and where similar views were held the reasons for the views were often different. Media entrepreneurs wanted to create private companies; the political opposition was looking for a communications channel; young people, ecologists, and public figures often wanted an avenue for expression of different opinions and values. Obviously, when unity of action does not involve unity of thought, the results can be unpredictable. Many things evolved out of this protest movement against state monopoly, but, in short, the traditional broadcasting arrangement as it had been known ceased to exist.

Cultural identity is a second major issue in the transformation of the broadcasting system. National broadcasting tends to express centralized national culture, either high-brow or mass oriented culture. Any serious reform of broadcasting is concerned with the fragmentation of the audience and a tendency to specialize media content toward cultural minorities.

Since the availability of additional radio frequencies, the number and variety of radio stations has also increased. Ethnic radio stations, homosexual, feminist, rock, and punk stations have all appeared on the air and and some have already disappeared, depending on the popularity of the issues they propagate and the bonds they create with listeners. In deviating from the model of traditional broadcasting, however, these stations, particulary those oriented around hobbies and social issues, are in danger of leaving the system of mass media completely. Some radio stations have become more similar to citizen band radio, juke boxes and telephone exchanges, and some television stations are nothing more than a long video clip or video club for viewers. This development is also accompanied by the danger that these stations occupy only a marginal position in a community or locality. By emphasizing the expressive function of radio at the expense of its function as a transmitter of information, speech is given preference to memory, attention to the present above concern for the past or for the future, and the transient above the permanent.

Decentralization of territory is another important issue in a country where communication developments of all kinds have been initiated from the capital city since the time of Napoleon. It took an entire century to establish the telephone network, in part because it was primarily intended for hierarchical and authoritarian transmission of information. The return to local initiatives is a top priority for many people in an era when national culture is being expanded throughout Europe and throughout the French speaking world. Television stations can be found broadcasting in low rent housing districts, counties, rural areas as well as in major cities.

Is the structure of local broadcasting a product of an administrative rationality or is there also an emotional or value-based structure to be found? Concepts such as being at 'home' are seen as the opposite of 'outside'; the 'inner' takes on meaning in relation to the 'exterior'. This is why 'local' not only refers to 'localism', a narcissistic return to oneself, but also represents a dialectic refusal of others, a tension between presence and absence. Local media cannot ignore the national and international environment. Even local radio stations make wide use of internationally produced and distributed music. The same development is anticipated with local television which depends on products from the audiovisual programming industry.

Some people believe that the local character of the media is provided by programming rather than production:

> If we consider the local as a social product, we treat the local as a *represented*

175

object, which is a misinterpretation because the main quality of what is local is that it *is present*. It cannot be considered as a 'text' because, first of all, it is a 'context'. (de Gournay, 1986: 11)

Local television programming in France, whether distributed via the cable or over-the-air, whether by private or public stations, does not constitute more than 30 to 60 minutes of daily station programming. Stations have little choice than to provide occasional (*rendez-vous télévision*), cyclic, and repetitive programmes while providing some amount of local origination and syndicated programming.

INDEPENDENT RADIO STATIONS

At the end of Giscard d'Estaing's administration in 1981 many people were eager to dismantle *Radio France*, the State monopoly which had sole authorization for broadcasting on French territory. Although the legal parameters of this monopoly were quite explicit, in actuality the situation was less clearcut in that many peripheral stations broadcast from outside the country (such as *RTL*, *Radio Monte-Carlo*, *Radio Andorre*) with approval and financial support from the French government.

Towards the end of the 1970s, a few pirate stations were commanding audiences around the country: *Radio Verte*, an environmentalist station, a labor movement station in Longwy, and stations subsidized by opposition parties. Both the Socialist and the Communist Parties were active participants in the struggle to develop independent stations during this decade. Court cases resulted from illegal use of radio frequencies, some of which involved political parties. Freedom for radio was included in the political platform of the Socialist Party candidate Mitterrand in 1981.

In the same year a new law authorized exceptions to the broadcasting monopoly, but these exceptions were restricted to local or community oriented low power stations. Fear of political control, in other words, was still present. In order to prevent political criticism of the government through the voice of local radio stations controlled by cities held by opposition parties, local authorities could only provide 25 per cent of the total funding. The *Haute Autorité* was commissioned to regulate local radio stations and over 1,800 licenses were issued.

But anarchy continued to reign, creating signal interference for the majority of the new radio stations. It was also virtually impossible to provide an official list of the wide variety of stations – those which were pirate, those operating on a semi-legal status, temporary stations and amateur and volunteer run stations. In 1982, the government tried to take measures to curb this state of anarchy. The broadcasting monopoly was terminated and a license to transmit was made compulsory in order to reduce the rate of increase in radio stations. Stations had to decide whether or not to accept advertising; those without advertising were entitled to relatively modest financial governmental assistance. The stations had a year in which to decide for a non-profit or commercial status. Tranmitters were not to produce more than 50 watts; larger transmitters required approval of the *Télédiffusion de France* (TDF) in order to permit orderly allocation of frequencies.

This 'freeing the airwaves' attracted many interested parties (see Cojean & Eskenazi, 1986). Those who believed in liberalizing the market and in freedom of enterprise invested in music and news format radio stations. Some, such as the station *NRJ*, now make a profit while others have been sold to large media conglomerates which provide financing until the stations become profitable. Political parties, particularly the Communist and Socialist Parties, as well as the Catholic Church set up quasi-municipal radio stations[22] and other groups introduced stations in specific geographical regions with well-defined socio-cultural features. The latter tend to be stations specializing in local news programming. After a promising start, most local news stations began to encounter difficulties related to financing activities, maintaining an audience and developing a programming formula. There is also a variety of other minority groups involved in station programming: homosexuals, feminists, environmentalists and various counter culture groups.

Ethnic groups were also attracted to the airwaves. They formed non-profit broadcasting associations and received special subsidies from the national government. The government believed ethnic radio stations could help integrate minority groups into society and lessen social tensions. Some of the programmes of these stations are produced in the language of the ethnic groups which contributes to the strong listener support these stations generally enjoy.

Ten years after the radio broadcasting revolution in France, the adventure is still continuing, although the initial fever has somewhat abated. The euphoric descriptions common in the early days are heard less frequently. Many radio stations which leaned heavily on such rhetoric ceased operation shortly after introduction; others stations have gone into hibernation and many have changed their audience focus or programming formula. In spite of such changes the French experiment in free broadcasting has remained alive and been the source of new impulses for the media in general.

The big winner, at least commercially, of the independent radio revolution was the *NRJ* network (pronounced as 'energy') which has refined the 'music and news' programming format to perfection. *NRJ* can be considered the antithesis of local, community or alternative radio. The revolution, in other words, has given birth to a monster, but the monster is doing much better than the legitimate children. NJR draws around 20 per cent of the overall radio audience. The *Radio France* stations have kept about 20 per cent of the audience, peripheral stations (such as *RTL* and *Europe No. 1*) about 50 per cent, and the various local radio stations from 1 to 6 per cent.

It is appropriate to dwell upon the phenomenon of *NRJ* as a counter example when evaluating the development of radio. *NRJ* is just as typically French as the television series *Dallas* is typical of America. It is a production and management formula invented elsewhere, but coming from nowhere and intended for listeners wanting to live in a musical, out-of-this-galaxy atmosphere. *NRJ* transforms sound by using special effects (equalizers, compressors, limiters) to give listeners 'unreal' audio perception. *NRJ* homogenizes sound and creates a structure in which music, voice, advertising and news intermingle. *NRJ* abhores live broadcasting which interrupts its sound pattern; it despises on-the-air telephone calls from listeners which localize the programming and it eliminates disc jockeys who tend to personify programming. *NRJ* is everywhere and nowhere. Anyone can tune in to it at any time, from the car,

---

22 *'Quasi-municipal' because local authorities were legally prevented from operating a station directly. Only non-profit organizations were allowed to operate stations, but it was still possible for municipalities to subsidize such organizations.*

the stereo at home, a walkman, or a ghetto blaster. It is like a hearing aid for people who want to stay within their own protective shells.

An important aspect to stress in the appearance of *NRJ* is the first alliance created between 'raw' market forces and consumers. In 1983 when the *Haute Autorité* refused to let the station increase its broadcasting power, it started a public campaign where freedom of expression was associated with free enterprise. The station succeeded in organizing a demonstration that brought thousands of young people (its target audience: ages 15 to 25) into the streets of Paris.[23] The situation became difficult for the administration which claimed to have liberated communications from the conservative parties. The government eventually backed down, however, and the law was modified.

Of all the stations that came into being when the airwaves were deregulated only those belonging to the *NRJ* network seem to have an economically secure future. The other stations, which attract less that 3 per cent of the audience in Paris, have two possible scenarios for survival. Either they look for a symbolic sort of 'iron lung' which will enable them to breathe for a while by establishing ties to a commercial network and being supported by a media industry interested in diversifying its possessions, or they continue struggling to maintain a marginal existence.

Less than ten years after the booming and blooming period of radio stations, the scenery has changed dramatically. Only 400 stations are still active and of these only about 100 are still committed to a pioneering spirit and community values. The other 300 stations are now owned by large communications firms which were already active and dominant before 1982 (*Europe No. 1*, *RTL*, *RMC*, the Hersant group) or newcomers like *Canal Plus*, the Swiss firm Nicole, or the British Crown group.

Ironically, the marginal existence of the community oriented stations is a consequence of the struggle to secure an audience which is willing to accept decentralization. The phenomenon of independent radio stations has forced *Radio France* to regionalize its operation and provide more specialized programming. Throughout the country decentralized public radio stations now operate and draw between 2 per cent to 5 per cent of the audience.

The course market out for local radio stations is not an easy one to follow. A large part of the material use for programming is not of local origin. The record and entertainment industries which provide much programming material is largely national and internationally oriented. National and international news also come from press agencies, newspapers and magazines, and not from the local station environment.

There are programming strategies which stations can employ to demonstrate alliance with their respective communities such as providing reports on local events, sports, entertainment, and producing programming using local dialects and accents. Other programming strategies incorporating live broadcasts, local advertising, quizzes,

---

23 *The target audience of the station is young people between 15 and 25 years. Over 100,000 people demonstrated according to the station, but less than 20,000 according to official sources. It was the worst possible time to hold a demonstration from the perspective of the government which was already caught up in an ideological fight for the 'freedom of education' (in France this means private religious schools) which led to another major demonstration.*

games and locally oriented public relations have already been claimed and perfected by commercial radio stations and offer little distinguishing value for community oriented stations.

LOCAL TELEVISION

The decentralization of television on a local basis is more complex, more problematic, and more time demanding than the decentralization of radio. Broadcasting methods and production techniques are more sophisticated and complicated, and transmission involves more contraints. Television companies are still quite monolithic organizations (see Charon & Simon, 1990).

Much has been written and even dreamed about local television. In addition to pioneering experiments such as the *Vidéo-gazette* in Grenoble or the *Vidéobus* in the Hérault area in the south of France (see Bonetti & Simon, 1983), it should be realized that many people fought against the broadcasting monopoly and centralization. Now that people are starting to fear the coming of multinational communication companies, however, local television is becoming seen as the universal remedy.

Certain changes have re-opened the question of localism. The launching of a cable plan which was initially intended to cover the entire country opened up the possibilities of transmitting television channels. In a country where only three to six channels can be received over-the-air, cable systems can now distribute as many as 24 channels. Local authorities were legally in charge of initiating the cable systems (see Simon, 1988). What town mayor has never dreamed of having 'his own' local television station? Independent of the answer to such a rhetorical question, empirical research suggests that local news ranks as the primary communication need by community residents (Lafrance, 1989). The privatization of *Channel 1* (*TF1*) in 1986 brought many people to hope for decentralization. Before 1980, there were three national channels and a decade later there were six, and an entire network of local television stations could possibly develop. The potential local advertising market has encouraged discussion of this last possible development.

The question of local television stations is brought up at virtually every convention for city government officials, at broadcasting conferences and even during some regional public events. About a dozen 'event' oriented television stations, remaining in operation only a short period of time, have been used to assess the feasibility of local transmissions, to test audiences for a future project or simply to acquire a broadcasting license. Examples include: *Télé-Avoriaz*, *Télé-Soleil* in Guadeloupe, *Télé-Martigues* in Provence, and various cable experiments in Villeneuve d'Asq, Lille and other cities.[24]

Multiplicity of formats: From télépuce to télébrouette

To speak in the jargon of communications specialists, developments have proceeded from micro to mega forms of communication. There seems, however, no lower limit to the geographic size of a locality. 'Local' takes on meaning in relation to 'national'.

---

24 *A portion of this section of the chapter appeared in a special issue of* Pouvoirs *devoted to television (Lafrance & Simon, 1989). That article includes an extensive description of the field trials with local television.*

It means *connection* just like outside compared with inside, exterior compared with interior, known compared with unknown. Some local television stations can be found in low-income housing projects, on a single floor of a high-rise apartment building, in towns, in the country. The variety of station types is protrayed in Table 2, some of which are discussed below.

Table 2. Local television stations types

Classified according to:

    –transmission mode

local cable channels, over-the-air stations, 'video wheelbarrows', low power stations

    –broadcasting area

local, regional, urban, district, community, rural

    –programme content

general entertainment, educational, topical, ethnic, family services

    –production staff

professional (journalist, programme producer), socio-cultural workers, volunteers, free access material provided by amateurs

    –programming format

Rendez-vous television, shared channels, repetitive programing with additional information available via a teletext system, network of independent local stations

    –programme origin

in-house production, subcontracts, wholesale or retail purchases

    –projected image

producers' or journalists' television, edited television, composite television with emphasis on electronic presentation and image

    –financing

government subsidies, local resources (integration in a cultural centre, use of municipal services and volunteers), local advertising and sponsoring, subscriptions, fund raising events, service fees, corporation financed stations

In Saint Ouen l'Aumone, 50 kilometres from Paris, there is an area full of dilapidated low income apartments, but they are connected to a cable system. The Vocational Training Centre of this city paid for the audiovisual training of several unemployed youths; the city's housing agency provided one of its apartments for use as station headquarters. The bedroom has become the editing and transmission center, the living room the studio (the ceiling being insulated with egg cartons) and the kitchen serves as office and reception room. Every Friday evening for a two hour period young people broadcast their own programmes on topics such as unemployment, sports, municipal politics, local news and current movies.

Unlike the youth of the 1960s and '70s, representatives of *Télépuce* do not describe their activities in socio-cultural terms, but as audiovisual technicians and programme producers, and many hope eventually to earn a living in these professions. The relationship between the station and its viewers is not whimsical; technology plays a mediating role, helping to counteract declining social conditions in the locality and the inacessible national and international focus given to the Parisian capital. Technology is, in other words, a symbol of modernization for the viewers in this small city.

Télébrouette (literally translated as 'video wheelbarrow') is the name given to local television stations which transport their programmes for showing in village movie theatres, cultural centres and schools. Using Super-8 film, these producers live in hard-to-reach areas such as valleys in the the Alps, Brittany, and in the southern most sections of the country. Once a month a new film is produced and circulated around the region in which the station is active. Since these stations cannot report timely news, they tend to produce magazine format programmes, combining more general news items with cultural information. The financing of these programmes is provided from subsidies from regional councils and the Ministry of Cultural Affairs. Generally, the salaries for two to three employees and for the equipment is funded by local authorities.

In the context of such activities it is important to discuss the Federation of Regional and Local Television Stations.[25] Is it an outgrowth of the former 'direct cinema' movement, a type of 'social' video, now looking for a broadcastlng outlet?

Whereas big cities are setting up sophisticated cable networks, the importance of local frequencies is making itself felt also. The relatively enclosed regions are trying to preserve their own characteristics. In contrast to efforts to unify Europe by 1992, these small regions are trying to project their differences, particularly regarding the centristic tendencies of the national French government. Trade and communications routes in tomorrow's Europe are changing; new regional capitals, such as Barcelona, Milan and Frankfurt, are transforming the flow of an invisible trade – people and information. Support for local cultural productions, the sometimes expensive construction of communications facilities (teleports, audiovisual centres, fully equipped conference halls), and the promotion of tourist attractions (festivals and conventions) are part of the strategy used to express and encourage local identity.

The image produced by local and regional television stations is not one of social struggle or folkloric return to nature. Rather, it is a reassuring self-portrait offered to others, of ecological and pastoral modernity.

'True' local television

The development of urban local television stations operating on a full-time basis is a much weightier and riskier undertaking. This development has resulted in heated discussions between local and national authorities in cities which have acquired power in the communications sector (particularly cable communications) and which have created a political image via the media. Many major cities – Paris, Metz, Montpellier, Rennes, Toulouse, Poitlers, Dunkerque and Marne-la-Vallée – seem to aspire to become the equivalent of Saint Jacques de Compostelle in the year 2000, with their media oriented cathedrals (technopoles) and 'High Masses' devoted to communications (see Bonetti & Simon, 1986).

---

25 *This federation involves about seven groups including* TéléSaugeais *in Montbenoit,* Cinétine *in Brittany and the* Beaufortain *television station in Savoie.*

Local television can either be broadcast on a cable channel[26] or on one of the available over-the-air frequencies.[27] Given the weight of initial investments and the size of the audience, cable operators who finance these channels try to achieve a combination of the two forms of signal distribution. Another combination found financially very attractive is the connection of several local channels belonging to the same cable operator.

Still, local television cannot be properly understood without placing it in the context of the entire broadcasting system. It would be misleading to believe that local television will someday replace national television. On the other hand, the broadcasting environment in France is still in development and it remains to be seen what role will emerge for local television. However, two observations can be made.

First, cable operators are playing a very ambiguous role. At the beginning of the introduction of cable plans, local governments had full responsibility for programing and production, whereas the PTT was the owner and constructor of the communication infrastructures. Because of a lack of knowledge on the part of municipalities, a new partner entered the scene: the cable operator (see Charon & Simon, 1989). This partner later became the manager of cable systems, then the broadcasters of programmes, and finally the programming producers. These roles are similar to those taken on by multiple system operators in the United States. To obtain local franchises, operators must promise to establish local television stations costing between 4 to 6 million francs per location. Subscriptions to cable have lagged behind expectations, however, and operators have begun considering more economical alternatives such as establishment of a central purchasing organization for programming rights, multipurpose production subsidiaries, foreign sales, and promotion of public access on community channels and leased access for corporate communications. It should be stressed that besides national and foreign channels, new programming is only being provided by the local stations. What also must be expected is a transfer of financial and technical resources from local to special interest channels – sports, news and music channels – which will be broadcast around France and perhaps elsewhere in Europe.

Second, the creation of local television was often conceived according to the model provided by national channels, either as a reaction to or as an imitation of them, but without taking into account transformations in the media systems: the fragmentation of the audience, specialization of programming, creation of a more and more internationalized network of audiovisual production.

For local television stations, whether they are independent or affiliated with a network, the problems are the same and can be summarized in a single question: Do local television stations have the means to develop an original, local medium, to acquire economic, financial, and political independence (Garin & Sainteny, 1988).

As far as local origination is concerned, what kind and how many programmes can a given environment produce? Can a local station produce more than entertainment

---

26 In 1988, there were local stations in operation on cable systems in Paris, Rennes, Montpellier, Nice, Biarritz, Avignon, Grande Synthe, Cergy-Pontoise and St. Cloud.

27 TéléToulouse was one of the first over-the-air local stations, later followed by Télé Huit Mont Blanc and Télé-Lyon-Métropole.

based programming, mimicking traditional television with its games, quizzes and talk shows? How can a policy of responsiveness to the community be developed, as seen on some Italian and Belgian stations such as *Télélombardie* in Milan and *Telébruxelles* in Belgium, characterized as journalists' rather than producers' television and which stress live coverage of events (Simon, 1987)?

As for purchased programmes, the problems are somewhat similar whether the station is a network affiliate or is attempting to establish buyers' cooperatives. The question is to evaluate the type, the nature, and the worth of the products used for programming without damaging the station's own personality. Is it possible to gain access to a market other than B or C class movies in an era when national and international networks are buying in bulk the rights to the best independent productions, producing their own movies and documentaries? Would it not be better to broadcast or rebroadcast only an hour each day instead of having local productions drown in a sea of externally produced programmes?

Regarding the financial and editorial independence of local television, these aspects are closely linked to station profitability. In the case of *TéléToulouse*, the cable operator owns over one-third of the company. The situatlon is similar in Lyon with the same operator.[28] So far, *Télé Huit Mont Blanc*, the programming of which can be received in two French Departments, is the only local station that is close to breaking even. The other over-the-air stations are still losing money (Charon *et al.*, 1990). There are examples of connections between local television stations and local newspapers, as well as of participation by local governments, municipalities and cultural organizations in station activities.[29]

The development of local radio and television in France is far from completed, and it must be stressed that it can only be understood by analysing the evolution of national – and on some matters, European – broadcasting. Media decentralization is partly related to the deregulation of communications, audience fragmentation and programme specialization. To discuss the development of radio and television without considering the connection, convergence and even merger of a large variety of media[30] is to discard significant factors for understanding the past, interpreting the present and predicting the future.

---

28 *This is already common in North America. In the United States most cable operators are also owners of television stations, and in Canada* Vidéotron *in Montréal has acquired* Télémetropole, *CPCF* Cable *and the* Quatre Saisons *network.*

29 *It is possible to give many examples of intra-, inter- and transmedia integration in today's media world. The connection between local television and newspapers is 'only natural' if we accept their dependance on the same advertising market and coverage of the same news. For further explanation of such cultural bonding see Lafrance (1989).*

30 *An increasing number of authors argue that telecommunications and local videotex must be taken into account in order to properly describe the decentralization of communications: Charon (1983); Guyot et al. (1984).*

APPENDIX: BROADCASTING IN FRANCE

Regulatory bodies

The *Conseil Supérieur de l'Audiovisuel* regulates cable, broadcasting and radio at both the national and local levels and for both private (regulation of licences, franchises, spectrum space and quotas) and public stations (programming and board of directors). The *Direction Générale à la Réglementation* (DGR), an executive agency of the PTT department, regulates telecommunications and the videotex service in the country.

Broadcasting organizations

National Level

Television

There are two public national broadcasting companies: *Antenne 2* and *France Régions 3* (FR3). There are also two public satellite channels available on cable systems: the French-German cultural channel *TDF1 also aired on FR3* every Saturday afternoon, and *TV-5* which is an international but French speaking channel and is received in Belgium, the Netherlands, Canada, France and Switzerland. There are also three private channels: *TF1, Cinq, M6,* and one private scrambled subscription television channel: *Canal Plus. Télédiffusion de France* (TDF) is the public organization responsible for distributing all television signals. *Société Francaise de Production* (SFP) is the public production unit for television programmes.

Radio

Radio-France operates four public radio channels (*France-Inter, France-Musique, France-Culture,* and *Radio-Bleue*), as well as a news programme (*France-Infos*) and a music and news programme (*FIP*).

Radio France Internationale (*RFI*) is in charge of French broadcasting conducted in foreign countries. There are four units of the *RFI* with headquarters and facilities located outside France: *RTL* a subsidiary of *Compagnie Luxembourgeoise de Télévision* (*CLT*), *Europe 1, Radio Monte-Carlo* (*RMC*), and *Sud Radio* in Andorra.

Regional and local levels

Television

FR3 provides regional news twice a day. *Radio France Outremer* (*RFO*) operates public radio and television stations in French territories abroad (Mayotte, Martinique, Guadeloupe, Guyane, Réunion, St Pierre and Miquelon, New Caledonia and French Polynesia). *Tele Monte Carlo* (*TMC*), a private television station, broadcasts in the South of France. Three local over-the-air stations are in operation: *Télé-Toulouse, Télé-Lyon Métropole,* and *Télé Huit Mont-Blanc.* There are 136 cable systems which serve most of the major cities in the country.

Radio

Radio France operates 36 decentralized public radio stations. There are eight networks of local radios: *NRJ* (with 100 affiliated stations), *Nostalgie* (200 affiliates), *Europe 2* (85 affiliates), *FUN* (97 affiliates), *Kiss FM* (60 affiliates), *Skyrock* (40 affiliates), *RFM* (40 affilites), and *Pacific FM* (40 affiliates). Finally, there are 800 local private community radio stations in the country.

References

Barbier-Bouvet, J.F., P. Beaud and P. Flichy (1979): *Communicatiion et pouvoir*, Paris: Anthropos.

Blumler, G., G. Thoveron and R. Cayrol (1978): *La télévision fait-elle l'élection? Une analyse comparative: France, Grande Bretagne, Belgique*, Paris: Presses de la Fondation Nationale des Sciences Politiques.

Bonetti, M. and J.P. Simon (1983): 'Ecrans pour tous. Démocratie locale et nouvelles technologies de communication', special issue, *Correspondance Municipale/Culture au Quotidien*, 239.

Bonetti, M. and J.P. Simon (1986): *Communication et dynamique urbaine*, Paris: CNET & Plan Urbain.

Charon, J.M. (1983): 'Le vidéotex, un nouveau média local? Enquete sur l'experimentation de Vélizy, 1980-1983', mimeo, Paris: Cems-EHESS.

Charon, J.M. and J.P. Simon (1989): *Histoire d'enfance: les réseaux câblés audiovisuels en France*, Paris: Documentation Francaise, CNET-ENST.

Charon, J.M., J.P. Lafrance and J.P. Simon (1990): 'Les médias du local', *Médiaspouvoirs* 18: 108-172.

Charon, J.M. and J.P. Simon (1990): 'Pour quelques dollars de plus. Les industries du contenu face au Plan Câble', in *Télévision/Mutations, Communications*, 51: 195-219.

Cohen-Tanugi, L. (1990): 'Les enjeux institutionnels de la déréglementation', *Réseaux d'Etat* 40: 27-34.

Cojean, A. and F. Eskenazi (1986): *FM, la folle histoire des radios libres*, Paris: Grasset.

Dagnaud, M. and D. Mehl (1988): *L'Elite rose: la sociologie du pouvoir socialiste 1981-1986*, Paris, Ramsay.

Dyson, K. (1990): 'Luxembourg: Changing anatomy of an international broadcasting power', in K. Dyson, P. Humphreys, *The political economy of communications: international and national dimensions*, London: Routledge.

Garin, J.C. and G. Sainteny (1988): 'L'implosion des telévisions locales', *Médiaspouvoirs* ll: 56-64.

Gournay, de C. (1986): 'Le local par la bande', report, Paris: CNET.

Guyot, B., P. Pajon and M. Valbot (1984): *Claire dans la communication sociale locale*, Grenoble: Gresec & INA.

Lafrance, J.P. (1989): *Le câble ou l'univers mediatique en mutation*, Montréal: Editions Québec-Amerique.

Lafrance, J.P. (1990): 'Les télévisions locales en Europe. Entreservice public et empires médiatiques, le tiers secteur de la télévision', *Télévisions/Mutations, Communications*, 51: 221-242.

Lafrance, J.P. and J.P. Simon (1989): 'Les télévisions locales,' *Télévision, Pouvoirs* 51: 61-75.

Moinot, P. (1981): *Pour une réforme de l'audiovisuel*, Paris: Documentation Francaise.

Rosanvallon, P. (1990): *L'Etat en France de 1789 à nos jours*, Paris: Le Seuil.

Simon, J.P. (ed.) (1984): 'Les enjeux des systemes de communication locale', special issue, *Correspondance Municipale*, 248.

Simon, J.P. (ed.) (1987): 'Télévisions locales', special issue, *Correspondance municipale* 280/281.

Simon, J.P. (1988): 'New media policies and the politics of central-local relations in France', in K. Dyson, P. Humphreys, R. Negrine and J.P. Simon *Broadcasting and new media in Western Europe*, London: Routledge.

Simon, J.P. (ed.) (1990): 'La communication locale. Premiere partie: les médias et les messages', *Territoires*, 313: 20-54.

Simon, J.P. (ed.) (1991a): 'Seconde partie: les hommes et les réseaux', *Territoires*, 314: 12-51.

Simon, J.P. (1991b): 'L'Esprit des regles, réseaux et réglementatiion aux Etats-Unis: Câble, électricité, télécommunications', Paris: l'Harmattan.

13. SPAIN, Catalonia: Media and democratic participation in local communiction

Miquel de Moragas Spà and Maria Corominas

Autonomous University of Barcelona, Spain

Catalonia, although lacking the political status of a full-fledged state, has created its own model of communication. In this model community radio and television – and the language of Catalonia – play a major role. We intend to summarize the local communication experiences of Catalonia and analyse the Catalan situation within the Spanish State in this chapter.[31] The local communication experiences described here should be seen within the context of the communication problems of minority nations or cultures lacking the infrastructure of a state within which communication policies can be formulated. These experiences illustrate how theoretical conditioning and conceptualization of social phenomena can impose practical and political restrictions on efforts to create more democratic societies.

The social processes which support the regional or local media result from political resistance by a population defending its own area of communication as a *sine qua non* of political autonomy. However, there are contradictions in this position: creation of local media space is necessary for cultural dynamics and political participation, but existence of such space does not guarantee effective results. This is the case because there are two sources for the 'logic' of communication which may function in different ways: the logic of commerce and the logic of politics and culture.

Local media are essential for a democratic society in that they facilitate distribution

---

31 *The original study on which this chapter is based was carried out with financial assistance from the* Diputació de Barcelona (*Barcelona County Council*), *and is available in English* (Moragas Spà & Corominas, 1988). *The authors wish to thank Daniel E. Jones for his contribution on local and regional press and Montserrat Llinés for hers on local radio.*

of information necessary and useful for debate and action. It is true, as demonstrated by many local commercial radio and television stations, that this sector can broadcast news of world interest or productions of cross-national cultural value. But it is also true that the ambit of cross-national reception could never accept news of local interest. And yet this news is essential for effective political action.

The technological and economic factors which influence modern media are altering the 'ecology' of the communication network, favouring the development of some sectors to the disadvantage of others. The technological transformation is bringing about a double transformation of the mass media in a seemingly contradictory fashion. On the one hand, there is expansion towards cross-national media. Increasing satellite transmission of television is an example of this development. Regarding Europe, this could mean creation of a new cross-national European communication space and, as a consequence, cultural and political homogeneity.

On the other hand, there is a tendency towards micro-reception, which may be further encouraged by introduction of glass fibre cables. Such cables are able to increase signal capacity substantially, thus making it possible to establish forms of two-way communication. This tendency is strengthened by the growth of the communication flow between institutions – especially companies, banks and large administrative units – with consequences for the control and management of social and economic resources.

THE REGIONAL PRESS IN CATALONIA

Although this chapter is devoted to the development of audiovisual media, specifically radio and television, this development should be situated within the older print oriented tradition of local communication media in Catalonia. Many local print media were already established in Catalonia before the appearance of local radio and television stations. In fact, these publications were reborn during the last years of Francoism as a part of the social struggle to break Franco's monopoly on the supply and distribution of information. In the 1960s, local press organizations appeared and disappeared, were shut down and fined on innumerable occasions. In the period of transition towards democracy, the local press was instrumental in that process and in the defense of the cultural identity of Catalonia, demonstrated by the predominant use of the Catalan language.[32]

The local press, specializing in general news in much the same manner as local radio and television stations, is characterized by limited circulation with a large number of distribution points. Also, there is a large diversity of publishers of the local and regional press in Catalonia. More and more numerous, however, is the upsurge of anonymous publications brought out by small groups and organizations. These publications have a greater rate of growth and higher circulation figures than those of the local and regional press. All in all, the associative and cultural wealth of Catalonia underlies this journalistic phenomenon: publications generated by neighbourhood organizations, schools, cultural and recreative associations, youth groups, religious organizations and non-professional writer's collectives.

---

32 For *additional information on the regional press, see: Guillamet, 1983; Huertas, 1981, 1982; Diputació de Barcelona, 1984, 1985; Generalitat de Catalunya, 1981, 1982, 1987. See also contributions in* Primeres Jornades sobre Meso-comunicació a Catalunya *(Anonymous, 1985).*

It is also significant that although the 1980s can be characterized as a period of unrestrained growth in local audiovisual media, this has not resulted in the disappearance of the local press (Moragas Spà, 1983). Here, and with local communication in general, the role of editors and reporters and their collaboration in both management and production has been of decisive importance. In fact, this phenomenon could be called 'editors in search of readers' – creative groups of people with an active concern in social and cultural affairs who obtain satisfaction from helping disseminate information and ideas. This notion is to a degree demonstrated by the unusual ownership patterns sketched above. The very versatility of the printed press, and the equally important determination to survive, has made many initiatives and small publications possible – without public financing, guidance or ownership.

LOCAL RADIO STATIONS IN CATALONIA

'Free' radio

In 1978, three years after the death of Franco, the first 'free' radio stations appeared in Catalonia. Basically, these stations were inspired by similar urban experiences in Europe, particularly in Italy (Prado, 1983). They remained in operation, however, for only a short period of time. Establishing such a communication mode without the support of a social movement proved difficult; spontaneity and determination were insufficient ingredients for survival. The unexpected appearance of these 'free' radio stations and the struggle to maintain them, however, was in no way futile. These stations stimulated widespread debate on the freedom of expression and demonstrated the importance of establishing both political and communication projects.

In 1979, at the height of this debate, initiated by citizen groups which supported the 'free' radio stations, three municipal stations were launched. On the basis of these initial experiences municipal radio stations have continued to increase in number: 11 new stations in 1980, 22 in 1981 and 35 more in 1982. There were a total of 103 by the beginning of 1985, and 138 by 1988. These experiences with radio and the conditions which brought about this local communication activity laid the groundwork for the subsequent introduction of local television stations, described later in this chapter.

Municipal radio stations

Foreign observers of the media in Catalonia are often surprized by the presence of more than a hundred radio stations acknowledged by the local government, but which, after more than ten years of operation, still lack legal authorization to transmit. Since 1990 the Spanish Parliament has been debating legislation to regulate this kind of radio broadcasting. These stations can be considered 'tolerated' or 'alegal' stations.[33]

The municipal radio stations, of which there were 150 in operation at the beginning of the 1990s, are grouped together in the EMUC association (the coordinating organ-

---

33 It should be pointed out that political parties across the political spectrum, including those supporting the government, operate municipal radio stations in some city halls where they constitute a majority. This is a fact of obvious political significance.

ization of municipal stations in Catalonia,) (Berrio & Saperas, 1984; *Primeres Jornades,* 1985). This association is based on:

> the principles of freedom of expression and municipal autonomy recognized by the Spanish Constitution and the Statute of Autonomy of Catalonia, by which all villages have the right to create their own communication media, including MF transmitters (Founding Declaration, Rubí, (Barcelona) 1 October 1980; in EMUC, 1982: 44).

In effect, these stations form a united movement in Catalonia, built around the ideals of democratic participation, decentralization of the media and municipal autonomy. But this unity should not be confused with homogeneity.

A classification of municipal radio stations may be made on the basis of population figures for the different areas where programming can be received (Prado, 1984). These figures, shown in Table 1, indicate a concentration of stations in locations with fewer than 15,000 residents. Also reflected is an abundance of stations in the counties surrounding Barcelona. In this region municipal radio stations also operate in municipalities with more than 50,000 residents. In contrast, in the counties of the western part of Catalonia, particularly around Lleida, there are many stations with fewer than 15,000 residents.

Table 1. Number of municipal radio stations per population category

Population	Regions of Catalonia				
	Barcelona	Girona	Lleida	Tarragona	Total
0–999		3	0	1	9
1000–4999	32	12	3	6	53
5000–14,999	30	8	3	8	49
15,000–24,999	6	2	0	2	10
25,000–49,999	9	0	0	1	10
50,000–99,999	3	0	0	0	3
100,000 and over	3	0	0	1	4
Total	88	255	6	19	138

Source: Compiled by authors with 1986 population figures.

Accent is placed on the percentage of transmission centres rather than audience size in order to reflect the abundance of stations which have developed in small population centres. This suggests that the logic for large audiences applied to commercial radio stations is less relevant to municipal radio stations.

It is also important to point out that radio stations with the smallest potential audience are those which have the greatest capacity to fulfill the objectives of communicative participation and decentralization. This suggests that the amount of bureaucracy in the organizational structure of the stations and the tendency to apply standardized cultural criteria in programming is directly related to the size of a city's population.

Municipal radio stations operating in areas with more than 60,000 residents tend to compete with the commercial stations in the same locations. In order to compete they allow audience growth to condition station development, and their working procedures and programming structures are adapted to those of commercial radio stations.

This situation suggests that the main problem and principal challenge facing the decentralization of communication in democratic societies today is to be found in the communication policies emerging in large urban centres. Analysis of this phenomenon is outside the scope of this study; suffice it to say that policy is related to competition between public and private media, and the commercial logic employed by large communication media.

Table 2. Municipal stations classified by population

Population in municipalities	Number of stations	Percentage municipal stations of total
Fewer than 15,000	112	81.2%
15,000–50,000	19	13.8%
More than 50,000	7	5.1%

Source: Compiled by authors.

Station financing and advertising

The economic data available on station budgets and advertising income support the above observations (Berrio & Saperas, 1984). The data related to advertising income constitute a particularly conflictive and polemical issue. The main threat to the continued tolerance of the municipal radio stations is that they may compete with commercial stations which have a licence to broadcast. In the initial draft of the new law for municipal stations and in legal studies commissioned by non-commercial stations, the underlying position was that advertising should not be allowed given the cultural and political objectives of the stations. The continued existence of local radio stations is best served, it is argued, by a policy where only territorially based limits would be imposed on advertising. The first administrative proceedings against municipal radio stations, interestingly, involved transmission of non-local advertising.

Table 3. Advertising income of municipal radio stations

	Number of stations	Percentage
60 per cent of station budget covered by advertising	13	12.6%
20–50 per cent of station budget covered by advertising	7	6.7%
Less than 20 per cent of station budget covered by advertising	7	6.7%
Stations with insignificant advertising (10 per cent or less)	76	73.7%

Source: Berrio & Saperas, 1984.

Cultural and political value of local radio

The experience of local radio stations in Catalonia has shown that not all the offers – and much less the needs – of local communication coincide with the planning and logic of creating economic markets. There are several commercial stations existing in Catalonia, but it is uncertain whether these stations would be able to operate in a less economically secure market. The logic of the relationship between market and media, in other words, cannot explain the development of mezo communication processes, particularly when these processes do not involve a specialized (consumer) public but a neighbourhood based public.

The experience of local radio stations in Catalonia can be seen as a positive contribution to social experiments in the field of communication. Most of the new local radio stations which have proliferated across Europe in recent years were created as a response to market expectations. A few stations, including the Catalan municipal radio stations, were developed as part of a quest for other objectives and have consequently adhered to other criteria:

- Alternative political criteria, particularly evident in the 'free' radio station movement;

- Democratic and administrative criteria, present in stations under direct or majority control from the city government;

- Cultural-political criteria, involving stations started by citizen groups which, without rejecting support from the political and commercial institutions, aim for station independence.

Stations emphasizing this last criterion are considered cultural institutions themselves. It is not surprising that these stations are located in areas where interest in local affairs is already well-developed and where the capacity for social and cultural organization already existed prior to the appearance of mass media. The survival of stations with a cultural-political element basically depends on the non-professional orientation of their supporters – in exactly the same way as recreational, sports and local cultural activities survived in these areas some years ago.

LOCAL TELEVISION STATIONS IN CATALONIA

Development of local television stations in Catalonia is part of a dynamic process. From the very beginning, these stations presented themselves as being in the service of their respective communities. After some time, however, this approach changed. The organizational structure of stations evolved and became more ambitious as the economic base improved. These changes have had influence on programming objectives and – in the final analysis – the cultural role of the stations. It is important, therefore, to distinguish the early from subsequent development of these stations (Prado & Moragas, 1991).

Introduction of local television

In June 1980 a group of people from Cardedeu decided to broadcast a television programme produced by residents of the town. Since that initiative, around 100 other groups have launched local television stations.

These pioneering initiatives, interesting though they may be, should be placed in the perspective of present-day strategies of media multinationals to penetrate local television markets. One frequently applied strategy is to offer television productions to local stations at a low price. The cost for the multinationals is minimal considering the benefits: access to local markets as well as contribution to a positive company image.

Regarding this stage of development, Prado (1985) distinguishes three groups of local television initiatives in Catalonia. First, some initiatives are simply strategies for facilitating introduction of private television. On the whole, these initiatives make extensive use of external television productions.

The second group of initiatives provides programming to areas inadequately served by the conventional television stations. A consequence of these initiatives has been introduction of cable systems in some villages which would otherwise not have been considered by cable companies. Residents in these villages, with between 700 and 3,000 residents, are now able to receive the Spanish, Catalan and French channels as well as a special movie channel.

The third group of stations aims to provide the public with access to television technology. These stations allow residents to make direct use of the television facilities for the production and broadcast of their own programmes. Local action groups generally run these stations, but city councils are sometimes also involved.

As the number of local stations increased need was felt for a coordinating body. In July 1985 the *Federació de Televisions Locals de Catalunya* (FTLC) was founded to lobby for the legalization of local stations, stimulate sponsorship and to preserve the ideal of community service by local television stations. Federation members were encouraged to promote local television as a public service and to use the Catalan language in programming. Federation stations were to restrict their transmission range so as not to overlap with other stations, and they were also to operate as non-profit organizations. Finally, programmes were to be locally produced and oriented.

Number of stations

It is difficult to say exactly how many local television stations exist in Catalonia. Although it may seem surprising and contrary to the very nature of the medium, the stations operate almost clandestinely. They broadcast openly, but avoid publicity and generally refuse to cooperate with journalists interested in reporting on their activities. The motive for this position is twofold: to avoid exposing contradictions in the government's tolerance of the stations, and to avoid being used by other interests for propaganda purposes.

Some station initiatives were abandonded in the design stage and others have only been able to broadcast sporadically. Inasmuch as the stations are not licenced, no official record is available as to their number. The Federation (FTLC) estimates, however, that some 100 stations are presently operational. These stations may be categorized into three types.

First, there are stations – 46 as of 1991 – belonging to the FTLC. These stations may be considered locally oriented, although this aspect is less prominent in stations active in large cities. Second, there are commercial stations which have a more limited programming policy. At present only two stations of this type are operational in Catalonia. The third and final station type is that which broadcasts more or less regularly, but which is not coordinated by the Federation (FTIC) because these stations are located either in towns far from Barcelona or in small villages.

Transmission frequency

Some stations broadcast only sporadically, often in conjunction with local festivals. About a quarter of the stations operate in this manner. Other stations transmit on a more regular basis, from monthly to daily transmission schedules. Whereas broadcasts tended to be sporadic in previous years, the current tendency is towards more frequent programming and, in major cities (more than 50,000 residents), daily programming.

Promotion

Local television stations in Catalonia can be distinguished by the type of organization which promotes them. The first local stations were initiated by various cultural organizations which have since then become involved in the promotion of local media generally. Local councils have also become involved, either officially through financial subsidies or more indirectly through provision of studio space, purchase of productions and occassional funding.

A second group of stations have been directly promoted by local government councils. In these cases, the stations generally have one or two professionals in service and tend to have better quality material at their disposal. These stations have broadcasted on a regular schedule since inception. The councils provide the bulk of financial support although other income, such as grants and sale of productions, is also acquired.

The third group of stations is commercial in nature and is sponsored by private individuals or companies. These stations are mainly located in urban centres with 50,000 or more residents. Station income is based entirely on advertising revenue and the sale of television productions. These stations are generally run by a professional staff, and productions are of correspondingly high quality.

Programming

Stations can also be differentiated by their programming. For local television stations with irregular transmissions, the very notion of programming seems inappropriate. Still, given this limitation, these stations can be seen as instruments of occasional communication.

In cases where stations have regular programming, there is a marked difference between the number of local productions transmitted and other types of productions. The latter include illegal reproduction of films, sports programming via satellite and productions from local video clubs. This programming format is particularly present in the case of commercial television stations. With other stations local productions are more commonplace and account for 60 per cent or more of the total programming time. Some local stations also rebroadcast television programmes received by satellite.

All television stations, even the commercial stations, devote much attention to topics of local interest. A typical broadcast includes a weekly news programme consisting of items directed at the local community. One of the basic attractions of local television is the fact that people can recognize and identify what they see. The kind of programme mentioned enables them to do this. Very often, programmes include interviews with people closely linked to life in the town or city and, where relevant, sports programmes are usually included.

MEDIA AND LOCAL TELEVISION IN CATALONIA

The Catalan experience is distinct from media practice elsewhere in Spain where local television and radio initiatives are rapidly and repeatedly shut down, in all likelihood to avoid repetition of the proliferation and popularity of such stations as has taken place in Catalonia.

Explanation of this difference in tolerance can be found in Catalan culture and the exceptional strength of the region's civil organizations. Within this framework three factors account for the multitude of local audiovisual experiences:

1 Democratic conditions for freedom of expression. After the death of Franco, with the recuperation of democratic liberties, people wanted to put their freedom of speech and communication into practice.

2 Participation of young people, orientated towards audiovisual media. Young people have traditionally been involved in cultural activities of a public nature. Traditionally they found an outlet in theatre groups and folklore activities, but now they have found a new form of expression in audiovisual creativity. Participation of groups of young people, as amateur contributors to radio and television productions, is a basic aspect of the local communication.

3 Contribution from cultural and electronic hobbyists. The development of so many radio and television transmitters would have been impossible without the presence of so-called 'cultural movers' and electronic hobbyists. Cultural movers are local personalities capable of projecting their utopian vision onto local cultural events. Radio and television provides them with the opportunity of challenging dominant political thinking and of encouraging young people to participate in their media projects. The technical aspects of these projects are attended to by electronic hobbyists. In Catalonia these persons are called 'sparks', and are able to solve a wide variety of electrical problems. Previously these technicians operated the lighting at popular theatres; now they assemble television transmitters and studios.

Political tolerance versus legal status

Until now, local television stations have been able to operate only because of a degree of political 'tolerance'; the stations have no legal status. Still, it is more difficult for local television to survive than for local radio stations because television in Spain is seen and used as a medium for political control. Another aspect making survival difficult is that the movement of community television stations is composed of different kinds of organizations: those backed by local councils, by public institutions, citizen groups and by private companies.

In order to understand the tolerance of some 100 local television stations in Catalonia several reasons and motives should be noted. Reference has already been made to the protagonism of economic, technological and political sectors interested in breaking the television monopoly in Spain and the support these sectors have given to local stations. In addition, popular initiatives have played a role. In Catalonia, these initiatives have been so active that considerable political pressure would be required to undermine them at this point in time.

The continued tolerance of local television stations is also a matter of political expediency: there are no political parties in Catalonia today which do not have 'illegal' stations in one or more city halls. In this respect, audiovisual information has become a necessity for all political groups within the local sphere.

CONCLUSIONS

For many years Catalonia has occupied a unique position within the country. Development of the Catalonian experiment with community radio and television has generated a degree of tolerance on the part of other Catalonian institutions, in contrast to the repression of similar community experiments held in other parts of Spain. Catalonia, in fact, has served as the nucleus for community radio and television experiments, particularly for initiatives operating as a form of public service. Elsewhere in Spain private or commercial objectives tend to dominate stations.

Future development of local radio and television is primarily in the hands of the Spanish Parliament. Presently, radio and television are regarded as essential public services and a responsibility of the Spanish state. Examples of legislative action in this regard are the Radio and Television Statute of 1980 and the Telecommunication Planning Act of 1987.

Formal recognition and regulation of municipal radio stations has come closer with legislation passed by the Spanish Parliament in April 1991. A subsequent step, to be performed in 1992 by the Catalonian Generalitat involves concession of transmission frequencies.[34]

The future of local television remains uncertain. It does not appear that the introduction in 1989–1990 of three commercial television channels has had any significant influence on local television. Present legislation makes local stations illegal, but this is not considered a real obstacle to their operation.

The evolution of community experiments (particularly television) has carried a great diversification. In cities with more than 50,000 residents there has been increasing professionalization which had an impact on the frequency of broadcasts, dependance on employed staff rather than volunteers, and the general quality of programming. This trend towards professionalization has also meant a loss of community identity among some stations.

Additional broadcast hours are often filled with satellite delivered programming. And, the use of paid personnel requires that stations secure regular sources of income, which basically means greater dependence on advertising. Limits on the amount of

---

34 *In Spain the situation is somewhat different from other European countries regarding assignment of frequencies. The power to assign frequencies, technically speaking, belongs to the central government, but the power to concede them belongs in some cases, including Catalonia, to the respective autonomous governments.*

advertising have been set by the Federation, but these guidelines are frequently ignored by stations.

Finally, local stations have shown little interest in new communication technologies such as videotex and teletext. This can in part be explained by the limited penetration of these communication forms in the country. The same can be said regarding cable television, for which future prospects are limited. In Catalonia cable television is seldom installed, and then only for the conventional reasons of improving over-the-air signal reception and removal of roof antennas. Local radio and television, in other words, will make little use of these technologies in the near future. They will, however, remain important communication media in Catalonia and serve as an example to the rest of the country as to how these media can be organized and operated.

APPENDIX: BACKGROUND INFORMATION ON CATALONIA

Catalonia is a historic region within the Spanish state. Encompassing an area of 32,000 square kilometres, Catalonia has a population of more than 6,000,000, about 16 per cent of the total population of Spain. Barcelona, capital of the region, has a population of aproximately 3,000,000.

Within the legal framework of the 1978 Spanish Constitution, Catalonia has been granted autonomous status (Statute of Autonomy, 1979) which recognizes part of Catalonia's historic position and establishes the Catalan Government (*Generalitat*) and Parliament with divisions for formulation of communication and cultural policy.

The official language is Catalan, a romance language common to several regions including France (the Balearic Islands, Valencia, Andorra, Rossello) as well as to Catalonia. The Catalan language is undergoing linguistic normalization and its use in public and the mass media is gradually increasing. It is far from having achieved the majority status which Spanish still commands in Catalonia.

Newspapers have a circulation of approximately 10 copies for every 100 inhabitants. Only two newspapers publish more than 150,000 copies: *La Vanguardia* and *El Periódico*. At present, out of the six daily newspapers issued in Barcelona, only two are published in Catalan: *Avui* and *Diari de Barcelona*. In addition, there are five other essentially local daily newspapers published in Catalan: *Diari de Girona, Diari de Lleida, El Punt, Nou Diari* and *Regió 7*. Since 1983 Catalonia has had its own radio and television public broadcasting company (CCRTV), which now has two television channels: TV3 and Canal 33, and three radio networks (*Catalunya Ràdio, Ràdio Associació de Catalunya* and *Catalunya Música*). There is also a government station, *Ràdio 4*, which broadcasts exclusively in Catalan.

The nationwide based communication media is amply represented in Catalonia, both through the public broadcasting companies – Channels 1 and 2 of Spanish Television, and Spanish National Radio – as well as through important private press (PRISA), radio (*Ser, Cope, Antena 3*) and television groups (*Antena 3-TV, Tele 5* and *Canal +*) (see further Corbella, 1988; Moragas Spà *et al.*, 1986).

References

Anonymous (1985): *Primeres Jornades sobre mesocomunicació a Catalunya*, Barcelona: Autonomous University of Barcelona.

Berrio, J. and E. Saperas (1984): 'Una experiencia de comunicación local. Las radios municipales en Catalunya', in M. de Moragas Spà (ed.) *La comunicació de masses a Catalunya*, Barcelona: Autonomous University of Barcelona.

Corbella, J. (1988): *La comunicació social a Catalunya*, Barcelona: Centre d'Investigació de la Comunicació, Catalan Autonomous Government.

Diputació de Barcelona (1984): 'La premsa comarcal. Cens', *Arrel* 8: 37-44.

Diputació de Barcelona (1985/86): *Llibre del cens de la premsa local i comarcal*, Barcelona: County Council.

EMUC (1982): 'Bases de funcionament i autoregulació de les emissores municipals de Catalunya', *Arrels* 3: 44-48.

Generalitat de Catalunya (1981/82): *Guia de la premsa local i comarcal*, Barcelona: Department of Culture, Catalan Autonomous Government.

Generalitat de Catalunya (1987): *Anuari de la premsa comarcal a Catalunya*, Barcelona: Department of Culture, Catalan Autonomous Government.

Guillamet, J. (1983): *La premsa comarcal. Un model català de periodisme popular*, Barcelona: Department of Culture, Catalan Autonomous Government.

Huertas Claveria, J.M. (1981): 'La premsa comarcal: 44,378 exemplars/dia', *Arrel* 1: 22-31.

Huertas Claveria, J.M. (1982): 'Cens de premsa local i comarcal', *Analisi* 6: 79-90.

Moragas Spà, M. de (1983): 'Mass communication and political change in Spain', in E. Wartella and D.C. Whitney (eds) *Mass communication review yearbook*, London: Sage.

Moragas Spà, M. de and M.C. Piulats (1988): *Local Communication in Catalonia (1975 – 1988); Media spaces and democratic participation*, Barcelona: County Council.

Moragas Spà, M. de, E. Prado and C. de Mateo (1986): *Electronic mass media in Spain*, Barcelona: Autonomous University of Barcelona.

Prado, E. (1983): *Las radios libres. Teoría y pràctica de un movimiento alternativo*, Barcelona: Editorial Mitre.

Prado, E. (1984): 'Radios municipales, una experiencia de comunicación popular', *Alfoz* 11: 43-48.

Prado, E. (1985): 'Television comunitaria en Catalunya', *Telos* 2: 53-58.

Prado, E. and M. de Moragas (1991): *Televisiones locales: Tipología y aportaciones de la experiencia catalana*, Barcelona: Col.legi de Periodistes de Catalunya.

14. YUGOSLAVIA until 1990: Liberalization, integration and local radio

Slavko Splichal

University of Ljubljana, Yugoslavia

To appreciate the development of mass and public communication in Yugoslavian society during the post-war period requires familiarity with changes in the social, economic and political relations in the country – all essential ingredients in the theory and practice of self-management. Since communication is a generic ability and need of humans, the practice of self-management can be considered the process for liberating communication activities from the privileges or 'freedoms' of the few and making such freedoms available to all citizens. Freedom of communication is clearly related to the development of human powers, culturally and economically, and the democratization of the political system.

The history of local radio in Yugoslavia exemplifies the importance of this broader context. Cultural diversity within Yugoslavia and changes in the country's political and economic systems have been major factors in the development of local radio.

Generally speaking, technological and social changes in communication seem to contradict the conventional notion of mass communication as a form of one-way, indirect communication in which the production process is controlled by complex organizations with extensive divisions of labour where the audience is seen as a 'mass' (e.g. Wright, 1966: 15, 49-50). In the late 1960s, the revolutionary idea of a transformation of mass communication into public communication was – at least partially – put into practice. The notion of public communication presupposes abolition of inequalities in social status and wealth, centralized and bureaucratic management systems, and political restrictions of rights and freedoms. The notion also implies development of new communication technologies, diffusion of knowledge and development of critical awareness. Mills (1959: 303-304) suggests that public communication entails four points:

(1) Virtually as many people express opinions as receive them;

(2) Public communications are so organized that there is a chance to immediately and effectively answer back any opinion expressed in public.
Opinion formed by such discussion;
(3) readily finds an outlet in effective action, even against – if necessary –
the prevailing system of authority; and
(4) authoritative institutions do not penetrate the public, which is thus more
or less autonomous in its operation.

Strictly speaking, the question remains, however, whether such a conception of public
communications is at all feasible, since there is no historical evidence of the existence
of public communication provided via the press or broadcasting. Nevertheless, the
idea of public communication is very much alive, particularly in local media experiments around Europe. In this regard, developments in Yugoslavia are parallel to those
found elsewhere.

The growth of local radio seems to be in line with the opposing societal tendencies
toward globalization (interconnection and internationalization through, for example,
satellite broadcasting) and toward individualization (increasing autonomy of individuals and groups through, for example, interactive media). These tendencies seem
to reinforce each other and weaken intermediary structures such as nationally
oriented media. On the one hand, new communication technologies extend the space
of individuals' interactions; on the other hand, they also provide new opportunities
for individualization and thus confront established institutions at the level of local
communities.

It is here that the essential difference between local and community radio becomes
visible. Local radio and local media denote, as opposed to mass oriented radio, a
relatively closed territorial unit in which geographical distribution and size of the
audience are the main differences – without any qualitative implications for the
nature of communication. Community radio, however, can be defined in qualitative
terms as a transformation from hierarchically organized, predominantly one-way
mass communication towards collaborative, not necessarily territorially defined (e.g.
communities of interest) public communication. In this sense, the development of
radio in Yugoslavia represents the more traditional, quantitative tendencies of growth
rather than a process of qualitative transformation into a new form of communication.
This may also be considered one of the reasons that radio research – based mainly on
social surveys – has not concentrated on critical issues of development, but rather on
the size and characteristics of the audience.

This chapter mainly discusses the development of local radio in Yugoslavia in the
period from the end of World War II until the political and economic upheaval which
began in 1990. Since the spring of 1990 major transformations have taken place in
what was once known as Yugoslavia. It is impossible, in the limited constraints of this
chapter, to describe these changes and their influence on local radio. The chapter
should be seen, in fact, as an historical sketch of local radio in Yugoslavia, neither of
which is any longer present in the same form.

NATIONAL CONTEXT

Yugoslavian society is composed of a wide variety of heritages, cultures, nationalities,
languages and religions. The federal state consists of six republics (Bosnia & Herzego-

vina, Croatia, Macedonia, Montenegro, Serbia, and Slovenia) and two autonomous provinces within Serbia (Kosovo and Voivodina). About 80 per cent of the total Yugoslavian population of 24 million stems from the ethnic groups deminant in the six republics (the largest groups being the Serbs and Croats); the remainder of the population is composed of various minorities and ethnic groups, the largest being of Albanian descent. Relations between these groups are complicated by the fact that, on the average, a quarter of the population resides outside the republics of which they are citizens. In addition, ten languages are spoken around the country, Serbo-Croatian, Slovenian, Macedonian and Albanian being the main ones. Two alphabets, Cyrillic and Latin, and three main religions – Serbian Orthodox, Roman Catholic and Moslem – introduce additional dimensions of cultural and political diversity.

Perhaps of greatest importance, however, are the differences in the economic structures of the republics. In Slovenia, the most economically developed republic in Yugoslavia, the labour force comprises about half of the population, while in Kosovo it constitutes less than a quarter. Such contrast is also found in the degree of urbanization, population density, birth rate and levels of literacy in the republics.

As for the political system, Yugoslavia was, since World War II, a federal state consisting of six republics and two autonomous provinces. Its social and historical base was normatively defined by two primary factors: (1) the autonomy, national identity and independence of the republics, and (2) the development of self-management in both the areas of labour and social institutions. Political reality, however, does not always reflect these principles.

Departure from the model of state socialism was formalised in 1953 under the Constitutional Law. This document established economic democracy as a cornerstone of the political system. From that point on, workers had the right to manage enterprises, and worker self-management was created. On the basis of the Constitutional Law, a system of institutions began to develop alongside state authorities (assemblies, people's committees and the governmental and legal units of these entities).

With the trend toward decentralization and democratization, authority was partially transferred from central state organs to specific sectors of society: cultural, educational, social, health and scientific institutions as well as organizations involved in public communication. The reduction of state and party monopoly allowed the media to become more economically independent, more differentiated in terms of content and more able to satisfy the communication needs and interests of citizens. However, administrative intervention in all of these areas, including communications, still prevails even though self-management was introduced nearly 40 years ago.

Democratic initiatives in the past two years have not essentially changed this practice. The new power actors – governments and political parties – still tend to reproduce the old form of hegemony based on the new, but still exclusive political and nationalistic ideology. They do not readily admit adversary power actors, such as the media, and other sectors of society into decision making processes. New political actors are interested in how to come into power rather than how to bring about structural change. As in previous periods, power has become a fetish of those who possess it. New governments are not able – or willing – to offer substantial participation in the new system. Again, instead of emancipation of the media, we are facing a new hyper-politicization; instead of depoliticization of the polity, we are facing a new, anti-communist dogmatism as the foundation of change in the media and in other spheres. The spirit of democracy is subverted by the fact that the media lack autonomy and are generally subservient to either the new (anti-communist) or the old (pro-communist) parties. One of the basic pre-conditions of democracy, the protection of less powerful groups from those with power, is far from fulfilled.

The expansion of the state is maintaining traditional domination of the state over society, although the forms of authoritative penetration have changed mainly because of the capitalistic orientation of present-day politics. The marketplace is becoming a common denominator of pluralism and democratic restructuring. As a consequence of restructuring centred on state and market economy principles, a kind of paternal media system is emerging. This media system is characterized by a tendency towards progressive privatization and commercialization (particularly the press) on the one hand, and by maximization of state power (particularly televison) on the other hand.

COMMUNICATION SYSTEM 1960–1990

After World War II and the liberation of Yugoslavia, one of the first laws enacted by the Federal Assembly was related to the press. Since that moment the process of democratization of society has been linked to freedom of communication. The principles of federalism and pluralism of interests are gradually materialising in a more decentralized mass media system. Publishing and broadcasting companies are managed by employees, particularly through workers' councils, and are controlled by a variety of legal regulations and social institutions, such as 'social organs of management' in communication companies and 'media councils'.

Nevertheless, new forms of media management, particularly those introduced after passage of constitutional amendments in 1971, do not prevent conflicts with 'old' forms of political and bureaucratic pressure, arising from contradictory developments in the social system. In this context, the 1960 Constitution introduced, probably for the first time in history, a new fundamental human right – the right to publish opinions. This right, together with the right to influence and participate in the management of communication companies, is the essential difference between self-management and other forms of management in communication systems. Although self-management in the area of communication has remained largely unexplored in the country, the challenge is clear and promising.

After the constitutional amendments inacted in 1971 and 1974, mass communication in Yugoslavia was reorganized to reflect the principles of self-management. Thus, social ownership of the media came to be the *conditio sine qua non* for the right to communicate. Consequently, the economic subordination of (mass) communication activities to the state (financing) and the market (commodity production) was to be replaced by common concerns and financed by a free exchange of labour amoung workers within media organizations and labourers in other spheres. Moreover, social influence was not to be defined as merely political influence; the socialization process of communication activities stands or falls with the universal democratization of social relations. By guaranteeing individual rights and freedoms, society as a whole becomes responsible for establishing facilities and providing resources for institutions able to secure these rights. Within this context, the question of access to the media is of prime importance.

Socialization may be considered a process of making individuals 'fit' in society. It refers to what, why, and how people learn to participate as more or less effective members of groups in society. Socialization studies (e.g. Lowery & DeFleur, 1983) have traditionally focused primarily on changes in the behavior of the learner, for example, the recipient in the communication process rather than the teacher or sender in that process. Accordingly, traditional communication theories were more concerned with audience behavior as (re)produced by the media than with the social nature of the media themselves, that is, in asking 'what?' rather than 'why?' regarding the communication process.

To understand the specific social role of the media, their particular place among agencies of socialization, and the actual possibilities of democratization of mass communication, the question should be rephrased: who makes the media 'fit' for what society, and how? Instead of increasing the ability of those who control the media to manipulate the audience, communication research should develop the understanding of and critical consciousness about economic, political, and social conditions of the development of the media.

In his discussion of controversies regarding development of the mass media and democratic communication, Williams (1976: 134) states that:

> There are two related considerations: the right to transmit and the right to receive....On the right to transmit, the basic principle of democracy is that since all are full members of the society, all have the right to speak as they wish or find.

This was precisely the idea behind the introduction of the federal Press Law in 1960. In addition to the traditional right of reply, this law emphasized the right of "Yugoslavian citizens, regardless of nationality, race, language or religion, to express and publish their opinions in the communication media" (art. 2 of Press Law). With the creation in 1963 of a Federal Constitution applicable to all of the republics, this right was elevated to constitutional status. However, the 1960 Press Law, the 1963 Federal Constitution (or the revised Constitution of 1974) and subsequent press laws (the latest drafted in 1985) have failed to specify precisely how this revolutionary right should be implemented.

One of the essential components of the process of democratization is the development of conditions for active participation of citizens. This involves the direct and indirect incorporation of citizens into the production and exchange of messages as well as into the management and control of communication processes in which individuals can develop their interests and meet their needs in collaboration with fellow citizens. Democratization increases not only the number of active participants in the communication process, but also the social basis and structure of communication through incorporation of formerly excluded social categories or groups – young people; women; socially, economically or politically deprived groups; and ethnic, linguistic and religious minorities. It also involves redistribution of (communication) power. As Young (1982: 2) notes in another context:

> In general, the major sources of distorted communications include class privilege, gender preference, racial discrimination, age grade exclusion,

and a division of labour which awards authority to a relatively few and mandates compliance to a large majority.

Among efforts to democratise communication, many different strategies have been developed, but with limited impact on the total sphere of communication (MacBride, 1980: 197). This is also the case in Yugoslavia, where ideas of a self-management type of socialist democracy in the area of mass communication have made little progress, due to discrepancies between revolutionary ideas on one hand, and restricted practices on the other.

Legal provisions concerning freedom of communication are unable to eliminate the practical restrictions on this freedom resulting from economic difficulties, political interests and pressures, fragmented consciousness, limited education and cultural obstacles. Nevertheless, the normative aspects of media socialization remain important. In Yugoslavia public communication is in a sense 'operationalised' in statutory regulations regarding four basic rights and freedom:

1. The right to publish opinions in the mass media, as an extension of the traditional freedoms of thought and expression, complementary to the right to receive information;

2. The right to participate in the management of the mass media and communication organizations;

3. The right of free association and mutual cooperation in order to realize individual and collective needs; and

4. Equality of citizens regarding rights and duties independent of social status.

The only way of achieving these rights and freedoms is to create self-managed media and communication organizations based on a public service model which places media in the service and under the control of citizens, inasmuch as "private ownership and/or party control of the media interferes with democratically organized communication" (Young, 1982: 11). The basic principle should be the abolition of all kinds of direct and indirect censorship, reflecting majority or minority interests.

While it is rather easy to identify and protest against these forms of censorship, it is far more difficult to counteract them. For instance, dominant groups legitimise their interests in the form of general or common interests, and oppositional interests and opinions are defined as abuses of the general and collective freedom, or as a "failure to respect higher values whose protection is largely guaranteed by the Constitution itself" (Krippas, 1982: 9). Such domination often appears in the Yugoslavian communication system in spite of decentralization of the system or the economical, cultural and ideological differences between federal units.

DEVELOPMENT AND EARLY DECENTRALIZATION OF RADIO

Before World War II there were only four radio stations in Yugoslavia providing a total of 40 hours of programming per day. By 1955 the amount of programming had increased to 193 hours daily, and by 1983 it has risen to more than 1,000 hours daily and was transmitted by 200 radio stations. In terms of both programme production and listener consumption, radio has certainly become the most developed and widespread medium in the country.

In 1983, the programming provided by the eight central radio stations (located in Belgrade, Ljubljana, Novi Sad, Prishtin, Sarajevo, Skopje, Titograd, and Zagreb) amounted to a third of the total programming time. The remaining two-thirds is distributed among 191 regional and local radio stations and *Radio Yugoslavia*. The ratio between talk and music programmes has not changed considerably with time: the amount of music programming has remained close to 63 per cent in the period between 1955 and 1983. This percentage is almost identical for both local and national programming. However, the eight central radio stations have specialised programmes. The first programme is conceived as a general, omnibus programme intended to satisfy the 'general needs' of mass audiences. These broadcasts technically cover the entire territory of a republic or province through AM and FM transmissions, while others, particularly third programmes, are mainly transmitted on FM channels. Second programmes are primarily devoted to light music stereo broadcasts, short news and call-in programmes. Additionally, third and fourth programmes of national radio stations started in the 1970s for only a few hours per day are directed at narrower, specific target groups (e.g. radio journals, science and culture and classical music).

As early as the 1960s, the development of radio broadcasting in Yugoslavia has been characterised not only by a more differentiated programme supply from central radio stations, but also by the development of regional and local radio stations. The process has spread to all regions of the country with the exception of Montenegro and Kosovo. Nowadays, the total number of radio broadcasts exceeds the number of television broadcasts in Yugoslavia by a factor of four. Since 1960, the number of radio stations has increased ten fold and the amount of radio programmes by three, a development particularly due to the establishment of local radio stations. Survey findings from the early 1960s (Bacevic *et al.*, 1965) suggest that over 90 per cent of the adult Yugoslavian population listens to radio, and a third attends to local radio stations.

Actually, the beginnings of local radio in Yugoslavia date back to the first days of 1941 when illegal stations of the resistance movement were set up in occupied cities and, later during the War, in liberated territories. During the final days of the conflict, numerous local radio stations began broadcasting in addition to the national stations located in the republic capitals. Some of these local stations stopped operation by the end of the 1940s due to the development of national radio stations, but they were reactivated during the 1960s when local radio expanded.

The first period of the development of local radio, between the 1940s and 1960s, occurred rather spontaneously. In Serbia, Voivodina and Croatia, close to 400 local pirate stations went on the air with transmission power ranging between 10 and 100 watts. These stations often caused signal interference with the legal local and national radio stations.

The financing of the legal local radio stations during this period was unclear. A portion of the funding was provided by the station founders, but the largest segment came from advertisements and 'music by request' programmes which frequently became the major form of local programming.

The second phase of the development of local radio started at the end of the 1960s. In 1968 alone, 33 new local stations were founded. This development reflected a break with political and administrative centralism, and introduced a process of searching for new ways to express differences, uniqueness and individuality. These new trends were based on the need for – even necessity of – decentralization in order to develop workers' self-management. According to the 1963 Constitution, the commune became the basic self-managed local community of citizens aimed at organising its own activities and satisfying collective needs. The Constitution also implied that being informed about the diversity of issues concerning everyday life, work and (local) management cannot be achieved through a centralized, uniform communication system. Consequently, local radio developed as a response to new political ideas and needs of citizens.

The development of local radio was not only the result of political democratization. It was also a reaction to the rise of television which has remained extremely centralized since the late 1950s. For radio, the introduction of television was a challenge which required reassessment of existing plans of development and initiated a search for comparative advantages. In the end, local radio actually received priority in a new developmental strategy designed to transform the centralized communication process.

INSTITUTIONALIZATION OF LOCAL RADIO

During the 1960s and early 1970s local radio stations were organized in autonomous associations in all the republics with the exception of Montenegro and Kosovo. Technological and financial cooperation between local and national radio stations ended a period of unorganized development of local radio. Because many local stations operated with antiquated and nonprofessional equipment and insufficient personnel, the programmes were often of poor quality. Cooperation among local stations and with national broadcasting companies raised the technical and programming standards. Yet, at the same time, it also weakened the authentic – 'alternative' or critical – contributions of the local stations.

In accordance with laws of the republic and the provinces, national broadcasting companies assumed responsibility for the construction and maintenance of distribution networks and for coordinating the technical development of all local and regional stations. Moreover, local transmitting capability was included in the uniform transmission procedures of the national stations, and several local radio stations began broadcasting programmes on national stations when local programmes were not available.

Actually, many local radio stations became part of the integrated national networks. Although not owned by or directly subordinated to national radio stations, these local radio stations transmited more programmes produced by national radio stations than by themselves. However, local radio stations simultaneously began to participate as 'collective local correspondents' in the production of national – mainly news – programmes with national radio stations.

Curiously, this cooperation does not result in a significant source of income for the local radio stations. The majority of local stations have never benefited from licence fees collected by republic and provincial broadcasting organizations, but have remained financially independent by relying on local advertisements and political authorities. The only exceptions have been local radio stations serving ethnic minorities, and regional stations which became an integral part of a national broadcasting organization. But irrespective of the type of cooperation with central radio stations, local stations have remained independent from them in terms of determination of the nature and amount of programmes transmitted. It is much more questionable whether local radio stations have achieved the same level of autonomy from commercial and political interests in their own local environment.

Paradoxically, the period of expansion of local radio ends in the mid-1970s when the idea of local radio was just emerging in Western Europe. At this time, television became generally accessible, and it was established as a national cultural institution with comprehensive programme offerings in the republic as well as the provinces. On the other hand, tendencies towards political and economic differentiation (with the wave of nationalism erupting in the early 1970s) have been replaced by ideas of centralization and integration. Local radio was to become 'mass' radio, a one-way communication medium and a 'commercial agent' instead of becoming public radio and a communication link among members within a particular social environment.

However, the relatively small number of listeners prevented local radio stations from becoming subordinated to commercial influences. Local advertising still has, if we paraphrase Habermas (1962: 14), a "feudal nature"; agents of economic activity do not perform local advertising to promote listeners' consumption, but rather to present to the audience their social status, their power, their 'common interest' in the local community and thereby the dependence of the local community and the radio on their 'charity'.

The contemporary distribution of local radio systems by republics and regions is uneven inasmuch as development of local radio not only depends on the general level of (economic) development, but also on administrative regulations (e.g. the number and size of communes). Currently, a local radio station in Yugoslavia has a potential of between 20,000 and 100,000 listeners, and transmits between one and four hours of local programmes per day. In 1984, there were 181 full-time employees worked for 18 local radio stations in Slovenia, and 193 for 18 local radio stations in Voivodina. However, the number of full-time employees varied considerably among local radio stations. Two local radio stations in Slovenia are operated entirely by amateurs. The majority of stations are staffed with fewer than 10 employees, but there are also stations in large towns (industrial or regional centers) with more than 20 employees. Curiously, smaller local stations transmit more programmes than larger stations relative to the number of employees. However, larger local radio stations are often associated with local weekly newspapers, and journalists work for both local radio and newspapers.

Journalists and newscasters generally comprise more than a third of all employees in local radio stations, the remainder being administrative and technical staff, editors and music programme presentators. In contrast to regional and central radio stations, and to the press, most journalists and other personnel in local radio stations do not have university degrees. Journalism and social sciences graduates prefer to work for national (metropolitan) media – a situation also found in other countries. A recent international comparative study (Sparks & Splichal, 1988: 18) reported that 59 per cent of the interviewed students in 22 countries (including Yugoslavia) preferred to find work with the higher status national media as opposed to less than 10 per cent who wanted to work for local media and some 13 per cent for regional media. Moreover, radio was not ranked among the preferred media; daily newspapers, television, and magazines were considered more desirable career paths than radio, news agencies and house organs.

In contrast, the professional criteria established by local media are lower and less demanding than those of major media. Such an unfavourable situation can be partially explained by the fact that editorial and managerial staff of local radio stations were formally recruited from local political structures without consideration of professional (journalistic) education; to preserve their own positions, these staff members tended to keep criteria for employment as low as possible. Unstable financial resources and personnel with limited education, however, effect the quality of local radio programming which tends to be dominated by music, advertisements, local news and entertainment.

For the most part, local radio stations did not arise as a result of functional but rather regional differentiation – with the exception of student and minority radio programmes. Local radio mainly directs attention to the closest geographical environment, thus reducing the dissonance between distribution of attention to national and international events which are prominent on central radio stations, and the interest most listeners have for local events.

A functionally specific (differentiated) programme is characteristic only for youth or student stations, such as those located in Ljubljana, Zagreb, and Belgrade. They emerged when young people ceased existing primarily as the 'future of society', and came to be considered an essential group in present-day society with a specific consciousness about the world and themselves. This rupture with the post-war conditions of 'waiting for the inheritance' of the older generation was especially expressed in the requirement for equal treatment of interests and opinions of the youth on key social issues. Subsequently, the 'new' youth press and radio have helped materialise the concept of democratic pluralism of interests and the right to communicate, as well as new methods and forms of journalism and radio programming.

While the development of the student radio stations widens the media horizon and contributes to the pluralism of ideas and interests, local radio stations generally operate within the traditional framework of one-way mass communication and tend to imitate the central radio stations. In addition, a close connection between local radio stations and local economic 'giants' (via advertising) as well as local authorities (via subsidies) represents a permanent danger to the democratic potential of the local media.

LOCAL RADIO AND LINGUISTIC PLURALISM

The development of local radio in Yugoslavia was particularly important from the point of view of a constitutional responsibility for the protection and universal development of national minorities. These minorities constitute sizeable portions of the population in Voivodina, Slovenia and Croatia. The Constitution guarantees education in the regional languages, integral development of national cultures and, in particular, the right to regionally autonomous media. Several media are directed at minority groups in the country: the newspapers *Magyar Szo* for the Hungarian and *La Voce del Popolo* for the Italian residents, other press (6 per cent of all Yugoslavian newspapers and 9 per cent of all periodicals), and the television programmes broadcast in Italian (TV Koper/capodistria), Hungarian, Rumanian, Slovak and Ruthenian (TV Novi Sad). In addition to these media, the development of local and regional radio has been of invaluable importance for national minorities. These radio stations enjoy direct financial assistance through state subsidies (budget of republics), and through allocation of licence fees.

Linguistic differentiation and multilingualism are the most significant characteristics of local radio in Voivodina, whose two million inhabitants represent over ten ethnic groups. Six language communities have very large memberships: Serbo-Croatian (91,262), Hungarian (385,356), Slovak (69,549), Rumanian (47,289), Ruthenian (19,305) and Macedonian (18,900). Of the 20 local radio stations in Voivodina, only three offer programmes in but one language (Serbo-Croatian). The provincial radio station *Radio Novi Sad* broadcasts in five languages and most local stations broadcast in three. A large proportion of the population is multilingual and attends to radio programmes in more than one language (Poppovic, 1983). Although language is the most apparent difference among the nations and nationalities, it becomes at the same time the essential foundation for collective development; that is, for an active process of creating and expanding knowledge, culture and mutual adaptation based on equality of languages and cultures, through independence as well as interdependence.

Although local or regional radio stations intended for and operated by national minorities also exist in other parts of the country, linguistic differentiation of local radio in Voivodina is of particular importance. Almost all of the 50 communes in Voivodina have statuary regulations providing for equality of languages and alphabets (Cyrillic and Latin). This practice is followed by the language policies of the central radio station *Novi Sad*, as well as by local radio stations in 26 communes. Actually, there is no commune in Voivodina without its 'own' local station or at least a joint radio station with neighbouring communes, and no minority without its 'representatives' among the staffs of local radio stations.

NATIONAL SIGNIFICANCE OF LOCAL RADIO

Local radio in Yugoslavia preserved a traditional uniformity regarding the establishment and organizational forms of the media. It was different from the press which is published by a variety of founders (i.e. political organizations, communities, associations, research and educational institutions, religious associations, unions and communication organizations). Although there were no legal restrictions for individuals to publish newspapers, this right had never been put into practice mainly for two reasons. First, interest in publishing a new journal or newspaper could be rather easily accommodated by existing communication organizations, already a fairly common practice among professional journals. Second, a relatively highly developed and diverse press published by public companies reduced realistic opportunities for the survival of a profitable private enterprise, especially since public communication organizations benefited from reduced postal and tax rates, low interest loans and special subsidies for a variety of newspapers and professional journals.

On the other hand, radio and television were much more uniformly and centrally organized. Although a state monopoly has been eliminated within the entire communication sphere, statutory regulation of broadcasting – in contrast to that for the press – remained restrictive. Radio and television programmes could only be broadcast by communication and related organizations, entities which cannot be established directly by individual citizens. This was true for central radio and television stations as well as for local radio stations. In practice, the majority of local stations was founded by local organizations of the Socialist Alliance or local governments in the form of specific communication organizations.

The Socialist Alliance which emerged after the political changes in 1990, a meta-political or 'umbrella' organization, has been transformed into a classic political party. In accordance with legal changes adopted in 1990, public service media became subordinated to the respective parliaments or even directly to the governments. Although some media, including local radio, became much more commercially oriented – already a trend developing in the 1980s – they are now largely dependent on the new national and local governments.

Due to such uniformity, programming format and content of local radio stations are still usually subordinated to political interests and lack a high degree of differentiation. An important reason why (local) radio did not follow a more pluralistic model of development like the print media is found in the prevailing political belief that radio is primarily a political force rather than a cultural institution or a vehicle for satisfying communicative needs. Federal and republic laws describe radio and other media as 'means of public information' and not as media of communication, although the programme structure of radio stations clearly shows that radio is much more than just a 'means of information'. Obviously, public communication is subordinated to the political sphere which prevents development of a non-hierarchical plurality of interests.

Such a position of (local) radio is not specific to Yugoslavia. Noncommercial local radio stations in Western Europe are in a similar situation. They have more than 'local importance' when:

> affiliated to political parties and organizations. Although operating in the fields of information and culture, their essential aim is all too often to carry on propaganda on behalf of their own positions and actions. (Richeri, 1983: 401).

Similarly, radio broadcasting in Yugoslavia was built on the model of a political organization, in which higher levels subsume lower ones. Accordingly, the thematic structure of local programmes often results in a reduced offering of central programmes. While the ideal function of local radio is that of a self-management system in which individual opinions and interests can be articulated, its actual dominant function is the distribution of themes and content with mass appeal – either produced by the political system or by commercial interests.

Indeed, after almost four decades of development, new forms of (local) public radio which Brecht (1983: 169) once called "the most wonderful public communication system" are still in their infancy in Yugoslavia and are far from integrated parts in a system of democratic pluralism. Brecht's classic idea of transforming radio from a distribution to a communication system still remains a utopian vision. Democratization of communication not only involves a relationship between communicators and the most immediate representatives of the ruling interests (i.e. the independence of communicators from political authorities), but also a relationship to the public. Local radio in Yugoslavia still acts as an intermediary between political elites and the masses rather than as an organizer of communication among listeners. Communicators are still 'collective organizers' in Lenin's sense of 'organizers of the masses', as opposed to organizers of actual possibilities for citizens and their right to communicate.

On the other hand, local radio is now facing a strong tendency toward commercialization. Although at other levels, radio is generally less influenced by commercial forces than print media and television, at the local level this tendency mainly applies to radio. This is simply due to the absence of print media and television at the local level.

CONCLUSIONS

Local radio in Yugoslavia developed, even during a period of rapid growth, rather spontaneously without coordination between larger territorial units, e.g. the republics or the entire country. Although local radio has a long tradition, after 40 years of development it still cannot be considered a form of community broadcasting. The majority of local radio stations exercise a pragmatic policy which inhibits experimentation with new programming forms and content. There is a tendency to rely on programmes already 'put to the test' by larger stations. Although local stations are integrated into national networks as direct transmitters of central programming, they do have full autonomy and independence from central radio stations in matters concerning financing and programming. Local radio is organized as a public service, operated by full-time salaried staff members, part-time contributors and occasionally by volunteers.

In any case, local radio does not function as open access radio even though local news and interactive programmes are produced. Listener participation is typically limited to call-in programmes. Station income is mostly generated by commercial advertising, local subsidies and paid messages. Throughout the development of local radio there have been no essential differences in style and programme structure between central, regional and local stations.

Nevertheless, local radio continues to be very attractive to listeners and advertisers, which helps explain the fact that only a few regions in Yugoslavia exist which are not served by local radio broadcasts. In recent years local radio has not attracted as much public and political attention as during the late 1960s and 1970s. This may be partially explained by the introduction of cable and satellite television which tend to attract more interest among local and regional authorities. Also, the media scene – particularly daily newspapers and quality magazines – have recently become much more differentiated and thus, again, local radio has lost some of its 'alternative' attractiveness.

Actually, and in spite of its emancipatory potentials and optimistic expectations, local radio never achieved the critical role or revolutionary political significance which 'alternative' print media have had in different periods and contexts since the Enlightment. The Yugoslavian case reaffirms this historical 'deficiency' of radio.

Although predictions were made that local radio would become a tool for the democratic transformation of society, it never really succeeded in challenging the mainstream development of national, large-scale radio broadcasting and its centralized organizational structure. Where (local) radio failed the alternative press succeeded in the mid-1980s: the latter significantly contributed to the processes of democratization in both the media sphere and society as a whole. This could, at least partly, explain why radio, although the most widely available of all the media, has been subjected to relatively little political concern in comparison to the daily press and television.

APPENDIX: Media Landscape in Yugoslavia

Expenses for culture and entertainment (including communication services) represents almost 4 per cent of the total personal consumption of Yugoslavians in 1983. Of this amount, 27 per cent was spent on books and newspapers, 65 per cent on broadcasting (radio and television sets and licence fees) and 17 per cent on other forms of culture and entertainment (e.g. movies, theatre and sports). This amount represents about one-tenth of all food expenditures, which suggests that consumption of communication services is an increasingly important part of the everyday life in Yugoslavia.

Radio and television broadcasting, with over 200 radio and 9 television stations reflects the pluralistic nature of Yugoslavian communication. In 1984, 202 radio stations produced over 418,000 hours of programming for about 5 million subscribers. One-third of all radio broadcasting was transmitted by 8 national radio stations (one in each republic and autonomous province), 14 per cent by regional and 53 per cent by local radio stations. National stations were founded by republican socialist alliances; regional and local stations have been created by specific social groups, e.g. national minorities, students, cultural organizations and local political organizations. Some of the are intended to serve local communities, others to cater to specific ethnic, language or special interest groups. There is almost no household in Yugoslavia without at least one radio receiver. All radio programmes are transmitted over-the-air; no attempts have yet been made to distribute radio by cable.

Nine national television stations around the country transmit 15 programmes, totalling over 50,000 hours per year to about 4 million Yugoslavian households with television sets. The number of households with television sets varies from nearly 80 per cent in the more developed parts of the country (Slovenia, Croatia and Voivodina) to less than 50 per cent in Montenegro and Kosovo. Four television stations transmit programming in Serbo-Croatian (Belgrade, Zagreb, Sarajevo, Titograd); other transmit in Slovenian (Ljubljana), Macedonian (Skopje), Italian (Koper/Capodistria – intended for Italian minorities living in Slovenia and Croatia) and Albanian (Prishtin – for Albanian minorities in Kosovo). Television *Novi Sad* in Voivodina transmits its programming in Serbo-Croatian (35 per cent), Hungarian (37 per cent), Rumanian (3 per cent), Slovakian (3 per cent) and Ruthenic (2 per cent). *TV Prishtin* also broadcasts in Turkish and Romani languages.

Less than one-fourth of the total television airtime is programmed with local productions. About 20 per cent comes from abroad and more than half from other Yugoslavian stations. The diversity is nevertheless limited because the programmes of individual television stations can be received within the republic of origin and in parts of the neighbouring republics, and because there are no essential differences among the 15 television programmes. Yugoslavian television must, however, compete with some foreign television programmes, particularly Austrian and Italian programmes which can be received in northern Yugoslavia.

Since the mid-1980s there is also an increasing tendency towards implementation of cable television (nearly 3 per cent of Yugoslavian households are already connected to cable systems and a large number of them are able to receive satellite delivered channels such as *Super Channel, Sky Channel, 3 Sat, Sat 1, RTL-plus, Music Box, Musik-kannal, World Net* and *Horizont*. In 1987 some 20 relative large cable systems had been developed and were available to more than 50,000 homes. Currently, all cable systems in operation are almost exclusively used for distribution of over-the-air signals; local origination progrmmina and two-way services are not yet available. The cable systems, however, are technically capable of providing local origination, and experiments have been conducted in Belgrade, Novi Sad, Maribor and Split.

An independent local television station, *Alternative Television*, started over-the-air operation in 1991 in Ljubljana and may break the monopoly of the central Slovene television station. Similar trends are present o other republics: two private television channels started operation in Serajevo in the spring of 1991, and two independent, though not privately owned, station in Zagreb (OTV) and Belgrade (Studio B).

Although the importance of advertising as a source of financing radio and television services in Yugoslavia is rising, the amount of commercials is no more than 4 per cent of the total broadcasting time (Splichal, 1987). The major source of income still comes from the licence fee paid by owners of radio and television sets. Regional and local radio stations, however, are more commercially oriented because they receive a smaller portion of the licence fee.

References

Bacevic, L., J. Danojlic, F. Dzinic and R. Mikasinovic (1965): *Masovno komuniciranje u jugoslaviji* (Mass Communication in Yugoslavia), Beograd: Institut drustvenih nauka

Brecht, B. (1983): 'Radio as means of communication', in A. Mattelart and S. Siegelaub (eds), *Communication and class struggle: 2 – Liberation, socialism*, New York: International General.

Habermas, J. (1962): *Strukturwandel der Öffentlichkeit*, Berlin: Luchterhand.

Krippas, G. (1982): *European press law in statutory regulation and self-regulation of the press*, Strassbourg: Council of Europe.

Lowery, S. and M.L. DeFleur (1983): *Milestones in mass communication research. Media effects*, London: Longman.

MacBride, S. (1980): *Many voices – one world*, Paris: Unesco.

Mattelart, A. and Piemme, J.M. (1984): 'Twenty-three guidelines for a political debate on communications in Europe', in V. Mosco and J. Wasko (eds) *Changing patterns in communications control*, Norwood, NJ: Ablex.

Mills, C.W. (1959): *Power elite*, London: Oxford University Press.

Popovic, D. (1983): *Radio u voivodini*, Novi Sad: Zajednica RDO Vojvodine.

Richeri, G. (1983): 'Local radio and television stations in Italy', in A. Mattelart and S. Sieglaub (eds) *Communication and Class Struggle: 2 – Liberation, Socialism*, New York: Bagnolet.

Splichal, S. and C. Sparks (1991): *Journalists for the 21st century*, Norwood, NJ: Ablex.

Splichal, S. (1987): 'Socialism limits advertising in Eastern Europe', *Media Development* 34, 2: 18-20.

Williams, R. (1976): *Communications*, Harmondsworth: Penguin Books.

Wright, C. (1966): *Mass communication; a sociological perspective*, New York: Random House.

Young, T.R. (1982): 'The structure of democratic communications: Interaction and information in public life', paper, Livermore, CA: Red Feather Institute.

Part III
Special themes

15. Women on the air. Community radio as a tool for feminist messages

Birgitte Jallov

Communication consultant

Since the late 1960s women have become increasingly active all around Europe, and in many instances this has resulted in a resurgence of feminist counter culture. Traditionally, European women have been excluded from participation in the public sphere and confined to exchanges with family and friends. Cultural expression by women has consequently developed and been appreciated primarily within this setting.

One of the basic aims of the new feminist movement in Western Europe is to end this confinement and encourage the visibility of women. In the course of the past decades women have come to take a more dominant role on 'public stages', in cultural, political and artistic life. And, as part of this struggle, feminist groups in several European countries became forerunners in the development of 'free radio'. Women began making use of radio broadcasting as yet another avenue for involvement in the public sphere.[35]

Radio Donna in Rome, *Les Nanas Radioteuses* in Paris and *Radio Pleine Lune* in Ferney-Voltaire in France along the Swiss border, were some of the groups which began experimenting with local radio, often as pirates, since the mid-1970s. Radio programmes were made on a variety of issues seldom considered in conventional radio programming. Abortion, for example, then virtually a taboo topic, was raised by these female radio pirates.

During this period, in 1978, a group of British women formed *Women's Airwaves* a

---

35 *This chapter is based on a comparative study of women's radio groups located around Europe (Jallov, 1983) and has been updated with personal correspondence and interviews with women involved. Documentation was also compiled during an international forum on women in community radio, held in Berlin in 1985. Additional resources include Baehr & Ryan (1984) and Gallagher's (1981) study of women and the media.*

collective of women who produced radio programming and lobbied for community radio. After a time in which women were mainly involved in pirate radio stations – as in France, Belgium and Italy – a second phase of pirating began to develop simultaneously in several countries. In the Netherlands *Vrouwenradio* went on the air in 1981, and the lesbian collective in Barcelona, *Onda Verde*, began producing programming in 1982.

In the Scandinavian countries developments proceeded differently in that there was no strong grassroots movement pushing for community or free radio stations. Instead, government-initiated experiments with community radio were launched: in 1979 in Sweden, in 1982 in Norway and in 1983 in Denmark. In spite of this more regulated start of the community radio movement in these countries, many women's groups reacted positively to the opportunity and created or took part in stations.

WOMEN'S PROGRAMMING ON NATIONAL BROADCASTING COMPANIES

The national broadcasting companies in most West European countries tend to stress traditional notions of balance and impartiality in their programming, and the women's programmes produced by these institutions reflect such conventions as well as the historical traditions and roles assigned to women in the respective countries. These programmes, in other words, have traditionally been directed towards the housewife and have dealt with topics such as homemaking, childcare, beauty and fashion. In most instances these programmes portray women in the roles of housewives and mothers, and as such cannot be considered serious efforts for strengthening women's own interpretations of and expectations in society.

In some places these traditional women's programmes have been transformed into programmes dealing with the lives of present-day women. The focus here is on the limitations and potential for conflict between traditional and new roles for women, rather than merely conservation of the status quo. Such programmes have been produced, for example, in Berlin, where *Frauenfunk* ('Women's Radio') presently broadcasts for two hours a day, five days a week, on *Sender Freies Berlin*. This programme receives among the highest audience ratings for programming on the station.

In spite of a few excellent examples demonstrating the transformation of women's programmes produced by national broadcasting companies, women in the new feminist movement knew all too well how easily progressive voices can be muted in such settings, how effective self-censorship takes hold, and how little possibility there is in actuality to attain a position of significant influence and role in decision making. For a time such initiatives may be tolerated, but after a while the (often male) editors believe that women's concerns have been adequately covered and that it is time to consider another theme or topic. Such a mind-set is difficult to combine with a more radical feminist perspective. At *Frauenfunk* this difficulty has been the source of frequent attempts to modify or eliminate the programming, and only strong listener support for *Frauenfunk* programming has prevented its demise.

EMERGENCE OF WOMEN'S RADIO STATIONS

Recognizing that there was little chance to rapidly transform attitudes within and accessibility to the national broadcasting companies, some European feminists decided to develop their own communication channels. The 'free' radio stations, either in an illegal pirate environment or in a state regulated experimental setting, provided opportunity for addressing the issues and concerns of feminists.

Most of the women's radio stations surfacing in Europe in this period, generally the early 1980s, were collectives which produced programming during scheduled time slots on community or movement oriented radio stations. The autonomy of these collectives and the possibility of producing and airing regularly scheduled programmes were major attractions of these stations for feminists. The geographical restrictions of low-power transmitters used by the stations were considered less important than the above mentioned advantages. Community radio stations have mainly been of interest by feminists to reach their own community-of-interest, members of the wider feminist movement. The ideal and sometimes intended audience, however, was all women, independent of their position on feminist issues.

The awareness and spirit of these groups is reflected in the names given to the programming initiatives. And, whether a women's group might have its own radio station, be an autonomous collective within a station serving many groups, or be a collective among other collectives in operating the station, they would refer to the enterprise as 'their station', 'the women's radio' or 'the collective' indiscriminately. These labels all describe the same phenomenon: a collective of women producing regularly scheduled radio programmes broadcast on a community oriented station.

Based on the assumption that senders and receivers have the same interests and concerns due to their common background, feminists have considered community radio a tool for organising the experiences and needs of the movement. As such, radio has been seen as a valuable channel for consciousness raising among both producers and listeners.

One of the top priorities of women's radio stations has been to increase the visibility of women and of women's experiences through use of the medium. Realizing women generally are not free to make crucial decisions in their lives, the women working in the stations attempt to organize the experiences of individual women into a collective unit of experience. By letting women speak for themselves, the individual experiences are transformed into a collective understanding of their life situation. Such understanding can contribute to further choice and action.

Rooted in the women's movement with a tradition of attaching equal value to tasks performed, hierarchical structures are seldom implemented. Managerial, journalistic and technical tasks are shared by all members of the collective. In some cases the technical quality of the programming has suffered, but this aspect is generally considered secondary to the opportunities created for self-expression and self-realization of the women involved.

In addition to this shared theoretical framework, there are differences among the women's radio stations. Some of the differences are a consequence of regional and national variations, but there are also differences based on the structure of the particular stations. These differences are illustrated in the examples below found in stations in France, Holland, Great Britain, Norway and Denmark.

Paris: *Les Nanas Radioteuses*

Originally part of the unregulated 'free' pirate French community radio stations, *les Nanas* and *les Radioteuses* joined forces in 1981 to become the major women's station in Paris. The following year it was granted an official broadcasting license by the government. A voice of the women's movement in Paris, *Les Nanas Radioteuses* moved from a women's center after theft of the studio equipment and shared premises with a grassroots station, *Canaille FM*. The women's group made use of the studio and other facilities, but maintained autonomy regarding programming policy and content.

A central objective of this station was to create a women's information channel and a forum for pluralistic, feminist discourse. They attempted to attain this objective by involving women from all walks of life in the programming. One programme was produced weekly. This programme, lasting six hours, was composed of items devoted to specific topics. There were items on employment, female chanson traditions, news from the women's movement, and portraits of known and unknown women. There were special programmes on women's culture and informational programmes on a wide range of themes: abortion, housework, childcare, legal matters and themes related to international solidarity among women.

Programme production was carried out by a core group of 10 women assisted by additional free-lancers. Production expenses were met through membership dues and self financing. The group was organized as a collective in which all members performed both the technical and journalist tasks. Programme planning and evaluation were also equally shared by group members.

Les Nanas Radioteuses was among the most productive of the women's community radio collectives in France. A change in legislation for community radio stations in the country, however, brought an end to this effort. *Canaille FM*, the station which had provided airtime to *Les Nanas Radioteuses*, decided to finance its own programming by selling airtime and cancelled the contract with the women's station. After a period of sporadic transmission on other frequencies, *Les Nanas Radioteuses* stopped production entirely in 1985.

Nijmegen: *Vrouwenzender*

While the Parisien feminists decided to abandon pirate radio activity and participate in the legalized community radio stations, Dutch feminists generally chose to avoid the legal stations and to instead maintain their own pirate stations. During the mid-1980s very few women were active in the 100-odd legal community radio stations then in operation (see Chapter 6 for a review of the Dutch stations). This was in spite of special training courses and other initiatives undertaken to attract women to the stations.

On the pirate stations, however, Dutch women have been a prominent element since around 1980, emerging from the squatter movement then active in the country. Nijmegen, a university dominated city, has been one of the more active centres of this development.

In the period between 1981 and 1987 seven women's collectives took part in the programming schedule of *Rataplan,* a pirate station whose programmes reached most parts of the city. These collectives concentrated on several facets of the women's movement: radical feminism, lesbianism, working class women, young girls, and a more general group which focused on in-depth features on women's lives and culture. Of these collectives only the last one continued producing programming as part of *Rataplan* by the end of the decade.

Much earlier, in 1984, two of the women's collectives left *Rataplan* to form an all women's radio station called *Vrouwenzender* (see Wiersma, 1988). The basic idea of this station was to fill one of the gaps of traditional media coverage and provide news and informational programming about women. The programming included in-depth interviews with prominent women and attention to cultural and musical programming involving women. The station, as in many other places, was primarily funded by the producers themselves and occasional grants.

Vrouwenzender began transmitting in late 1986, producing around 5 hours of programming, aired one day each month. Later, the group attempted to produce a weekly programme, but in the course of the following year the collective was forced to close down. Economic problems and attrition among collective members proved too great for the initiative.

London: Women's Airwaves

British women, in contrast to French and Dutch feminists who chose the alternative of pirate broadcasting, decided to engage in political battle with the government in order to create a legal community radio alternative within the British broadcasting system. While engaged in this enterprise, the women involved also began training themselves and other women in the production of quality radio programmes.

Women's Airwaves was one of the collectives involved in these undertakings. The group originated during a feminist conference held in London in 1979. Its basic objective was to make the lives and perspectives of women more visible. The group felt it important to create a sphere of openness and confidence when approaching a new, technically oriented profession such as radio programming, and decided the best manner to acheive this was by restricting their activities to women only.

Because of the absence of legislation for community stations at that time, the collective chose to work on three fronts simultaneously: lobbying for new legislation, providing training in radio production, and producing audio cassettes which could be used by women's groups. The collective also wanted to develop more open and less hierarchical programming formats, such as modifying the conventional roles of interviewer and interviewee and letting, for example, the interviewee participate in the editing process after a taped discussion along with the interviewer.

Inasmuch as legislation for community radio stations was slow in coming, *Women's Airwaves* came to concentrate less on programming production and more on training activities. Demand for such training has been increasing, particularly among teachers and women advisors of youth clubs. The training activities are used to help young city girls formulate employment options and to consider other lifestyle alternatives than those offered by traditional role models.

219

Initially, *Women's Airwaves* was a large group composed entirely of volunteers. As the demand for training increased, the collective hired a full-time staff member and considered a second paid position. Additional forms of professionalism in the activities of the group were also implemented.

With no opportunity to broadcast programmes, then, *Women's Airwaves* was unable to achieve its primary goal: making women more visible through community radio. But through the training activities, the collective has been able to achieve extensive contact with groups in and around London. It is unlikely that as many groups could have been trained had there also been demands on *Women's Airwaves* to produce regular radio programmes.

Oslo: RadiOrakel

RadiOrakel began broadcasting in 1982 from studios situated in a women's cultural centre in Oslo. From the beginning *RadiOrakel* was distinct from most other women's radio collectives in Europe. They considered themselves less a movement radio station than one in competition with other stations for listeners. Committed to reflecting women's lives and activities, the choice of this station was to produce high quality professional programming. In this manner *RadiOrakel* hoped to attract listeners as well as provide information and awareness regarding women's issues.

During the mid-1980s *RadiOrakel* was the fifth most popular radio station in Oslo; the other four stations were all economically secure music oriented stations. The original seven hours of programming per week was increased to 26 hours per week by 1988.

RadiOrakel was at that time the only known women's radio station in Europe which allowed men to participate in station activities. The number, however, was limited to no more than a third of the entire group. Initially, there were five men and 80 women. Five years later, in 1987, the ratio was 8 men and 27 women.

RadiOrakel is financed through a diversity of sources: membership fees, listener donations, city subsidies, benefit concerts, studio rental fees, and sale of airtime to non-profit organizations. Indications were, should advertising become legalized for community radio stations, that *RadiOrakel* would expand its economic base through broadcast of selected commercials.

Although *RadiOrakel* considers its organizational structure non-hierarchical, some 'functional hierarchies' have been established in order to produce programming of high technical quality in an efficient manner. The programme editors plan and evaluate in closed weekly meetings; decisions are then passed on to the rest of the staff. Three positions – chief editor, station manager and one journalist – are salaried. In addition, a special governmentally funded unemployment scheme provides salaries for five technicians.

Training consists of 'learning by doing'. Experienced producers work together with new volunteers in order to maintain a high level of professionalism. In addition, production courses are established as needed and discussion evenings are organized with representatives from other media. These discussions are intended to help re-examine and renew perspectives within the collective.

Copenhagen: *Kvindeboelgerne*

In the early 1980s, about half of all community radio producers in the larger cities in Denmark were women, and women played a very active role in the government initiated experiment with community radio and television launched in 1983 (see Chapter 4 for information on this experiment). A number of women's collectives were also formed and special women's programmes were launched in many places around the country.

One of the first of these initiatives to go on the air was *Kvindeboelgerne*, ('Woman Waves') in Copenhagen. *Kvindeboelgerne* is part of a Copenhagen grassroots radio station, *Sokkelund Radio*, the latter being an initiative of some 15 groups and organizations. Three of these were women's groups: 'The Redstockings' (part of the new feminist movement), 'The Lesbians' and 'Women over 40'. These three groups composed *Kvindeboelgerne*, and one day a week was reserved on the station for women's programming, with a 1.5 hour-long broadcast each evening, a transmission repeated the following morning.

The original 25 women active in the station formed three groups responsible for the programming in alternating weeks. This created the time and space necessary for learning to use the equipment and for the volunteers, most of whom were new to radio production, to produce programmes. The collective was also organized with a horizontal organizational structure, with no editors or divisions between technical and journalistic positions. Since 1986 the number of women active in the station has decreased by about half, and some of the production groups have reduced their programming frequency.

The intention of *Kvindeboelgerne* was to reflect the lives and concerns of different groups of women in the Copenhagen area. During the first two years of programming about two-thirds of the programming concentrated on activities in and around the feminist movement: actions, cultural manifestations, women's role in society, women's politics, and health issues. Whether the group's objective was achieved with these programmes is uncertain. The volunteer producers, affiliated with the women's movement, produced meaningful programmes about issues that interested them. Whether these programmes reached a wider audience, however, is uncertain.

INCREASING THE VISIBILITY OF WOMEN

Part of the ideology of most of the women's collectives was to develop an open, horizontal organizational structure which would reflect the ideas and concerns of the active participants at any given time. One of the few rules of *Les Nanas Radioteuses* was, that only the women currently active in the radio collective could have a say in the planning and evaluation sessions. This notion was also practiced in most other collectives. This means, that the amount of enthusiasm and energy in the group of producers at any given moment in time would determine expansion or termination of a particular programme.

This organizational structure of women's radio groups stems from the history and ideas of the feminist movement, with all its strengths and weaknesses. The feminists in the collectives did not intend to create institutions which would last any longer than needed. Involvement in a radio station was, for them, not for the sake of the radio, but for creation of a communication channel able to convey messages important to women in general. This conviction certainly holds for women's radio groups during the process of development and when they were active in broadcasting programming. But when a station is faced with closure, does this ideology remain intact? Would, for example, the French *Nanas Radioteuses* or the Dutch *Vrouwenzender* stations have wanted to cease programming if they had not been forced to do so by circumstances?

The silence and invisibility of women within society – the eradication of which was the motivating force behind women becoming involved in community radio – are not aspects which can be changed overnight. When overt physical repression or severe financial problems are present, along with the continuous threat of attrition caused by personnel burn-out, it may be relevant to question the suitability of the organizational structure chosen. It is not at all clear whether a non-authoritian structure is the best organizational form for confronting and changing imbalances and injustices in the society at large.

In an institutional setting very different from that of community radio, *Frauenfunk* in Berlin has for a number of years been producing two hours of women's radio on a daily basis as part of the state sponsored *Sender Freies Berlin*. The staff is paid, the technical quality of the equipment is high, and the programme has many listeners. Still, the women involved in *Frauenfunk* talk about forms of self-censorship which occur, where topics and programming angles are chosen which they feel will not jeopardize the other activities of *Frauenfunk*.

In choosing community radio as a medium for expression, European feminists found what they were initially looking for: autonomy and the absence of censorship. This was a choice taken, knowing there was little opportunity for creating a suitable platform within the established media, at least in the short run. In the present situation, however, none of the available choices seems to adequately provide a communication medium able to satisfy both the objective and subjective needs of listeners. Whether community radio, by providing opportunity for working in the margins of the media, has contributed towards increasing the visibility of women, or whether real changes can only be brought about by securing space in the established media is uncertain. What has emerged from these experiences, however, is that women need and want structures which can more directly be used to address their concerns and within which they can operate more effectively than is now possible.

FUTURE PROSPECTS

One of the women's radio stations discussed earlier, *RadiOrakel*, seems to contain important elements for solving some of the above problems. By combining elements from grassroots radio stations as well as from professional media traditions, this women's station seems to be able to combine the 'best of both worlds'. The formal structure is that of a community station: a 'free' radio station with no obligations towards 'balanced and impartial programming' and with no decision makers elsewhere in the organization who determine the fate of a particular programme. *RadiO-rakel* is an independent station which shares a single frequency with other groups. The station is run in a collective spirit, but with aspects of a hierarchical structure: there are some paid staff members and there are editors responsible for certain programming areas. This structure ensures a stable daily routine. *RadiOrakel* is the only collective examined in this chapter which has during the past years been able to expand its transmission hours.

RadiOrakel is defined as a women's radio station, but has discarded one of the fundamental principles in the feminist movement: the importance of women working together without the influence of men. *RadiOrakel* women argue that they are perfectly able to work together in a respectful and productive atmosphere with the kind of men wanting to work inside a women's radio station. The editors are, incidently, women and the point-of-view taken on topics discussed is that of women.

In another area *RadiOrakel* deviates from the conventions of the women's radio movement. The original collectives were concerned about producing programming significant to the producers as well as the listeners, and where the process was as important as the final result. *RadiOrakel*, however, aspires to high professional standards, and wants to compete with popular disc-jockey programmes in terms of content and of technical quality. A horizontal structure in which everyone may perform all tasks is not a feature of the *RadiOrakel* station.

In a sense, community radio has provided an ideal opportunity for women to get on the air and contribute women's voices and perspectives to public debate. Channels became available and, given the audience was local and initially interested in content rather than form, there was less difficulty for women without experience to begin producing programming.

In terms of programming content, however, most women's collectives have not been locally oriented. The programming themes could just as easily have been the basis of national radio programming. Realistically, though, the programmes produced on these themes would not have been broadcast by national stations. In this sense, then, community radio has very much been a tool, rather than an end in itself, for the women's collectives.

Movement radio can best be seen as reflections of activity and discussion in the movement and the society in which the station is based. These radio stations are the bearers of the original ideas of free community radio with open access and maximum participation for everyone in all areas of activity.

These 'carriers of messages' exist as long as there are messages, or until external pressures forces a collective to abandon operation. This type of radio station comes and goes as the need for communication arises.

The free and professionalised women's radio, as in the case of *RadiOrakel*, demonstrates a trend in the opposite direction. Here, a choice has been made to professionalise and compete with commercial radio stations for space on the airwaves. Although they continue to operate from within the women's movement, they do so with a professional approach and structure.

These different approaches to women's radio are well defined, each in its own world, following its own regularities. In this respect the developments and discussions within the women's radio movement are similar to those in the community radio movement generally. A central issue remains that of determing the proper balance between public access and democratization of the airwaves on the one hand, and the desire to reach a wider audience with women's programming on the other.

One approach to securing such balance can be found in strategies employed by American women active in community radio stations. The production of messages remains central; volunteers are involved in radio production, but with assistance from professional staff. Such an approach maintains the freedom of community media while complementing it with programming continuity and quality found on the more traditional and established media.

Visibility of women seems, in this manner, to be insured. What is uncertain is whether such a structure will permit radio programming, grounded in enthusiasm and desire to communicate significant societal messages, to survive. Removed from its movement basis, such radio activity may have nothing to serve as a tool. The challenge for women's radio groups today, then, is to maintain both affinity with that basis and to perfect the communicative tool at their disposal.

References

Baehr, H. and M Ryan (1984): *Shut up and listen! Women and local radio; a view from the inside*, London: Comedia.

Gallagher, M. (1981): *Unequal opportunities: the case of women and the media*, Paris: UNESCO.

Jallov, B. (1983): *Women on the air; women in (community) radio in Europe*, Roskilde, Denmark: Roskilde University Centre.

Wiersma, A. (1988): *Dan liever de lucht in! Nijmeegse vrouwenradio's en hun feministiese ideologie*, Nijmegen: Institute of Mass Communication, University of Nijmegen.

16. Experimenting with minority television in Amsterdam

Ineke Gooskens

DG Research Company, Landsmeer, The Netherlands

In the early 1980s the Dutch government felt more resources should be directed at promoting involvement of ethnic minorities in the media, and with this in mind an experiment was proposed for minority television. The aim of the experiment was to encourage participation of ethnic minorities in local television. Participation was hoped for not only within the organizational affairs of the station but also – and more importantly – in the production of television programmes.

Suitable sites for this experiment were to meet three general criteria: that a substantial ethnic minority population resided in the city, that a cable television net was installed with a local station licensed to cablecast programming, and finally that a relatively large number of ethnic minorities were subscribers to the cable services. Five cities were chosen as sites for the experiment: three relatively small cities – Deventer, Gouda and Zaltbommel – and two major municipalities – Amsterdam and Rotterdam.

Television programming for ethnic minorities living in these cities was funded by the Ministry of Culture for a period of three years, from 1984 through 1986. The Ministry commissioned a study of the experiment (Reubsaet & Boekhoorn, 1986) and the city of Amsterdam financed a separate study of the first two years. The evaluation of the minority television experiment in Amsterdam focused on three aspects:

– the structure, functioning and objectives of the project (reported in Reubsaet & Boekhoorn, 1986);

– the (potential) audience of the minority television programmes (Gooskens, 1984a, 1984b, 1984c, 1985);

– and a production training programme initiated in January 1985 (Gooskens, 1986).

Before discussing the results of the research on minority television in Amsterdam background information is provided on ethnic minorities in the country and on the decisions which led up to the experiment. At the end of the chapter a brief sketch is given of developments which have transpired since the experimental period.

ETHNIC MINORITIES IN THE NETHERLANDS

In 1985 Some 615,000 persons of ethnic minority origin resided in the Netherlands. At that time they represented 4.3 per cent of the total Dutch population. Since 1975 this number has more than doubled (see Table 1).

Table 1. Ethnic minorities in the Netherlands

	1975	1985
Turks	62,587	155,579
Moroccans	33,156	111,579
Other Mediterraneans	77,094	ca. 67,000
Surinamese	68,700	ca. 181,000
Antilleans	19,300	ca. 47,000
Moluccans	ca. 29,000	ca. 40,000
Vietnamese	-	6,772
Others	ca. 3,000	6,369
	293,000	615,000

Source: Van Praag (1986).

During the course of the 1960s immigration of guest workers from Mediterranean countries increased steadily. In the 1970s the families of these guest workers also came to the country with the intent of settling more or less permanently. By the middle of that decade large numbers of former residents of Surinam had moved to the Netherlands. This emigration was the result of political and socio-economic upheaval in Surinam related to independence of the colony in 1975.

Since 1980 immigration of minority groups to the Netherlands has decreased substantially. However, high birthrate, especially among Turks and Moroccans, has caused a rapid increase of ethnic minority residents in the country.

In general, ethnic minorities in the Netherlands, have completed little formal education and their socio-economic status is low. The cultural distance between them and the Dutch community is often great. This situation varies with each ethnic group and with other factors such as religion, culture and language. What all ethnic minorities have in common, however, is a high unemployment rate – two to four times higher than that of comparable autochthonic Dutch residents.

Ethnic residents live predominantly in urban centres around the country. Half of them reside in the four major cities (Amsterdam, Rotterdam, The Hague, Utrecht), where they constitute 12-15 per cent of the city population. In certain age groups this proportion is even higher. For example, in Amsterdam 35 per cent of the population younger than 15 years belongs to an ethnic minority. In 1985 about 80 per cent of the Amsterdam population was autochthonic Dutch and 20 per cent were allochthons (see Table 2).

Table 2. Composition of Amsterdam population

Resident group	Size
Autochthonic Dutch	543,291
Surinamese	43,372
Antilleans	5,193
Turks	16,640
Moroccans	26,110
Other Mediterraneans	10,900
Other foreign residents	30,064
Total	675,570

Source: City of Amsterdam (1985).

NATIONAL MINORITY TELEVISION EXPERIMENT

The idea for an experiment with minority television originated during a policy review of media and minority relations in the country. Government commissioned reports (Medianota, 1983; Minderhedennota, 1983) stressed the disadvantaged position of ethnic minorities and the important role of the media in diminishing, if not eliminating, this deprivation. The mass media, it was stated, were intended to provide a pluralistic reflection of contemporary Dutch society. Ethnic minorities, however, have had little influence on media programming. Recognition of ethnic groups in general media programming has been very limited. If members of minority groups were involved in television production, it was argued, awareness of the place of ethnic groups within Dutch society might increase. And through participation, minorities might gain more responsibility for programme content.

Study of mass media use by migrants (e.g. Wentholt, 1982) suggests that first generation migrants live quite isolated lives. The flow of information in Dutch society hardly reaches them. Measures recommended to alleviate this situation include:

– more information about Dutch society in general, and about policy measurements related to migrants in particular;

– more educational opportunities in order to improve language skills and reduce illiteracy;

– more news and information about (cultural) developments in ethnic communities in the Netherlands and in their countries of origin.

The best medium for providing information to most minority groups is television. The majority of Turks and Moroccans, at least first generation members and in particular women, can hardly read or write. They rely on oral and face-to-face communication rather than on print media. Television can be considered a form of oral communication with a visual element.

This medium, it was believed, could be a powerful tool in improving the images of the diverse groups which compose Dutch society.

There was also a feeling, expressed in policy statements on minority relations, that an experiment with television could help stimulate participation and emancipation of ethnic minorities in Dutch society and strengthen cultural identities. Because participation of minorities could be stimulated most easily at the local level, it was decided to locate the experiment with minority television in several communities around the country.

Proposals were also made for media activity at the national level. It was recommended that additional transmission time be allotted to informational and educational programmes aimed at minority groups. And at the same time, a facility for training minorities in audio-visual production techniques, Studio Information Minorities (Studio IM), which has the task of producing audio-visual programming on Dutch society for minority groups, was to be strengthened.

As for the minority television experiment, it was designed with three objectives in mind: to stimulate participation of minority groups in local cablecasting organizations, to encourage participation of minority groups in the production of television programmes in local stations, and to improve the audio-visual skills and knowledge of minority groups. These objectives were also meant to guide the evaluation research which accompanied the experiment.

AMSTERDAM EXPERIENCE WITH MINORITY TELEVISION

Research around the minority television experiment in Amsterdam focused on the project organization, audience reactions, and the training programme.

Project organization and programming

Before this experiment began the local radio station, *Radio Stad Amsterdam*, had no experience in producing television programmes and very little experience in working with minority groups. This situation contributed to a decision to allow the experiment to operate with considerable autonomy, even though the radio station was formally responsible for all radio and television programming transmitted on the cable.

Three groups were organized at the start of the experiment: a board of advisors called the 'Project Group,' an independent Editorial Team, and a Policy Council composed of representatives from minority organizations.

Project group

The Project Group was installed once approval was granted for Amsterdam to participate in the national experiment with minority television. The group, appointed by *Radio Stad*, did not have representatives from minority organizations, and six of the eight members were autochthonic Dutch. The group's main task was to get the experiment started and ensure that it progressed satisfactorily.

The Project Group placed emphasis on practical and technical matters, and on establishing a structure for the experiment as rapidly as possible. Two principles guided the formulation of this structure. First, as many persons as possible from ethnic minority groups were to be allowed to participate in the project. Second, the programming was to be of high professional quality.

After the first months of operation effort was made to alter the ethnic composition of the Project Group so that at least half of its members belonged to minority groups.

New representatives from minorities were recruited, but these persons never became intensively involved, and after a few months they ceased attending meetings.

Several explanations were given to account for this phenomenon. There are, first of all, relatively few persons from ethnic minority groups who have the experiences and interests required for such voluntary work. And most qualified persons were already involved in comparable functions in other organizations. Second, it was difficult for newcomers to become involved in the project to the same extent as initiators of the minority television experiment. The momentum and direction of the experiment had already been set and could not be changed easily. The central figures in the Project Group remained, then, the same as those as at the start of the experiment – autochthons.

Editorial team

The Editorial Team, an independent unit within the experiment, had the task of organizing and co-ordinating production of the television programmes. A single editor-in-chief, of Surinam origin, was among the paid staff. He was assisted by three volunteer editorial teams of Turkish, Surinamese/Antillean and Moroccan nationalities. Two additional teams were formed to produce Italian and Spanish programming, but only incidental productions resulted for these language groups.

Initially, the editor-in-chief wanted to work with only one multicultural editorial team rather than separate ones for different minorities. After several months of attempting to produce a single team, however, he concluded that such a strategy was unworkable. The differences in cultural background and language between the Turks, the Surinamese/Antilleans and the Moroccans were simply too large. A consequence of this editorial structure was that three separate hour-long television programmes were produced weekly, differing in subject matter, emphasis and style. In the course of the experiment, though, the actual production of these programmes was increasingly taken on by multicultural teams.

Policy council

The Policy Council was created to encourage participation in the experiment of minority organizations active in Amsterdam. Members of the Policy Council, as representatives of their respective organizations, advised *Radio Stad* on programme policy, planning, and possible topics for specific programmes. Difficulties were encountered by the Policy Council in performing these tasks throughout the experiment. In all likelihood this organizational form was inappropriate for encouraging minority group participation. Most Council members either lacked interest or experience in developing media policy, or were already actively engaged in other minority organizations.

Television programmes

The first programmes were completed and transmitted two months after the start of the experiment, in early 1984. These programmes, however, had not been produced entirely by minority group members. This compromise was made in order to initiate the experiment as quickly as possible. A decision taken in this period was to produce separate programmes for the three largest minority groups in Amsterdam – for the Turkish, Surinamese/Antillean, and Moroccan communities. These programmes were transmitted during the first three days of the month. The programmes lasted 50 minutes and were repeated hourly, from 4 in the afternoon until midnight. When appropriate, the programmes were subtitled in Dutch in order to make them accessible to other Dutch speaking viewers. Subtitling in the language of the minority target group was provided when Dutch was spoken in the programmes.

Although a systematic content analysis of the programmes was not performed, on the basis of regular viewing of most programmes during the first 18 months of the experiment it was evident that the migrant programme producers were attempting to change the one-sided stereotypical image of minority groups. Effort was devoted to creating a programming formula which would be attractive to the target audiences. Attention was given to initiatives taken by minorities in the city; the intent seemed one of promoting cultural pride, self-confidence and co-operation.

The programmes presented not only informational and news items, but social and cultural events were also filmed, and examples of successful individuals were shown. The formula of an hour-long programme, alternating serious and light items within that time, appeared – as indicated in the next section – to satisfy large numbers of minority viewers.

Audience

During the first years of the experiment two 'street surveys' and a series of group discussions were carried out among the three main minority groups, the Turks, the Surinamese and the Moroccans. In addition, several questions about the minority television programmes were included in two general surveys (Gooskens, 1984c). Respondents to these general surveys are almost all autochthonic Dutch.

Street surveys

The first street survey (N = 380), conducted after two transmissions, showed that acquaintance with the minority television experiment (MTV) varied substantially. Of the Moroccan respondents 80 per cent had seen one or both Moroccan programmes; of the Turkish respondents 25 per cent had seen the Turkish programmes; and of the Surinamese respondents 20 per cent had viewed programmes produced for them.

Appreciation of the programmes also varied. Although most respondents were rather positive about the new local television programmes for minorities, there were also critical comments, and many respondents made suggestions for improving future programmes. One frequently-heard remark was that the technical standards of the programmes should remain high inasmuch as viewers were accustomed to such quality. If the quality should deteriorate, the feeling was that minority television would quickly acquire a negative image. The initiators of the MTV experiment, on the basis of this reaction, decided to give high priority to a technical training programme.

The second street survey (N = 1200) was conducted a year after the initial survey. The aim was not only to measure acquaintance with and appreciation of the MTV programmes, but also to gain an idea of the viewing frequency, the general opinion of the MTV experiment, and suggestions for future programmes.

After a year of monthly transmissions, only 8 per cent of the Moroccan respondents had not heard about MTV. Among Surinamers this figure was 25 per cent and among the Turks 20 per cent. Almost 20 per cent of all migrants assessed MTV programmes positively and considered them worth watching. Almost 30 per cent (especially Moroccan viewers) thought the MTV programmes had improved since the beginning of the experiment. Only 10 per cent (mostly Turkish and Moroccan respondents) thought the MTV programmes were declining in quality or not worth watching. This criticism was directed more to the general programming and organization of MTV than to special items in the programmes.

All three minority groups made requests for more information and education in the programmes: 66 per cent of the Turkish, 50 per cent of the Surinamese and 30 per cent of the Moroccan respondents. The specific information requested, and the preferred mode of presentation differed substantially between and within the three groups. These differences seemed related to ethnic origin, subculture, sex and age of the respondents. Overall, the Moroccans, many of whom were illiterate women, wanted a more accessible and entertaining programme than the Surinamese and the Turkish viewers.

As for frequency of viewing, respondents could be classified into three groups: regular viewers (persons who watched the MTV programming almost every month), occasional viewers (those who watch or have watched the MTV programme now and then) and non-viewers (those who have never seen a MTV programme). Since the first street survey the audience had grown substantially. Of the Moroccans, 69 per cent were among the regular audience members (especially women: 82 per cent) and 17 per cent were occasional viewers. Of the Surinamese/Antilleans 38 per cent belonged to the regular viewers and 31 per cent were casual viewers. Of the Turkish residents, those figures were respectively 46 per cent and 27 per cent. The regular audience of the latter two migrant groups consisted of relatively more women then men; the casual audience contained more men then women.

When these percentages are translated into population figures, the MTV audience, taking the three minorities as a whole, consisted of about 45,000 persons. The total MTV audience after the first year amounted to nearly 100,000 men and women, when the other allochthon and Dutch viewers of MTV programmes are included. About half of the Dutch, 10 per cent of the Moroccans, 20 per cent of the Turks and 25 per cent of the Surinamers/Antilleans residents in Amsterdam were unable to describe the experiment in the surveys conducted after a year of programming (Gooskens, 1984c, 1985). Findings from another survey suggest that one out of ten Amsterdam residents occasionally views MVT programmes (Gooskens, 1984c).

Training programme

From the beginning of the experiment it was clear that much of the production work would have to be performed by volunteers recruited from minority groups. Only two paid professionals could be financed with available funding. Two months after the first request for volunteers 150 applications had been received. A year later this number had risen to 250, and by December 1986 some 450 persons had volunteered to work on productions. A problem, however, was that almost no migrants had experience working with audio-visual media.

Since the MTV directors had chosen for quality programmes – a decision supported by audience reactions – it was necessary to train a sufficiently large staff of migrants capable of producing high quality television programmes. There were then few professional audio-visual training centres in the country, and the existing ones were insufficiently accessible to migrants.

The only viable alternative was that MTV establish its own audio-visual training programme. Developing such a programme, it was argued, would not only serve the project, but might also stimulate employment possibilities for ethnic minorities. Both the MTV directors and participants considered such a training programme a worthwhile investment given the expanding audio-visual market in the country.

Since most (85 per cent) of the migrants interested in the training programme were unemployed, funding requests were made at both national and local levels to subsidize the training. The national department of labour agreed to finance a full-time 12-month training course for 16 persons. The funding was made available for a three-year period, 1985 through 1987. The municipal department of employment agreed to finance a half-time training course for 30 persons during the same three-year period. The half-time training course aimed to give the participants an initial introduction to and acquaintance with producing television programmes. If, after the first year, participants wanted to pursue professional instruction, and this request was supported by staff recommendations, provisions were made to continue with the full-time training course. Participants who successfully finished the full-time course, 14 of the 16 participants, were given the opportunity to expand their experience as paid assistants in various video and broadcasting companies for another year.

Several tentative conclusions can be drawn from the initial experiences with the programme. First, much interest was expressed by migrants in the audio-visual training courses. This interest did not differ substantially between the three primary minority target groups – Turks, Moroccans, and Surinamese/Antilleans. The age of participants was slightly above the usual age for this level of education. Of the 450 applications submitted by the end of 1985, 60 per cent was around 30 years old. Some 20 per cent was younger than 27 years. The educational level of the participants was higher than that for minorities as a whole.

Second, expectations of participants was high regarding the course. Disappointment was voiced by some participants, largely attributable to the experimental nature of the training. The structure and content of the programme during the first year were not fully developed.

Third, all participants who finished the full-time training course (14 of 16) and the part-time course (17 of 24) indicated appreciation for the general characteristics of television production: the teamwork required, the tension of deadlines, the reactions from other viewers. Appreciation was also expressed for the training programme as a whole and the emphasis on practical skills.

Fourth, the majority of participants developed a bond to MTV. More than half wanted to keep working, if necessary as volunteers, to help the station grow and develop. In the long run, however, participants were interested in securing paid positions.

Finally, those who finished the training course generally felt as if their professional perspectives had been renewed – understandable given that many had experienced long periods of unemployment prior to the course. They also felt their awareness of other ethnic cultures had increased during the training programme.

CONCLUSIONS

The minority television experiment in Amsterdam developed independently from the already existing local broadcasting station, *Radio Stad*. MTV represented one of the first initiatives to produce local television programmes on a regular basis for cable distribution. In the process minority groups have secured an advantageous position regarding local television production in the city.

The production and transmission of ethnic minority television programmes provide an important function given the cultural and language barriers between Dutch and minority group residents. For the intended audience a gap has been filled in the television programming directed at minority residents. Should programme producers maintain contact with their audiences, MTV has the potential of developing into an important force for motivating and supporting minority groups.

After two years of experimentation equal participation by minorities in the production of television programmes had been essentially achieved. During that period programme quality also improved. This improvement was largely due to the training programme initiated. That programme, along with the television studio and programming demands, has the potential of creating a new cadre of minorities professionally trained in audio-visual techniques which could have influence on the nature of television programming – locally and nationally.

EPILOGUE: FROM EXPERIMENT TO INSTITUTION

The three-year experiment with minority television in the Netherlands terminated at the end of 1986. The experience in Amsterdam was considered successful, and both the local television programming and the audio-visual training programme have remained in operation.

Since 1987 MTV has become an independent foundation with its own board of directors. Other aspects of the organizational structure and programming formula have hardly changed. The board of directors is composed primarily of representatives of ethnic minorities. The annual budget in 1991 totalled dfl 1.5 million (about $750,000) of which half is provided by the city of Amsterdam, a quarter by the Ministry of Culture and the rest is earned through production fees.

The number of paid staff has expanded from a single position during the experimental period to five positions in 1991: the editor-in-chief, programme producer, and three editors for the editorial teams of the Turkish, Moroccan, and Surinamese/Antillean programmes. These staff members are further assisted by paid freelance personnel. Volunteer labour, common during the experiment, has now all but vanished. The Policy Council, which functioned unsatisfactorily during the experiment, has been replaced by a commission composed of persons participating without organizational affiliation.

The programming formula developed during the experiment, basically a magazine-type format, has not changed substantially. A 50-minute programme for each of the three main ethnic minority groups is broadcast once a week on Thursdays. This programme is transmitted every hour between 4 p.m. and midnight. In addition, a multicultural programme is broadcast once a month which attempts to portray the pluriform character of the Amsterdam population.

Surveys conducted by the city in the first half of 1990 suggest that attendance to MTV programmes has remained at the level achieved during the experiment. Some 45-55 per cent of the Moroccan and Turkish residents, and 25-30 per cent of the Surinam/Antillean residents are regular viewers of MTV programming. Some 18 per cent of all Amsterdam residents attend regularly to this programming, which means an increasingly large number of autochthonic residents is among the viewers.

Since 1989 the training programme has also become an independent foundation. The national department of employment extended financial support for another three-year full-time training programme. In this new programme the focus has been enlarged to include training in various media applicable to public relations and educational settings.

Since the experimental period Migrant Television Amsterdam has become one of the established media institutions in the city. It is, along with other media organizations and with the city government, involved in plans to develop a professional and commercially funded local television station. In addition to programmes designed for specific ethnic groups in the city, future plans involve production of multi-cultural programming directed at all Amsterdam residents, providing a platform for allochthonic perspectives.

References

Amsterdam, City of (1985): *De Amsterdammers in zeven bevolkingskategorieen*, Amsterdam: afdeling Bestuursinformatie.

Gooskens, J.T. and M. Freeman (1984a): *MTV, Verslag van een straatenquete*, Amsterdam: afdeling Bestuursinformatie.

Gooskens, J.T. (1984b): *MTV, Verslag van enige groepsdiscussies*, Amsterdam: afdeling Bestuursinformatie.

Gooskens, J.T. (1984c): *MTV, Verslag van een omnibusenquete*, Amsterdam: afdeling Bestuursinformatie.

Gooskens, J.T. (1985): *MTV, Verslag tweede straatenquete*, Amsterdam: afdeling Bestuursinformatie.

Gooskens, J.T. (1986): *MTV, De start van een nieuwe beroepsopleiding voor Migranten*. Amsterdam: afdeling Bestuursinformatie.

Medianota (1983): The Hague: Ministry of Internal Affairs.

Minderhedennota (1983): Rijswijk: Ministry of Culture.

Reubsaet, T.J. and P.F. Boekhoorn (1986): *Minderheden in beeld. Experimenten voor en door etnische groepen bij lokale omroepen*, Nijmegen: Institute of Applied Sociology.

Van Praag, C.S. (1986): 'Minderheden voor en na de Nota', *Migrantenstudies*, **4**: 2-53.

Wentholt, H. (1982): *Massamedia en buitenlandse werknemers in Nederland*, Hilversum: NOS.

17. Legal and policy aspects of community broadcasting

Nico van Eijk

Institute for Information Law, University of Amsterdam, The Netherlands

In contrast to print media, broadcasting has always been subject to extensive regulation. According to the position commonly held, freedom of the press implies that government should not regulate the activities of print media. In most cases, the press is left to operate on the open market; broadcasting, on the other hand, is considered part of the public sector and thereby subject to regulation and protection.

When radio began developing in the 1920s in Europe it was matter-of-factly assumed governments would be involved in its regulation as they were already regulating other parts of the telecommunications infrastructure. Two specific arguments were put forward in support of this position. In the first place, regulation was considered necessary because of the then limited number of frequencies. Scarcity of frequencies required an equitable form of distribution. In the second place, radio was considered by many observers to be a potentially powerful medium which should be used and developed with care. With these considerations in mind European governments generally chose for the simplest form of regulation: prohibition. Transmission of signals was restricted and only allowed with official permission. In most cases permission was given to one national organization, often state controlled, which could be easily supervised.

The original arguments for regulation and control of broadcasting lost meaning in the course of time with technical developments (FM transmitters and receivers, and cable distribution systems) and with change in opinion regarding the potential influence of radio programming. In this new climate it was possible for forms of decentralized and private broadcasting to develop.

Apart from provisionary regulations which had mostly an experimental character, legislation of small scale broadcasting appeared for the first time during the 1980s. The emergence of specific regulations for community radio and television is not something which came about exclusively because of a particular need or because of rejection of the originally posed arguments. It was rather part of an overall reformulation and restructuring of national broadcasting systems.

In nearly all West European countries the broadcasting systems have been partially or totally revised during the past years; in many cases the systems are still undergoing revision. France, for example, renewed its broadcasting system in 1982, 1986, and 1990; Belgium in the period 1984 – 1988; in the Netherlands, Spain and Portugal revisions were approved in 1988; and the United Kingdom modified its legislation in 1990.

Most of these renewed systems have, for the purposes of this volume, two similar characteristics: (1) small scale broadcasting is, in one form or another, permitted; and (2) potential links have been investigated with private commercial initiatives.

The regulation of community radio and television differs for each country, suggesting that development is still in progress. Future experience will undoubtedly lead to further adjustment of the legal framework for community broadcasting. Moreover, the regulation of broadcasting – including community radio and television – is no longer the exclusive domain of individual countries. Domestic issues are increasingly determined by European-wide concerns which are in part taken up by the EEC and the Council of Europe.

In this chapter general legal principles such as freedom of expression will be first considered inasmuch as they have special implications for community radio and television. How different the implementation of such principles can be in practice will become evident during a comparison of the regulations for community radio and television in the Netherlands, Belgium, and France.

Finally, anticipated regulatory changes are considered. Obviously, in the confines of this chapter, such a review must be broad and consequently incomplete. Furthermore, emphasis is placed on community radio for the simple reason that regulation of community television is much less developed.

COMMUNITY BROADCASTING AND FREEDOM OF EXPRESSION

Freedom of expression belongs to the most fundamental of legal principles and civil rights, and in every European state the freedom of citizens to receive and impart opinions is guaranteed in a constitution or similar document. In addition, freedom of expression is safeguarded in the European Convention on Human Rights (ECHR), Article 10:

> 1. Everyone has the right to freedom of expression. This right shall include freedom to hold opinions and to receive or impart information and ideas without interference by public authority and regardless of frontiers. This Article shall not prevent States from requiring the licensing of broadcasting, television or cinema enterprises.

> 2. The exercise of these freedoms, since it carries with it duties and responsibilities, may be subject to such formalities, conditions, restrictions or penalties as are prescribed by law and are necessary in a democratic society, in the interest of national security, territorial integrity or public safety, for the prevention of disorder or crime, for the protection of health or morals, for the protection of the reputation or rights of others, for preventing the disclosure of information received in confidence, or for maintaining the authority and impartiality of the judiciary.

The European Convention on Human Rights has been signed by all West European countries and represents the highest level of regulation for freedom of expression. A distinction is suggested between the press and broadcasting, which is also noted in the introduction to this chapter. In the first part of the Article explicit mention is made that broadcasting may be subjected to a form of licensing.

In the second part of Article 10 it is stated that restrictions on freedom of expression (and thus on community broadcasting) can only be imposed for very specific reasons. Before discussing the relationship between freedom of expression and community broadcasting, some remarks on the character of constitutional rights must be made.

In jurisprudence a distinction is made between so-called classical and social constitutional rights. Freedom of expression has always been considered a classical constitutional right designed to protect citizens against authorities. In current legal opinion freedom of expression also has the characteristic of a social constitutional right. This is understood to mean that, apart from a passive task (i.e., no interference by the state), the government also has an active role to play in ensuring citizens are able to gain access to the media. Both elements of freedom of expression are elaborated below.

Freedom to impart information

The principle to impart information freely, embedded in Article 10, is extremely important. It requires governments to ensure opportunity for citizen expression of opinion. Community broadcasting in fact derives partial justification from this principle (the concept of 'public access'). However, Article 10 also implies that regulation is necessary in order to specify how and to what extent the interest of the individual is to be ensured. This mandate, in turn, involves the concept of pluralism.

Pluralism

Safeguarding pluralism implies that it is important to ensure that at least prevailing views and opinions can be broadcast. Community broadcasting is one important medium for this purpose. A special task is reserved for community broadcasting particularly regarding issues to which other media cannot or will not attend. Community broadcasting can contribute to a pluralistic communication system, especially in 'one-paper' cities. Community broadcasting not only can contribute to pluralism with regard to content and quality, but also as an addition to existing local media. Two pluralistic models are available from which legislators can chose: internal and external.

The internal pluralistic model assumes that only a limited number of broadcasting possibilities are available and, in any case, this is less than the number of interested parties. Since the idea of 'one-man, one-transmitter' is not feasible, an alternative is necessary to ensure 'internal pluralism.' Those granted a license for community broadcasting also have the duty not only to report what they think relevant, but also to allow – if not ensure – propagation of other views. This can be realized by means of direct access, such as when a group or an individual makes a production and is granted broadcasting time on the licensee's transmitter, or by means of indirect access. An example of indirect access is when a resident provides an idea for a programme which is subsequently produced and broadcasted, while responsibility for the broadcast is borne by the station licensee.

Restrictions like one broadcasting license per service area can in this manner be compatible with the principle of internal pluralism. The objection against monopolising is anticipated in this construction through imposition of additional obligations on the licensee concerning programmes, and through provision of third party access to the medium.

Conversely, 'external pluralism' involves activities of several community broadcasting stations within one service area. Regulations to ensure pluralism are not as necessary in an external pluralistic model. The existence of several community broadcasting stations in the same service area, however, can lead to a destructive competitive situation. In cases where this has been attempted programming has actually deteriorated. Also, principles like the obligation to hear both sides of an issue – when one party is allowed to speak, the opposite party must be given a chance to respond – sometimes results in what is called 'stopwatch pluralism.' This term refers to compulsive forms of pluralism in which party 'y' is entitled to five minutes of broadcasting time if party 'x' also had five minutes time.

Transparency

French media law contains at least three fundamental principles (*Les grands principes du droit de l'audiovisuel*). Two of them have already been discussed: freedom of communication and pluralism. The third principle is 'transparency' which is directly linked to the concept of broadcasting as a market activity of business enterprises. When community broadcasting is left to the mercy of commercial powers, this principle becomes of special significance. According to Drouot (1988: 143) transparency is especially aimed at ensuring pluralism and implies, for example, that it must be clear who has authority over a medium or several media. For if it is known who actually controls a (community) radio or television station, it can be ascertained whether the pluralistic function of broadcasting is threatened and the public can be aware of its existence.

A logical consequence of this approach is the formulation of regulations which contribute to transparency in media ownership, or to ensuring the underlying principle of pluralism. In the first place, there are regulations with regard to the registration of owners and shareholders of broadcasting corporations, and rules for accumulation of shares in media and cross-ownership. But also on the production level transparency can be ensured. Later in this chapter, in discussing networks of stations, it will become apparent that such arrangements have valuable aspects.

Active government involvement

Even if a government prefers not to be concerned with the content of broadcasting, it is – or should be – involved in the realization and viability of community broadcasting. Particularly when it is acknowledged that community broadcasting is desired for reasons of pluralism, it is not enough to simply allow community broadcasting through creation of a system of licensing. It is equally important to formulate legal and policy conditions under which community broadcasting can develop.

This is where the previously mentioned responsibility of government with respect to freedom of expression lies.

This responsibility can be expressed in various forms – from direct financial support to the supply of technical equipment. The extent to which government contributes to safeguarding community broadcasting depends on the position taken regarding the function of this kind of broadcasting in the media system as a whole. An approach in which community stations are considered part of public service broadcasting leads to other consequences than an approach in which community broadcasting is part of a privately oriented media environment. Recent developments in regulation suggest a renewed interest in the non-commercial (public service) aspects of local broadcasting.

COMMUNITY BROADCASTING REGULATIONS

Two theoretical models can be distinguished in the legal design of community broadcasting. When attention is focused on a passive role for government, it is obvious that regulation of community broadcasting is minimized and is in principle left to market forces. Detailed regulations related to access of available frequencies or to programming content are not components of this minimalistic model.

When government plays an active role, particularly in situations where pluralism is emphasized, regulations for constructive intervention are desirable. Such a maximalistic model implies a broadcasting system regulated in detail, with little space for private initiative. Objections to this situation can be met by stressing the self-regulating character of the model. For, if it is possible to draw up rules which can lead to the presence of checks and balances within the community broadcasting system which safeguard pluralism, the role of the government can remain restricted. In such a 'black box' approach attention is focused on both aspects of input (e.g. regulation and financial arrangements) and output (e.g. assessment of activities). There is hardly any interference in the internal organization of community broadcasting or of programming content.

In most cases, however, neither model is found in its pure form, but as a mixture of the two. On the basis of the regulations developed it is generally apparent which of the two models has been emphasized. Without intending to assess the purposes and consequences of a particular model, the legislation approaches in Belgium, France and the Netherlands are examined below.

Belgium

In Belgium community broadcasting is mainly left to private initiative. Insofar as technical requirements are met, requests for authorization may be granted. The legal term used for community broadcasting in Belgium, 'non-public radio', implies that community broadcasting does not fill the same public function as national public broadcasting.

However, it would be incorrect to classify community broadcasting simply as a business enterprise. Only non-profit associations are eligible to apply for authorization. In practice, however, there is no preventive measure to keep associations from transforming community broadcasting into a profit-making enterprise. The fact that community stations may legally broadcast advertisements contributes to the commercial quality of the medium. Such commercial activity was initially prohibited, but practice superseded theory, and by means of additional legislation community stations had to be granted the right to broadcast advertising. Inasmuch as commercials are an essential source of income for stations given the absence of other financial sources, these determine the existence of community broadcasting. However, because several stations may operate in the same region – and inasmuch as they all draw on the same pool of commercial resources – stiff competition may result among stations in a particular region. It is therefore inevitable that stations consider the financial consequences programming policy may have. As a result, community broadcasting stations increasingly have developed identical – most often popular, middle-of-the-road – programming. The formation of networks, to be dealt with below, is another result of this competitive economic environment.

To safeguard pluralism the Belgian system distinguishes two guarantees. An association is not allowed to operate more than one station. It is also required that the programming be aimed at a specific geographic community, and that there is opportunity for involvement by listeners, and social and cultural organizations. Regulations for 'non-public radios' stipulate that these stations must offer a variety of information, animation, education and entertainment with an intention of supporting communication within their transmitting area and of contributing to general knowledge.

Community television is of no great significance in Belgium, with the exception of Wallonia where community television has become quite successful. In Flanders, broadcasts still take place on an incidental basis, and in terms of the overall media structure, community television plays only a minor role. Regulations formulated in 1987 do permit community cable television broadcasting – again on a 'non-public' basis – but it is uncertain what direction this development may take.

The Belgian community broadcasting system displays minimal governmental involvement through encouragement of private initiative. On the other hand, community broadcasting has been reserved for non-commercial organizations which have a legal obligation to contribute to a pluralistic programming policy. (See Chapter 8 for further information on developments in Belgium.)

France

France is a remarkable country, particularly regarding the way in which recent broadcasting regulations have developed. Until 1981 the system of state broadcasting in the country was quite rigid. Although radio pirates already enjoyed a certain reputation, it was not until the presidential elections in 1981 that they began to play a prominent role. Given the nature of the broadcasting system there were few or no possibilities for opposition parties, particularly for the socialist party, to address voters. Illegal radio stations, however, did provide some opportunity. Not surprisingly, one of the socialists' campaign promises that year was to legalize community broadcasting (*radio libre*). In a provisionary regulation passed in November 1981, with the poignant title *Loi portant derogation au monopole d'Etat de la radiodiffusion* (Act Concerning Cession of the Government's Monopoly of Radio), a special committee was charged to oversee distribution of frequencies. No further definition of the objective of community broadcasting was stated in the Act (this was to be described in the license conditions), but it was specified that licenses would only be granted to institutions and non-profit associations. Advertising was not to be allowed.

In an entirely new media regulation, the *Loi sur la communication audiovisuelle* (Audiovisual Communication Act) of 1982, which fundamentally changed the character of national broadcasting and partly privatized it, the private community broadcasting system (*les radios locales privées*, RLP) was definitely regulated. A special body, *La Haute Autorité de la communication audiovisuelle* (High Authority for Audiovisual Communication), was charged with the distribution of frequencies. As in Belgium, community broadcasting was not really considered a public service. Programming requirements were not specified, but geographical and socio-cultural conditions were to be taken into account as well as general guarantees for freedom of expression and pluralism. To prevent networking, 80 per cent of the programming was to be of local origin. In order to limit external influence, financial contributions from third parties were not to exceed 25 per cent. Moreover, stations could claim financial support from a fund generated by a tax placed on national broadcast advertising.

In 1984 this financing system was modified. Support from the special fund proved insufficient, and other commercial funding sources were considered. The revised law permitted advertising, but stations that chose to broadcast commercials could no longer lay claim to full support from the special fund.

Particularly in Paris the scarcity of frequencies caused substantial problems inasmuch as requests had to be turned down and frequencies shared. Competition also developed between community stations, and license conditions were sometimes violated (e.g. use of high power transmitters). As a result, the large variety of community stations originally broadcasting, characterized by the presence of action radio stations and involvement of diverse interest groups, disappeared.

In 1986 a new government took power and one of the first projects of the conservative Chirac cabinet was reorganization of the broadcasting system. Community broadcasting was, for all intent, eliminated. The licensing system for community broadcasting was replaced by a general regulation for the distribution of radio and television frequencies. Another change permitted companies, in addition to institutions and associations, to apply for 'community' broadcasting licenses.

The task of granting licenses was assigned to a new institution with wide powers, the *Commission Nationale de la Communication et des Libertés* (National Commission for Communication and Freedom), or CNCL. Inasmuch as previously granted licenses had or were about to expire, the CNCL was soon able to exert its authority. In accordance with the government's philosophy, commercial exploitation of community broadcasting was given a clear field in the distribution of frequencies.

Furthermore, the CNCL permitted an increase in more powerful transmitters and networking of stations, thereby making a development already initiated under the previous regulation legal. The fact that French broadcasting is subject to a market-orientated commercial approach explains the detailed regulation of cross-ownership. There are, for example, restrictions on the ownership of radio transmitters by the press, and prohibitions to own more than a certain percentage of all broadcasting facilities within a given area.

The Conseil supérieur de l'audiovisuel, CSA, which succeeded the CNCL in 1988, recently adopted a new policy allowing more attention to be given to distribution of community radio licenses. And, in contrast to earlier developments, further expansion of networks has been limited.

In France, community television is still in its infancy. This is evident from regulations which essentially place community cable broadcasts under the responsibility of the cable system operator. Furthermore, very few areas are cabled and television frequencies are scarce since they are primarily reserved for the six national channels.

As with radio, no distinction is made in the new law between community television broadcasts via the ether and national broadcasts. Contrary to radio, television broadcasts cannot be operated by non-commercial organizations; these are explicitly reserved for business enterprises. Financially speaking, the three existing commercial local television stations have not been very successful.

The French system is a good example of a regulatory system in transition from a situation of state-domination to one where government policy is being limited or withdrawn. Non-commercial aspects in the regulations have made commercial exploitation possible. It is remarkable that non-commercial initiatives could still appeal to a special fund for assistance, but this is clearly advantageous for a pluralistic media policy.

The Netherlands

All broadcasting, with the exception of pay television, is considered in the Netherlands to be in the public interest and therefore part of the public broadcasting service (national commercial broadcasting will be allowed by the end of 1991). This perspective is characteristic of countries in which the principle of a social welfare state is prominent. The Media Act which took effect in 1988 is not much different from the provisionary rules dating from 1982 – at least regarding community broadcasting. Unlike procedures in Belgium and France, pluralism is ensured through means of a single community station licensed for each municipality or cable system. This organization is required to ensure participation of groups and organizations considered representative for the particular community. To obtain a license for community broadcasting it is therefore necessary that the programming policy be determined by a body made up of representatives from local social and cultural groups.

Furthermore, the Media Act states that the community station's programming must be oriented to the locality in which a license has been granted. By means of these conditions government interference with programming content is prevented. The Media Authority (*Commissariaat voor de Media*), charged with issuing licenses, may also exercise marginal control over station activity.

Although community stations are considered part of the public broadcasting service, there is no arrangement for structural financing. Advertising on community programming will be introduced in 1991. And regulations preventing stations from developing collective programming policy, i.e. formation of networks, do not yet exist.

No distinction is made in the regulations between radio and television, and community stations are entitled to produce both types of programming for distribution by cable. Since 1988 low power ether radio is also permissible; see Chapter 7 for further information on recent developments.

In the Netherlands a clear decision bas been made in favour of a model in which the government is directly involved in the organization of community broadcasting, particularly evident in a system of restricted licensing. Through introduction of various checks and balances far-reaching interference in programming content is prevented. As community stations are considered part of the public broadcasting service, regulations intended to curb commercialization are considered less necessary than in other models.

ANTICIPATED DEVELOPMENTS

As noted earlier, there is a wide variety of regulations for community broadcasting, and the regulating framework here, partly in contrast to that for national broadcasting, is still in development. Some countries like France have distinct forms of community broadcasting in which efforts have been made to achieve a balance between practice, theory and policy. In other countries emphasis is placed on what is considered desirable in accordance with policy (the law as an instrument to realize social developments), but which is not always in accordance with everyday practice. The resulting area of tension is, among other things, recognisable in the Dutch community broadcasting system. Expectations are that further development of community broadcasting will be influenced by four interrelated factors: Europe-wide regulations, commercialization of programming, increase in scale of operation, and development of networking.

Europe-wide regulations

The EEC and the Council of Europe have drawn up rules aimed at harmonising and co-ordinating the different national rules with respect to broadcasting. These European broadcasting regulations all have in common that they contain provisions concerning advertising, sponsorship and programming content. According to Europe-wide regulation, member states may retain authority to prohibit commercials in national broadcasting or contributions by sponsors. However, foreign programmes which meet the European regulations (e.g. no more than 15 to 20 per cent advertising) may no longer be barred. Consequently, when programmes from Luxemburg are directed at France or the Netherlands, these programmes can be freely distributed in the receiving country. If the receiving country (in the above example the Netherlands or France) has stricter rules for advertising than the broadcasting country (Luxemburg) it can be lucrative for advertisers to broadcast commercials for the home market from abroad.

This development is of importance to community broadcasting in that stations located along national borders face tough competition from stations operating just on the other side of the border in a national broadcasting system with more liberal legislation allowing advertising. To improve the position of national broadcasting, the same financial conditions must be created as in a neighbouring country where the programming is directed across the borders. For example, if community stations in the Netherlands and France do not want to lose their audiences because of 'unfair competition', the same sources of income must be made available as in Luxemburg. In addition to regulations related to the harmonization of advertising and sponsoring practices, Europe-wide regulations are also required in order that programming content meets certain minimal standards regarding, for example, portrayal of violence, pornography and the protection of children from specific types of programming.

Regulations regarding harmonization and co-ordination can be at odds with the general intention of allowing community stations to develop their own character and to protect them from commercial influences. Acceptance of such regulations, in whatever eventual form, will most likely have substantial consequences for community broadcasting.

Commercialization of activity

Apart from possible consequences to the character of community broadcasting due to European-wide regulations, these developments may also involve a trend towards increasing commercialization of station activity. This is a logical consequence of the privatization of community broadcasting. If community broadcasting is to be self-supporting and if at the same time stations are unable to secure subsidies or levy license fees, then commercial arguments will play an increasingly important role in programming decisions. The extent to which this happens may also influence the pluralistic character of station programming.

This trend toward commercialization of community broadcasting is well illustrated by the uncontrolled introduction of advertising in community broadcasting in certain countries. Both in France and Belgium commercials were initially prohibited, but lack of alternative financing soon led stations to solicit advertising in spite of the prohibition. Since enforcement of this prohibition became impracticable because of the large number of stations, the regulatory agencies in both countries soon decided to formally allow such commercial activity.

Scale of operation

Belgian legislation limits transmitter power to a maximum of 100 watts. The same power limitation applies in principle to community radio stations in the Netherlands. The original French broadcasting regulation of 1982 designated that station signals could be received within a 30 kilometre radius from the transmitter. Such technical restrictions were related to the character of community broadcasting, i.e. that station programming was intended for geographic communities. This idea that community broadcasting should be confined to a geographically limited area has since been criticized, not because of any need for a change in the content of programmes but because of pragmatic considerations.

As a result of the commercialization of activities and subsequent decrease in programming variety, there is also a tendency towards increasing the scale of operation and of transmission power. In France the CNCL and CSA have already permitted 'community' broadcasting with 1000-watt or larger transmitters, and in Belgium similar plans exists to allow such transmitters. The Dutch Media Act, in contrast, restricts the service area of radio stations to either the limited range capable with 100-watt transmitters or, if programming is distributed by cable, to the neighbouring municipalities sharing a single cable infrastructure.

Particularly in countries where community broadcasting was aimed at the realization of a (limited) privatization of broadcasting activities generally, an increase in scale of operation also involves economic and strategic considerations. There is a reduction in costs when the same programme is used in a larger service area, and 'community' stations are then better able to compete with national broadcasting corporations. The possibility should not be discounted that some European community stations could become so-called 'superstations' like CNN; in a sense CNN is no more than a local broadcasting station located in Atlanta, Georgia, but with a world-wide distribution network.

Networks of stations

The idea that community broadcasting is 'big business' is most evident from the development of so-called networks of stations. This form of co-operation between small scale forms of broadcasting is frequently found in the United States, and was introduced in Europe during the late 1980s in Italy. Then, entrepreneurs began purchasing and linking individual community television stations, thereby creating a new national network which directly competed with the national broadcasting corporation. In France such networking is in an advanced state of development with community radio stations. Creation of radio chains is acknowledged by the government and regulated through restrictions on media cross- ownership.

Various radio chains such as *FUN*, *Nostalgie* and *Europe 2* have branches in all important cities in France. Media barons and concerns such as Hersant and RTL-Luxemburg mainly exercise authority over these chains. The largest network *NRJ* (pronounced 'Energy') has become the third radio station in France in less than 5 years. *NRJ* uses a sophisticated franchise formula which requires participating stations to use identical programming, adopt the name of the chain and employ a similar form of presentation. In return for these concessions these stations may share the profits of the chain. Profit-making is, of course, the principle reason for the emergence of networks. Advertisers are interested in the largest possible distribution of their commercials among members of the target audience. Chains which can offer advertisers broadcast outlets around the country are, thus, extremely attractive.

Also in countries where commercial motives (earnings from advertising and/or internal competition) play a role, there is a tendency towards formation of chains. Belgium is following the French example, and in Germany similar steps are being taken, although the national media authority is not encouraging such development (see Chapter 9 for information on trends in Germany).

CONCLUSION

The regulation of community broadcasting in Europe is a recent development and is far from complete. The general objective of this regulatory activity is either primarily directed at privatization of broadcasting or at creation of a new means of community expression. In this respect, the law offers a choice between the principles of government withdrawal or government interference. The first choice implies primarily a system which propagates community broadcasting as a sort of business enterprise able to compete with the protected public broadcasting system. However, where community broadcasting is highlighted as a new means of expression, explicit safeguards are generally instituted to regulate access to the medium.

On the basis of a limited analysis of regulatory activity, it appears that the notion of community broadcasting as part of a public broadcasting service is no longer dominant. Community broadcasting seems rather to serve the function of breaking through the present system in order to facilitate privatization of broadcasting. In legal terms, 'Community' in community broadcasting refers less to the content of programmes than to a technical criterion. This is not surprising from a legal point of view: nothing is more difficult in the field of law than refining and enforcing substantive criteria.

It seems, though, that governments are becoming more aware of the need for a balance between private and public interests. Community broadcasting with a public service character might, then, receive more attention in the future.

References

Benhaim. J., F. Bonvoisin, and R. Dubois (1985): *Les radios locales privées*, Paris: Enterprise Moderne d'édition.

Boon, P.J. (1983): *Zonder voorafgaand verlof*, Nijmegen: Ars Aequi.

Breways, E., S. Desmet, J. Opdebeeck, P. Voets, and D. Voorhoof (1987): *Persvrijheid, omroeprecht en nieuwe media*, Antwerpen: Kluwer.

Drouot, G. (1988): *Le nouveau droit de l'audiovisuel*, Paris: éditions Siney.

Eijk, N.A. van. (1983): 'Lokale omroep: een heet hangijzer in 'omroepland', in A. van de Felz, M. Göbbels, M. Polak, M. Sommer, M. Vos and R. Zeldenrust (eds) *Mediarecht*, Nijmegen: Ars Aequi.

Hollander, E.H. (1982): *Kleinschalige massacommunicatie: Lokale omroepvormen in West-Europa*, The Hague: State Publ. Co.

Luhmann, N. (1986): 'The self-reproduction of Law and its limits', in Teuber, G. (ed.) *Dilemmas of law in the welfare state*, New York: Walter de Gruyter.

Meij, J.M. de (1984): *Van zender naar ontvanger*, Amsterdam: Cramwinckel.

Meij, J.M. de (1990): *Uitingsvrijheid*. Amsterdam: Cramwinckel.

Nonet, P. and P. Selznick (1978): *Law and society in transition; towards responsive law*, New York: Harper & Row.

Teubner, G. (1986): 'After legal instrumentalism?' in G. Teubner (ed.) *Dilemmas of law in the welfare state*, New York: Walter de Gruyter.

18. From small scale utopianism to large scale pragmatism.
Trends and prospects for community oriented local radio and television

Ole Prehn

Aalborg University, Denmark

CREATION OF A NEW STRUCTURE

During the past 15 years Western European countries have experienced an unparalleled explosion of new radio and television stations. In the beginning of the 1970s most stations were part of national public service institutions, with only a small number of private outlets funded commercially. Today, in contrast, there are at least 12,000 private radio stations (Loensman, 1990). The number of private television stations is much smaller, but their proliferation has clearly marked developments. The main media issues on the political agenda in Western Europe have centred on the development of nationwide television companies, transfrontier satellite television and establishment of cable television networks. In recent years, though, there has been a significant expansion of local radio and television programming distributed both by cable and Hertzian waves.

This volume focuses on the development of community oriented local radio and television. The chapters in Part I of the volume treat the historical development of these small scale media and some of the theoretical perspectives which have guided research. Chapters in Part II concentrate on specific development in several European countries, and chapters in Part III analyse overarching concerns such as legal structures and use of the media by women and minority groups. Much of this work has demonstrated that community oriented local radio and television is only one of many elements in the changing scene of electronic media in Europe. Generally speaking, the main trends in Western Europe revolve around the privatization, commercialization and internationalization of the broadcasting media, politically enforced by deregulatory initiatives. An undercurrent in this development, though, is an ongoing effort to secure a position for small scale, non-commercial community oriented media in the newly emerging electronic media landscape.

As repeatedly demonstrated in this volume the task has not been easy for the thousands of volunteers of community oriented radio and television stations to achieve substantial control of the media. Even if the various schemes for testing and evaluating the viability of such media had been introduced prior to general reformulation of media policy, even if the original scarcity of frequencies which prohibited a differentiated media structure had disappeared and the monopolies had vanished, difficult times would still have been faced by those committed to the idea of giving a voice to the voiceless through these small scale media.

FROM STATE REGULATED MONOPOLIES TO COMMERCIAL NETWORKS

Broadcasting monopolies

In the years immediately following introduction of wireless transmission radio was seen as an extension of telegraphy. It soon became clear, however, that radio could be used for other purposes than furthering telegraphic transmissions, and both in North America and Europe radio amateurs began transmitting radio programming directed at the general public.

There also developed a widely felt need for regulation of frequency space. The European approach to satisfying this need was establishment of national, state regulated transmission monopolies. The main argument for monopolizing broadcasting was to protect other services making use of frequencies, particularly military and telegraph services. This argument eventually led to formation of de facto monopolies responsible not only for transmission, but also for programme production. There was also fear that private firms, such as the Marconi Company in England, would become too powerful. To avoid such development the government created the British Broadcasting Company in 1922 (Crisell, 1986: 20; Lewis & Booth, 1989: 53).

Another reason for monopolization of broadcasting was the conviction among politicians and cultural leaders that broadcasting was a potential force of influence which should be controlled and kept in line with dominant ideas and tastes. Thus, broadcasting was seen as a tool for general education and enlightenment, and not as a form of commercial activity.

Although emerging from different legislative and organizational structures, broadcasting in Western European countries developed between the 1920s and 1970s into public service institutions for both radio and television. These institutions were regulated and administered differently for each country; a common denominator, nevertheless, was the strict limitation as to who should run the radio and television services as well as the public service obligations requiring diversity, objectivity and good taste in programming.

Despite introduction of advertising in several countries as a supplementary source of income to licence fees and introduction of privately owned radio and television companies, the concept of politically defined monopolies as opposed to market-based monopolies (McQuail & Siune, 1986: 116) was generally left undisturbed until the late 1950s and '60s.

Challenge of the pirates

The ideal of the public service monopolies has always been to keep the broadcasting media at arm's length from private capital and ideologically or politically vested interests. The concept of public service was based upon the premise that only through a politically controlled structure would it be possible to guarantee freedom of speech and diversity. As things turned out, the monopolies became increasingly difficult to defend inasmuch as technological developments became less of a hinderance for establishing additional channels without frequency congestion and interference.

Parallel to the emergence of new technological possibilities a growing crisis of legitimacy was faced by the public service institutions which were accused of approaching listeners and viewers from a high-brow, top-down attitude. Founded in the tradition of high culture and good taste, the companies were considered by large parts of the audience as paternalistic or authoritarian institutions which, embedded in an elitist approach, neglected the tastes and preferences of the general public.

The monopolies were also questioned by the private sector especially because of the limited amount of advertising time and, indeed, because the monopolistic structure made investments in a potentially profitable sector impossible. As indicated above, the political climate changed radically in the 1970s towards a more liberal and market oriented broadcasting policy, but before that phase, the public service companies were challenged by several attempts to introduce alternative broadcasting services directed more explicitly at satisfying audience needs and concerns.

In searching for the roots of community oriented local stations, the early pirates are important in that they expressed dissatisfaction with the public broadcasting companies and their programming policies. It is important to stress that, in contrast to the situation in the United States where community stations were established as an alternative to entertainment oriented middle-of-the-road stations (Barlow, 1988; Spark, 1987; Kellner, 1987), the European radio scene was characterized by a lack of entertainment programming. Accordingly, the first examples of 'free' radio stations were American-style stations with light music, soap operas and commercials, such as *Radio Normandie* in 1931 and *Radio Luxembourg* in 1933, both reaching countries across the European continent as well as Britain. These stations had an extensive impact on their audiences, often attracting more listeners than the *BBC* (Crisell, 1986: 24). This success, however, did not substantially affect the predominant policy of the public broadcasting companies.

The pirates did, however, achieve much more impact during the 1950s and 1960s. Two notable examples are *Radio Caroline*, established in 1964, which transmitted from a ship in international waters close to Britain and *Radio Mercury*, transmitting in the same manner between Sweden and Denmark from 1958. Both stations eventually were closed down by state authorities, but the discontent with the programming offered by the public broadcasting companies was so manifestly demonstrated by these and many other stations that the monopolies were forced to change their policies. In both Britain and Denmark new popular channels (Radio One in Britain and *Program 3* in Denmark) resulted which offered previously neglected pop music programming and other fast moving formats. In both cases the companies hired former pirate station employees to run the new services (Boyd, 1986).

Perhaps such "commercial pirates" (McCain & Lowe, 1990: 88) seem far removed from community oriented stations, but their anti-establishment attitude and programming formats were, to an extent, a pre-echo of many community stations of the 1970s and '80s.

During the 1960s pirate stations were frequently set up and just as frequently closed down by authorities in all parts of Western Europe. Although the first examples of pirate stations were found in northern European countries, the real breakthrough took place in Italy in the mid-1970s. It was no coincidence that this 'second wave' of pirate radios emerged in southern Europe: the broadcasting monopolies there were far more politicized and governmentally controlled than elsewhere.

Contrary to the pirates of the 1960s, those of the '70s in Italy were affiliated with the Socialist and Communist Parties, trade unions, and political and social movements of the late 1960s. When the Italian Constitutional Court ruled in 1976 that the monopoly of the public broadcasting company *RAI* was only valid at the national level the number of local radio stations increased at an explosive rate. Some 2,275 radio stations were in operation in 1978 according to an official survey (Lewis & Booth, 1989: 141). Without regulations, the situation in Italy rapidly changed from one with heavy political control to that of a *laissez faire* state where virtually everyone with the finances began to establish a radio station. Although Italian leftist groups were the first to make use of clandestine radios, the political right and commercial interests eventually became the dominant forces of local radio in the country.

The same point of departure was found in France where the broadcasting monopoly traditionally was in the hands of the government which allotted only limited airtime to the political opposition and minority groups. In response, the French Ecology Party introduced one of the first well-known clandestine radios in 1978. Shortly thereafter, hundreds of illegal stations were started, often supported by opposition parties and the labour movement. Like in Italy, the local radios were within a short period of time, in 1981, recognised by law. In contrast to Italy, France established a regulatory framework for issuance of licences. The number of licences available was limited, though, and legalization of local radio did not mean the end of pirates in France.

The pirate or clandestine period of local radio was also part of the media landscape in many other countries: Spain, Portugal, Ireland, Britain, the Netherlands and Belgium. In these countries hundreds – in some cases thousands – of illegal radios could be heard. Only countries in the central and eastern regions of Western Europe – in Germany, Austria and Switzerland – and in the Nordic countries – Finland, Sweden, Norway and Denmark – were pirate radios a relatively minor phenomenon.

Apart from the fact that the stations were illegal and that generally inexpensive equipment was used with a limited range of transmission, it is hard to find a common denominator among the thousands of new voices which were being heard in Western Europe. As already mentioned, many of the new stations had relations with various social movements and had explicit political goals. Sometimes the stations were affiliated to political parties and sometimes programming was directed at societal or environmental issues. Even when the goals of these stations went further than the direct concerns of specific localities, it was often the case that programming was meant to serve as a vehicle for stimulating local initiatives. First and foremost, however, these stations considered themselves non-commercial, non-profit and non-professional.

Many other stations had more commercial ambitions and accordingly concentrated on broadcasting music, disc jockey chatter and phone-in programmes. Finally, some stations claimed to be pure public service institutions for their communities, and emphasized a pluralistic and non-political approach.

Whatever the differences in background and goals, the illegal radio stations, and to a lesser extent the cablecast television initiatives, had a profound impact on the formation of media policy. In Italy and France the authorities legalized local radio; in Italy local television was also legalized. In other countries political decisions were postponed through introduction of a period of experimentation.

Period of experimentation

The situation in Western Europe in the 1970s resembled the era prior to establishment of the public broadcasting monopolies in the 1920s in that large numbers of radio stations were operating illegally. Contrary to this pioneering period, however, activities in the 1970s were initiated by groups which lacked access to established broadcasting institutions. These groups had been denied access even though there was no longer technical justification for protecting the monopolies. More transmission space had become available both for over-the-air and cable delivered signals, initially one of the most persuasive arguments in favour of the monopolies.

In order to allow time for finding a new regulatory framework, several governments initiated an experimental period aimed at assessing the prospects of local radio and television. As mentioned earlier, developments in France and Italy proceeded much more quickly with legal recognition of pirate initiatives. Experiments were introduced in Britain, the Netherlands, Switzerland, Germany and in the Nordic countries. Britain was the first to introduce such experiments and they were based on a governmental proposal dating back to 1951. Ironically, Britain has been one of the last countries to pass legislation providing a more permanent status for commmunity oriented local radio and television stations.

The British experiments began in 1972 with primarily cable distributed community television, but there was also some experimentation with cablecasted community radio (Partridge, 1982; Lewis, 1978). The experiments, a compromise between the interests of cable companies and community groups, were based on the assumption that there was a need among people to have access to electronic media and a need to provide local information and discussion based on programming produced by non-professionals. The experiments were later discontinued because of financial problems when the cable companies terminated support. The experiments remained, nevertheless, a source of inspiration for initiatives elsewhere in Europe because of their pluralistic and community orientation.

Shortly afterwards, between 1974 and 1978, the Dutch government introduced an experiment with cable delivered community oriented radio and television in six localities. Some years after termination of this experiment, in 1984, community radio and television were legalized and other initiatives were allowed to apply for licences.

In Switzerland experiments with local television have taken place since 1977, and with local radio between 1982 and 1988. Whereas the experiments in the Netherlands were based on a community oriented non-commercial concept, the experiments with local radio in Switzerland were mainly a testing ground for local stations with commercial affiliations; advertising was one of the primary sources of income (Langenbucher, 1989).

In Germany experiments with local radio and television were included in the so-called *Pilot-Projekte* in the form of open channels. These pilot projects were primarily concerned with developing cable services; except for various pirate stations, which were quickly shut down by the German PTT authorities, over-the-air distribution of community radio programming has not been an issue in the country.

In the Nordic countries similar experiments took place during the 1980s, starting in Sweden in 1979 with the introduction of 'neighbourhood radio'. The Swedish approach has strived to guarantee community orientation through issuance of licences for neighbourhood radio or local television only to recognized organizations. In Denmark and Norway experiments were started in 1981, but contrary to the Swedish model the regulations inacted were quite liberal and only excluded private companies from applying for broadcasting licences. Advertising was not allowed in these three countries, but in Finland privately owned local radio stations have been permitted to broadcast advertising since 1985. In Finland there was also no period of experimentation as elsewhere in Scandinavia.

The general aim of all these experiments, with the exception of those in Switzerland, was to assess the viability of community oriented stations operating within a limited geographical area. The stations were to function without advertising and to be open for input from residents in the area. The stations, in other words, were to be non-commercial and non-professional in nature, and to rely primarily on volunteers for programme production. The general policy was to exclude commercially oriented entrepreneurs from the experiments in order to allow opportunity for local participation to develop.

The experiments were not only media experiments, but social laboratories for testing the degree of participatory potential in the respective communities. In all cases, the experiments were evaluated on the basis of findings collected from social science research, employing a diversity of methodological and conceptual approaches.

The experimental period is the focal point of this volume, and in general terms it can be said that the experiences demonstrated interest in the community oriented radio and television stations among local populations, both as audience members and as participants in station activities. The experiments also revealed many of the problems faced by stations operating from the concepts of community orientation and non-professionalism, particularly problems related to financing station activities, and attracting and maintaining an audience. Even during the experimental period there was a strong effort to professionalize these media and to modify the principle of maintaining an open and participation-rich station.

In the Netherlands and Sweden this development was not as outspoken as in Denmark and Norway, perhaps due to the fact that the regulatory basis in the latter two countries was more open and less restrictive as to who was elegible for obtaining a licence. Thus, both community radio and television stations in Denmark and Norway quickly developed into quasi-commercial outlets, biding time until permanent legislation would legalize advertising and reduce restrictions on programme content.

Period of institutionalization

Developments in the southern countries of Western Europe and experiences gathered during the period of experimentation in northern European countries have demonstrated, on the one hand, the viability and importance of community oriented radio and television and, on the other, the fragility of these media. In nearly all Western European countries, with the exception of Austria and Portugal, local radio and television are now developing within an established regulatory framework. Only in Sweden, however, are stations protected from commercial interests through a prohibition on advertising.

Following the deregulatory development in France and Italy and the experimental period in other countries in Western Europe, community radio and television became accepted elements in national media legislation by the end of the 1980s. Even though recognized as part of the media landscape, in very few countries is community oriented local radio and television treated as the only outlet for local programming. Formulation of new legislation coincided with the general trend in European media policy debates towards privatization and commercialization of both radio and television.

The community radio and television stations began to form national associations and lobby groups: OLON in the Netherlands, The Association of Local Radio and Television Stations in Denmark, The Community Radio Association in Britain, The National Association of Community Broadcasters in Ireland, Vidéotram (television) and ALO-VEBE (radio) in Belgium, EMUC (radio) in Catalonia, and the *Association Nationales des Radio Libres Noncommerciales* in France. Most of these organizations have joined the worldwide, loosely organized association of community radio stations AMARC (Association Mondiale des Radiodiffuseurs Communautaires) which was established in 1985 during the first world conference for community oriented broadcasters in Montreal. In 1986 the European association of 'free radios' *Federation Européenne des Radio Libres* was created, and in 1991 a pan-European organization of local television stations was formed: *Organization Européenne des Télévisions Locales*.

These organizations were established mainly to represent the interests of local radio and television with a non-commercial and community orientation at a period when commercial interests were securing frequencies. Although reasonably well organized and generally with non-commercial statements of purpose, community stations around Western Europe began to experience an ideologically difficult situation inasmuch as public funding for such stations was diminishing.

In the Netherlands, until the prohibition on advertising was lifted in 1991, community stations were completely dependent on funding from their respective municipalities. In Belgium advertising has been allowed since the early 1980s, but public financial support is minimal. In Ireland community stations were an accepted phenomenon, but operated outside the law until 1988 when advertising for local radio was legalized. In Spain stations were frequently established by municipalities even though such broadcasting was, strictly speaking, illegal. In Italy a sphere of 'survival of the fittest' reigned, and stations with commercial support, or those with political party, interest group and trade union affiliations were able to survive. In Finland the primary source of support is advertising, as is it in Switzerland and Germany. Only in France and Norway have an alternative to commercialism been implemented. Here, a tax or levy has been established at the national level which serves as a form of cross subsidy, from the commercial to the non-commercial stations.

In a situation where the market forces primarily dictate who is to win and who is to lose, the policy of remaining non-commercial is, understandably, difficult to maintain. In the face of insufficient funding many non-commercial stations have modified their community oriented principles rather than cease activity altogether.

Towards a two-tiered system of local broadcasting

The general trend in Western Europe – and since recently a trend also evident in former Eastern European countries – has been to lift the broadcasting monopolies and establish privately owned channels. Especially in political debates focus has been on transfrontier television destributed by satellite and the future of the European film and television industry (European Institute for the Media, 1987, 1988; Lange & Renaud, 1989). The development of local radio and television, on the other hand, has until recently been nearly totally neglected despite the fact that the most profound changes and experiments have taken place at the local level (Council of Europe, 1990).

Many people initially expressed high expectations regarding the possibilities of community television, especially when used in combination with portable video equipment and multiple channel cable networks. Local community oriented television, however, has remained in embryonic form partially because the medium is relatively expensive and because audiences generally prefer entertainment programming of high technical quality (Vidéotrame, 1990).

Even though television has the basis for becoming a community oriented medium and even though there have been hundreds of initiatives to implement community television in Western Europe during the past two decades, it is radio which has become the dominant and revitalized medium (Lewis & Booth, 1989). Starting with pirate initiatives, often with conflicting objectives, the challenge against the public service broadcasting monopolies succeeded in paving the way for a new structure of radio with the local level as its point of departure.

Apart from the relatively few commercial pirates of the 1960s, the radio stations in the 1970s were the ones which gave substance to the concept of non-professional programming. The aim of these stations was to promote points of view never heard on the monopoly channels and to create station organizations based on the principles of self-management. These pioneering stations are now being confronted by commercial stations and radio networks emerging across Western Europe.

In all European countries except Sweden and Austria advertising on local radio has been allowed, making radio a potentially – if somewhat overestimated – profitable market for newspapers, publishers and other investors in electronic media (see Pürer, 1988). Inasmuch as the locality for which a broadcasting licence has been issued is often too limited for stations dependent on advertising, the trend is to increase the transmission area by using stronger transmitters and by creating country-wide networks of stations as in Italy, France (Oehler, 1988), Belgium and Germany (Jens, 1989; Röper, 1989; Wöste, 1989). Specialized networks broadcasting identical news programmes also exist in Norway and Belgium, and advertising for local stations is sold on a national scale in Norway, Finland and Denmark. In some cases – in Belgium, France and Denmark – foreign capital has also entered the marketplace. Only the Flemish section of Belgium seems to be developing in a direction which emphasizes the geographical parameters of local radio. As for recent developments in the Netherlands, it is uncertain how the legalization of low power ether radio and advertising will influence the further course of events once hundreds of such stations commence operation.

As shown in Table 1, thousands of local radio stations and hundreds of local television stations are currently operating in Western Europe.

Table 1. Number of local radio and television stations in Western European countries

Country	Local radio ( ) = non-commercial		Local TV
Austria	0		0
Belgium (French)	250	(70)	11
Belgium (Flemish)	400	(?)	4
Denmark	300	(150)	85
Finland	66	(7)	0
France	1600	(400)	3*
Germany ('FRG')	100	(1)	17
Greece	670		12
Iceland	70	(70)	0
Ireland	22	(9)	0
Italy	4530	(500)	950
Netherlands	240	(240)	76
Norway	400	(100)	160
Portugal	400	(?)	0
Spain	1000	(?)	150
Sweden	150	(150)	18
Switzerland	36	(2)	8
United Kingdom	74	(0)	15

(*) = Terrestrial stations only.
Sources: In many countries no reliable data exist on the number of local radio and television stations. The figures in this table are estimates based upon Gear (1990), Udvalget vedr. lokalradio og -tv (1990a, 1990b), Familie- og forbrukerdepartementet (1990), Moring (1991), Prehn (1990), OLON (1990), Vidéo-trame (1990), Loensmann (1989), Heretakis (1990), Traquina (1989, 1990), Woldt (1989), Leoponieni, (1990) and Kleinsteuber & Sonnenberg (1990).

Although reliable data are not available for all countries, more than a thousand radio stations and some hundred television stations still insist that there are other ways of using radio and television than those emphasizing commercial and para-local. By attracting small but specialized audiences and by giving thousands of people the opportunity to produce and air programmes, these stations are trying to maintain the concept of community orientation and to survive in the increasingly limited space between public broadcasting and private local radios (Kleinsteuber & Sonnenberg, 1989, 1990; McCain & Lowe, 1990).

SMALL BUT BEAUTIFUL – THE COMMUNITY CONCEPT

Back to basics

In the Anglo-Saxon literature, non-commercial and local radio, as well as local television stations, are often referred to collectively as 'community stations'. In a pan-European context it is difficult to justify use of this label. Most Europeans do not speak English as their native language and do not use the term 'community stations' to describe the emerging local media. In Spain emphasis is placed on *radio municipales* or 'municipal radios'; in the Netherlands the term *lokale omroep* or 'local broadcasting' is used; in Denmark *naerradio* or 'close radios'; in France *radio libres* refers to 'free radios' or 'non-commercial radios'.

The different terms are not only due to linguistic differences, but are also based on ideological and conceptual distinctions. Historically, the phrase 'community radio and television' was imported from North America and was related to the principle behind establishment of community radio stations in the United States since the late 1940s as non-commercial, democratic organizations aiming at community involvement (Barlow, 1988). This principle was later applied to community television channels operating on cable television networks. The Canadian National Film Board's Challenge for Change programme, and the successive policy statements by the Canadian regulatory body CRTC were also of importance for developments in Europe (Council of Europe, 1977: 3).

In Europe, the turbulent period of pirate radios and to a lesser extent the development of local television, with emphasis on access to the airwaves and cable channels, in many ways resembles the initiatives in North America. The development suggests further that freedom of expression, diversity and pluralism as laid down in most public service broadcasting charters had not, in fact, been realized (Shaughnessy & Cobo, 1990). Although the broadcasting structure in the United States is quite different from the European tradition of public service companies, both cases generated a call for more diversity, more access and more participation. In both cases there was a rejection of a top-down, uniformistic system of mass communication, be it monocentrically organized as in Western Europe, or polycentrically structured as in the United States (Jakubowicz, 1988).

Until the development of inexpensive lightweight video and radio equipment and until additional frequencies and channels on cable systems had been made available, the monopoly situation in Western Europe was accepted as a technical fact of life. Even such 'natural monopolies', however, were strongly felt as 'unnatural', and with the advent of new technological possibilities they came to be considered obsolete.

The first prominent public figure to criticize the monocentric organization of broadcasting was Bertolt Brecht:

> Radio should be converted from a distribution system to a communication system. Radio could be the most wonderful public communication system imaginable, a gigantic system of channels – could be, that is, if it were capable not only of transmitting but of receiving, of making the listener not only hear but also speak, not of isolating him but of connecting him. (Brecht, 1930/1983: 169)

What Brecht thus challenged was the one-way and top-down approach characterizing the organization of radio which overlooked the true potential of this new information technology. Brecht called for consideration as to how radio could be utilized under other technical and societal conditions.

As described by Lewis and Booth (1989: 21-25), the question of frequencies is perhaps more political than technical, and in all Western European countries there was reluctance to make frequencies available for community radio. The possibility of providing access to the airwaves had, of course, been known for many years. In Great Britain, for example, the Beveridge Committee, reporting on the future of broadcasting in 1951, stated that:

> Use of VHF could make it possible not merely to give the existing *BBC* programmes to people who now fail to get them, but to establish local stations with independent programmes of their own. How large a scope there would be in Britain for local stations broadcasting programmes controlled by Universities or Local Authorities or public service organizations is not known, but the experiment of setting up some local stations should be tried without delay... (quoted in Partridge, 1982: 10)

Reluctance to establish new outlets outside the broadcasting monopolies was, as indicated by Brecht, not only due to technical but also political and ideological considerations regarding the potential power ascribed to broadcasting media (Jakubowicz, 1985: 41). That broadcasting media have an ideological, activating, and even revolutionary potential was not only a belief of the establishment; the 'new left' also felt in the late 1960s that electronic media could be important tools for generating societal change.

One of the most influential documents calling for alternative use of broadcasting media is an essay by Hans Magnus Enzensberger entitled "Constituents of a Theory of the Media". Enzensberger argues that the new left neglected the potentials of the electronic media and notes the limitations of these media as presently employed:

> For the first time in history, the media are making possible mass participation in a social and socialized productive process, the practical means of which are in the hands of the masses themselves. Such a use of them would bring the communications media, which up to now have not deserved the name, into their own. In its present form, equipment like television or films does not serve communication but prevents it. It allows no reciprocal action between transmitter and receiver; technically speaking it reduces feedback to the lowest point compatible with the system. (Enzensberger, 1972: 101)

Enzensberger presents a simple – in many ways simplistic – dichotomy for organizing

257

the media. In spite of its limitations the typology reflects the utopian visions of a decentralized and democratized use of electronic media (Enzensberger, 1972: 115-116):

Repressive use of media	*Emancipatory use of media*
Centrally controlled programme	Decentralized programme
One transmitter, many receivers	Each receiver a potential transmitter
Immobilization of isolated individuals	Mobilization of the masses
Passive consumer behaviour	Interaction of those involved, feedback
Depolitization	A political learning process
Production by specialists	Collective production
Control by property owners or bureaucracy	Social control by self-organization

In Enzensberger's conception of a new media structure demand for change was not limited to merely broadcasting other programmes based on alternative ideologies and political messages, but it also implied a collective process of production and self-organization. The aim of this media structure was to establish new forms of controlling the media, while contributing to political awareness.

This vision of decentralizating the media and of reforming media organizations from vertical to horizontal structures was noted in policy statements of many of the new stations. It also found expression in international documents such as the report of UNESCO's General Conference held in 1976 in Nairobi:

> In the past, the role of communication in human society was seen essentially as to inform and influence people. It is now being proposed that communication should be understood as a process of social interaction through a balanced exchange of information and experience....This shift in perception implies the predominance of dialogue over monologue. The aim is to achieve a system of horizontal communication based upon an equitable distribution of resources and facilities enabling all persons to send as well as to receive messages (Quoted from Jouet (1977: 3).

The aim was not only to introduce access or participatory programmes in the broadcasting monopolies, as the *BBC* had done with its programme *Open Door* and *Danmarks Radio* had developed with its *Radio Workshop*. In these cases lay persons are given help from professionals to produce their own programmes which are later aired. The aim, rather, was to establish new programming outlets for contributions from active citizens, where assistance from professional staff was limited or even nonexistent.

This approach to organizing the broadcasting media was in line with a general trend calling for participatory democracy involving 'ordinary' people in policy and decision making (Groombridge, 1972). The core of the concept was thus a conviction in the mobilizing and dynamic forces of the broadcasting media and a belief that producing and disseminating alternative information would alter the social and political structure (Jankowski, 1988). This idealistic concept draws on a tradition from the Enlightenment where the public sphere is seen as the true battlefield of social change (Habermas, 1962). It also draws on the classical – and limited – notion of the communication process as a linear relationship between sender and receiver (see e.g. McQuail & Windahl, 1981).

The promotion of the ideas of public access and participation was not meant only for determing the goals of new stations, but it also was a frontal critique against the broadcasting monopolies for not living up to their social responsibilities as public service institutions. Only by increasing broadcasting outlets, it was assumed, would it be possible to transform radio and television from mass oriented communication media into small scale media operating within a structure of polycentric pluralism (Jakubowicz, 1988).

Some public service institutions have for many years provided programming aimed at involving people in societal matters, at providing opportunities for lifelong learning, and at offering advice on general concerns. The tradition of social action broadcasting in Great Britain (see Prehn, forthcoming) is an example of this undertaking. In spite of these developments, hostility towards the monoplies remained strong among many new social movements. For them, new technical possibilities of broadcasting in localities, either with cable networks or low power VHF transmitters, were seen as means for profoundly changing the broadcasting system.

The technological developments and the critique against the monopolies coincided with an awareness of the locality or community as a potential basis for social renewal. The call for locally situated radio and television stations based upon the principles of access and participation must be understood as but one of several efforts to reverse the societal trend towards still larger units and concentrations of power. Social movements for more democracy and decentralization are, in this respect, examples of a complicated nexus between concentration and totalization on the one hand, and deconcentration and division on the other.

The euphoric ambition was to demonstrate that if the overall structure of broadcasting media were changed and if the media were defined as non-commercial, non-professional and non-national institutions, then the involvement of people in radio and television production would increase along with their social and political awareness and participation in society. It is no coincidence, then, that the movement for changing the structure of broadcasting media had as its point of departure the local context. Only on the basis of everyday life, it was felt, would it be possible for non-professional programmes to function as vehicles for strenghtening local identity and interest in local affairs. Producing and airing programmes offering authenticity and personal experience were only possible within a limited geographical area, it was believed, even when the issues were trans-local in nature. The concept 'community' was accordingly interpreted both as 'community area' and as 'community of interest'.

In addition to the scale of operation as a common core of the new local stations, a wide variety of structures have been implemented reflecting different aims and ambitions. As Jouet (1977: 3) has noted, however, it is necessary to make distinctions between two of the most frequently cited terms: access and participation. Whereas access primarily refers to the relation between the public and the established broadcasting institutions, participation implies a wider range of activities related to involving people directly in station programming, administration and policy activities.

Community oriented local stations tend to focus on the participatory aspect, but there are many different models which have been proposed for achieving community involvement. In this regard Jankowski (1988: 6–7) notes three main station philosophies: a philosophy stressing the importance of diversity of expression, a radical philosophy where radio and television are incorporated into social and political actions, and a public service philosophy where residents are informed of institutional and organizational activitites in their area. Although situations vary from country to country regarding the relevance and importance of these philosophies, it is still possible to identify three main types of stations: (1) community stations with emancipatory intentions, (2) community stations which stress free speech, and (3) public service oriented community stations (Jankowski, 1988: 171-175).

It is not possible, however, on the basis of this typology of ideal types to easily fit actual stations into one of the three types. There are many cases where all three types have developed in a particular country, and in some cases in a particular station (Browne, 1988). At one end of the scale, the development of free radios and militant radios in Italy and France exemplifies the emancipatory and politically defined stations operating to promote their respective political positions. At the other end of the scale is the Swedish model which places emphasis on established organizations and associations. In the middle is the Dutch model of issuing only one licence to a given locality which is to be shared by all interests in the area, be they organizational or individual.

A fourth station type should be added to the above typology: stations attempting to serve a locality with programming designed to attract the largest audience. This is not always a goal in itself, but is sometimes based on the philosophy that people in a region should be able to view or listen to the types of programmes they want.

Concepts and reality

The results of the various experiments with community oriented radio and television throughout Western Europe demonstrate that people are interested in taking part in the production of programmes and running of stations. It is also evident that community oriented stations have, in spite of unfavourable odds, managed to survive.

Too little research has been conducted to give a detailed evaluation of the development of the hundreds of initiatives. It is nevertheless clear that, in spite of the distinctiveness of the service provided, community stations have not been able to avoid commercialization and professionalization of programming activities. Although hundreds of stations around Western Europe still operate on a non-commercial basis, many stations initially established as non-commercial and non-professional have been forced to adopt a more pragmatic policy. Five factors account for this transformation.

First, the ideas of the pioneers – media activists, researchers and theoreticians – overestimated the need by people to take part in station activities. Many of these pioneers also seemed to have lost ability to take distance and reflect on developments (Jankowksi, 1988: 9). Because of the original high expectations, many stations came to face a problem of legitimacy when it turned out that the facilities were used by far fewer people than originally anticipated. Moreover, those who did use the stations were not persons in some way neglected by the established media, but generally middle class citizens who already had easy access to the media.

Warning signals were sounded early in the development of these media by various individuals and institutions. A Council of Europe (1977: 17) report expressed such concern relatively early:

> There are experiments, on the other hand, which seem to indicate that direct participation of the public in CTV (community television) corresponds to a less pressing need than was first thought. These experiments may lead one to believe that it is unrealistic to want to accustom a community to continous self-expression. Participation quickly runs out of steam and becomes artificial.

Still, many of the experiments of the 1980s were based on the assumption that there was strong need for self-expression by residents in communities.

Second, all stations – both the experimental stations and the free, community oriented stations with participatory objectives -found it difficult to implement organizational changes in the face of withering support. Once stations had been established it seemed as if survival became an end in itself.

Third, an inflexible logic of institutional development took its toll. The core of station staff, volunteers and paid personnel, which insured continuity in operations came to favour professionalization of programming activities and station management. The early experiments in Britain demonstrated such a tendency very early in the history of community oriented television. The need to fill available airtime increased dependence on the few paid staff, and the need for a 'station identity' tended to support production of certain types of programming. Both of these needs brought stations into conflict with the initial intention of operating differently from traditional media (Bibby *et al.*, 1979).

The fourth factor is an extension of the above and has to do with the original position of stations in disregarding audience size. Community oriented stations were not established originally to attract the largest possible audience, but to facilitate community action and awareness. This position eventually was confronted with the quite natural interest of programme makers in securing an audience for their work. This need for an audience resulted in policy compromises between the position of open access and a more selective programming policy.

Finally, economic restraints forced many stations to make compromises regarding the non-commercial philosophy. In an early Council of Europe (1977: 2) report the importance of station financing was stressed:

> Obviously, financing is a key to control. If it is thought that communities should have a greater share in controlling their own activities, local financing of local cable TV programming becomes a central factor. In this perspective the issue must also be faced whether television is too expensive a medium to be afforded at local levels and thus less amenable to local control and funding than the cheaper medium of radio.

This report was issued prior to major changes in the broadcasting landscape of Western Europe. Most countries introduced private and commercial stations at all levels soon afterwards. The structural and economic context, then, within which community oriented stations had to develop was quite different from the situation when utopian visions had been formulated. Community oriented stations were no longer the only alternative to the national and regional public service channels; localities were suddenly served by a multitude of commercial stations supported by local companies and businesses. It is no wonder, then, that many municipalities were reluctant to finance stations broadcasting unconventional programmes with low audience interest:

> Over the past ten years, extreme segmentation has often·proved self-defeating. Many 'community' stations in France, Italy, Holland and Belgium, have complacently locked themselves up in deliberately marginal structures. The systematic refusal of advertising revenue, the rejection of a professional approach to broadcasting for ideological reasons, the use of low power transmitters and of poor wave bands, the parochialism of programme content, have condemned them to the outer fringes of the system and, therefore, sometimes to extinction. (Crookes & Vittet-Philippe, 1986: 13)

This description of community oriented stations certainly reflects the attitudes among many observers, politicians and journalists involved in broadcast media. The charactarization of community stations as cited above does not, however, take into account that community oriented stations were never meant to be compared to professional media. Instead, they were considered to be extra-commercial facilities for local residents.

TRENDS FOR THE OUTER FRINGE

The advent of community oriented radio and television stations in Western Europe took place during the period of crisis and transistion experienced by broadcasting since the late 1960s. Following the allotment of more frequency space in 1979 for radio transmission and the deregulatory policies implemented in most European countries during the 1980s, the political and economic situation for small scale stations changed dramatically.

When the broadcasting monopolies began to be lifted in the 1970s, generally at the same time as the introduction of community radio and television, observers felt the main changes within the broadcasting structure would be in the direction of specialization, decentralization and democratization (Jakubowicz, 1988). The role of local radio and television was seen as one – if not the primary – area of importance and expansion. This position was, for example, taken by the British Annan Committee (1977).

The focus on local or regional broadcasting embraced not only the emerging non-commercial initiatives and commercially oriented pirate stations; public service institutions also started operating at a sub-national level. These institutions began introduction of local or regional broadcasting services in line with a general policy of decentralization and reinforcement of regional and local autonomy.

This "early devolution" (Crookes & Vittet-Phillippe, 1986: 15-17), mainly concerning the public monopolies, was followed by an explosive deregulation in Italy in 1974 and later in Greece, Spain and Portugal. Developments in France, Belgium and Finland initially involved a re-regulatory process, and in countries such as the Netherlands, Sweden, Denmark and Norway a period of experimentation preceded changes in media policy.

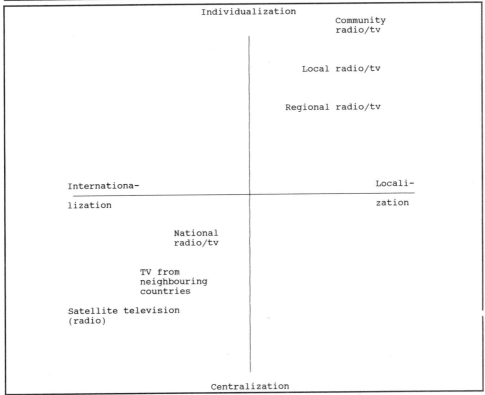

Fig. 1. Distribution of electronic media in two-dimensional matrix
Source: Prehn, 1989

Different models and policies emerged across Western Europe (see Kleinsteuber & Sonnenberg, 1989). During the 1980s after the experimental periods and in line with the liberalization of broadcasting regulations sweeping across all European countries, the tendency now seems to be one of convergence. As far as local radio and television is concerned, the crucial factor has been legalization of advertising, establishment of networks, and a flexible attitude toward cross-ownership allowing newspapers and other companies to enter the field of local broadcasting.

Although expansion of local broadcasting media has been one of the major media developments during the last decade, it has been surprisingly neglected in pan-European policy considerations. The Council of Europe, interestingly, was quite active during the period of experimentation in the 1970s, but in the following decade devoted minor attention to these media. Only since 1990 have the European Community and Council of Europe begun again to consider the policy issues related to these small scale media.

The proliferation of television and radio channels throughout Western Europe based upon privatization and commercialization is not without dangers. Repeated warnings have been voiced that this development might adversely affect the amount and kind of public service programming for minorities. The overall responsibility to provide cultural and educational programmes by public service broadcasting companies seems to be diminishing (European Institute for the Media, 1988; Prehn, in press).

As important as this development is regarding the old broadcasting monopolies, it is even more significant for local radio and television. These media began with policies emphasizing openness, participation and non-profit orientation in the best tradition of public service, and the objective was to counterbalance tendencies toward concentration and metropolization of the broadcast media.

These developments can be graphically illustrated as in Figure 1. Four main tendencies are evident in the changing structure of broadcasting. Regarding programme content, both internationalization and localization have increased. With expansion of satellite television and importation of programming especially from the United States, internationalization of broadcasting is becoming stronger. And with proliferation of local and regional channels there is a trend in the opposite direction of localization.

Regarding programme production and public involvement in the production process, centralization is increasing. At the same time there is also an increase in individualization through greater access and participatory possibilities. Examining the distribution of broadcasting forms along the axes in Figure 1, it appears that the commercialization of local radio and television is tending to de-individualize and de-localize these media. This development is exerting pressure on these media so that they are moving from the upper right cell in the typology towards the lower right cell and perhaps even in the direction of the lower left cell. Such displacement will tend to disrupt the relative equilibrium achieved by the original pattern of broadcasting forms.

This development is manifestly evident in Italy, France, Greece, Spain and Belgium with the creation of programming and station networks. In Denmark and Norway networks are also appearing, even though prohibited by law. And with the new legislation in the Netherlands allowing advertising the community oriented structure, stations in this country may be in the first phase of decline. Sweden, the only country in Europe still insisting local radio should be community oriented without advertising, may be the next to shift in the direction sketched above: as of this writing, in late 1991, legislation is being considered to permit advertising.

The general tendency, in other words, is that three types of local outlets for programming are developing at the local or community level. One type is run by or affiliated with public service institutions. A second type is private, commercial stations operating within national networks or close collaborative structures. And a third type is non-commercial stations continuously struggling to survive because of insufficient funds (McCain & Lowe, 1990). This last type of station is marked for extinction unless financial resources and spectrum availability is secured by national and local authorities (Widlok, 1988).

RESEARCH AND POLICY

During the period of experimentation community oriented local radio and television preoccupied policy makers, media activists, broadcasters and researchers. A wide variety of projects, studies and reports resulted from this attention, and the chapters of this volume represent a considered selection of the knowledge derived from this work. Developments related to local radio and television have not ceased, however, and further research is essential.

Considering the number of stations operating as non-commercial radio and television outlets around Western Europe – not to mention those being planned in former Eastern European countries – it is remarkable how limited information is on even basic questions (see e.g. Parliamentary Assembly of the Council of Europe, 1991a; Contamine, 1991). There is, for example, uncertainity on the number of stations operating in some countries, on their financial situation, on the forms of operation and organization, on audience reactions to programmes, and on programme content and policy.

With the trend toward commercialization not only is the existence of non-commercial stations at stake, but also research directed at understanding these forms of broad-casting media. The danger is that future research will only be financed on the condition that 'hard data' are produced on audience ratings – the only form of research considered valuable for commercial stations. Such quantitative research lacks sensitivity to the issues of importance for community oriented media; these media are seldom striving for the highest possible ratings, but in creating a medium of communication for citizens.

There are, admittedly, situations where quantitative empirical research is valuable. Still, a qualitative and multi-disciplinary approach seems more applicable when involved in researching the dynamic interaction between local communication, identity and participation. As emphasized in the first two chapters of this volume, community media are a challenge not only for those involved in policy making, but also for those concerned with the theoretical and methodological issues of media research. Recent trends in mass communication research emphasizing ethnographic and cultural studies, and qualitative reception analysis (e.g. Jensen & Rosengren, 1990; Ang, 1990) provide points of departure for more substantive analysis of access, participation and democratization (Jankowski, 1991).

Research is not an end in itself, however; it is also essential for the development of media policy in the coming years, a point made by the European Parliament (1989) in a resolution stressing the importance of increased knowledge about national legal structures and conditions for development of local radio. The Parliamentary Assembly of the Council of Europe has also considered the issue of local radio. In its report 'On the situation of local radio in Europe' (Parliamentary Assembly, 1990) the importance of local radio is stressed, particularly the need for attention to regulation, access to the airwaves and financing of stations. As followup to this report, the Parliamentary Assembly passed a resolution on local radio in January 1991 stating that '...local radio is an ideal potential means of fostering freedom of expression and information...' and that '(m)ember states not yet having done so should accordingly permit local radio to exist' (Parliamentary Assembly, 1991b: par. 3-4). The resolution calls further for better planning of frequencies and regulations regarding programming independence and responsibility.

In the light of this recent emphasis on policy, future research of community oriented media is accordingly faced with a need for more elaborate and innovative theories and methodologies. These new approaches must be both sensitive to the object of study and yet be able to maintain a critical approach; they must also be both valuable for 'the outer fringe' and for national and international policy makers – a delicate and difficult objective.

Community oriented radio and television, although relegated by the dominant forces in society to the fringe of media activity, still have an important mission, and seem committed to continuing: 'We are, however, here to stay, determined to resist political and economic pressure and conscious of the role we have to play in the defence of fundamental liberties' (FERL, 1989). In spite of such assertions the future of these media remains problematic and complicated.

Community oriented radio and television originally came as a challenge to the broadcasting monopolies. These small scale media were determined to change the alienating approach of traditional media intent on generalizing the concrete (Horkheimer & Adorno, 1969) into a setting involving closeness and concern for concretizing the general.

The need for locally oriented media to confront oligopolistic and transnational cultural industries will become more urgent in the coming years. Non-commercial and locally oriented media as social and cultural tools – and not as mass media in local disguise – can play an important role in strengthening local identity and self-respect. In the dialectic nexus of internationalization and localization, local media with a community orientation along with a trans-local perspective supported with international programme exchange networks can contribute to both local self-awareness and international understanding.

This "social dream" (Kleinsteuber & Sonneberg, 1990: 105) can only become reality if community oriented media are recognized for what they are – communicative tools – as well as for what they are not – serious contenders in a Darwinistic struggle among commercially oriented media. The question is not whether European countries can afford to support such small scale media as an alternative to the commercial cacophony of other electronic media; the question is whether they can afford not to.

References

Ang, I. (1990) 'Culture and communication: Towards an ethnographic critique of media consumption in the transnational media system', in *European Journal of Communication* 5, 2-3: 239-260.

Annan Committee (1977) *Report of the committee on the future of broadcasting*, London: HMSO.

Barlow, W. (1988) 'Community radio in the US: The struggle for a democratic medium', in *Media, Culture and Society* 10: 81-105.

Bibby, A., C. Denford and J. Cross (1979) *Local television. Piped dreams?* London: Redwing Press.

Boyd, D.A. (1986) 'Pirate radio in Britain: a programming alternative', in *Journal of Communication* spring issue: 83-94.

Brecht, B. (1930/1983) 'Radio as a means of communication: a talk of the function of radio', in A. Mattelart and S. Siegelaub (eds) *Communication and class struggle: 2. liberation, socialism*, New York: International General.

Browne, D.R. (1988) *What's local about local radio? A cross-national comparative study*, London: International Institute of Communications.

Contamine, C. (ed.) (1991) *Media in Eastern and Western Europe. Shared problems, shared solutions?*, proceedings, European Television and Film Forum, European Institute for the Media, Manchester.

Council of Europe (1977a) *European experiments in cable television. Local radio and video: lessons to be learned and prospects for the future*, Strasbourg: Council of Europe.

Council of Europe (1977b) *The financing of community and public access channels on cable television networks*, Strasbourg: Council of Europe.

Crisell, A. (1986) *Understanding radio*, London: Methuen.

Croll, P. and C. Husband (1975) *Communication and community. A study of the Swindon community television experiment*, Leicester: Centre for Mass Communication Research.

Crookes, P. and P. Vittet-Philippe (1986) *Local radio and regional development in Europe*, Manchester: European Institute for the Media.

Enzensberger, H.M. (1972) 'Constituents of a theory of the media', in D. McQuail (ed.) *Sociology of Mass Communications*, Harmondsworth: Penguin.

European Institute for the Media (1987) *Towards a European common market for television*, Manchester: European Institute for the Media.

European Institute for the Media (1988) *Europe 2000: what kind of television?* Manchester: European Institute for the Media.

European Parliament (1989) 'Beslutning om radiospredning.' *De europaeiske faellesskabers Tidende*, Brussels.

Familie- og forbrukerdepartementet (1990) Stortingsmelding nr. 12, Om pressestötten, Oslo.

FERL (1989) Proposed Community Radio Charter.

GEAR (1990): *Euro-Factbook. Basic hardware & audience data*, publisher unknown.

Groombridge, B. (1972) *Television and the people. A programme for democratic participation*, Harmondsworth, Penguin.

Habermas, J. (1962) *Strukturwandel der Öffentlichkeit. Untersuchungen zur einer Kategorie der bürgerlichen Gesellschaft*, Berlin: Hermann Luchtherhand Verlag.

Heretakis, E. (1990) 'The Greek radio marketplace', in *Media Bulletin 7*, 4: 14.

Horkheimer, M. and T.W. Adorno (1969/1944) *Dialektik der Aufklärung*, Frankfurt am Main: Fischer Verlag.

Jakubowicz, K. (1985) 'Mass(?) communication(?) as contemporary broadcasting evolves, both terms are acquiring quite new meanings', in *Gazette* 36: 39-53.

Jakubowicz, K. (1988) 'Gazing into the crystal ball: radio in the new media age', in *Theory and Practice* 3: 20-47.

Jankowski, N.W. (1988) *Community television in Amsterdam. Access to, participation in and use of the 'Lokale Omroep Bijlmermeer'*, Amsterdam: University of Amsterdam.

Jankowski, N.W. (1991) 'Qualitative research and community media', in K.B. Jensen and N.W. Jankowski (eds) *A handbook of qualitative methodologies for mass communication research*, London: Routledge.

Jens, C. (1989) 'Privater Hörfunk – eine Verlegerdomäne. Ergebnisse einer Dokumentation über Verlagsbeteiligungen an Privatradios in der Bundesrepublik Deutschland', in *Media Perspektiven* 1: 23-37.

Jensen, K.B. and K.E. Rosengren (1990) 'Five traditions in search of the audience', in *European Journal of Communication 5*, 2-3: 207-238.

Jouet, J. (1977) *Community media and development: problems of adaption*, Paris: UNESCO.

Kellner, D. (1987): Public access television: alternative views', in D. Lazere (ed.) *American media and mass culture. Left perspectives*, Berkeley: University of California Press.

Kleinsteuber, H.J. and U. Sonnenberg (1989) 'Radio in Grenzen – Nicht-Kommerzielles Lokalradio in Westeuropa', in *Rundfunk und Fernsehen 37*, 2-3: 283-294.

Kleinsteuber, H.J. and U. Sonnenberg (1990) 'Beyond public service and private profit: International experience with non-commercial local radio', in *European Journal of Communication* 5: 87-106.

Lange, A. and J.L. Renaud (1990) *The future of the European audiovisual industry*, Manchester: European Institute for the Media.

Langenbucher, W.R. (1989) 'Musikteppiche für Dialektkommunikation am 'Neuen Dorfbrunnen'. Lokaleradios in der Schweiz', in *Media Perspektiven* 10: 618-631.

Leponiemi, T. (1990) *European FM handbook 1990*, Helsinki.

Lewis, P.M. (1976) *Community control of local radio*, Strasbourg: Council of Europe.

Lewis, P.M. (1978) *Community television and cable in Britain*, London: British Film Institute.

Lewis, P.M. and J. Booth (1989) *The invisible medium. Public, commercial and community radio*, London: Macmillan.

Loensmann, L. (1989) 'Radiosituationen i Vesteuropa land for land', mimeo, Copenhagen.

Loensmann, L. (1990) 'Community radio and cultural identity – the development of independent radio in Europe', paper, International Communication Association, Dublin.

McCain, T. and G.F. Lowe (1990) 'Localism in Western European radio broadcasting: Untangling the wireless', in *Journal of Communication* 40, 1: 86-101.

McQuail, D. and K. Siune (eds) (1986) *New media politics. Comparative perspectives in Western Europe*, London: Sage.

McQuail, D. and S. Windahl (1981) *Communication models for the study of mass communications*, London: Longman.

Moring, T. (1991) 'Finska medier 1989-90. Publik och reklam i centrum. Politisk reklam på väg', in *Pressens Årbog*, Odense: Pressehistorisk Selskab.

Negt, O. (1971) *Soziologische Phantasie und exemplarisches Lernen. Zur Theorie und Praxis der Arbeiterbildung*, Frankfurt am Main: Europäische Verlagsanstalt.

Oehler, T. (1988) 'Lokale Radio-Networks in Frankreich', in *Media Perspektiven*, 6: 358-365.

OLON (1990) 'Local radio and television in the Netherlands and the OLON', brochure, Nijmegen: OLON.

Parliamentary Assembly of the Council of Europe (1990) 'Report on the situation of local radio in Europe', Strasbourg: Council of Europe.

Parliamentary Assembly of the Council of Europe (1991a) 'Provisional report on parliamentary responsibility for the democratic reform of broadcasting,' Strasbourg: Council of Europe.

Parliamentary Assembly of the Council of Europe (1991b) 'Resolution 957 on the situation of local radio in Europe', Strasbourg: Council of Europe.

Partridge, S. (1982) *Not the BBC/IBA. The case for community radio*, London: Comedia.

Prehn, O. (1989) 'Kommer de gode gamle dage igen?' in *NordREFO* 2: 90-128.

Prehn, O. (1990) 'Community radio or just local airwaves. The development of community radio in Denmark', paper, International Communication Association, Dublin.

Prehn, O. (forthcoming) *Broadcasting for employment*, Manchester: European Institute for the Media.

Pürer, H. (1988) 'Österreichs Mediensystem im Wandel. Ein aktueller Lagebericht', in *Media Perspektiven* 11: 673-682.

Röper, H. (1989) 'Stand der Verflechtung von privatem Rundfunk und Presse 1989', in *Media Perspektiven* 9: 533-551.

Shaughnessy, H. and C.F. Cobo (1990) *The cultural obligations of broadcasting*, Manchester: European Institute for the Media.

Spark, C. (1987) 'Pacifica Radio and the politics of culture', in D. Lazere (ed.) *American media and mass culture. Left perspectives*, Berkeley: University of California Press.

Traquina, N. (1989) 'Radio: A period of growth', in *Media Bulletin*, 6, 4: 10-11.

Traquina, N. (1990) 'Portugal', in *Media Bulletin* 7, 3: 14-15.

Udvalget vedr. lokal radio og tv (1990a): Status over ordningen for lokal radio og tv. Copenhagen.

Udvalget vedr. Lokal Radio og TV (1990b): Notat om de nordiske ordninger for lokal radio og tv. J. Nr. 90.8641-4, Copenhagen.

Vidéotrame (1990) 'Community, local and regional television stations in the EEC', proceedings of Colloque International, Namur.

Widlok, P. (1988) 'A voice for the voiceless. Community radio: Everyman at the microphone', in *Transatlantic Perspectives* 18: 10-12.

Woldt, R. (1989) 'Private radio in Germany', in *Media Bulletin* 6, 3: 11-12.

Wöste, M. (1989) 'Networkbildung durch die Hintertür? Programmzulieferer für privaten Hörfunk in der Bundesrepublik – Eine Bestandsaufnahme', in *Media Perspektiven* 1: 9-22.

Indexes

SUBJECT INDEX

Media titles available from John Libbey

ACAMEDIA RESEARCH MONOGRAPHS

Satellite Television in Western Europe
Richard Collins
Hardback ISBN 0 86196 203 6

Beyond the Berne Convention
Copyright, Broadcasting and the Single European Market
Vincent Porter
Hardback ISBN 0 86196 267 2

The Media Dilemma:
Freedom and Choice or Concentrated Power?
Gareth Locksley
Hardback ISBN 0 86196 230 3

Nuclear Reactions: A Study in Public Issue Television
John Corner, Kay Richardson and Natalie Fenton
Hardback ISBN 0 86196 251 6

Transnationalization of Television in Western Europe
Preben Sepstrup
Hardback ISBN 0 86196 280 X

The People's Voice: Local Television and Radio in Europe
Nick Jankowski, Ole Prehn and James Stappers
Hardback ISBN 0 86196 322 9

BBC ANNUAL REVIEWS

Annual Review of BBC Broadcasting Research: No XV - 1989
Peter Menneer (ed)
Paperback ISBN 0 86196 209 5

Annual Review of BBC Broadcasting Research: No XVI - 1990
Peter Menneer (ed)
Paperback ISBN 0 86196 265 6

Annual Review of BBC Broadcasting Research: No XVII - 1991
Peter Menneer (ed)
Paperback ISBN 0 86196 319 9

Media titles available from John Libbey

BROADCASTING STANDARDS COUNCIL PUBLICATIONS

A Measure of Uncertainty: The Effects of the Mass Media
Guy Cumberbatch and Dennis Howitt
Hardback ISBN 0 86196 231 1

Violence in Television Fiction: Public Opinion and Broadcasting Standards
David Docherty
Paperback ISBN 0 86196 284 2

Survivors and the Media
Ann Shearer
Paperback ISBN 0 86196 332 6

Taste and Decency in Broadcasting
Andrea Millwood Hargrave
Paperback ISBN 0 86196 331 8

A Matter of Manners? – The Limits of Broadcast Language
Edited by Andrea Millwood Hargrave
Paperback ISBN 0 86196 337 7

BROADCASTING RESEARCH UNIT MONOGRAPHS

**Quality in Television –
Programmes, Programme-makers, Systems**
Richard Hoggart (ed)
Paperback ISBN 0 86196 237 0

Keeping Faith? Channel Four and its Audience
David Docherty, David E. Morrison and Michael Tracey
Paperback ISBN 0 86196 158 7

**Invisible Citizens:
British Public Opinion and the Future of Broadcasting**
David E. Morrison
Paperback ISBN 0 86196 111 0

School Television in Use
Diana Moses and Paul Croll
Paperback ISBN 0 86196 308 3

Media titles available from John Libbey

UNIVERSITY OF MANCHESTER BROADCASTING SYMPOSIUM

And Now for the BBC ...
Proceedings of the 22nd Symposium 1991
Nod Miller and Rod Allen (eds)
Paperback ISBN 0 86196 318 0

Published in association with UNESCO

Video World-Wide: An International Study
Manuel Alvarado (ed)
Paperback ISBN 0 86196 143 9

Published in association with
THE ARTS COUNCIL of GREAT BRITAIN

Picture This: Media Representations of Visual Art and Artists
Philip Hayward (ed)
Paperback ISBN 0 86196 126 9

Culture, Technology and Creativity
Philip Hayward (ed)
Paperback ISBN 0 86196 266 4

ITC TELEVISION RESEARCH MONOGRAPHS

Television in Schools
Robin Moss, Christopher Jones and Barrie Gunter
Hardback ISBN 0 86196 314 8

Media titles available from John Libbey